INNOVATION FOR GREEN GROWTH

Mu Rongping, Reinhard Meckl

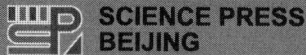

SCIENCE PRESS
BEIJING

Responsible Editors: Hou Junlin, Niu Ling, Zhang Cuixia

图书在版编目（CIP）数据

面向绿色增长的创新 = Innovation for Green Growth：英文/穆荣平，（德）梅克（Meckl，R.）主编. —北京：科学出版社，2014.1
　ISBN 978-7-03-039240-4

Ⅰ. ①面… Ⅱ. ①穆…②梅… Ⅲ. ①经济增长-研究-英文 Ⅳ. ①F061.2

中国版本图书馆 CIP 数据核字（2013）第 286340 号

Innovation for Green Growth

Copyright © 2014 by Science Press, Beijing

Published by Science Press
16 Donghuangchenggen North Street
Beijing 100717, China

Printed in Beijing

All right reserved. No part of this publication
may be reproduced, stored in a retrieval system,
or transmitted in any form or by any means,
electronic, mechanical, photocopying, recording
or otherwise, without the prior written permission
of the copyright owner.
ISBN：978-7-03-039240-4
Price：158.00RMB

Introduction

With the challenges of a series of global issues, such as the global climate change and the financial crisis, how to make the transformation of economic development pattern become increasingly more important than ever. Therefore, green growth has drawn great attention from governments, academia and enterprises in recent years, while eco-innovation is recognized as a key to green growth. In order to facilitate knowledge sharing, joint learning and capacity building on the innovation policy for green growth, we coorganized the "4th Sino-German Conference on Technological Innovation and Management" at Institute of Policy and Management, Chinese Academy of Sciences from September 26-29, 2011 in Beijing.

This book "*Innovation for Green Growth*" mainly contains articles based on papers presented during the conference. The main objectives of the book are to deepen the dialogue, communication and cooperation among researchers from two countries, and to enhance knowledge transfer and exchange of information for green growth. The book consists of four parts, namely: (1) Innovative strategy for green growth; (2) Innovation policy for green growth; (3) Industrial innovation for green growth; (4) Enterprise technical innovation and future challenges for green growth. The articles in the book enhance policymakers' and business leaders' understanding of innovation policies for green growth and provide a platform for sharing policy experiences to facilitate implementation and improve efficacy of innovation policies for green growth.

The conference was financed by the "Sino-German Center for the Promotion of Sciences" in Beijing. We thank the center for the generous support and the help in organizing the conference. We also thank the center's financial support for publishing this book. We also thank Dr. Song Hefa and Ms. Niu Ling for their support for and great effort in editing this book.

Mu Rongping, Reinhard Meckl
Beijing, Bayreuth
November, 2013

Content

Introduction

Part 1 Innovation Strategy for Green Growth / 1

    1 Green Development and Innovation in China / 3
    2 Green Innovations and CO_2 Emissions in a Growth Perspective:
        Competition, Growth, Welfare Analysis and Policy Implications / 19
    3 Are There Any First and Second Mover Advantages for Eco-pioneers?
        Lead Market Strategies for Environmental Innovation / 41
    4 Exporting Green Technologies: Prerequisites and Perspectives for China and Germany / 64
    5 An Evaluation on Driving Forces for Green Innovation in China / 83
    6 Will the European Emission Trading Scheme Promote Green Innovation in the European Industry? / 96

Part 2 Innovation Policies for Green Growth / 117

    7 Innovation Policies for Green Growth in China / 119
    8 Governance of Innovation Alliances in Green Industries / 135
    9 The Regional Innovation Capacity Construction for Green Growth: An Essential Way to be an Innovative Country/ 156
    10 Are Regional Clusters Necessary for Innovation? Case of German Wind Turbine Innovation Clusters/ 171

Part 3 Industrial Innovation for Green Growth / 189

    11 The Competitive Position of German and Chinese Photovoltaic Companies in International Markets / 191
    12 Role of Entrepreneurial Region in Development of Photovoltaic Industry of China / 210
    13 Innovations for Electro-mobility and Renewable Energies: Prospects

for Chinese and German Firms / 227
14 Low Carbon Industrial Development in Chongqing: Automotive Industry as Example / 244

Part 4 Enterprise Technology Innovation and Future Challenges for Green Growth / 257

15 Green Technologies—Germany's and China's Activities in Renewable Energies / 259
16 Lead Market Potential for Phosphorus Recycling Technologies in Germany / 275
17 The Greening of Human Resources Management in China / 297
18 Firms' Innovation Strategies in Relation to Green Growth / 314

Part 1

Innovation Strategy for Green Growth

Green Development and Innovation in China

Wang Yi

With its peaceful rising in international arena, China has become a major player in the process of global economic growth and sustainable development. In the context of globalization, the experiences got and challenges faced by China in its course of development are of global implications due to its large population and size of economy. Over the last sixty years, particularly over the past three decades, China has achieved outstanding results in its economic development. Even in 2009 against a backdrop of global financial and economic crisis, China's GDP still grew by over 8%, triggering another round of heated discussion on "the China Model". However, it should be noted that due to a number of factors(e. g. its specific development stage, national conditions, and international division of labor), China is confronted with a series of challenges in addressing such issues as poverty reduction, employment, population ageing, and, in particular, the negative impacts of resources and energy consumption and pollution on the global environment. For this reason, China is expected to play a crucial role in re-shaping the sustainable development worldwide, i. e. a green China is also needed(Friedman, 2008).

In addressing various challenges both at home and abroad and promoting sustainable development, China is trying to explore the way of sustainable development with Chinese characteristics. In recent years, based on our research, we have put forward the concepts that China has to achieve "sustainable rising" (CAS Sustainable Development Strategy Study Group, 2006); it should transform with a sustainable development strategy under the new circumstances (CAS Sustainable Development Strategy Study Group, 2008); it should follow the path of low-carbon development with Chinese characteristics (CAS Sustainable Development Strategy Study Group, 2009); and green innovation and green transition will be key elements of the transformation of economic development pattern in China, Asian countries and the world(CAS Sustainable Development Strategy Study Group, 2010; CAS Sustainable Development Strategy Study Group, 2011; CAS Sustainable Development Strategy Study Group, 2012 ; AASA, 2011). All the conclusions were made on the basis of reviewing and reflecting the state of growth and environment over the last three decades, as well as the lessons and experiences learned in meeting various new challenges. These findings are expected to provide inspirations for the global community to develop green economy, ecologically-efficient economy and low-carbon economy under the context of financial crisis and climate change, and to offer guidance for China in its future reform and growth.

1.1 Three major challenges to China's sustainable development in the new era

1.1.1 Ongoing challenges of global financial crisis

Due to global financial and economic imbalances, in particular the long-term economic imbalance of developed economies, many countries in the world have been battered by the economic crisis that has never been seen over the last decades. To address this issue, many economies(both developed countries and developing countries including China) have launched financial stimulus packages in the effort to recover their economy at the earliest date possibly. So far, the global economy seems to have struggled out of the most difficult period and some countries have begun to recover, although the prospect of recovery is still uncertain and the recovery for the real economy is yet to be maintained. With the exit of stimulus policies and tightening of monetary policies, the world economy is still vulnerable to financial turmoil, and its long-term, sustainable growth is hard to be predicted.

What is unique for this crisis is that the financial crisis and global climate change have interwoven to complicate the issue, and addressing financial crisis has, to some extent, adversely affected the process of mitigating climate change. As a result, some experts and international organizations have recommended that all the major economies should integrate the short-term actions with long-term measures for sustainable growth to achieve so-called *Green New Deal* and *Green Recovery* (Edenhofer et al.,2009;UNEP,2009a;UNEP,2008). In reality,no significant results have been made, and the existing industry structure and energy use remain little changed, which are quite different from the situation when the energy crisis took place in 1970s. In this case, if no effective measures are taken after the economic growth is re-launched, the demand for natural resources and energy and greenhouse gas emission may rise again.

China was also severely hit by the global financial crisis. Although China has achieved its target of "maintaining economic growth" through a series of measures, such as the economic stimulus package of 4 trillion yuan, the plan for invigorating ten major industries, as well as the action to develop new energy industry, some short-term economic problems have been transformed into long-term and local debts. New problems may emerge if the financial sustainability cannot be ensured. More importantly, while the economic stimulus package focuses more on traditional industries and large-sized state-owned enterprises, the new industries of strategic importance are far from being mature, the small- and medium-sized enterprises suffer from many difficulties, and China is still confronted with various structural conflicts. In addition, it has to address a number of issues such as the rising production costs, poor innovation capacity and the unsustainable extensive growth mode. Despite the fact that the Chinese central government has attached great importance to these problems, accelerating the structural reform and transforming the growth mode remain the most challenging task for China in the post-financial crisis era under the existing conditions and institutional framework.

1.1.2 Long-term challenges of climate change

No legally-bound agreement has been reached at the UN Summit on Climate Change in Copenhagen by the end of 2009. The prospect for UN Climate Change Conference which is held in Mexico in late 2010 is still gloomy amid many disagreements on funding, technology and equity. While the developing countries including China need to further defend their basic human right and development right, they should also make their due contributions to protecting the global climate under the principle of "common but differentiated responsibilities".

Although more and more countries have recognized the importance of developing low-carbon economy, it should be noted that most of the wealth of developed countries is generated on the basis of relatively cheaper fossil energy sources. For the large economies, no best practices and models are available for them to expedite the industrialization and urbanization drive by mainly depending on non-fossil energy sources, and to maintain high quality living standards under the scenario of low-carbon emission. Only defining an objective on transforming towards low-carbon development is far from being enough. It is also necessary for us to understand the pathway, constraints, technical tools and approaches, practical ways for international cooperation to achieve this objective, and who will bear the costs.

In the next decade, it is essential for China to explore the low-carbon pathway if it expects to achieve its goal of promoting industrialization and urbanization drive and addressing climate change. Although China does not have to commit any quantified emission reduction targets by 2020, and its per-capita energy consumption and emission is far lower than that of the developed countries, China, as the world's top carbon emitter, is bound to face increasing pressure from the international community. Under such context, China needs courage, wisdom and stamina to find an innovative pathway that is responsible and meets its actual conditions.

1.1.3 Challenges of a variety of domestic resources and environmental problems

As a large developing country, China's sustainable development is mostly threatened by the growing domestic resources and environmental problems. Against a backdrop of fast economic growth and upgraded consumption structure, the strategic energies(in particular the quality energy sources such as oil and gas) and the key mineral resources(e.g. iron, copper, aluminum and uranium) in China will be in tight supply in the long run. On the one hand, China's external dependence of the above-mentioned energies and resources is likely to grow further. On the other hand, China's overseas development of natural resources will be confronted with increasing constraints, posing a major risk to the energy and resource security in China. Therefore, it is imperative for the Chinese government to change its foreign economic cooperation strategy.

Compared with two decades ago, the existing eco-environmental problems in China have experienced significant changes, evidenced by more complex pollution pattern and the large area of ecological degradation. Due to the underlying causes of economic benefits-driven strategy, poor monitoring and supervision capacities, the overall environmental pollution in China has yet to be fully contained, which has extended into regional atmospheric pollution and river basin water pollution that are cross-sectoral and trans-administrative boundary. As a result, an integrated solution needs to be developed in no time. In addition, although a series of large-scale ecological programs have been implemented in China and some results have been made, the ecosystems in the ecologically vulnerable central and western areas will face emerging pressures with the rising of the central regions and the advancing of western development program.

To simultaneously address various resources and environmental problems, the institutional arrangement and management matters more than technology and funding. It calls for the government to be accountable, shift its traditional ideas, coordinate different interests, innovate the institutions and mechanisms, and involve various stakeholders in the process. Only by integrating energy saving and environmental protection into the socio-economic activities can China fundamentally develop a comprehensive control framework and ultimately transform the environmental externality into the internal driving force of development for the country.

Challenges also herald opportunities. When the human society is shifting towards the post-financial crisis era, post-fossil fuel era and post-industrialization era, the global community is faced with a common problem: while meeting the challenge of financial crisis, how to explore new strategic opportunities, restructure the economic architecture and build new competitive advantages to address the aforementioned three challenges at minimum costs and with integrated and coordinated approaches. One solution behind these challenges is clear: green development and innovation.

1.2 What is green development?

To combat global financial crisis and climate change, the United Nations Environment Programme(UNEP) launched the initiative of *Global Green New Deal* and *Green Economy* in October 2008(UNEP,2008), released the policy brief on *Green New Deal* in March 2009(UNEP,2009a) and submitted the updated version on *Global Green New Deal* to G20 Summit in September 2009(UNEP,2009b). Its core concept is to "green" the economy by re-shaping and re-focusing on the policies, investment and expenditures of some key sectors, and to accelerate the pace to address climate change while working on economic recovery and jobs growth. Those sectors include: energy efficiency, renewable energy, green transport, green building, water service and management, sustainable agriculture and forestry, among others.

In June 2009, the Ministerial Council of the Organization for Economic Co-operation and Development (OECD) adopted the Declaration on Green Growth to encourage economic recovery through policy instruments and green investment in the short term, and help to build the environmentally friendly infrastructure required for a green economy, promote sustainable growth and shift towards sustainable, low-carbon economy in the long term.

In October 2009, the European Council adopted the decision of developing "eco-efficient economy" under the post-Lisbon Agenda and EU sustainable development strategy. This indicates that in addition to advocating low-carbon economy, EU also proposed a longer-term and more inclusive eco-efficient economy, i.e. to build a safe, sustainable, low-carbon and energy-saving economy by transforming towards sustainable production and life style.

As a matter of fact, "green economy" is not a newly coined word, and no uniform definition has been provided. The concept of "green economy" can be traced back to 1960s when the US scholar Boulding put forward the idea of "spaceship earth economics"(Boulding, 1966), as well as the ideas of Daly and Pearce et al. on steady state economy, green economy and ecological economy since then(Daly et al., 2004; Pearce et al., 1989; Daly, 1973). In addition, many domestic and foreign scholars have addressed the topics related to the green development in China, including green economy, circular economy, low-carbon economy, *and Green New Deal* (Liu, 2001; UNDP China, 2002; Hu, 2004; Zhou, 2005; Zhuang, 2007; Zhu, 2008).

The connotation of green economy is constantly changing. Compared with the traditional development mode depending on fossil fuels, green growth or green economy is a new economic growth pattern that contributes to energy conservation and environmental protection. In China, all the discussions on green economy or green growth are focused on different aspects of sustainable development or the tasks at specific stages. They are aimed to achieve a win-win situation in economic development and environmental protection by shaking off the constraints of limited environmental carrying capacity and decoupling the economic growth and resources consumption.

Since the beginning of 21st century, China has been in a new development stage. At the same time, it is also confronted with a series of new problems. During the period of "11th Five-Year Plan"(2006 – 2010), China's sustainable development was mainly focused on energy conservation, emission reduction and building a resources saving-based society. Under the new circumstances, China has to address growing challenges in sustainable development. As mentioned above, it has to tackle many domestic resources and environmental problems while having to meet the challenges of global climate change and international financial crisis; it has to focus on environmental protection while having to focus on socio-economic development; it has to "maintain the economic growth" while having to "adjust the economic structure". In his speech at the opening ceremony of UN Summit on Climate Change at

Copenhagen by the end of 2009, former Chinese President Hu Jintao pointed out that China will "make great efforts to develop green economy, actively pursue low-carbon economy and circular economy, study and promote climate-friendly technologies". This is a succinct summary by the Chinese top leaders on the ways ahead for China to tackle various challenges in the future (Hu, 2009).

For this reason, we have re-proposed developing green economy to achieve green growth in the new stage. This is done to realize three fundamental objectives: (1) giving top priority to solving the domestic resources and environmental problems; (2) leveraging technical progress to enhance the energy efficiency and green competitiveness, achieve green recovery, and address such issues as economic growth, poverty reduction and employment, among others; (3) shifting gradually from fossil fuels to new, low-carbon or carbon-free energies to develop energy conserving and environment-friendly industries, and to promote the "greening" of the economic system by means of transforming the growth mode, in particular the green transformation, with an ultimate goal of addressing long-term challenges in climate change and sustainable development.

The years between 2010 and 2020 are a key decade for China to accelerate its pace of industrialization and urbanization drive, and transform its development mode. By 2020, China is expected to fulfill its commitment of reducing carbon dioxide emission intensity and other indicators in addressing climate change, implement the *Circular Economy Promotion Law of the People's Republic of China*, and build a resources-saving, environment-friendly and low carbon-oriented society by constantly improving the efficiency of resources utilization and the environment quality. As a result, we believe it is necessary to integrate the development of green economy, low-carbon economy and circular economy into the framework of green growth, and highlight green growth as a key component of sustainable development strategy, in order to address the aforementioned three challenges. Great efforts should be made to accelerate the process of industrialization and urbanization through green transformation, and to explore a low-carbon growth mode with Chinese characteristics and achieve green revitalization and sustainable growth by building green industry, construction and transportation systems.

1.3 Promoting green growth needs to leverage green innovation

Innovation in all aspects is required to build a green China, achieve green transformation and follow a pathway of green growth. Meanwhile, the innovative activities and their road map at the new stage have to fit into the needs of the actual situation in China, the global trend and green growth. Therefore, the innovative activities that are green-based and are aimed to address the above-mentioned three challenges are called green innovation or sustainable innovation. Achieving the goal of green growth calls for green innovation, which, in turn, can promote the green growth.

So far, innovation has become a core component of development strategy in each country worldwide, and green innovation will become a major trend in future innovation. In the next one and two decades, a new technological and industrial revolution that features green, intelligent and sustainable development is likely to take shape(Lu, 2009). "Green" could possibly serve as a key element in driving the new technological revolution and guiding the trend of innovation. This is a major challenge to China, as well as a historic opportunity for her to achieve sustainable development. We cannot afford to miss the opportunities offered by green innovation and the ensuing technological and industrial revolution.

Over the last thirty years, China's growth was mainly based on the extensive growth mode. In the next decade, China will undergo a process of transforming towards an innovation-based, intensive growth mode. Extensive growth mode is labor-intensive and at the cost of high consumption of resources and environmental degradation, with poor innovation capacity. In the future, external conditions of the extensive growth will experience some changes: (1) If the current population policy is still maintained, the working-age population in China will reach its peak within the next ten years, and the period of unlimited supply of labor is about to come to an end. (2) The resources and energy of strategic importance will be in tight supply, and the carrying capacity of environment will reach its limit. As a result, on the one hand, innovation has become an intrinsic factor for economic growth, while improving resources and environmental performance and achieving high-level development under the context of limited per-capita resources and carbon emission permits are defined to be a key indicator to measure the innovation capacity. On the other hand, against a backdrop of addressing financial crisis and growing external environmental pressures, it has become an inevitable option for China to adjust its economic structure, boost domestic demand, promote technological advancement and transform the development mode through innovation at all aspects. This will pose a major challenge to China for its green innovation in the days ahead.

At the same time, we have to note that new demands and markets are created for developing green economy and low-carbon economy in the course of addressing the problems in environmental protection and climate change and meeting the challenges of financial crisis, which also provides new opportunities for green innovation. China's market demand for the solution of green technology is enormous (Kirkham et al., 2009), so is the global market demand for green innovation to mitigate climate change. Green innovation will not only benefit the general public, create new jobs and enhance the market competitiveness, but also build up the basis for China to be competitive in the global green market.

The enabling policy environment is needed for innovation and implementing a green growth strategy can drive the green innovation. Under the era of globalization, all the major countries worldwide are actively adjusting their strategies and policies in scientific and technological innovation, and promoting their development and enhancing their international competitiveness through innovation (China Innovation and Development of Chinese Academy of Sciences, 2010). The best practice in China during the period of "11th Five-Year Plan" (2006 - 2010) suggests that significant results have been achieved in terms of energy conservation, emission reduction and in addressing climate change. For example, some technologies, equipment and engineering construction in some areas (e.g. clean coal-fired power generation, renewable energy and high-speed railway) in the country have already reached world-class level, and even contain the core technologies developed by China. It is no doubt that as long as China follows the pathway of energy conservation and emission reduction and develops incentive policies to overcome the obstacles in market, financing and regulation, it will be ranked among the groups of top class worldwide in terms of energy conservation and emission reduction in the major industries in another one or two decades.

Innovation does not just mean technological innovation. It also involves institutional, policy and managerial innovation, and even cultural innovation. In the past, institutional innovation and managerial innovation were often regarded as the enabling conditions for technological innovation. Instead, they should be integrated as major components of innovation. In addition, green innovation is also a systematic process. Interaction, coordination, and cooperation are needed among different innovation activities in the open, competitive environment to reduce the risks of technological transformation, and ultimately to provide integrated solutions.

In his speech titled *Leading the Sustainable Development of China with Science and Technology* delivered to the scientific community in Beijing in November 2009, former Chinese Premier Wen Jiabao stressed that, to promote the all-round, coordinated and sustainable economic development of China in a longer-term basis, and follow the track of innovation-driven and endogenous growth, China needs to integrate the building of an innovation-oriented nation as one of its strategic objectives and sustainable development as one of its strategic goals(Wen, 2009). Therefore, we have to fully understand the inherent relations between sustainable development and innovation, seize the opportunities of innovation, enhance the innovation capacity and accelerate the pace of green transformation and green development.

1.4 Investing in green innovation to realize green growth

Against a backdrop of rapidly changing conditions at home and abroad, China needs to develop a practical green development strategy and invest in green innovation in order to achieve its goal of green growth and provide favorable conditions for its long-term sustainable growth in the period of "12th Five-Year Plan"(2011 – 2015) and beyond. As many areas are involved in green development and innovation, China should give top priority to the following aspects.

1.4.1 Developing a comprehensive strategic plan on China's green development and the priority action plan in the "12th Five-Year Plan"(2011 – 2015)

So far, under the guidance of the *Scientific Outlook on Development*, China has put forward many new concepts on green development, including new-type industrialization, energy conservation and pollution reduction, green economy, circular economy, low-carbon economy, emerging industries of strategic importance, resources-efficient and environment-friendly society, in which there is an overlap between each other in terms of their contents and multiple government departments are involved in terms of their implementation and supervision. Therefore, while incorporating green development as a key guiding principle in the "12th Five-Year Plan", it is necessary to develop a comprehensive strategic plan framework to integrate the green development strategy, road map and priority areas, as well as the green investment and green innovation-related incentive policy, institutional arrangement and demonstration programs, and to give top priority to such long-term restructuring related key tasks as transforming towards low-carbon energy use, etc.

1.4.2 Speeding up institutional innovation, and giving top priority to the development of green development-related policies

Developing green economy needs to fully leverage the legal, administrative and economic means, and constantly adjust and make innovation in the policy instruments. During the period of "11th Five-Year Plan"(2006 – 2010) in China, more administrative means have been adopted to promote the efforts of energy conservation and emission reduction. However, in the next decade, it is necessary to use more economic instruments with supported by appropriate administrative measures.

First, China needs to consider developing the "Guideline on Green Development" at the national level, which should identify the basic connotation of green development and the relationship between green development and other concepts, define the respective responsibilities and obligations of the governments, enterprises and various stakeholders, highlight the leading role of the governments in green development, and establish a national integrated coordination mechanism on green development.

Second, China should give priority to addressing the prices formation mechanism of resources, energy and environmental factors, and reverse the distortion of resources allocation in order to make the prices truly reflect the scarcity of resources, supply-demand relations and external costs of pollutants discharge. Under such context, it is necessary to understand the opinions of various stakeholders on resources and environmental pricing mechanisms through fair and transparent procedures, reduce the over-intervention of the government, and regulate the pricing with market-based tools.

Third, resources and environmental taxation such as energy tax, environmental tax and carbon tax should be considered comprehensively and implemented in tandem with relevant financial policies and overall taxation reform in an orderly manner, while reducing human resources-related taxes so as to balance the overall level of tax burden and mitigate negative impacts on corporate competitiveness.

Last, it should continue to use the Resources and Environmental Performance Index (i.e. the efficiency index) as the core administrative means during the "12th Five-Year Plan" period (2011 – 2015), and appropriately identify these indicators as binding indicators according to the specific conditions, resources and environmental features of different regions (e.g. the water pollution at river basin scale).

1.4.3 Investing in green scientific and technological innovation

To strengthen the role of policy in guiding green innovation, the government is required to increase the related scientific and technological input and improve the national capacity in this area. Meanwhile, emphasis should be put on enhancing the efficiency of research and development (R&D) through appropriate institutional arrangement, creating the model of integrating government, industry, education and research, as well as the model of public-private partnership (particularly combine the strength of relevant research institutions, enterprises and capital market), coordinating different actions to promote the corporate innovation capacity and competitiveness, and facilitating the growth of strategic, emerging industries. In addition, efforts should be made to expand opening to the outside world, learn from the international best practices, and strive to be the leader and provider of technologies in energy conservation, emission reduction and green innovation. Special attention should be paid to the following three aspects.

First, further deepening reform on public research institutions, accelerating the reform on supporting systems such as budget and personnel systems, and promoting the appropriate flow and efficient use of scientific and technological resources in line with the characters of professional areas and on the basis of survey.

Second, implementing key scientific and technological programs on green development. Efforts need to be made in coordinating the different R&D projects related to energy conservation, environmental protection, and low-carbon economy, developing scientific and technological road map on green growth, and arranging other special programs under this framework, while focusing on the commercialized demonstration projects and engaging more enterprises in this process.

Third, as to the R&D of low-carbon technologies, (1) focusing on the development and demonstration of low-carbon technological systems (e. g. IGCC, CCS and coal-based poly-generation systems) that meet the actual conditions and are in the long-term interests of China; (2) conducting development on the energy conservation and emission reduction technologies (i. e. applicable renewable energy, bio-charcoal, and carbon sink technologies) that are fit for being expanded across the developing countries, in line with the Copenhagen agreement and the trend.

The government should adjust the foreign economic cooperation strategy and promote the social and environmental responsibility in overseas development. With the increasing international focus on China's rise, it is critical for the country to adjust its strategy of foreign economic cooperation against the new circumstances. Four priority areas need to be paid attention to: (1) developing new strategy in foreign economic cooperation (including China's new global resources and energy strategies) in the new era; the energy conservation and emission reduction and that of addressing climate change should be taken into account as the key factors in guiding the foreign economic cooperation, and speeding up the transformation of foreign economic development mode; (2) more wisely use the overseas resources and energy, and leverage overseas assistance funds to directly or indirectly boost the development and use of overseas resources and energy; (3) adjusting the strategy of foreign investment, developing guidelines on the corporate behavior for the Chinese companies to operate overseas, in which the Chinese companies are not only requested to follow necessary business rules and international practice, but also to shoulder their social and environmental responsibilities in the local areas where they operate; (4) transforming its overseas assistance pattern, making energy conservation, environmental protection, and addressing climate change as key components in overseas assistance to build a new green image for its enterprises and the nation as a whole.

The government should also boos the development of strategic emerging industries that are resources-saving and environment friendly. These industries include new energy, energy conservation and environmental protection, electric cars, new materials, as well as the industries that are related to green industry, construction and transportation. Specific plans will be developed at the national and local levels to define the development objectives, technical road map, spatial layout and incentive policy, enhance the building up of talent and technologies, and avoid redundant construction. In addition, those industries will gradually grow up on the basis of implementing related plans, accelerating the demonstration process, and the building of markets.

Take the environmental protection industry for instance, it plays a crucial role in addressing the domestic environmental protection challenges in China. However, it is confronted with many problems such as single investment and financing channel, poor innovation capacity, and low industry concentration. For this reason, it is necessary to strengthen the policies in environmental industry. These include: expanding the investment and financing channel; standardizing the industry system; improving the scientific and technological standards of the companies; implementing favorable taxation policies for the industries; and improving the charging system for sewage and waste discharge. In particular, emphasis should be put on: deepening the market-based reform on municipal utilities; encouraging the entry of private capital and the financial service innovation while increasing the input of public fund; improving the license-based operation model and the pricing mechanism of municipal utilities; enhancing the government's supervision on market-based reforms; and engaging the general public in environmental protection.

References

AASA. 2011. *Towards a Sustainable Asia: Green Transition and Innovation*. Beijing: Science Press and Springer.

Boulding, K. E. 1966. The economics of the coming spaceship earth. In: Jarrett, H. (Ed.), *Environ-

mental *Quality in a Growing Economy*. Baltimore:Johns Hopkins University Press,3-14.
CAS Innovation Development Research Center. 2009. *The Report on Innovation and Development in China* 2009. Beijing:Science Press.
CAS Sustainable Development Strategy Study Group. 2006. *China Sustainable Development Report* 2006: *Building a Resource-Efficient and Environment-Friendly Society*. Beijing:Science Press.
CAS Sustainable Development Strategy Study Group. 2008. *China Sustainable Development Report* 2008: *Policy Review and Outlook*. Beijing:Science Press.
CAS Sustainable Development Strategy Study Group. 2009. *China Sustainable Development Report* 2009: *China's Approach towards a Low Carbon Future*. Beijing:Science Press.
CAS Sustainable Development Strategy Study Group. 2010. *China Sustainable Development Report* 2010—*Green Development and Innovation*. Beijing:Science Press.
CAS Sustainable Development Strategy Study Group. 2011. *China Sustainable Development Report* 2011—*Greening the Economic Transformation*. Beijing:Science Press.
CAS Sustainable Development Strategy Study Group. 2012. *China Sustainable Development Report* 2012—*China's Sustainable Development in the Shifting Global Context*. Beijing:Science Press.
China Innovation and Development of Chinese Academy of Science. 2010. *China Innovation and Development*:2009. Beijing:Science Press.
Climate Group. 2009. *China's Clean Revolution* Ⅱ: *Opportunities for a Low Carbon Future*. Beijing:Climate Group.
Council of the European Union. 2009. *Towards Sustainability*: *Eco-Efficient Economy in the Context of the Post* 2010 *Lisbon Agenda and the EU Sustainable Development Strategy*. Brussels:The Council of the European Union.
Daly,H. E. ,Farley,J. 2004. *Ecological Economics*: *Principles and Applications*. Washington D. C. :Island Press.
Daly,H. E. 1973. *Toward a Steady-State Economy*. San Francisco:W. H. Freeman Publishers.
Eco-efficiency. 1996. Task force reports from first phase of the President's Council on Sustainable Development (PCSD). http://clinton2. nara. gov/PCSD/Publications/TF_Reports/eco-top. html.
Edenhofer,O. ,et al. 2009. *Towards a Global Green Recovery*: *Recommendations for Immediate G*20 *Action*(*Report Submitted to the G*20 *London Summit*). Report on behalf of German Foreign Office.
Friedman,T. L. 2008. *Hot*,*Flat and Crowded*. New York:Farrar,Straus and Giroux.
Hu,A. G. 2004. *New Development Concept in China*. Hangzhou: Zhejiang People's Publishing House-in Chinese.
Hu,J. T. 2009. Joining hands to address the challenge of climate change:speech at the opening ceremony of UN Summit on Climate Change. http://news. xinhuanet. com/world/2009-09/23/content_12098887. htm-in Chinese.
Hu,J. T. 2010. The speech of Hu Jintao at the seminar on implementing the scientific outlook

on development for the cadres at the ministerial and provincial levels. http://news.xinhuanet.com/politics/2010-02/03/content_12926039.htm-in Chinese.

Kirkham, et al. 2009. *China Greentech Report* 2009. Shanghai: Mangao Strategy.

Liu, S. H. 2001. *Green Economics*. Beijing: China Financial and Economic Publishing House-in Chinese.

Lu, Y. X. 2009. Speech at the news conference on release of strategic study reports titled "science & technology in China: a road map to 2050". http://www.bps.cas.cn/zlyj/gzdt/200906/t20090625_1818996.html-in Chinese.

McKinsey & Company. 2009. *China's Green Revolution: Prioritizing Technologies to Achieve Energy and Environmental Sustainability*. Chicago: McKinsey & Company.

Nilsson, M., et al. 2009. *A European Eco-Efficient Economy: Governing Climate, Energy and Competitiveness*. Stockholm: Stockholm Environment Institute.

OECD. 2009. *Declaration on Green Growth*. Adopted at the Meeting of the Council at Ministerial Level on 25 June 2009. C/MIN(2009)5/ADDI/FINAL.

Pearce, D., et al. 1989. *Blueprint for a Green Economy*. London: Earthscan.

UNDP. 2002. *China Human Development Report* 2002: *Making Green Development a Choice*. Beijing: China Financial and Economic Publishing House.

UNEP. 2009a. *Global Green New Deal: Policy Brief*. Nairobi: UNEP.

UNEP. 2009b. *Global Green New Deal: An Update for the G20 Pittsburgh Summit*. Nairobi: UNEP.

UNEP. 2008. Global Green New Deal—environmentally-focused investment historic opportunity for 21st century prosperity and job generation. http://www.unep.org/documents.multilingual/default.asp?documentid=548&articleid=5957&l=en[2011-9-20].

Wen, J. B. 2009. Leading China's sustainable development with science and technology. http://news.xinhuanet.com/politics/2009-11/23/content_12526569.htm-in Chinese[2009-11-23].

Zhou, H. C. 2005. *Circular Economics*. Beijing: China Development Press-in Chinese.

Zhuang, G. Y. 2007. *Low-carbon Economy*. Beijing: China Meteorological Press-in Chinese.

Zhu, D. J. 2008. *Ecological Civilization and Green Development*. Shanghai: Shanghai People's Publishing House-in Chinese.

Author

Prof. Dr. Wang Yi was born in 1962 in Beijing and graduated from Tsinghua University and Graduate University of Chinese Academy of Sciences(CAS). He is currently served as the Deputy Director-General of the CAS Institute of Policy and Management(IPM), and Deputy of the National People's Congress of China since 2008.

Prof. Wang is actively engaging in many aspects of China's policy studies. His research interests include strategic issues and public policy studies of sustainable development, especially in the fields of climate change and energy package, integrated river basin management, and comprehensive plan for the environment and development. He is now in charge of several key programs, such as CAS Strategic Leading Program: Policy Research for Carbon Budget, the National Major S & T Special Program: Reform of Water Management System and Demonstration Research, the project sponsored by the Energy Foundation: On the Legislation of Addressing Climate Change. His research result has been contributed to forming and shaping many China's current policy making and institutional arrangements. He is also the author and editor of numerous publications including more than 30 books and more than 100 technical papers. His major publications include the annual *China Sustainable Development Strategy Report* and the *China Study Report* series. His works have won several ministerial-level awards including the 4th Chinese Youth Science and Technology Award in 1994.

Prof. Wang is currently holding the following posts: Team Leader and Chief Scientist of CAS China Sustainable Development Strategy Study Program(Annual China Sustainable Development Report) since 2006, Deputy Director of the CAS Climate Change Research Center since 2009, Deputy Director of the CAS Center for Sustainable Development Research since 2006, Deputy Director of the CAS Center for Interdisciplinary Studies of Social and Natural Sciences since 2007, Adjunct Professor of the Center for China Studies of CAS and Tsinghua University since 2005, Adjunct Professor of Graduate School of the CAS since 2002. He is also serving as the standing member of the board of directors of several academic societies, the member of the editorial board of several academic journals, and the project adviser to a dozen of international organizations and foundations such as the United Nations Development Program(UNDP), United Nations Industrial Development Organization(UNIDO), Global Environmental Facility(GEF), World Bank, Asian Development Bank(ADB), EU Delegation in China, AusAID(International Development), CIDA(Canadian International Development Agency), WWF-China, WRI(World Resources Institute), Energy Foundation, and Ford Foundation.

Green Innovations and CO_2 Emissions in a Growth Perspective: Competition, Growth, Welfare Analysis and Policy Implications

Paul J.J. Welfens

2.1 Introduction

People have a natural interest to achieve high living standards, which generates analytical interest in the topic of economic growth. At the beginning of the 21st century, the dynamics of global warming have added one important element, namely to consider the role of CO_2 emissions and other greenhouse gas emissions, respectively. Innovation dynamics—including green innovations—can be considered in various ways in growth models(Bretschger, 1999; Bretschger, 2008; Bretschger, 2011); some economists have argued that green innovations and diffusion of environmental-friendly new products could contribute to climate change mitigation in an efficient manner and create new opportunities for economic growth(Aghion et al., 2009; Popp et al., 2009). Environmental issues and growth dynamics can also be considered in the broader context of trade(WTO, 1999) and foreign direct investment(Welfens, 2011; Erdem, 2010). In a broader perspective, issues may also be raised related to capital markets and investment incentives—subsequently part of the analytical focus will be on the role of green ratings: Companies are rated on the basis of sustainability of production processes and products sold; the questions arise to which extent capital market developments affect capital formation and innovation dynamics, respectively. Moreover, there is the question to which extent growth of output and consumption are associated with rising greenhouse gas emissions—and hence negative external effects that can be considered as a negative value-added; and how green technological progress can be achieved in a growing economy. An important analytical question arises once we define "net gross domestic product" which stands for net GDP minus the imputed(negative)real value of CO_2 emissions; referring to a modified neoclassical growth model, one may ask how maximum sustainable per capita consumption—net of emissions—can be achieved. This specific question of a modified golden rule(in the context of CO_2 emissions) is analyzed here for the first time, namely within a simple and convenient framework. One also may point out that a consistent index of sustainability is required(Welfens et al., 2010).

Green innovations are not easy to launch since innovation risks and costs are often high thus established, less environmentally friendly technologies and products dominate many markets. However, once green innovations have successfully been launched, there are good prospects that competition in markets will lead to rapid diffusion of more environmental-friendly products (Acemoglu et al., 2009; Aghion et al.,2009). If companies with a green innovation project are afraid that they cannot fully capture the Schumpeterian innovation rents, because policymakers will effectively push for accelerated diffusion, there is risk of underinvestment in green innovations(Newell,2009;Jaffe et al.,2005). The role of innovations for sustainable growth—sustainable consumption and production—has been emphasized by many authors (Erdem, 2010; IGES, 2010). Furthermore, the role of information and communication technology, including concepts of green IT, has also been emphasized (Welfens, 2010).

With some degree of uncertainty, green innovations(Walz,2010) can be measured and countries can also be identified on the basis of their innovation dynamics. International patent applications are highly correlated with per capita income, except for most member countries of the Organization of Petroleum Exporting Countries (OPEC). It is well known that resource-rich countries face Dutch disease problems, which means that the high share of value added in the capital-intensive resource extraction sector gives only weak impulses for the modernization of the industry—and only with a relatively high share of modern manufacturing industries and a modern innovation system will a country generate significant contributions to green innovations. The EU is more concerned with energy security and would like to reinforce the regional diversification of energy imports in the long run, not least because the share of energy imports in total energy use is expected to rise over the coming decades. The EU's main goal in the field of energy policy comes under the heading 20∶20∶20, namely that the share of renewable should reach at least 20% by 2020, energy efficiency should be improved by 20% and the CO_2 emissions should be reduced by at least 20% compared to the benchmark year 1990. High-energy prices and OPEC market power, indirectly give an incentive to the EU countries to save energy and to adopt more energy-efficiency enhancing innovations.

The market power of OPEC countries has, however, ambiguous effects on CO_2 emissions and global innovation dynamics: As regards impulses for reducing CO_2-emissions, it might be argued that OPEC countries' market power indirectly stimulates CO_2-emission-saving technologies in OECD countries and some newly industrialized countries(NICs).

While the above argument may be valid to some extent, it should not be overlooked that the industrial modernization of OPEC countries in a world economy with lower prices of nonrenewable energy sources is likely to have advanced faster than it currently is and this would mean that global innovation dynamics might be stronger without OPEC market power; whether a general increase in innovation dynamics implies more green innovation dynamics has to be clarified on the basis of empirical analysis.

A typical problem concerning the raise of relative oil/energy prices is the so-called Dutch disease problem which means that a natural resource boom will distract part of production factors from the tradable sector and raise the ratio of non-tradable wages to the wages in the tradable sector—and as the tradable sector expands in relative size, the country will suffer from a current account deficit and possibly even from lower long run growth(an effect which typically will incur if the tradable sector is more competitive than the non-tradable sector). The analysis of van der Ploeg (2011) shows that the size of the economy also plays a role: If the natural resource windfall is large, capital goods have to be produced at home and, of course, adjustment to natural resource windfall takes time. In the case of a small open economy facing a considerable windfall gain from a natural resource boom, it might be possible for the respective country to import capital and to attract sufficient migrant labor so that the Dutch disease will be avoided. Note that one may add: If the importing country(Ⅰ) is big, there will be a rise of the world real interest rate as the rising import of capital goods from country(Ⅱ) implies an increasing scarcity of capital abroad.

The broad international consensus to limit greenhouse gas emissions in the medium term and to cut emissions in the very long run has contributed to a broad policy debate in OECD countries on how energy efficiency and resource productivity could be raised. The implementation of eco-efficiency principles in production implies certain adjustment requirements and the need to adopt new initiatives for green innovation dynamics. The OECD(2009) with respect to the EU and the US notes: "Such tasks are not trivial for manufacturing companies and place great demands on their organizational management capability. The development of environmental management systems(EMSs) has tied many of the environmental monitoring and management principles together, providing a framework to move towards eco-efficient production... An EMS is meant to provide companies with a comprehensive and systematic management system for continuous improvement of its environmental performance. Once implemented, the system relies on a structure that is typically characterized by four cyclical, action-oriented steps: (1) plan; (2) implement; (3) monitor and check; (4) review and improve..."; and with respect to the EU, the OECD analysis states: "In the last few years, many companies and consulting firms have started using eco-innovation or similar terms to present positive contributions by business to sustainable development through innovation and improvements in production processes and products/services. A few governments and the EU are now promoting the concept as a way to meet sustainable development targets that keep the industry and the economy competitive. In the EU, eco-innovation has been considered to support the wider objectives of its Lisbon Strategy for competitiveness and economic growth. In 2004, the Environmental Technology Action Plan(ETAP) was introduced to promote the development and implementation of eco-innovation. The ETAP defines eco-innovation as 'the production, assimilation or exploitation of a novelty in products, production processes, services or in management and business methods, which aims, throughout its life cycle, to prevent or substantially reduce environmental risk, pollution and other negative impacts of resource use (including energy)'. The action plan provides a general road map for promoting environmental technologies and business competitiveness by focusing on bridging the gap between research and markets, improving market conditions for environmental technologies, and acting globally. Eco-innovation is now part of the EU's Competitiveness and Innovation Framework Program 2007-13, which offered € 28 million in funding in 2008 to stimulate the uptake of environmental products, processes and services especially among small medium enterprises(SMEs). In the United States, environmental technologies are also seen as a promising means of improving environmental conditions without impeding economic growth, and are promoted through various public private partnership programs and tax credits... In 2002, the Environmental Protection Agency laid out a strategy for achieving better environmental results through innovation... Based on this strategy, it set up the National Center for Environmental Innovation and is promoting the research, development and demonstration of technologies... In Japan, the government's Industrial Science Technology Policy Committee introduced the term 'eco-innovation' in 2007 as an overarching concept which provides direction and a vision for the societal and technological changes needed to achieve sustainable development."

A study by the European Commission(Conte et al., 2010) presented a model-based approach for cost-efficiency of alternative EU climate policy options through which innovation dynamics could be encouraged to contribute to an environmentally sustainable growth path. The innovative model, which is based on the Commission's QUEST Dynamic Stochastic General Equilibrium Model, assesses different policy options in order to identify the best policy mix of environment and innovation market instruments in terms of their cost-effectiveness. The key finding of the authors is that an adequate policy mix should strongly stimulate research and development in the short term and phase it out by spreading the innovation support to all sectors in the economy in the medium run. Moreover, these authors emphasized the role of the supply chain(Conte et al., 2010): "The essential contribution of our approach is to consider that green innovation occurs along the supply chain and is not necessarily bounded within a single sector. The introduction of an exhaustive sectoral input-output matrix allows us to capture the development and use of environmentally friendly products substituting dirty products across different sectors of the economy. Such a 'green' multi-sectoral version of the model allows us to evaluate the marginal economic effects of sector-wide measures compared to economy-wide policy intervention in the environment and innovation markets. In applied terms, this model is calibrated on our newly constructed dataset that includes green R&D and CO_2 emissions for five sectors with a distinctive potential for nesting green activities."

Sustainable growth is a key challenge for Europe, Asia and other regions of the globe in the 21st century. The concept of double sustainability will be emphasized here; sustainability in the traditional sense of environmental economics means that future generations should have the opportunity to enjoy at least the same level of well-being as current generation(a nation of sustainability developed in the Brundtland Report, which largely shows the perspective of industrialized countries and does not emphasize the obvious desire and need of developing countries to catch up with OECD countries). The second notion of sustainability emphasized here is related to financial markets—sustainability means that banks, investment funds and insurance companies as well as other investors have a long-run perspective. This second notion suggests emphasizing a stronger role for the green rating of companies listed on the stock market. Such a rating would be a signal to investors interested in thoughtful long-run decision-making. Sustainable development has a natural connotation with growth analysis, namely in the sense that growth modeling typically looks into the conditions of long-run growth and a stable steady state solution.

Besides the long-run growth analysis, medium-term adjustment and growth dynamics can also be looked into. Barbier (2009) has argued that governments' spending programs aiming to overcome the Transatlantic Banking Crisis should be more focused on the promotion of environmental-friendly growth so that not only the global economy could be stimulated and new employment would be created, but also, carbon dependency could be reduced, the degradation of the ecosystem could be reduced and the problem of water scarcity could be tackled more effectively.

The bottom line is, analytical progress is developed subsequently and some rough calculations on the impact of CO_2 emissions on true gross domestic product are also presented; for many OECD countries the corrected gross domestic product figure—taking into account the quasi-negative value-added of CO_2 emissions—is rather small relative to official figures from the System of National Accounts. However, there are also industrialized countries in which imputed negative value-added from CO_2 emissions are rather big: China, a country where CO_2 emissions have not been internalized through policy intervention so far, is an interesting case where the negative value-added from CO_2 emission is in the range of 2%–3% of official gross domestic product (the range is a function of the opportunity costs of CO_2 emission reduction). The outcome is that the analysis presented argues that green innovation dynamics could play a crucial role in sustainability and long-run growth. Information and communication technology is a sector that is highly innovative and could particularly contribute to green growth—despite some rebound effects in the field of green ICT. One of the most important green potentials that could be exploited by ICT is a more efficient use of machinery and equipment: by introducing virtual markets and creating virtual machines, individual demand curves at any point in time can be aggregated effectively, namely in a way that raises the capacity utilization of real machinery and equipment. The demand collected via computer systems and assigned to virtual machines can be assigned in a second step to real machines. This two-stage system will manage the existing capital stock in many sectors in a much more efficient way than prior to the expansion of ICT. This special aspect will subsequently be neglected. However, many other key aspects of green innovation and green growth will be discussed. It will be argued that simple growth models allow an important new insight into the field of green growth analysis.

2.2 A rational approach to promotion of green innovation

2.2.1 Taxation and subsidies as a means to internalize external effects

A government in a market economy has several tasks: creating institutions necessary for transactions in markets, stabilizing the economy and internalizing of negative as well as positive external effects. In addition, promoting innovations is a standard task of the government, however, before paying subsidies for research and development, the economy should be open to trade and competition should be introduced in the goods and factor markets; China has been among the countries that have made enormous progress in this field since 1990 and membership in WTO in 2001 has been an important signal. EU eastern enlargement also stands for a remarkable experience in the field of trade liberalization, privatization and competition. With the ongoing discussion about global warming and other environmental problems—including nuclear risks—there is a special need to emphasize green innovation dynamics. Innovation dynamics will be high if there are five key elements.

(1) Strong competition: as regards sustainability this refers to green product innovations and process innovation in green technology.

(2) Sufficient emphasis on human capital formation and expansion of digital networks that are important for both fast diffusion of technologies and for creating internet-based innovation networks (with more emphasis on technology-intensive production, there will be a growing demand for human capital so that there is some trade-off between rising government expenditures on education and rising promotion of innovation).

(3) Efficient innovation systems—with emphasis on sustainability.

(4) International technology flows—typically partly related to trade and foreign direct investment inflows.

(5) Adequate incentives: such incentives should tax emissions and provide R&D subsidies.

As regards innovations, there are often positive external effects from innovations in a certain sector (or from certain innovative firms in this sector) so that subsidies for innovators and R&D are justified. A Pigou tax should be imposed on activities with negative external effects and the revenues thus obtained can be used to finance government incentive schemes for innovation.

2.2.2 Economic growth

Among the leading economies—including China (and India)—there seems to be an ongoing quest for high growth rates. For countries with a low per capita income, high economic growth seems to be a natural goal of policymakers since growth is the way for economic catching up. High investment-GDP ratios are typically considered to be crucial pillars of high economic growth (g_Y) for real GDP because $g_Y = (I'/Y)\partial Y/\partial K$, where I' is real net investment and K is the capital stock. It should be noted that the growth rate of GDP could be raised by increasing the net investment-GDP ratio.

Raising the marginal product of capital (with a Cobb Douglas production function $\partial Y/\partial K = \beta Y/K$; the parameter $0 < \beta < 1$); an important aspect of the marginal product of capital is that it does not only depend on net investment, rather it also depends on the gross investment output ratio with technological progress in a vintage model. Stoleru (1978) has shown that in the case of the Cobb Douglas function, higher technological progress amounts to raising the capital depreciation rate δ.

It should also be noted that traditional growth theory—read the Solow model and many refinements following this approach—has ignored the fact that production is associated with emissions and hence a "true national accounting system" would have to consider that one should consider at least three output data in an enhanced system of economic statistics.

2.2.3 GDP(Y)

Net domestic product which could be defined as $Y - \delta K - V$ where V is the economic negative value added of emissions (and waste); innovations would help to reduce V and if $V = v''Y$ the key challenge is to reduce v'' over time.

The latter aspect has been ignored so far in official statistics and in the literature. The traditional growth literature has, however, developed an important concept, which is indirectly related to the emission problem of many countries—the concept is normative and comes under the heading of maximum per capita consumption C/L (C is real consumption, L is the population and the workforce, respectively) in the steady state. If it is assumed that the individuals' utility function is $U(C)$, it seems wise for the government to maximize steady state per capita consumption $(C/L)\#$, where $\#$ denotes the steady state—read: the long-run equilibrium.

Capital accumulation is crucial for economic growth. The investment-GDP ratio of Germany and Japan have declined in the two decades after 1990; the investment-GDP ratio was about 20% in 2009/2010, slightly higher than in the US. This is much in contrast to the rising investment-GDP ratio of China, which reached about 40% at the beginning of the 21st century. (Figure 2.1, Figure 2.2)

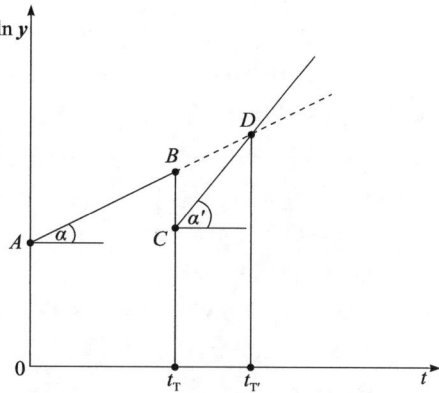

Figure 2.1 Gross investment-GDP ratios in selected countries
Source: International Monatery Fund, World Economic Outlook Database(2010)

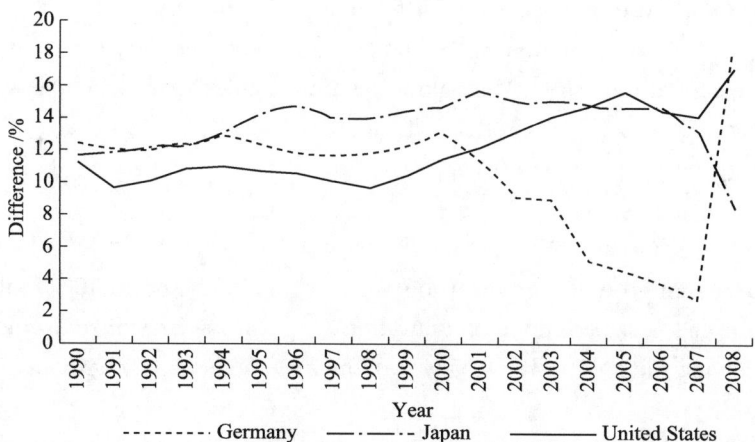

Figure 2.2 Investment-GDP ratio and net savings ratio in selected countries
Source: World Bank, World Development Indicators & Global Development Finance; International Monatery Fund, World Economic Outlook Database(2010)

Besides physical capital accumulation, focus may be placed on accumulation dynamics in human capital, which has been emphasized in the Lucas-Uzawa approach. While the Lucas-Uzawa approach—with emphasis on human capital—is useful for certain questions, it may be pointed out that refinements of the traditional Solow model also has its merits and therefore the subsequent analysis looks at key aspects of refining the approach of Solow(1956).

2.2.4 Traditional neoclassical growth modeling

The growth model of Solow(1956) is based on the assumptions that savings $S = sY$ (and hence $S/L = sY/L$ where L is labor and the size of the population, respectively) and that there is a well-behaved neoclassical production function $F(K, L)$; assuming a linear-homogeneous production function, we can write for per capita output $Y/L := y = f(k)$—where $k := K/L$ is the capital intensity—and imposing the goods market equilibrium condition $\delta K + dK/dt = sY$ (t is time and δ is the depreciation of capital) yields a different equation for the capital intensity k. Assuming a constant growth rate (n) of the population and considering that $dk/dt = (dK/dt)/L - nk$ and imposing the equilibrium condition that savings per capita should be equal to gross investment per capita, namely $S/L = (dK/dt)/L + \delta k$, we can write:

(1) $dk/dt = sf(k) - [n + \delta]k$

This equation can be used to determine the equilibrium condition, namely the steady state value $k\#$ [a stable $k\#$ implies $dk/dt = 0$; if $dk/dt = 0$, the gross investment-GDP ratio is equal to $sf(k\#)$ and this term is equal to $(n + \delta)k\#$; therefore $(n + \delta)k\#$ is the amount of per capita investment needed to maintain the steady state capital intensity]. The Solow equation is modified in a simple way, namely by assuming a Cobb Douglas production function $Y = K^\beta L^{1-\beta}$ so that $y = k^\beta$ ($0 < \beta < 1$). The steady state solution for $k\#$ is:

(2) $k\# = [s/(n + \delta)]^{1/(1-\beta)}$

(3) $y\# = [s/(n + \delta)]^{\beta/(1-\beta)}$

The optimum growth literature (von Weizsäcker, 1962; Phelps, 1961) puts focus on the equation and how per capita consumption C/L can be maximized, which is given by the following function in the steady state of a closed economy without government consumption:

(4) $C/L = y(k\#) - (n + \delta)k\#$

Maximizing C/L is obtained under the golden rule; here this requires for the case of the Cobb Douglas function $y = k^\beta$ that

(5) $d(C/L)/dk = \beta k^{\beta-1} - (n + \delta) = 0$

If profit maximization of firms brings about the equality of the real interest rate r and the net marginal product of capital $\beta k^{\beta-1} - \delta$, we get the golden rule that r must equal the growth rate of output (here the growth rate is n); alternatively, we can state that in the golden age—equivalent to the golden rule—the sum of $(n + \delta)y$ is equal to the marginal product of capital. If initially per capita savings are given by $s_0 y(k)$, the steady state capital intensity is equal to $k\#_0$. However, the golden rule—maximizing per capita consumption in the steady state—requires that we choose that capital intensity, which is characterized by a tangent to the production function $y(k)$, where the slope must be equal to that of $n + \delta$ (point E_1). The capital intensity k^{gold} brings about the maximum sustainable per capita consumption, which is equal to the distance $E_1 F$. This capital intensity can be reached if the savings rate s is reduced to s_1 (Figure 2.3).

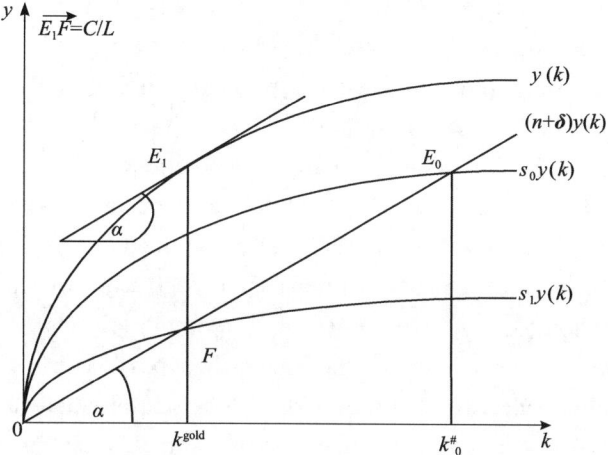

Figure 2.3 Golden rule in a standard neoclassical growth model ($E_1 F = C/L$)

Alternatively to the condition $r = n$ we can state that $s = \beta$, because from $d(C/L)/dk = \beta k^{\beta-1} - (n + \delta) = 0$ we have the equation $k\#^{gold} = [\beta/(n + \delta)]^{1/1-\beta}$, while the accumulation dynamics of the growth model for the steady state imply that $k\# = [s/(n + \delta)]^{1/1-\beta}$ and this implies (Welfens, 2011):

(6)(8') $s = \beta$

Assuming that β is given, it may be assumed that the government can manipulate the savings rate s in a way that the golden $k\#$ is reached. If the initial savings ratio s were too high—that is $k\# > k\#^{gold}$—the government should reduce the savings rate. If the initial savings rate s were too low—that is $k\# < k\#^{gold}$—the government should raise the savings rate.

If the actual steady state capital intensity exceeds the capital intensity required by the golden rule, the per capita consumption and the ratio C/Y will be lower than it would be possible in the "golden age". Since $C + I = Y$, it holds—with g denoting growth rate—that $g_Y = (C/Y)g_C + (I/Y)g_I$ and in the steady state $g_Y = g_C = g_I$. Therefore it holds that if the I/Y is higher than required by the golden rule (and $I/Y = S/Y$), we can draw the following conclusion: $d\ln(k'\#/k'^{gold})/d\ln s = 1/s$—if the savings rate is compatible with the golden rule capital intensity and we then increase the savings rate s by 1% the elasticity, $1/s$ indicates that an increase in the savings rate by 1% raises $k'\#/k'^{gold}$ by 2.5%. At the same time we know that "an excess savings rate" of 1 percentage point will reduce the consumption GDP ratio C/Y by 1 percentage point (we will pick this up in the case of China subsequently).

The standard assumption for the size of the output elasticity of capital is that it is about 1/3 in OECD countries. Hence if $s = I^{gross}/Y$, any investment-GDP above 33% would seem excessive. Excessive investment is not only a doubtful exercise from the perspective of maximum per capita consumption but also because an excess capital intensity implies an excess per capita GDP and—assuming that CO_2/L is proportionate to y—an unnecessarily high level of emissions per capita. The emission aspect has never been considered in the traditional neoclassical growth theory, but it will be covered subsequently. Note that if Germany, the US or China raises its gross investment-GDP ratio and the capital intensity, respectively, beyond the value that is compatible with the golden rule, there will be three main effects:

The consumption per capita will be lower than possible in principle; if $k\# > k^{gold}$, we get an abundance of resources and C/L is smaller than it could be under a more optimal government and economic system—and this can bring about political instability since the politico-economic system will not be judged on the basis of per capita GDP but on the basis of long-run per capita consumption.

Emissions will be higher than necessary, therefore the respective country's contribution to global warming will be higher than necessary; and the price of CO_2 emissions certificates will be higher than it would be under the (modified) golden rule (the necessary modification is considered subsequently).

This basic logic applies to all countries and therefore it is particularly necessary to reduce the capital intensity in those countries that face excess capital intensity (there could be symmetrical problems in some countries, namely that the capital intensity is below the golden rule capital intensity, but it seems likely that both politicians and investors would rather have a tendency for overinvestment than for underinvestment).

A crucial question in reality concerns the size of the savings rate and the size of the depreciation rate. Following the World Bank concept of genuine savings, serious doubts may be raised about the significance of the official savings rate. The genuine savings rate that takes a broader definition of capital into account—physical capital, human capital and the stock of natural resources—often looks different from the official savings rate. Countries with huge depletion rates of natural resources typically have genuine savings rates that are lower than the official savings rates from traditional statistics. The savings rate is, of course, of key importance in growth modeling. It should be pointed out that the difference between the gross savings rate from the system of national accounts and the genuine savings rate is large in many countries.

Since emissions enter a hybrid welfare function—with per capita consumption and emissions per capita—with a negative sign it is important to consider the share of renewable(almost zero CO_2 emissions within the life cycle analysis).

The international specialization of countries in the field of innovation matters for green progress. Here it is interesting to see how specialization patterns change. Looking at revealed comparative advantage, it is clear that some countries are positively specialized while others are negatively specialized.

Policymakers' focus on the maximum C/L in the steady state is only plausible to some extent. The problem that any given capital intensity k and GDP per capita, respectively, is associated with certain emissions need to be considered and it may be assumed that emissions enter the individual utility function with a negative sign. Raising per capita consumption over time is a natural goal of policymakers and this should be achieved in a sustainable way which will require some specific innovation efforts on the one hand, and on the other hand, a key idea here is the neoclassical golden rule which emphasizes that there is a specific capital intensity—the ratio K/L [or $K/(AL)$ in a model which includes knowledge A so that AL is labor in efficiency units]—which maximizes the long run per capita consumption.

2.2.5 Technological progress and R&D

Subsequently we will use the production function $Y = K^\beta (AL)^{1-\beta}$—where A is knowledge and L is labor, $0 < \beta < 1$; by assumption knowledge is labor-augmenting, but other types of technological progress also can be considered. Note that $\partial Y/\partial K = \beta Y/K$. Using the production function $Y = K^\beta (AL)^{1-\beta}$ and assuming that the growth rate of knowledge $d\ln A/dt = a$ is exogenous and has a specific advantage, we can write (with $k' := K/(AL)$):

(7) $y' := Y/(AL)$

Here AL is dubbed labor in efficiency units; therefore the mechanics of the neoclassical model are roughly the same as in the simple Solow model. Using a savings function $S = s(1-\tau)Y$—where τ is the income tax rate—and hence $S/(AL) = s(1-\tau)y'$, we obtain a differential equation in k', namely $dk'/dt = s(1-\tau)y' - (a+n+\delta)k'$ and taking into account that $y' = k'^\beta$, the solution of the Bernoulli differential equation is(with C' to be determined from initial conditions in $t = 0$; e' is the Euler number):

(8) $k'(t) = [C'e^{-(a+n+\delta)(1-\beta)t} + s(1-\tau)/(a+n+\delta)]^{1/1-\beta}$

This differential equation is converging to the steady state value $k'\#$ if $0<\beta<1$ which has been assumed. Setting $t = 0$ we get $k'(0) = [C' + s(1-\tau)/(a+n+\delta)]^{1/1-\beta}$ and therefore $(k'_0)^{1-\beta} = C' + s(1-\tau)/(a+n+\delta)$, which implies that $C' = (k'_0)^{1-\beta} - s(1-\tau)/(a+n+\delta)$.

The steady state solution is:

(9) $k'\# = [s(1-\tau)/(a+n+\delta)]^{1/(1-\beta)}$

(10) $y'\# = [s(1-\tau)/(a+n+\delta)]^{\beta/(1-\beta)}$

Since $A(t) = A_0 e^{'at}$—where A_0 is knowledge in the initial time period $t = 0$—we can write the following for per capita income:

(11) $y = \{A_0[s(1-\tau)/(n+a+\delta)]^{\beta/(1-\beta)}\}e^{'at}$

Since $L(t) = L_0 e^{'nt}$

(12) $Y = \{L_0 A_0[s(1-\tau)/(n+a+\delta)]^{\beta/(1-\beta)}\}e^{'(a+n)t}$

The level of the growth path in y-t space is determined by the expression $\{A_0[s(1-\tau)/(n+a+\delta)]^{\beta/(1-\beta)}\}$. The growth rate of output per capita in the steady state is given by the parameter a, the growth rate of Y in the steady state is $(a+n)$.

The role of the rate of technological progress rate (a) is important and in particular it holds that (see the subsequent figure where the initial path is ABD):

(1) A rise in the progress rate a (in t_T) will reduce the level of the growth path.

(2) At the same time, a rise in the increase of the steady state growth rate of y.

If the government's time horizon is sufficiently long, the government will undertake measures that raise the rate of technological progress: government will understand that the short-term impact of a rise in the progress rate is that the level of the growth path is reduced, while the long-term impact implies—due to the rise in the permanent growth rate—that a higher per capita income can be reached than without the rise in the progress rate. Only in countries where the government extremely discounts future income gains associated with a higher rate of technological progress will the government likely to not have an increased progress rate (Figure 2.4).

2.2.6 Golden Rule Aspects in an Economy with Technological Progress

In a world with technological progress, the golden rule capital intensity requires:

(13) $\beta k'^{\beta-1} = (n+a+\delta)$

If firms are profit maximizing, the net marginal product must equal r and therefore $(\beta k'^{\beta-1} - \delta) = r$, we get the implication $r = (n+a)$. If capital markets bring about the condition $r = (n+a)$, the society is in the golden steady state. While it might be argued that China's economy is not in a steady state, the subsequent graph

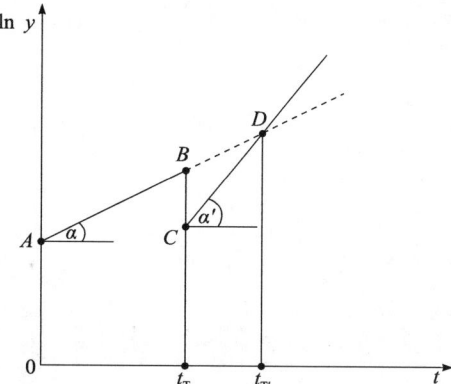

Figure 2.4　Impact of a rise of the growth rate of knowledge on the level of per capita income (y) and the growth rate of per capita income(tg $\alpha = a$)

raises some doubts about the wisdom of China's growth policy: as the real GDP growth rate has been above the real interest rate for 30 years, the hypothesis might state that China's aggressive growth policy has raised the capital intensity systematically above a level which is consistent with the golden rule. The elasticity of ($k' \# / k'^{\text{gold}}$) with respect to the savings rate is 2.5 has already been pointed out(assuming that China's savings rate is initially 0.4 which already is high; there are some good arguments why the elasticity could be even higher). Thus China's government faces the risk that its policy contributes to high growth rates of output, while households/voters are partially dissatisfied because per capita consumption is relatively low (China's increasing investment-GDP ratio mainly benefits Germany, Japan and the US as major exporters of machinery and equipment). Looking at the subsequent figures for Germany, Japan, Russia and the US, it seems that Germany, Japan and the US have an economic performance, which is largely in line with the golden rule. (Figure 2.5)

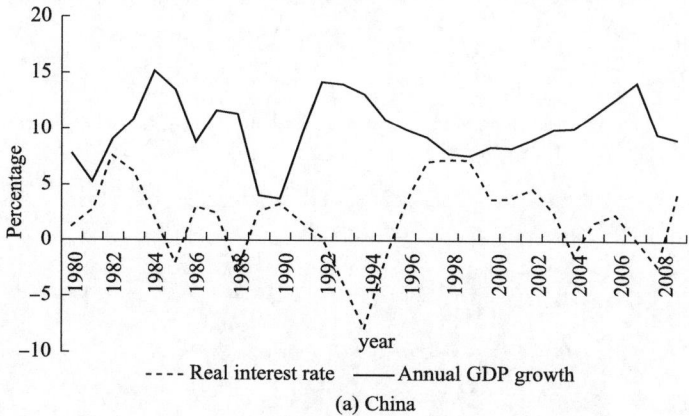

(a) China

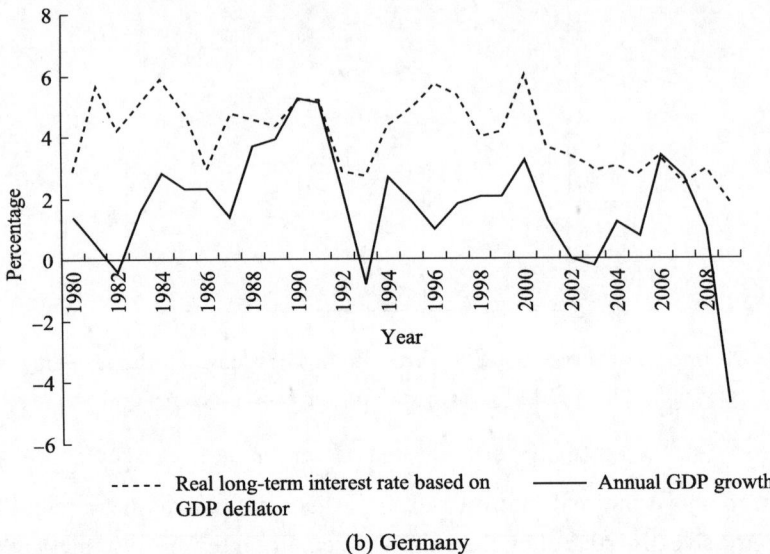

(b) Germany

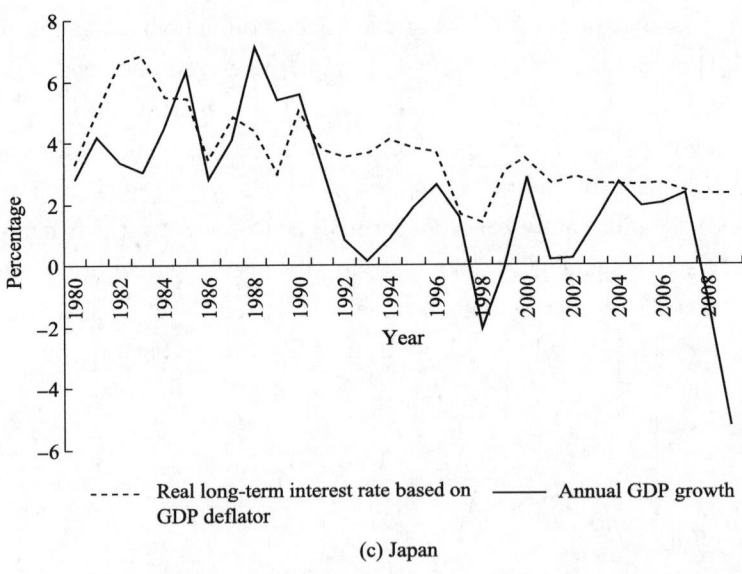

(c) Japan

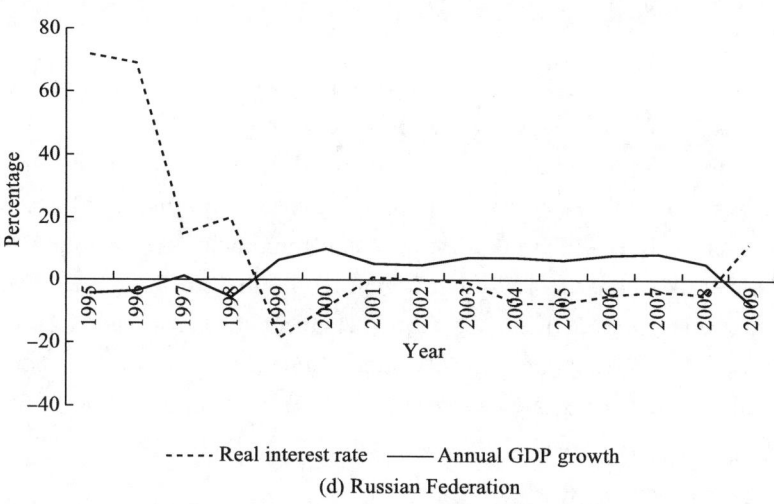

(d) Russian Federation

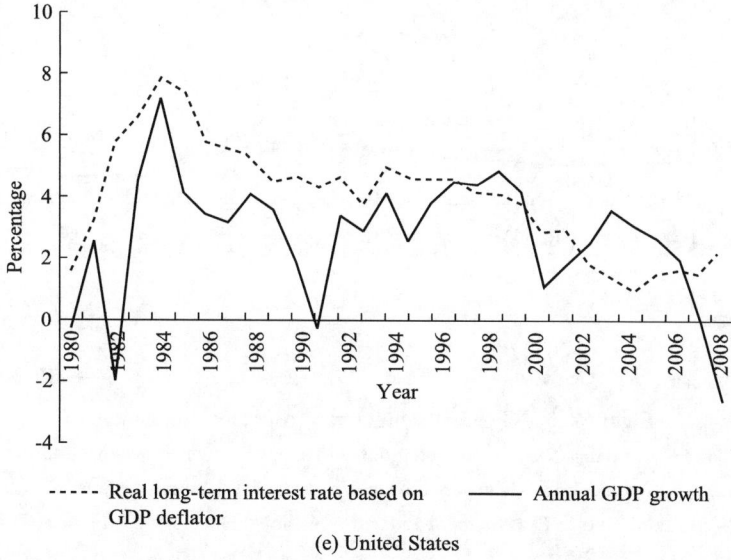

(e) United States

Figure 2.5 Real interest rate and growth rate of real GDP in selected countries

Source: European Commission Ameco database [real long-term interest rate based on GDP deflator (%)]; World Bank, World Development Indicators & Global Development Finance [real interest rate/ real lending rate(%), GDP growth(annual %)]

Note that from the steady state solution for $k'\#$, we can draw the following conclusion for the steady state:

(14) $s(1-\tau) = \beta$

Thus the optimum tax rate (golden tax rate) is given by:

(15) $1 - \tau = \beta/s$

(16) $1 - \beta/s = \tau$

If β exceeds s—a typical perception based on standard statistics of the OECD—the income tax rate should be negative. However, the government must have some tax revenues in order to be able to run the political system; without a stable political system there is no stable economic system and therefore no sustainable growth.

A broader analysis which takes into account the genuine savings ratio—as published by the World Bank—however, leads to different results: the genuine savings ratio considers not only standard savings activities but also investment in human capital (this raises the savings rate) and the depletion rate of natural resources (depletion of non-renewable resources reduces the savings rate) as well as some other activities (Figure 2.6).

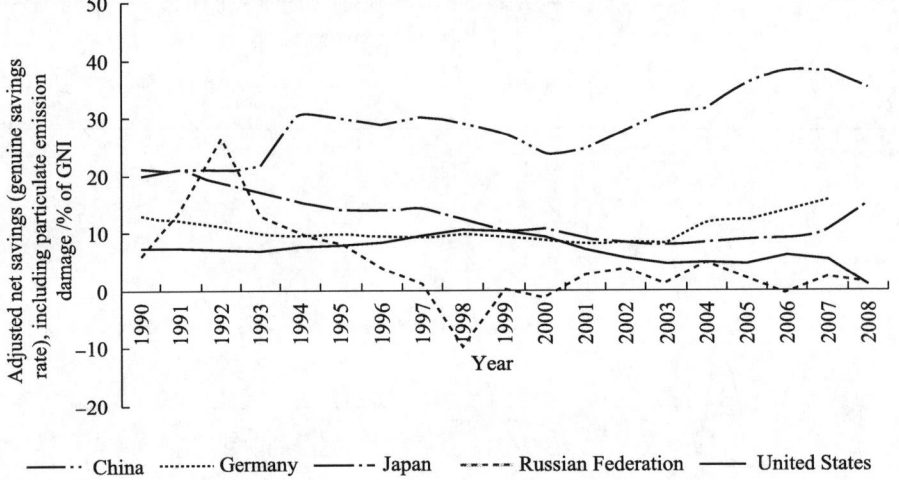

Figure 2.6 Genuine savings rate for selected countries

Note: Adjusted net savings are equal to net national savings plus education expenditure, minus energy, mineral and net forest depletion, and carbon dioxide and particulate emissions damage

Source: World Bank, World Development Indicators & Global Development Finance (2010)

2.3 Growth in a world with negative external effects: CO_2 emissions and hybrid welfare

If it is assumed that CO_2 emissions per unit of AL are proportionate to y', the maximization of the difference between y' and investment per unit of labor in efficiency units in the steady state will no longer be desirable. Rather, $y'(1 - \psi)$ minus the investment relative to AL will be considered, where ψ stands for the imputed marginal negative CO_2 welfare effect of y'; ψ is a parameter in the interval $(0,1)$ and it indicates the negative external effects—the marginal negative welfare effect related to CO_2 per unit of AL—from production related emissions. In a nutshell, the government wants to maximize hybrid welfare $C/(AL) - \psi CO_2/(AL) = y' - \Omega CO_2/(AL) - (a + n + \delta)k'$ which under the simple assumption gives that $CO_2/(AL) = \psi' y'$ the expression (with $\Omega := \psi\psi'$):

(17) $C/(AL) = y'(1 - \Omega) - (a + n + \delta)k'$

It will be assumed that the size of the negative externality is a negative function of the share of workers employed in (green) R&D and we may specify $\Omega = \Omega'(1 - \Omega''\rho)$ where Ω' is the environmental externality parameter in the absence of an R&D sector ($0 < \Omega'' < 1$). The specification $\Omega = \Omega'(1 - \Omega''\rho)$ postulates that the innovation system is organized in a pro-ecological way. Thus the result we get for the golden rule is:

(18) $\beta[1 - \Omega'(1 - \rho)]k'^{\beta-1} = (\rho'\rho - \rho'' + n + \delta)k'$

(19) $k'\#^{gold} = \{\beta[1 - \Omega'(1 - \rho)]/(\rho'\rho - \rho'' + n + \delta)\}^{1/(1-\beta)}$

The CO_2 emission effect reduces the golden capital intensity $k\#^{gold}$. The reduction is the term $(1 - \Omega)$ where Ω is the combined parameter from negative utility ψ and the emission parameter ψ' (green innovations that reduce ψ' imply that the golden capital intensity will increase).

Taking the result for the steady state into account, we can write:

(20) $s(1 - \tau) = \beta[1 - \Omega'(1 - \Omega''\rho)]$

Taking logs [assuming that $\ln(1 + x) \approx x$; τ and $\Omega'(1 - \Omega''\rho)$ have to be small here] we get:

(21) $\ln(s/\beta) - \tau = -\Omega'(1 - \Omega''\rho)$

(22) $[-\ln(s/\beta) + \tau]/\Omega' = (1 - \Omega''\rho)$

(23) $\rho = \{1 - [\ln(s/\beta) - \tau]/\Omega'\}/\Omega''$

This equation gives the optimal share of workers employed in the R&D sector; this share is thus a positive function of the output elasticity, a negative function of the savings rate and Ω'' (the effectiveness at which a higher share of researchers in overall employment reduces emissions) and a positive function of the autonomous externality parameter Ω'. This analysis has broad implications for economic policy.

2.4 Policy perspectives

Many developing countries are catching up with leading OECD countries. Typical ingredients of the catching-up process are the following: (1) Improvement of the level of education. (2) Foreign direct investment inflows that bring about an international technology transfer. (3) High investment output ratio partly stimulated by government and government firms, respectively.

In China (and possibly in other countries) there is a tendency for overinvestment. Such overinvestment has two negative aspects:

(1) Output growth and capital accumulation are higher than required by the golden rule; therefore per capital consumption is not optimal—it is lower than it could be. (2) As per capita output growth is too high, the CO_2 per capita emissions are also too high. This is not only a problem for China as it contributes to global warming so that negative international externalities occur.

The topic of optimal taxation should be picked up in a new way: The inherent logic of the government budget constraint and the ideas developed here suggests a careful look into the determination of an adequate subsidy rate and Pigou rate, on the one hand, and the determination of the income tax rate, on the other hand. If the income tax rate can be lowered, this will stimulate economic development, which should be discussed in Europe, Asia and North America.

With rising per capita income, there will typically be a growing interest in a clean environment—the income elasticity of the demand for a clean environment is positive—and at the same time, higher per capita income often goes along with higher emissions per capita; if green innovations increase parallel to per capita income (once a critical minimum per capita income and a minimum R&D-GDP have been achieved), there could be some decoupling between the growth of per capita income and emissions per capita.

References

Acemoglu, et al. 2009. The environment and directed technical change. *NBER Working Papers*, 15451, 1-66.
Aghion, et al. 2009. No green growth without innovation. *Bruegel Policy Briefs*, 7, 1-8.
Barbier, E. B. 2009. A global green new deal. Report prepared for the Economics and Trade Branch, Division of Technology, Industry and Economics, United Nations Environment Programme, mimeo.
Bretschger, L. 2010. Economic growth, structural change, and global sustainability. Paper presented at the 3rd International Wuppertal Colloquium on "Sustainable Growth and Resource Productivity—Harnessing Industry and Policy towards Eco-Innovation", Brussels.
Bretschger, L. 1999. *Growth Theory and Sustainable Development*. Northhampton: Edward Elgar Publishing.

Bretschger, L. 2008. Wachstumstheoretische perspektiven der wirtschaftsintegration: Neuere ansätze. *Jahrbücher für Nationalökonomie und Statistik*, 222, 64-79.

Conte, A., Labat, A., Varga, J., et al. 2010. What is the growth potential of green innovations? An Assessment of EU Climate Policy Options, European Economy, Economic Papers No. 413, European Commission.

Erdem, D. 2010. FDIs, energy efficiency and innovation dynamics. Paper presented at the 3rd International Wuppertal Colloquium on "Sustainable Growth and Resource Productivity—Harnessing Industry and Policy Towards eco-Innovation", Brussels.

IGES. 2010. Sustainable consumption and production in the Asia-Pacific region. IGES White Paper Ⅲ.

Jaffe, et al. 2005. A tale of two market failures: technology and environmental policy. *Ecological Economics*, 54, 164-174.

Newell, R. G. 2009. Literature review of recent trends and future prospects for innovation in climate change mitigation. *OECD Environment Working Papers*, 9, 1-51.

OECD. 2009. *Eco-Innovation in Industry: Enabling Green Growth*. Paris.

Phelps, E. S. 1961. The golden rule of accumulation: a fable for growthmen. *American Economic Review*, 51, 638-643.

Popp, et al. 2009. Energy, the environment, and the technological change. *NBER Working Papers*, 14832, 1-74.

Solow, R. M. 1956. A contribution to the theory of economic growth. *Quarterly Journal of Economics*, 70, 65-94.

Stoleru, L. 1978. *L'Équilibreet la Croissanceéconomique*. Paris: Dunod Éditeur.

van der Ploeg, F. 2011. Fiscal policy and Dutch disease. *International Economics and Economic Policy*, 8, 121-138.

von Weizsäcker, C. C. 1962. *Wachstum, Zins und Optimale Investitionsquote*. Tübingen: Mohr Siebeck.

Walz, R. 2010. Benchmarking green innovation. Paper presented at the 3rd International Wuppertal Colloquium on "Sustainable Growth and Resource Productivity—Harnessing Industry and Policy towards Eco-Innovation", Brussels.

Welfens, P. J. J. 2010. Green ICT dynamics and double sustainability. Paper presented at the 3rd International Wuppertal Colloquium on "Sustainable Growth and Resource Productivity—Harnessing Industry and Policy towards Eco-Innovation", Brussels.

Welfens, P. J. J. 2011. *Innovations in Macroeconomics* (3rd revised and enlarged edition). Heidelberg and New York: Springer.

Welfens, P. J. J., Perret, J., Erdem, D. 2010. Global economic sustainability indicator: analysis and policy options for the Copenhagen process. *International Economics and Economic Policy*, 7, 153-186.

WTO. 1999. *Environment and Trade*. Special Studies 4, Geneva.

Author

Prof. Paul Welfens, born on January 29th, 1957 in Düren, studied economics in Duisburg, Wuppertal, Berkeley and Paris. He obtained his Ph. D. in 1985 from the University of Duisburg. He obtained his habilitation in 1989 with a study on the internationalization of economies and perspectives for economic policy. From 1992 to 1994, he has been Professor for European and International Economics at the University of Münster, and from 1995 to 2004 at the University of Potsdam. Since 2004, he holds the Chair for Macroeconomics at the University of Wuppertal. In addition, he has been awarded the Jean Monnet Chair for European Economic Integration, and is the Founding Director of the European Institute of International Economics. In 2007, he took a visiting professorship at the Institute d'Etudes Politiques de Paris. In the same year he was the first German to be awarded the silver medal of the International N. D. Kondratiev Foundation. Prof. Welfens has been, among others, a distinguished Mc Cloy Research Fellow and a DaimlerChrysler Research Fellow at Johns Hopkins University. Welfens has published over 160 works and academic papers, and is one of the managing editors of the journal *International Economics and Economic Policy*.

Are There Any First and Second Mover Advantages for Eco-pioneers? Lead Market Strategies for Environmental Innovation

Klaus Rennings, Thomas Cleff

3.1 Introduction

The term first mover advantage is often cited in documents of environmental policy. For example, in the justification of the *Renewable Energy Act*, the German government states that it will realize first mover advantages due to the use of renewable energy with modern technology(Bundesregierung,2007). Another example from the German Ministry of Environment(2008) is the report *Investments for a Climate Friendly Germany* which mentions these technology investments will create first mover advantages for the domestic industry. At the European level, the President of the European Commission, Jose Manuel Barroso(2008), argues that the European energy and climate change package should be seen as an opportunity to Europe in economic terms:"It will encourage innovation and it will increase competitiveness. It is a mistake to oppose the fight against climate change to the competitiveness of European industries. The Union should lead the global efforts to tackle climate change. And European industries should continue to be world leaders. At the same time, we will also create new markets and new jobs, and make sure that we have the first mover advantage in many sectors."

It seems that in the political arena first mover advantages for environmental technologies are taken for granted. It is a popular view to see the state as a political entrepreneur who introduces a certain environmental policy instrument such as feed-in tariffs for renewable energies, and thus creates a profitable market for the respective technology. However, with regard to lead markets, the question should be allowed if it can be attractive for a country to invest in the development of a market where the majority of goods and services have imported from other countries, such as in the case of photovoltaics in Germany(Frondel et al. ,2010). There would also be an alternative strategy for government strategies in environmental technology markets to wait and to catch up quickly later by leapfrogging, being a second mover or a late follower, with likely giants steps in catching up(Hilton,2001). This is a strategic option especially for emerging countries such as China and India(but the question of being a 2nd mover seems also be realistic e. g. for many southern or eastern European countries in the European Union).

Against this background, this paper wants to find out if first mover advantages for pioneering firms are confirmed by theories and empirical evidence from the relevant literature of industrial organization, business management, environment and development economics. It starts with an analysis of market-oriented innovation strategies of innovating companies. It has however to be asked if such strategies can easily be transferred to eco-innovations and to the level of national policy strategies. In a second step we look at the case of wind energy in China as an example for successful leapfrogging strategies at country level. The second case of the feed-in tariffs policy in Germany will show that a too narrowly defined national lead market policy—only focusing on the demand advantage of the market—may not necessarily lead to advantages of the German photovoltaic industry. Industry policy has to take into account the whole range of all lead market factors of the lead market approach and the supply-side of the industry at the same time. Only if the supply-side is able to develop high lead market potentials for all lead market factors, the country's industry may benefit from a governmental lead market strategy.

Therefore the structure of this paper is as follows: While section 3.2 introduces the concept of lead markets, section 3.3 reviews the theoretical reasons for first and second mover advantages; Section 3.4 gives an overview about the empirical literature on econometric analyses and case studies for first and second mover advantages, country lead market strategies and leapfrogging; In section 3.5 the question of lead markets vs. lead suppliers will be discussed; Finally we will draw some conclusions regarding national lead market policies.

3.2 The lead market approach

3.2.1 Lead market factors

The lead market approach suggests focusing customer interaction on those regions, which are likely to be ahead in international demand trends and show demand preferences that are later adopted in other regions, too. It was first suggested in the 1980s by Porter(1986) and Bartlett and Ghoshal(1990), and is receiving increasing attention worldwide during the last years (Cleff et al., 2009; Commission of the European Communities,2006;Johansson,2000). Bartlett and Ghoshal(1990) consider lead markets as "markets that provide the stimuli for most global products and processes of a multinational company"..."Innovation in such markets become useful elsewhere as the environmental characteristics that stimulated such innovations diffuse to other locations."

A lead market can be defined as a country where users prefer and demand a specific innovation design that not only appeals to domestic users, but can subsequently be commercialized successfully in other countries as well. The technical design preferred by the lead market squeezes out other designs initially preferred in other countries and becomes the globally dominant design. The innovation designs adopted in the lead market have an advantage over other country-specific innovation designs competing globally to set the international standard. This advantage makes consumers from other countries follow the technological standard of the lead market and adopt the design preferred by users there. In some cases this means abandoning a design that was previously preferred on the national market (Beise et al., 2002). Where the scientific and technical knowledge for this purpose was actually generated is mostly not relevant, as companies in the lead market are able to appropriate this knowledge. More important for competitiveness is the ability to learn on the lead market about the applications and production of innovations(Meyer-Krahmer,1997).

Therefore, lead markets have specific properties (lead market factors) that increase the probability of a wide take-up of the same innovation design in other countries(Commission of the European Communities,2006). A theoretical lead market model has to provide these lead market factors. Moreover, it has to give an answer to the question under which market circumstances a country's market characteristics are appropriate to the adoption of technological innovations that will succeed internationally and mark out the technological path to be followed worldwide.

At the moment there is no consistent and stringent lead market theory. However, Beise(2006,2001)and Cleff et al. (2007) were able to develop an eclectic approach of a lead market model. They have been investigating lead markets on the basis of detailed ex-post case studies focusing on the mechanisms at a national level and how these mechanisms are leading to global designs. Beise(2001) himself has derived a system of five particular country-specific success factors for lead markets. A study on lead markets of environmental innovations has added a sixth success factor, the so-called regulation advantage(Beise and Rennings, 2005). These factors are influencing the international competitiveness of innovations and a good performance of these factors at the national level increases the probability of the market becoming a lead market. The six factors, as shown in Figure 3.1, are price advantage, demand advantage, transfer advantage, export advantage, market structure advantage and regulation advantage.

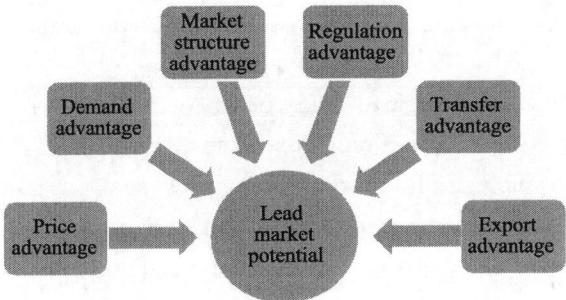

Figure 3.1 Lead market factors
Source: Rennings and Smidt(2010)

A price advantage arises from national conditions that result either in relative reductions in the price of a nationally preferred innovation design compared with designs preferred in other countries or in anticipation of international factor price changes. Countries can gain a price advantage if the relative price of the nationally preferred innovation design decreases, thus compensating for differences in demand preference to foreign countries. This price mechanism is the centerpiece of Levitt's (1983) globalization hypothesis, according to which consumers in foreign markets "capitulate" to the attraction of lower prices and abandon their initial endowment of goods. Price reductions are mainly due to cost reductions based on static and dynamic economies of scale (learning-by-doing). Market size and growth are examples of country-specific factors creating economies of scale. Another price advantage emerges from anticipatory factor prices in the lead market. Factor price changes can induce innovation. If the new relative prices occur worldwide, the same innovations are adopted worldwide as well. Price advantages also play an important role in leapfrogging strategies in emerging countries due to low labor costs.

Demand advantages originate from national conditions which result in the anticipation of the benefits of an innovation design emerging at a global level. A good example is provided by off-grid solutions in the energy and telecommunication sector. Such innovations are more beneficial and thus more likely to be adopted first in industrialized, geographically large countries with a low population density, such as in Scandinavia(Beise and Rennings, 2005). When other countries catch up, they demand the same innovation that has already been used in the country at the forefront of the trend. Another example is provided by trends related to environmental problems such as climate change. Some countries are more exposed to the risks of rising temperatures (e.g. countries with above-average risks of flooding like the Netherlands) than others and will thus anticipate these trends earlier.

Transfer advantages are national conditions that increase the perceived benefit of a nationally preferred innovation design for users in other countries or by which national demand conditions are actively transferred abroad. The perceived benefit increases when information on the usability of the innovation design is made available. The initial adoption of an innovation of unknown merit reduces the uncertainty and therefore the risk for subsequent adopters and kicks off a bandwagon effect—also referred to as the demonstration effect of adoption (Mansfield, 1968). With regard to eco-innovation, international reputation in the field of environmental technologies plays an important role.

Conditions which promote the inclusion of foreign demand preferences in nationally preferred innovation designs constitute a national export advantage. Three national export advantage factors can be identified: domestic demand that is sensitive to the problems and needs of foreign countries, the established export experience of national firms, and the similarity of local market conditions to foreign market conditions. Dekimpe et al. (1998) support the hypothesis already proposed by Vernon (1979) that the greater the cultural, social and economic similarities are between two countries, the greater is the likelihood that an innovation design adopted by one of the two countries will be adopted by the other country as well.

The market structure effect focuses mainly on the degree of competition. Competition and entrepreneurial effort have been described as two of the main determinants of international patterns of innovations by researchers such as Posner (1961) and Dosi et al. (1990). The lead market is usually highly competitive. This is due to the fact that faster development and more market-oriented innovations are supported by competitive market structures. Firstly, companies engaged in fierce competition will demand more innovations from suppliers because they are able to reap greater competitive rewards from using innovative parts than monopolies (Porter,1990). Secondly, competing firms are under more pressure to emulate firms which have already adopted a new technology(Mansfield,1968). Thirdly, and possibly most importantly, more innovation designs are tested in a competitive market than in a monopoly market.

Regulation advantage is a specific determinant of environmental innovations (Rennings,2000), thus it will be explained separately in the next section.

3.2.2 Lead markets, eco-innovation and regulation

In this paper we define environmental innovation (or eco-innovation) as innovation of new or modified processes, techniques, practices, systems and products which are more environmental friendly compared to earlier innovations(Rennings and Zwick,2002;Kemp and Arundel,1998)[①]. Beise and Rennings(2005) have shown that lead markets exist for environmental innovations, with demand advantages being especially relevant e. g. for eco-efficient cars. However, for other eco-innovations such as renewable energies innovations are strongly driven by regulation. Beise and Rennings added regulation advantages of a country as a sixth lead market factor specifically for eco-innovations. Due to the—at least partial—public good character of new environmental products and processes, it is evident that regulation will have an important influence on the innovation process and therefore on the lead market position. Two different types of eco-innovations can be distinguished as follows.

Environmental innovations can have a typical business objective with the aim to reduce the costs in the production process or the product characteristics, to raise the product quality and thus to improve the competitive situation—with a reduction of environmental impact at the same time. This type of eco-innovation does not differ in its primary focus from other product or process innovations, which also have as target the increase of process or market efficiency. Porter and van der Linde(1995) see this form of eco-innovation especially there, where resources are privately owned or possess a regular market price and savings of respective resources are immediately cost-effective. Several eco-innovations have this "triple-benefit" for the environment, the firm and the user. Examples for such eco-innovations are innovation in energy and

---

[①] Innovation in the organization of firms as it is described in the OECD(2005)guidelines on the collection and interpretation of innovation data is not within the scope of this paper.

material efficiency(Rennings and Rammer,2009).

On the other hand,eco-innovations can have the exclusive focus on the reduction of environmental impacts. This is the case when policy regulations interfere in the economy and thus cause innovations. The prohibitions to use certain harmful products, resources or end-of pipe technologies are examples for this. This type of regulation can improve the international competitive situation for the home industry when the regulation policy is adopted by other countries so that the innovation design established on the home market can develop into a global design. One can speak—in terms of the lead market language—of an anticipation of existing regulatory trends by a national government. It is not very difficult to observe such long term regulation trends if we look at the issues of international agreements: low carbon economy, energy and material savings are for example megatrends of the current and future decades(Jänicke,2008). Regulation can pick up such regulatory trends and lead to the development of new markets,for example for energy efficient refrigerators,dishwashers or washing machines. These new markets, however, must orient themselves along the lead market factors and allow the development of a global design on the home market. However,there is the risk that other countries will not follow the regulation process or that they will choose another form of regulation and that there develops an idiosyncratic innovation design on the home market. But the development of environmental markets such as the rapid worldwide diffusion of energy efficiency labels shows that there is a quick adoption of innovative regulation in the area of eco-innovations.

3.2.3　Innovation timing advantage

3.2.3.1　Sources of first mover advantages

The "first mover" in theory is the very first firm to bring an innovative product or service to markets,but in practice it means one of the first to do. Therefore,Gilbert and Birnbaum-More(1996) recommend to use the term "early mover" since it might be a more accurate description of most situations, which are discussed as "first mover". "Second mover"or"late mover"means all firms entering the market after the "first mover(s)". They typically imitate or adapt the innovation design.

Only the profits for innovation with well specified and protected intellectual property rights(IPRs) are limited to a single first user. Where do the first mover advantages result from and why don't they come up in specific situations? Three basic sources of first mover advantages and another three of second mover advantages are often described in literature of business strategies(Gilbert and Birnbaum-More,1996;

Lieberman and Montgomery, 1988).

The first source of a first mover advantage is technological leadership due to a quick reduction of costs, the learning or experience curve (Lieberman, 1987) or a success in R&D or patent races (Mansfield, 1986). When IPRs are well-specified and protected, a firm gains competitive advantages through patenting or copyright, or as a trade secret. Theoretically this leads to a temporary monopoly. Mansfield (1985) however has found that successful protection of IPRs against imitation by other firms is a rare case.

Secondly, a source of first mover advantages can be the pre-emption of physical or spatial assets such as skilled workers, unique channels of distribution or manufacturing facilities. It is seldom the case however that those assets are completely appropriated by a single firm (Lieberman and Montgomery, 1988). It can thus be argued that pre-emption of assets is a kind of timing advantage available to several "first movers", i. e. "first movers" securing anchor locations in a new shopping mall in a desirable area gain advantages over latecomers.

The third category of advantages is buyer switching costs. Switching costs develop due to initial transaction costs or investments when a user has to adapt to the new product. First of all, the user must be convinced of learning another system. This step demands for non-superior products specific marketing skills and additional costs from the followers. Additionally, there arise user-related qualification costs, which must be covered by the supplier or the user. All these costs have to be raised by the follower in order to compete with the "first mover" on the market. In case the "first mover" is able to convince the buyer of the uncertainty of the follower's product quality, then the user will seldom turn away from the first brand, which has already proven its quality. Switching costs may also arise through the users' contractual restraints with the "first mover" (Lieberman and Montgomery, 1988).

It can be summarized that out of the three sources of first mover advantages, only technological leadership—if at all—is restricted to a single firm. And in the case of technological leadership it depends on the existence and protection of IPRs, and on the time potential imitators need to find ways around the restriction.

3.2.3.2 Sources of second mover advantages

"Second movers" have a competitive advantage in specific situations, which are based on three theoretical arguments. There is no indication in the literature that second mover advantages may be limited to a single firm.

The competitive advantage for "second movers" is simply to free-ride on first mover investments. This is possible due to the positive spillover of the "first mover", especially when IPRs are not well-defined and specified. Many products and services can be easily and inexpensively imitated. In many cases "second movers" can also profit from improvements of the "first mover" regarding the learning and experience curve(Lieberman,1987).

A second source of advantages is technological developments or customer needs, which arise after the introduction made by the "first mover". They may be overlooked by the "first mover" due to incumbent inertia. This argument is taken up by Markides and Geroski(2005) who argue that a "first mover" is colonizing the product and typically has a different—in most cases technology—driven mindset, while a fast second firm focuses on consolidation from niche to mass markets.

The third main advantage for "second movers" is leapfrogging(Fudenberg et al., 1983), i.e. catching up to the "first mover" in fast, big or even giant steps. While the developer of the new product or service had to experiment with a lot of different variations of the original innovation design, and thus had to pay a large amount of development costs, which are now sunk costs, the "second mover" has the advantage of reduced market, technological and regulatory uncertainty.

In the following we want to present the results of some empirical studies that have analyzed, which factors influence the innovation success of market pioneers/of a follower in dependency on different factors.

3.2.4 Empirical evidence from the literature

3.2.4.1 Business management literature: evidence on first vs. second mover advantages of firms

The empirical literature brings up reasons for and against first mover advantages, which have been analyzed broadly during the past decades. An analysis of studies shows that until the mid 1980s the opinion prevailed that only the market pioneer can secure a long-lived market share advantage(Urban et. al, 1986; Robinson and Fornell, 1985; Yip, 1982). Biggadike(1979) was convinced of having proved in his study that even after 5 to 8 years later entrants were not able to catch up with the disadvantage.

This apparently natural symbiosis between the "first mover" and the innovation success was questioned by more recent studies. Studies conducted by Tellis and Golder (1996), Lellien and Yoon(1990), and Lambkin and Day(1989) confirm a higher failure rate of market pioneers. Golder and Tellis (1993) ask rightly whether the pioneer advantages are a "Marketing Logic or Marketing Legend". Olleros(1986) even states that "we see industries emerge over the dead bodies of their early pioneers".

Markides and Geroski(2005) give a great number of anecdotic examples for unsuccessful pioneers, contributing to the discussion of first mover advantages for radical innovation. The authors show anecdotically that the process for radical innovations is mainly driven from small firms or startups, very often without an established brand name. Main criteria from Markides and Geroski are shown in Table 3.1.

Table 3.1 First and second mover strategies for radical innovations

Item	First mover	Fast second
Focus of activity	Exploration and creation of product on niche market	Creation of mass market
Firm characterization	Young, small	Established, big
Major role	Colonization(creation of product)	Consolidation(of market)
Innovation driver	Technology push	Market pull
Object of competition	Rival innovation designs	Rival variants of dominant design
Dominant innovation design	Variation, exploration	Selection
Market structure	Large firm population	Concentration, shakeout

Source: Own overview according to Markides and Geroski(2005)

According to Markides and Geroski (2005), "first movers" typically develop a technology-pushed innovation over a long period in niche markets and they feel less risky to pioneer a radical innovation. The innovation design is being developed in an elaborate exploration process, during which different variations have to be checked with regard to the market preference. The major role of the pioneer is the colonization of the new market. The established firms free-ride on the technological and market experience of the pioneer. They make use of the developing mass market and the dominant designs, by trying to drive out the "first mover" with rival variants of the dominant design, and to consolidate the market into a mass market.

This can also be seen in the area of eco-innovations, e. g. in the case of E-Mobility. Up to now it is not decided, which engine technology—if at all—will win the race for a sustainable transport technology, if it will be e. g. hybrid, fuel cell or battery cars? Thus, following Markides and Geroski, big firms should aim at a strategy of consolidating markets, i. e. taking up a radical innovation early enough to be able to develop it from niche to mass markets.

However, it is not the case that these results speak against a first mover advantage. Robinson and Min(2002) observe a 66 percent survival rate during the same time for market pioneers, whereas early followers only have a 48 precent chance. The results could not be more diverging, so that Min et al. (2006) come to the conclusion that first mover advantages depend on the respective environmental circumstances.

One of the first studies that took into account the environmental circumstances of the market is the study conducted by Urban et al. (1986). Data bases were the sales of 38 and in a later analysis 44 brands of frequently purchased consumer goods in connection with information from media audits and interviews. On the basis of regression analyses, the authors analyzed the influence of the order of entry, the years between the entry, the product positioning, the preference of a brand of interviewees, and the advertising intensity on the market share of "first movers". The authors assess that a later entrance has less market share on average than the market pioneer, but the pioneer's share decreases with each new firm entering the market. This decline is higher if other brands can achieve superior price and product positioning. In order to avoid this, the market pioneer should occupy and defend the preferred product positioning.

Another regression analyses approach was chosen by Robinson(1988). On the data basis of 1.209 companies from mature industrial goods manufacturing businesses, he confirms that market pioneers gain a sustainable market share advantage. In addition, their products have a better quality and show a broader product line. While the product quality advantage decreases over the time, the advantage of the breadth of product line remains. Robinson(1988) differentiates the results with regard to the different velocities of the technological development on markets. The market share of the pioneer decreases when the technological competition increases on the market. Only if the value added of an industry is high, the market pioneer is able to resist the technological competition and to extend the market share.

Some years later, Gilbert and Birnbaum-More(1996) took up the findings of the influence of dynamics in technology and on the market in the framework of a meta study, in which they bring together the empirical results of different surveys. On the basis of different sources of competitive advantages, they propose the important influencing factors on the industry and technology level as well as on the product and service level(Table 3.2).

Table 3.2 Correlation directions between factors and timing advantages

Level	Factor	Correlation with first mover advantage	Correlation with second mover advantage
Industry and technology	Degree of fragmentation	+	−
	Velocity of innovation	+	−
	Rate of innovation diffusion	−	+
Product and service	Connection to technological infrastructure	+	+
	Degree of novelty	−	+
	Difficulty of production/complexity of technology	−	+
	Customer resources invested(lock in)/switching costs	+	−
Firm strategy	Cost leadership	−	+
	Differentiation	+	−
	Core competence	+	+

Source: According to Gilbert and Birnbaum-More(1996)

With increasing fragmentation of the industry and increasing velocity of the innovation, the first mover advantage rises. This effect is being emphasized when switching costs are high and technological infrastructure is sufficiently available. The implementation of a first mover strategy is successful under these circumstances only by taking-over technological leadership and the herewith connected R&D expenditures. The diffusion rate, the degree of novelty and the complexity of the product, however, have negative effects on the first mover advantage. The "second mover" has the advantage that the pioneer has already found technological solutions and has developed these for the market preference. There are no such costs for the followers, so that a cost leadership strategy is promising.

Min et al. (2006) look at radical and incremental innovation. The latter is "designed to satisfy a felt market need and uses an existing technology or refinement of it"(Min et al., 2006). Using the Thomas' Register of American Manufacturers, they identified 264 new industrial markets and analyzed the influence of different factors on the survival rate of "first movers". Indeed, the multivariate hazard rate analysis shows that market pioneers have a greater survival risk for radical than for incremental innovation. This context is not significant for early followers. For radical innovations the market pioneers show a significantly higher survival risk than the early follower. For incremental innovation it is vice versa. "In conclusion, market pioneers are often the first to fail in really new product-markets. However, this is not true in incremental new markets, in which market pioneers have consistently lower survival risks than the early follower."(Min et al., 2006)

Summing up, it can be ascertained from the literature of business management that the successful innovator is not necessarily the first but very often one of the "early movers" within the competition of different innovation designs. The empirical literature on the firm level finds evidence that there is no simple yes or no answer to the question of first vs. second mover advantages. The studies based on correlation or regression analysis are inconsistent in the choice of factors, which are finally responsible for the development of successful global designs, but the results of the empirical studies find different factors leading to a successful timing strategy. They range from "Luck", to technological leadership, pre-emption of assets and buyer switching costs(Lieberman and Montgomery, 1988) to industry, technology, firm and product-specific factors(Gilbert and Birnbaum-More, 1996) and leading time, market dynamic, and type of innovation(Min et al., 2006). It seems that radically new technologies are difficult to defend for a "first mover", while it seems to be easier for incremental innovations.

3.2.4.2 Innovation and environmental economics literature: evidence on first mover advantages of countries

Characteristics of different national country markets for the global success of an innovation design have hardly gained importance in the discussion. Although Beise (2006) and Beise and Cleff(2003) carried out an ex-post analysis of successful global innovation designs and identified typical patterns on the country level. According to this anectdotical evidence, "successful" global designs can be characterized by the following patterns (Beise, 2006; Beise and Cleff, 2003). They firstly enjoy early national success, then are successfully commercialized worldwide and force other innovation designs out of the market in the medium term, to become the global design or the world standard respectively.

There are many examples of global innovation designs emerging from the adoption in one country, e. g. the cellular mobile telephony in the Scandinavian countries, the personal computer in the USA, the industrial robot or the fax machine in Japan, the airbag in Germany and the smart card in France (Beise, 2001). All these examples show that the first country that adopts a specific design becoming the global dominant design is often not the country where the innovation was invented or the technology used for it mostly developed. On the contrary it is often another country that is leading the worldwide adoption of an innovation: this country can be called the lead market.

The pattern of successful lead market strategies was also confirmed by Beise and Rennings(2005) for environmental innovations. They have applied the lead market approach to the world market for renewable energies and especially wind energy which has grown rapidly in recent decades(Figure 3.2). The developing world market was in the nineties dominated by countries that introduced feed-in tariffs, especially by the small Nordic country of Denmark. Substantial differences can be identified where regulation systems are related to the development of a national wind industry. A wind industry tends to develop rapidly in countries with a feed-in tariff system, such as in Denmark, Germany and Spain. Figure 3.2 shows the penetration rate of wind energy use in different countries and identifies Denmark as the lead market. Germany follows closely, while other countries are developing wind energy with a considerable lag. The penetration rate has been measured as the percentage of exploitation of on-shore wind potential.

It remains however unclear if a lead market position is really profitable for a certain country. The discussion on this issue usually is very general and refers to the so-called Porter hypothesis postulating improved competitiveness for a country due to environmental regulation in the long run. A literature review on the Porter hypothesis

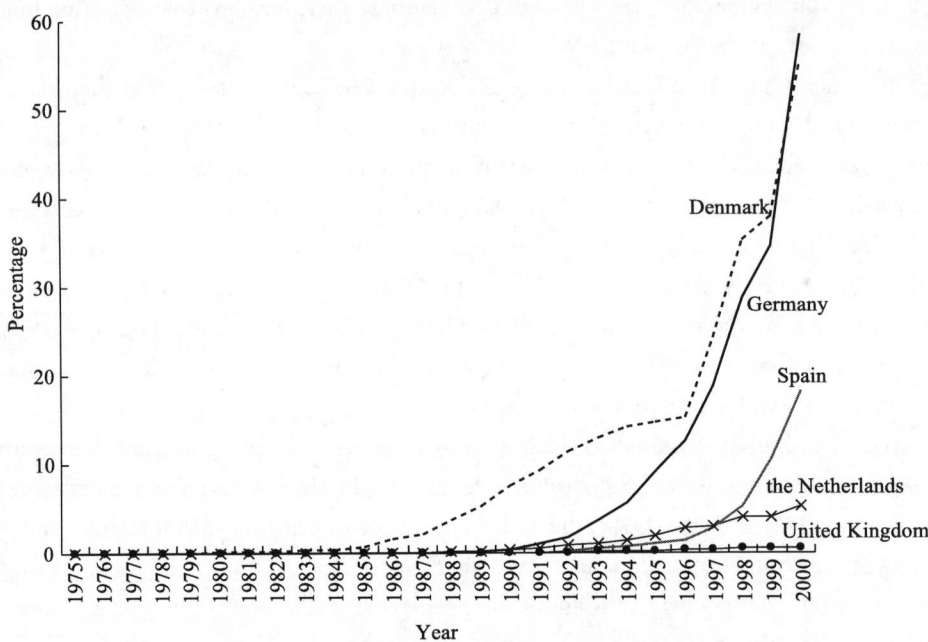

Figure 3.2 International diffusion of wind energy
Source: Beise and Rennings(2005)

faces however the problem that a "...systematic economic analysis is hindered by ambiguity as to exactly what the hypothesis is"(Jaffe and Palmer, 1997). This critique refers to the initial paper of Porter(1991), where he claims: "Strict environmental regulations do not inevitably hinder competitive advantage against foreign rivals; indeed, they often enhance it. Tough standards trigger innovation and upgrading." In the literature the positive link from environmental regulation to competitiveness is known as the strong version of the Porter hypothesis(Ambec et al. ,2011).

In their recent comprehensive survey of the hypothesis, Ambec et al. (2011) state that the overwhelming part of the literature does not find evidence for the strong Porter hypothesis. However, Rexhäuser and Rammer (2011) find evidence that the Porter hypothesis is true only for innovations in energy and material efficiency(i. e. for type 1 mentioned in section 3.2.2, in contrast to eco-innovations aiming at a general reduction of external effects which may only produce a public benefits but not firm profits, i. e. type 2 in section 3.2.2.

3.2.4.3 Development economics literature: empirical evidence on leapfrogging

While a lead market strategy may be attractive for countries with a high reputation in environmental technology, others as for example eastern European or emerging countries start from a "catching up" position. For them a first mover strategy is not realistic since they are latecomers. And a late follower strategy is more attractive for those countries since it allows to "leave the initial risks of developing new products to and establishing a market for a new product to industrialized frontrunner countries" (Watson, 2011). This advantage of technological leapfrogging has been formulated by Soete (1985) as follows: "The opportunities offered by the international diffusion of technology to jump particular technological paradigms and import the more if not most, sophisticated technologies that will neither displace the capital invested nor the skilled labor of the previous technological paradigm, constitute one of the most crucial advantages of newly industrialized countries in their bid for rapid industrialization."

Watson reviews the evidence on successful leapfrogging strategies by reviewing three cases: the Korean steel industry, the Korean automotive industry and wind energy in China and India. He concludes that "key factors for success are different in each case, but important latecomer advantages were in all three cases the cost advantage due to cheap labor costs. It is therefore not possible to generalize to a larger degree" (Watson, 2011). But he also perceives barriers to successful leapfrogging such as the lack of innovative capacities, lack of technological expertise, missing access to markets and the missing appropriate institutions.

This explains to a large degree the international differences in the diffusion of environmental technologies regarding abatement times. In a case study on the worldwide lead phase Hilton (2001), using data for 48 countries, observes a faster abatement of latecomers that is triggered by lower costs and lower innovation risks. The countries who started early with their abatement activities took about 50 percent more time (on average 15 instead of 10 years) than late abaters to complete their abatement. The quick catching up was enabled by "giant steps", i.e. at least one very large reduction in a 2-year period. While none of the early abaters has ever taken a giant step, 13 out of 20 latecomers have taken such a step. This is explained by innovation spillovers or, in the words of Hilton (2001), by accrued wisdom. As empirical studies show, historically late diffusion has been accompanied by faster diffusion, e.g. already in the case of railroads and channels in the 19th century. This accrued wisdom means that early abaters have demonstrated not only the feasibility of a new technology, but also showed how to implement the policy in practice.

The catching up of the Chinese and Indian wind industry is an impressive example of a successful leapfrogging strategy. Both countries have established a home wind industry within a decade. This was enforced by national renewable legislation and policies in support of domestic industries(Watson, 2011). According to Zhang et al. (2009) the progress can be explained by a bundle of domestic policies(such as a mandatory renewable market share) and international support(such as the Clean Development Mechanism). Jänicke and Rennings(2011) and Jin et al. (2010) see the main driver of the success story in a policy push in terms of ambitious domestic target setting. The Chinese renewable energy development plan from 1997 introduced a targeted share of renewable energy which was quantified as 10 percent of the total energy consumption by 2010 and 15 percent by 2020.

The change from a market dominated by foreign-owned manufacturers to a domestic wind industry is shown in Figure 3.3. The success can be mainly explained by a requirement of the wind concession program that 70 percent of the added value of the components of the wind turbine should be manufactured by domestic firms(Zhang et al., 2009).

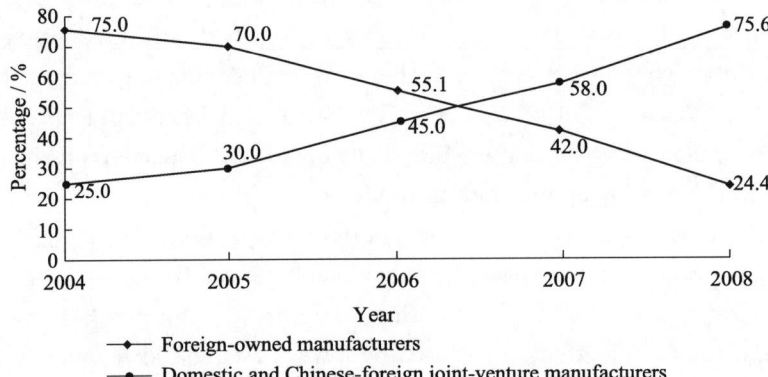

Figure 3.3　Changes in market shares in China's wind energy market
Source: Zhang et al. (2009)

3.2.5　From lead markets to lead suppliers

3.2.5.1　Cost-benefit analysis of lead markets: the case of feed-in tariffs

While there is agreement in the literature that lead markets for environmental innovations exist, and that Germany has successfully established such a lead market for renewable resources due to the system of feed-in tariffs, it is still controversial if it is profitable to be such a lead market. It is argued that subsidies for suppliers of renewable resources are much too expensive, and that the lead market position does not lead to a dominant position for German exporting firms. Thus this section will discuss the case of feed-in tariffs, and based on this experience it will analyze if a lead market strategy is sufficient in terms of industrial policy targets.

German's renewable industry is rapidly increasing, and is exceeding its policy targets. This is mainly a consequence of a subsidy policy based on feed-in tariffs which was established in 1991, the year when the *Electricity Feed-in Law* was introduced (Frondel et al., 2010). The government provided excellent investment conditions in this law by guaranteeing stable feed-in tariffs for up to 20 years, i. e. a price up to 43 cents/kW · h for solar electricity.

This brought the German market quickly into a demand advantage position, see also section 4.2. However, this did not lead necessarily to advantages for the German industry. Most modules for photovoltaic energy are imports from Japan or China. While the imports in the era of solar electricity were € 1.44 bn. in total, exports had only a value of € 0.2 bn. (Frondel et al., 2010). As is shown in Table 3.3, the domestic production of installed capacities started in 2000 with only 16 percent. Although the share of German production has grown substantially over the past decade (the average growth rate is pgeom = 61%), it is still lower than the growth of the domestic PV capacity (the average growth rate is pgeom = 75%), i. e. Germany is still a net importer of photovoltaic cells. It seems that the German photovoltaic industry is not able to develop relative export or price advantages compared to producers from other countries such as China.

Table 3.3 Photovoltaics capacities and solar cell production in Germany

Year	2000	2001	2002	2003	2004	2005	2006	2007	2008
Capacity installed in MW	100	178	258	408	1018	1881	2711	3811	5311
Annual increase in MW	—	78	80	150	610	863	830	1100	1500
Annual cell production in Germany in MW	16	33	54	98	187	319	530	842	1450

Source: BMU(2009) and BSW(2009), cited in Frondel et al. (2010)

The debate on the cost efficiency of feed-in tariffs is still ongoing. Wackerbauer (2009) for example argues that in 2007 one employee in the renewable resources sector needed public support between around € 28.000 for biomass and € 41.000 for solar energy. Frondel et al. (2010) count even € 175.000 as per capita subsidy for photovoltaics. According to Wackerbauer, the abatement costs of CO_2 for photovoltaics in the year 2007 are estimated between 420 and 611 €/t CO_2 since the subsidies have crowded out much cheaper investments in the area of e. g. residential buildings and heating systems. Frondel et al. (2010) estimate even higher abatement costs for photovoltaics of 716 €/t CO_2.

3.2.5.2 A lead supplier strategy: the case of e-mobility in Germany

The experiences from the renewable resources market have obviously motivated a change of the German policy approach from an unexceptional demand-oriented towards a broader approach, taking all lead market factors of the lead market model and the supply-side of the innovation into consideration. We have also seen in the example of the wind energy market in China that emerging countries do not follow an eco-innovation policy without considering the interests of the domestic industry, but more an industrial policy ensures a certain share of the production from Chinese firms.

The best example of the revised and broader German lead market strategy is the case of e-mobility. The German government follows the target of developing a domestic lead market for e-mobility. Until the year 2020 one million e-cars should drive on German roads. However, the concept is not only demand oriented. Maybe due to the negative experiences with the renewable resources market, a focus of the German strategy lies on either market pull measures such as tax reductions or technology push measures such as R&D and qualification(Acatech, 2010).

The German National Platform E-mobility aims explicitly at becoming a market with high lead market potentials for all lead market factors, including both, the development of lead supplier structures by realizing price advantages through cost reductions in first market phase until 2014, and a demand advantage by developing a pilot market for cars and infrastructure until 2017, and starts a mass market later (Nationale Plattform Elektromobilität, 2011). A list of the foreseen policy mix is listed in Table 3.4.

Table 3.4 German measures for becoming a lead supplier in e-mobility

Technology push measures	Market pull measures
R&D programme and networking in battery, engine, lightweight, information and communication technologies, recycling and integration	Privileges of e-cars regarding parking
Academic and occupational qualification and education	Compensation for users of company e-cars
Harmonisation of international standards and norms	Tax depreciations for firms
/	Programs from the Kreditanstalt für Wiederaufbau for private use of e-cars
/	Annual tax incentives

Source: Acatech(2010)

3.3 Conclusion

In this paper the sources of first mover advantages were presented. There is agreement in the business management literature that first mover advantages depend on the respective environmental circumstances. It can be ascertained that the successful innovator is not necessarily the first but very often one of the early movers within the competition of different innovation designs.

The results of the empirical studies of successful timing strategies of firms find different factors leading to a successful timing strategy. They range from technological leadership, pre-emption of assets and buyer switching costs to industry, technology, firm and product-specific factors, and leading time, market dynamic, and type of innovation. It seems that radically new technologies are difficult to defend for a "first mover", while it seems to be easier for incremental innovations.

There is also anecdotical evidence on the country level of both successful lead market and leapfrogging strategies. For countries with high reputation in environmental technology, it is attractive to join the race for a lead market. For emerging countries however it seems reasonable to apply a leapfrogging strategy approach, by jumping into a first mover position when innovation capacities exist, and when there is large innovation pressure. However, the question under which conditions a country may switch from a second mover to a first mover position can't be answered by the existing literature. With regard to these questions, research needs can be stated.

The case of the German renewable policy showed that a strong demand-pull policy alone does not guarantee sufficient value added to the domestic industry. Industrial policy has to take into account the whole range of the lead market approach and the supply-side of the industry at the same time. Only if the supply-side is able to develop high lead market potentials for all lead market factors, country's industry may benefit from a governmental lead market strategy. This is also an important aspect for emerging countries, as it was demonstrated by the case of wind energy in China.

Interestingly, in all cases industrial policy played an important role. In the case of Germany, this aspect can be identified as the reason why the country switched from a strict demand-oriented strategy with regard to renewable resources to a complementary lead supplier strategy with regard to e-mobility. Thus, if industrial policy targets are also relevant, a lead market strategy should be at least complemented by a lead supplier strategy, leading to a policy mix of technology push and market pull measures.

References

Acatech. 2010. Wie Deutschland zum Leitanbieter für Elektromobilität werden kann—Status Quo, Herausforderungen, offene Fragen. Acatech bezieht Position, Nr. 6, Berlin.

Ambec, S. , Cohen, M. , Elgie, S. , et al. 2011. The Porter hypothesis at 20. Can environmental regulation enhance competitiveness? Resources for the Future Discussion Paper, Washington.

Barroso, J. M. 2008. Presentation of the priorities of the Slovenian Presidency of the Council of the EU. Speech at the European Parliament, Strasbourg.

Bartlett, C. A. , Ghoshal, S. 1990. Managing innovation in the transnational corporation. In: Doz, C. Y. , Hedlund G. , (Eds.), *Managing the Global Firm*. London: Routledge, 215-255.

Beise, M. , Cleff, T. 2003. Assessing the lead market potential of countries for innovation projects. Discussion Paper Series No. 142, Research Institute for Economics and Business Administration, Kobe University.

Beise, M. , Cleff, T. , Heneric, O. , et al. 2002. Lead Market Deutschland. Zur Position Deutschlands als führender Absatzmarkt für Innovationen—Endbericht. ZEW-Dokumentation Nr. 02-02, Mannheim.

Beise, M. 2006. Die Lead-Market-Strategie. Das Geheimnis weltweit erfolgreicher Innovationen. Heidelberg.

Beise, M. 2001. Lead markets: country specific success factors of the global diffusion of innovations. *ZEW Economic Studies*, 14.

Beise, M. , Rennings, K. 2005. Lead markets and regulation: a framework for analyzing the international diffusion of environmental innovation. *Ecological Economics*, 52(1), 5-17.

Biggadike, E. R. 1979. Corporate Diversification: Entry, Strategy and Performance. Cambridge.

Bundesministerium für Umwelt (BMU), Naturschutz und Reaktorsicherheit. 2008. *Investitionen in ein klimafreundliches Deutschland*. Berlin.

Bundesregierung. 2007. Die Begründung der Bundesregierung für ihren Gesetzentwurf für das Erneuerbare-Energien-Gesetz(EEG) vom 5. Dezember 2007, *Bundestags-Drucksache* Bd. 16 (8148), o. O.

Cleff, T. , Grimpe, C. , Rammer, C. 2009. Demand-oriented innovation strategy in the European energy production sector. *The International Journal of Energy Sector Management*, 3(2), 108-130.

Cleff, T. , Grimpe, C. , Rammer, C. 2007. *The Role of Demand in Innovation—A Lead Market Analysis for High-tech Industries in the EU-25*. ZEW Dokumentation Nr. 07-02, Mannheim.

Commission of the European Communities. 2006. European Competitiveness Report 2006: Economic reforms and competitiveness: Key messages from the European Competitiveness

Report 2006 COM(2006)697 final, location N/A.

Dekimpe, M. G., Parker, P. M., Sarvary, M. 1998. Globalisation: Modeling Technology Adoption Timing across Countries. INSEAD working paper No. 98/69/MKT, location N/A.

Dosi, G., Pavitt, K., Soete, L. 1990. *The Economics of Technical Change and International Trade*. New York.

Elektromobilität N. P. 2011. Zweiter bericht nationale plattform elektromobilität. Berlin.

Frondel, M., Ritter, N., Schmidt, C. M., et al. 2010. Economic impacts from the promotion of renewable energy technologies: the German experience. *Energy Policy*, 38, 4048-4056.

Fudenberg, D., Gilbert, R., Stiglitz, J., et al. 1983. Pre-emption, leapfrogging and competition in patent races. *European Economic review*, 22, 3-31.

Gilbert, J. T., Birnbaum-More, P. H. 1996. Innovation timing advantages: from economic theory to strategic application. *Journal of Engineering and Technology Management*, 12(4), 245-266.

Golder, P., Tellis, G. J. 1993. Pioneer advantage: marketing logic or marketing legend? *Journal of Marketing Research*, 30, 158-170.

Hilton, F. H. 2001. Later abatement, faster abatement: evidence and explanations from the global phase out of leaded gasoline. *Journal of Environment and Development*, 10(3), 246-265.

Jaffe, A. B., Palmer, K. 1997. Envionmental regulation and innovation: a panel data study. *Review of Economics and Statistics*, 79(4), 610-619.

Jin, J., Dong, Y., Chen, J. 2012. Incentive policies to address climate change in China. *International Journal of Innovation and Technology Management*, 9(04).

Jänicke, M. 2008. *Megatrend Umweltinnovation: Zur ökologischen Modernisierung von Wirtschaft und Staat*. oekom verlag.

Jänicke, M., Rennings, K. 2011. Ecosystem dynamics: the principle of co-evolution and success stories from climate policy. *International Journal of Technology Policy and Management*.

Johansson, J. K. 2000. *Global Marketing: Foreign Entry, Local Marketing, & Global Management*. Boston.

Kemp, R., Arundel, A. 1998. Survey indicators for environmental innovation. *Indicators and Data for European Analysis*, 8.

Lambkin, M., Day, G. S. 1989. Evolutionary processes in competitive markets: beyond the product life cycle. *Journal of Marketing*, 53(3), 4-20.

Lellien, G. L., Yoon, E. 1990. The timing of competitive market entry: an exploratory study of new industrial products. *Management Science*, 36(5), 568-585.

Levitt, T. 1983. The globalization of markets. *Harvard Business Review*, 61(3), 92-102.

Lieberman, M. B., Montgomery, D. B. 1988. First-mover advantages. *Strategic Management Journal*, 9, 41-58.

Lieberman, M. 1987. The learning curve, diffusion and competitive strategy. *Strategic*

Management Journal, 8, 441-452.

Mansfield, E. 1985. How rapidly does new industrial technology leaks out? *Journal of Industrial Economics*, 34, 217-223.

Mansfield, E. 1968. *Industrial Research and Technological Innovation: An Econometric Analysis*. New York: Norton.

Mansfield, E. 1986. Patents and innovation: an empirical study. *Management Science*, 32(2), 173-181.

Markides, C. C., Geroski, P. A. 2005. *Fast Second—How Smart Companies Bypass Radical Innovation to Enter and Dominate New Markets*. San Francisco: Wiley.

Meyer-Krahmer, F. 1997. Lead märkte und innovationsstandort. *FhG Nachrichten*, 1/97, o. S..

Min, S., Kalwani, M. U., Robinson, W. T. 2006. Market pioneer and early follower survival risks: a contingency analysis of really new versus incrementally new product-markets. *Journal of Marketing*, 70(1), 15-33.

Olleros, F. J. 1986. Emerging industries and he burnout of pioneers. *Journal of Product Innovation Management*, 1(1), 5-18.

Porter, M. E. 1991. America's green strategy. *Scientific American*, 168(4), page N/A.

Porter, M. E. 1986. Changing patterns of international competition. *California Management Review*, 28(2), 9-40.

Porter, M. E. 1990. *The Competitive Advantage of Nations*. New York(free press).

Porter, M. E., van der Linde, C. 1995. Towards a new conception of the environment-competitiveness relationship. *Journal of Economic Perspectives*, 9(4), 97-118.

Posner, M. V. 1961. International trade and technical change. Oxford Economic Papers, 30, 323-341.

Rennings, K., Rammer, C. 2009. Increasing energy and resource efficiency through innovation—an explorative analysis using innovation survey data. *Czech Journal of Economics and Finance*, 59(5), 442-459.

Rennings, K. 2000. Redefining innovation—eco-innovation research and the contribution from ecological economics. *Ecological Economics*, 32, 319-332.

Rennings, K., Smidt, W. 2010. A lead market approach towards the emergence and diffusion of coal-fired power plant technology. *Politica Economia*, XXVII (2), 301-327.

Rennings, K., Zwick, T. 2002. The employment impact of cleaner production on the firm level—empirical evidence from a survey in five European countries. *International Journal of Innovation Management*, 6(3), 319-342.

Rexhäuser, S., Rammer, C. 2011. Unmasking the Porter hypothesis: environmental innovations and firm-profitability. ZEW Discussion Paper No. 11-036, Mannheim.

Robinson, W. T., Fornell, C. 1985. Sources of market pioneer advantages in consumer goods industries. *Journal of Marketing Research*, 22, 305-317.

Robinson, W. T., Min, S. 2002. Is the first to market the first to fail? Empirical evidence for industrial goods business. *Journal of Marketing Research*, 34, 120-128.

Soete, L. 1985. International diffusion of technology, industrial development and technological leapfrogging. *World Development*, 13(3), 409-422.

Tellis, G. J., Golder, P. 1996. First to market, first to fail? Real causes of enduring market leadership. *Sloan Management Review*, 2, 65-75.

Urban, et al. 1986. Market share rewards to pioneering brands: an empirical analysis and strategic implications. *Management Sciences*, 32, 645-659.

Vernon, R. 1979. The product cycle hypothesis in a new international environment. *Oxford Bulletin of Economics and Statistics*, 41(4), 255-267.

Watson, J. 2011. Sustainale innovation through leapfrogging: a review of the evidence. *International Journal of Technology and Globalization*, 5(3/4), 170-189.

Yip, G. S. 1982. *Barriers to Entry*. Lexington(free press).

Zhang, X., Chang, S., Huo, M., et al. 2009. China's wind industry: policy lessons for domestic government interventions and international support. *Climate Policy*, 9(5), 553-564.

Author

Dr. Klaus Rennings has been senior researcher at the Centre for European Economic Research(ZEW) since 1994 and deputy head of the department "Environmental and Resource Economics, Environmental Management". From 1990 to 1994, he worked at the University of Münster as a researcher at the Institute for Transport Economics. In the same time, from 1992 to 1994, he was an assistant at the German Council of Environmental Advisors, an interdisciplinary advisory council of environmental scientists for the Federal Government. His main fields of research are innovation-oriented environmental policy and sustainability impacts assessment.

Klaus Rennings has co-ordinated several big national and international research projects, including the EU Strata Network Blueprint("Blueprints for an Integration of Science, Technology and Environmental Policy") and the EU Project I. Q. Tools("Indicators and Quantitative Tools for Improving the Process of Impact Assessment for Sustainability").

Exporting Green Technologies: Prerequisites and Perspectives for China and Germany

Rainer Walz, Michael Krail, Jonathan Köhler, Frank Marscheider-Weidemann

4.1 Introduction

Markets for more environmentally products and services have been recognized as major areas of growth. An important argument in the policy debate is that countries and/or industrial sectors which develop green technologies will gain several advantages. They will have the potential for a major reduction in environmental pressure and resource needs. Also, they will be well placed to export goods into the expanding international markets for clean intermediate and consumption goods, thus securing economic growth and generating new employment.

Traditionally, it is thought that countries of the North will be the supplier of green technologies. However, with increasing globalization, and the growing strength of the technological capabilities in the countries of the South, the integration of these innovations into the development process in the rapidly growing economies becomes an additional option for a transition strategy which combines both economic catch-up with environmental sustainability. Green technologies are seen as a possible field in which Newly Industrializing Countries (NICs) might more rapidly achieve a leading position (Walz and Meyer-Krahmer, 2003). Indeed, both China and Germany are already major exporters of green technologies.

In a narrow interpretation, lead markets denote the country in which a later globally successful innovation takes off(Beise,2004). This perspective concentrates on the factors which make a later globally successful innovation happen first in a specific country. In a broader interpretation, lead markets are linked to the notion of first-mover advantages in foreign trade: It is argued that the trade patterns for technologies are also determined by the quality of the technology and its innovative character. Thus, high international market shares depend on the innovation ability and the achieved learning effects. If a country forges ahead in a specific technology, it tends to specialize early in the supply of the necessary technologies. According to the logic of a first-mover advantage, these countries are then in a good position to dominate international competition due to their early presence in this field (Porter and van der Linde,1995).

The paper will start with an exploration of the lead market factors which are vital to realize first mover advantages. These factors are condensed into a conceptual model of explaining lead -market- based export shares. In the second part of the paper, indicators for these factors are presented from a top-down perspective for green technologies. This chapter has a methodological focus on the one hand: The factors for which indicators are available and which can be collected and applied on the aggregate level of green technologies will be outlined, and those factors identified for which only a disaggregate technology specific evaluation can be performed. On the other hand, this chapter will yield a first overview of the position of Germany and China and will compare it with other countries with regard to important lead market factors for green technologies. The chapter will conclude with a summary of results and an outlook towards future research needs.

4.2 Lead-market-based factors for a first-mover advantage

For first-mover advantages to be realized, the domestic suppliers of green technologies have to be competitive internationally so that they—and not foreign suppliers—meet the demand. Taking the globalization of markets into account, this requires establishing competence clusters which are difficult to transfer to other countries with lower production costs. These competence clusters must consist of high technological capabilities linked to a demand which is open to new innovations and horizontally and vertically integrated production structures. The following factors have to be taken into account when assessing the potential of countries to benefit from a first-mover advantage(Walz, 2006): (1) characteristics of the technology which form obstacles to international relocation; (2) demand conditions in the country; (3) innovation-friendly regulation in the country; (4) technological capability of the country; (5) competitiveness of related industry clusters in the country.

4.2.1 Characteristics of the technology

A first-mover advantage requires that at least a niche market exists where competition is driven not so much by cost differentials and the resulting attractiveness of international production location alone, but also by quality and/or performance aspects. Knowledge always has tacit components, which makes the acquisition of capabilities in the relocation of knowledge-intensive production more difficult (Archibugi and Pietrobelli, 2004). Thus, especially goods which can be characterized as knowledge-intensive can form the basis for long-lasting first-mover advantages.

However, knowledge is necessary not only to create, but also to maintain export advantages. Thus, high innovation dynamics and high potential learning effects of the technology work against cost-driven relocation of production facilities. Otherwise an erosion of the importance of the quality component of the technology would take place, which in line with the Product Cycle Theory of Vernon(1966) or the seminal works of Krugman(1979) or Grossman and Helpman(1991a) would be equivalent to no longer climbing up the quality ladder and would lead to a subsequent relocation of production facilities towards imitating countries with lower production costs.

4.2.2 Demand conditions

The importance of the demand side can be traced to the work of Linder(1961), and is emphasized by authors such as von Hippel(1988), Porter(1990) or Dosi et al. (1990). There are various market factors which influence the chances of a country developing a lead market position. Beise(2004) and Beise and Cleff(2004) classify them in the 5 categories demand and price advantage, market structure, and transfer and export advantage.

In general, a growing demand oriented towards innovations and readily supporting new technological solutions benefit a country in developing a lead-market position. One underlying mechanism is called price advantage. With growing demand, economies of scale drive the costs of the technology down. In the line of the work of von Hippel (1988) and Lundvall (1985), this effect is augmented by knowledge exchanged between users and producers during the use of the technology. This user-producer interaction leads to further innovations, which enable additional learning effects and further price advantages.

The demand advantages focus on the ability of a country to develop a market which takes up global demands earlier than others. It is linked to the concept of lead users, which are interested in novel approaches and willing to accept higher prices. Thus, quite often it is assumed that high income countries can support a higher percentage of new approaches. However, the situation might be different with regard to green technologies. They address a global societal need, which is much more triggered by societal concern and regulation than "normal" innovation. Thus, green technologies also open up the opportunity for other countries than the traditional high-income countries to establish a demand advantage.

A third factor is a market structure which facilitates competition. Here it is assumed that a higher level of competition increases the innovativeness among the suppliers and pushes them towards looking for new markets. This mechanism is dependent on the technology still being immature, so that there are competing technological solutions. However, if one wants to assess a niche, the sheer existence of strong domestic players in the field of the technology seems to be of importance as well. Thus, this factor can also be labeled as structure of suppliers.

The transfer advantage is based on a kind of demonstration effect. If countries show a high level of successful technological applications, they will find it easier to export their products. Thus, the transfer effect works in favor of countries which enjoy a high technological reputation. This factor can also be positioned at the landscape level. An export advantage, finally results from the degree to which the preferences in one country are similar to the preferences on the world market. Thus, countries which are more open to the world will enjoy an export advantage compared to countries which are moving towards idiosyncratic solutions for their own market. Again, this factor is more general and is positioned at the landscape level.

4.2.3 Innovation friendly regulation

A lead market situation must also be supported by regulation which at the same time is innovation-friendly and sets the example for other countries to follow the same regulatory path. This relates to different aspects.

First, for environmentally friendly technologies, the demand depends very much on the extent by which regulation leads to a correction of the market failures. Without such regulation, the demand will be much lower, and the various demand effects are less likely to be strong.

Second, the national regulation should not lead to an idiosyncratic innovation, in other words an innovation that can be only applied under the very specific national regulatory regime. In contrast, the regulation should be open to diverse technical solutions, which increase the chance that they fit into the preferences of importing countries.

Third, the national regulation should set the standard for the regulatory regime, which other countries are likely to adopt. Examples for this are product standards or testing procedures, which have to be fulfilled before a technology becomes classified as environmentally benign. If the procedure from the lead country is adopted in other countries, the national suppliers from the lead country have additional advantages on the world market, because they have adapted their technologies early on to pass the requirements of such a regulatory regime and have developed administrative capabilities how to deal with all the procedures.

However, even though there has been some clarification of the mechanisms which make regulation an important parameter for a lead market, there is a lot of additional research necessary to develop a clear methodology on how to operationalize the empirical evaluation of an existing regulatory regime with regard to its innovation friendliness.

The need for an innovation - friendly regulatory regime is especially strong for green technologies. They are very often applied in infrastructure fields such as energy, water or transportation, which are characterized by monopolistic bottlenecks. In these fields, the innovation-friendliness of the general regulatory regime, e. g. with regard to IPR or the supply of venture capital, must not only be accompanied by an innovation-friendly environmental regulation, but also by an economic sector regulation resulting in a triple regulatory challenge(Walz, 2007). However, the regulation of monopolistic bottlenecks is clearly shaped by the dominant technological regime.

4.2.4 Technological capabilities

The ability of a country to utilize a lead market for a first-mover advantage also depends on its comparative technological capability. If a country has a comparatively high knowledge base, it also has an additional advantage in developing and marketing future technologies.

Despite all the problems and caveats associated with measuring technological capabilities, indicators on R&D expenditures and patent indicators such as share of patents or the relative patent advantage are among the most widely used indicators. The empirical importance of these indicators for trade patterns, which was already concluded in the past(Table 4.1), is also supported by more recent empirical research (Madsen, 2008; Lachenmaier and Wössmann, 2006; Sanyal, 2004; Blind, 2001).

Madsen(2008)underlines the importance especially of transnational patents.

Table 4.1　Impact of technology and other factors on export performance

R&D intensity (expenditure in % of production, 1985)		Technology					Price/cost			Investment				Scale	
		R&D		Patents											
		L	F	M	S	F	A	F	M	A	L	S	F	M	A	S	F
Aerospace	20	—	—	x	x	—	—	—	x	—	—	—	—	(—)	x	—	x
Computers	10	x^e	—	x	x	—	x	—	x	—	—^{e}	—	—	x	x	—	x
Electronics	8	x^e	x	—	x	—	—	x^d	x	—	—^{e}	—	—	x	—	—	x^d
Instruments	6	x^e	x	—	x	x	x	—	x	x	—^{e}	—	—	x	—	—	—
Electrical machinery	3	x^e		—	x	x	—	x	—	—	—^{e}	—	—	—	—	—	—
Non-electrical machinery	2	x		x	x	x	x	x^b	—	—	—	—	—	—	—	x/—	x^e
Cars	3	x^f	—	x	x	—	x	—	—	—	—^{f}	—	—	—	(—)	x	x
Other transport	3	x^f		—			—	x	—	—^{f}			—				
Ships	0	x^f	—		—	—	—	—	—	—^{f}	—	x	—	—	—	—	—
Drugs	9	x		—	x	x	x	x	x	—	—	—	(—)	x	—	—	(—)
Industrial chemicals	3	x	x^a	x	x			x	x^a	x	x	—	—^{a}	—	—	x	—^{a}
Plastics	1	x	x	—	x		x	x	—	x	—	x	—	x	—	x	—
Petroleum refining	1	—		—	—			x		—	x			—			
Ferrous metals	1	x^g	—		x	—	x	x	x	—	—^{g}	—	—	—	—	x	—
Non-ferrous metals	1	x^g	—	—	x	—	—	—	x	—	—^{g}	x	—	—	—	—	(—)
Metal products	1	x^g		x	x	x	—	x	x	x	—^{g}	—	—	—	—	x	—
Stone glass and clay	1	—		—	x		x	—	—	x	—		—	(—)		x	
Wood and wood products	0	—		x			x		x	x	—			—			
Paper	0	x	—	x		—		—	x		—		—		—			
Textiles clothing	0	—	—	x	—	—	x	x	x	x	—			—			x	—
Food and drinks	0	x		x	—		x		x	x	—							

Symbols: x=significant, correct sign; x/—=conflicting evidence; —=not significant; (—)=significant. incorrect sign; blank=not included

Notes: ^{a} Organic chemicals. ^{b} Special machinery. ^{c} Power-generating machinery. ^{d} Semiconductours. ^{e} Electrical machinery(broadly defined) and instruments. ^{f} Transport equipment (excluding aerospace). ^{g} Metals and metal products

Sources: R&D intensity=Fagerberg (1995).
L=Lacroix and Scheuer (1976); 15 sectors/12-17 countries, 1968.
F=Fagerberg (1995); 28 sectors/19 countries, 1960-83(average values).
M=Magnier and Toujas-Bernate (1994); 20 sectors/5 countries. 1980-1987.
S=Soete (1981); 40 sectors/22 countries, 1977.
A=Amable and Verspagen (1995), 18 sectors/5 countries, 1970-1991.
Source: Fagerberg 1995, p. 47.

4.2.5　Complementary Sectors

It is widely held that innovation and economic success also depend on how a specific technology is embedded into other relevant industry clusters. Learning effects, expectations of the users of the technology and knowledge spillovers are more easily realized if the flow of (tacit) knowledge is facilitated by proximity and a common knowledge of language and institutions (Archibugi and Pietrobelli, 2004). Furthermore, there is strong empirical evidence that the international competitiveness of sectors and technologies is greatly influenced by the competitiveness of interlinked sectors (Fagerberg, 1995).

4.2.6 International knowledge spillover

There are also factors which work towards the erosion of a first mover advantage. One such approach is also implied by the product cycle theory. There it is argued that the characteristics of a technology change over time to make the technology more easily reproducible and hence more subject to price competition. Thus, in the context of the product cycle theory, the erosion of a first-mover advantage is brought forward by a change in the characteristics of the technology.

Since the seminal paper of Grossman and Helpman (1991b), the importance of international knowledge spillover via trade is widely acknowledged in the literature. The mechanisms of how the trade of technologies affects knowledge spillover have been further analyzed by Griliches (1991) and Archibugi and Pietrobelli (2004). The knowledge embodied in patents, which are published, has become codified and accessible. The export of technologies makes knowledge embodied in the physical technology also partially accessible to the users. Spatial proximity with the technologies facilitates user-producer communication in the importing countries. Furthermore, there is empirical evidence that the inflow of FDI and the resulting production in host countries lead to knowledge spillovers towards the host countries (Pain and Wakelin, 2004; Greenaway et al., 2004). However, there is also evidence which supports knowledge spillovers towards the supplying companies (Wei et al., 2008; Wagner, 2007), leading to the effect of learning by exporting. Depending on the absorptive capacities and the emergence of competing technology providers in the importing countries, the knowledge spillovers lead to an erosion of technological leads. This erosion is further facilitated, if the importing countries start to implement also the other success factors such as innovation-friendly regulation patterns within their countries.

4.2.7 Conceptual model

The variables described above can be condensed in the conceptual model shown in Figure 4.1. The model consists of the factors described above. They can be influenced directly by the stringency and the design of policies. Thus, the R&D levels (R&D programs for the technology), the diffusion of the technology (which is driven due to the externality problems by environmental policy) and the regulatory advantage are classified as policy factors. Other factors are rather exogenous from the technology analyzed. The factors are linked to each other by either positive or negative impacts (negative meaning that the increase in the causing factor leads to a decrease in the dependent factor). These impacts are not unidirectional; there are also positive and negative feedback, which leads to feedback loops within the system.

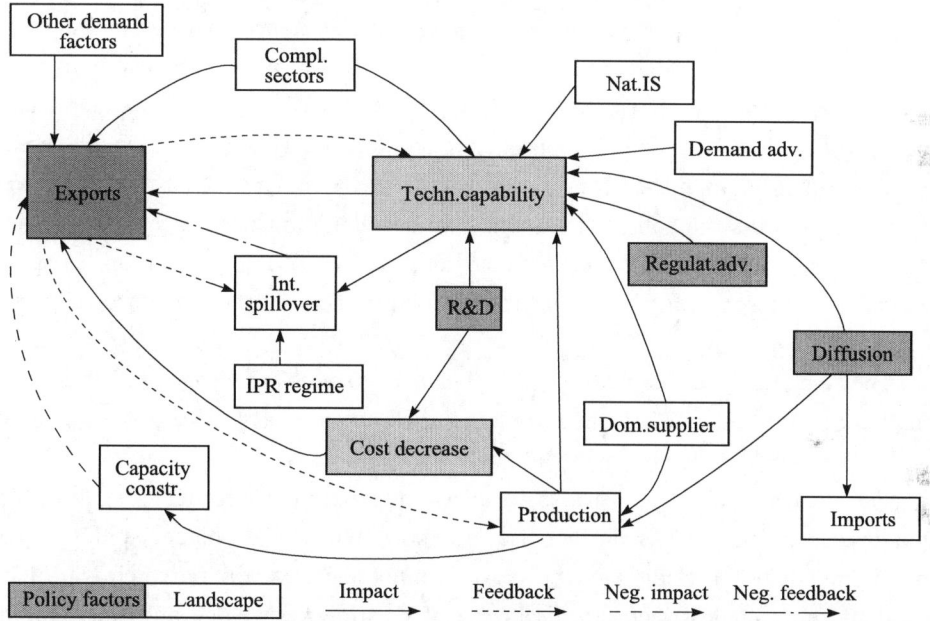

Figure 4.1 Conceptual model for explaining export shares for green technologies

The conceptual model consists of the following factors and impacts.

The exports are influenced by technological competences (which can be described as patents) and cost decreases.

R&D subsidies are an important policy factor, which enhances both the number of patents and cost decreases.

The diffusion of the technology in the country is directly influenced by environmental and sector policies. It leads to demand for the technology, which can be either produced domestically or is imported. Furthermore, exports must also be produced domestically.

The level of domestic production leads to scale effects and thus cost/price advantages. Furthermore, it enables learning by doing leading to new patents.

The level of domestic diffusion will also influence user-producer interaction, which will lead to additional knowledge and increases in technological capability.

The national innovation system (NIS) influences the innovation capability of a country as a whole. Thus, even though this factor is not technology specific, it also influences the level of increase in technological capability in a country in the analyzed technology.

The regulatory advantage consists of an innovation friendly regulatory regime. This will lead to a better innovation performance and higher technological capability.

The level of domestic production requires the existence of domestic suppliers. Furthermore, the level of technological capability is also influenced by the structure among these key actors. Thus, if domestic suppliers and a competitive market structure emerge, the level of both domestic production and technological capability will increase.

The other demand factors described above (demand, transfer and export advantage) address the ability of a country to develop a market which takes up global demands and international preferences earlier than others, and the demonstration and credibility of these advantages. Thus, they directly influence the amount of exports of the country.

The technological capability also benefits from knowledge spillovers from complementary sectors. Thus, the stronger the complementary sectors, the higher will be the technological capability in the analyzed technology.

The importance of the various forms of international knowledge spillovers has been described above. Thus, an increase in exports will lead to higher spillovers from capital embodied knowledge. Furthermore, technological capability which is protected by patents nevertheless leads to disclosure of existing knowledge and thus potential knowledge spillover. However, the stronger the protection of intellectual property rights, the less pronounced are these effects.

The capacity constraints described above are impeding the level of exports. They are acting as an upper limit to exports as long as the increase in domestic production capability cannot keep pace with the increase in demand.

4.3 Lead market characteristics of green technologies: a top-down indicator perspective

4.3.1 Characteristics of the technology

A technological breakdown of green technologies shows that they very often consist of technologies which are medium-to-high with regard to R&D intensity, or even high tech such as photovoltaics. Another indicator is the patent dynamic: For green technologies such as sustainable transport and green energy supply, the dynamic exceeds the average of all patents(which is shaped, among others, by fields such as life science and nano technology). However, a closer look indicates important differences between various forms of technology classes, which are even stronger if single technologies are distinguished(Figure 4.2). These results should caution against an interpretation which assigns a high innovation dynamic to all fields of green technologies. Instead, it underlines the need to perform a technology specific analysis of the lead market characteristics of a selected technology.

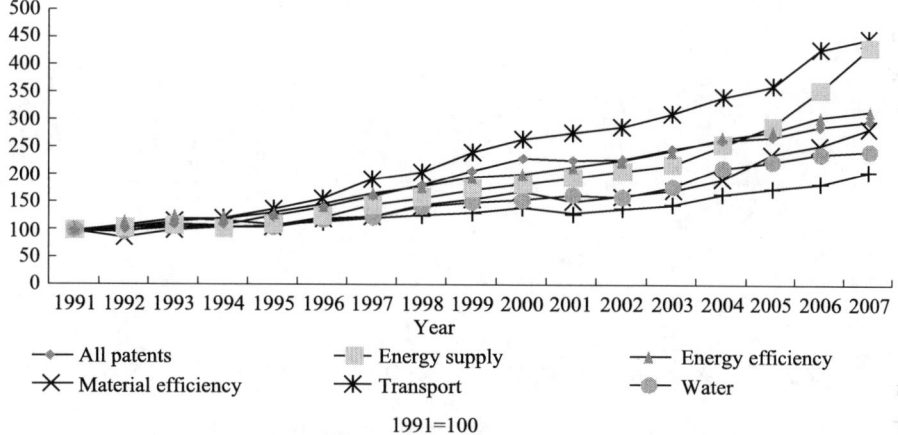

Figure 4.2 Patent dynamics for fields of green technologies

Source: Calculations from Fraunhofer ISI

4.3.2 Demand conditions

The price advantage indicates the extent to which an increase in demand drives down costs and enables suppliers to reduce prices. A typical approach to assess the reduction in costs according to increasing demand is the concept of learning curves. However, the values are very technology specific. Overviews on renewable energy technologies show already substantial. Typically, learning rates between 10% and 30% are assumed, which lead to a vast difference especially for technologies in their earlier phase of development. However, it is also criticized that learning curves systematically underestimate the learning rates for established technologies(Jamasb and Köhler, 2008; Pan and Köhler, 2007). To sum up the argument it is not possible to assess the aggregate level of green technologies with regard to the price advantage countries might achieve if they forge ahead with deploying green technologies in their home market.

The demand advantage is attributed to countries where society and markets are more open than others towards future challenges. Green technologies are tackling a global need: reducing the environmental burden to strive towards sustainability. Thus, from a top-down perspective, countries forging ahead with regard to taking sustainability issues into account can be adjudged in general to have a demand advantage. Using factor analysis, a sustainability index has been constructed by Peuckert(2011). For this index,55 countries are taken into account, comprising OECD countries as well as NICs and a few developing countries for which the indicator values are available. Figure 4.3 shows the resulting values for selected countries. Based on this approach, Germany is among the leaders, and China is in the lower midfield.

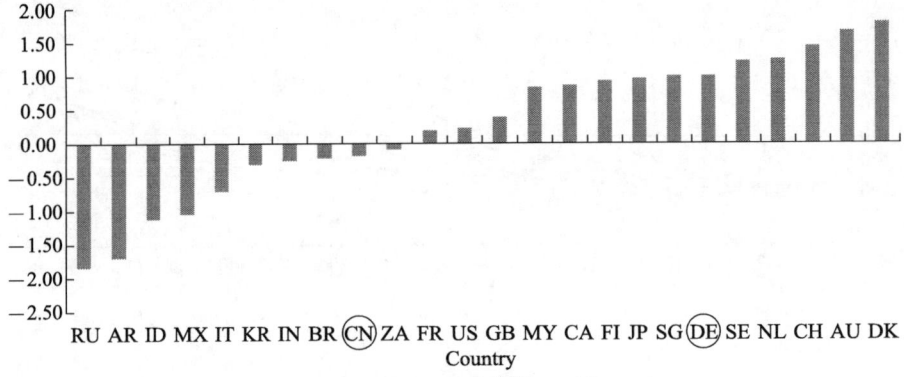

Figure 4.3 Sustainability index
Source: Data from Peuckert(2011)

The market structure advantage looks at competition among the technology suppliers. However, this is also a highly technology specific characteristic. Thus, the market structure cannot be assessed for the aggregate of green technologies.

The transfer advantage depicts a demonstration effect and also depends on the technological reputation of the country. If countries are assigned a high technological reputation, they also have a transfer advantage. One approach of measuring the technological reputation of countries are subjective values. The expert opinion surveys of the World Economic Forum offer various questions, which point towards technological reputation. Using factor analysis, an index has been constructed which condenses the different indicators(Peuckert,2011). Thus, according to the results of Figure 4.4, Germany is among the top, and China is at the lower end of the midfield.

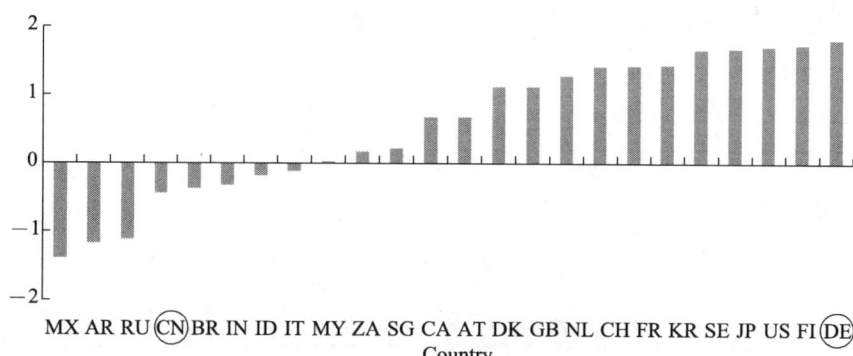

0 = average of 55 countries

Figure 4.4 Technological competence

Source: Data from Peuckert(2011)

The export advantage describes the advantages of a country due to its openness. However, the opinion based data which typically can be found under this label concentrates more on inward openness, that is the inflow of capital and knowledge from abroad to foster internal innovations. Thus, this data seems less suited to the assessment of export advantage, which looks more at how international preferences in demand are taken into account in the domestic market. Therefore trade data is used to present a top-down perspective on this factor. The share of R&D intensive exports at the GDP of the countries is used as an indicator (Figure 4.5). The higher this value, the stronger is the economy shaped by the demands from abroad. Using high-tech goods also gives a better correlation with green technologies, which are also judged as falling under this category.

The data shows the highest values for Singapore and Malaysia. Most countries, e.g. China and Germany, show indicator values in the order of magnitude of 10%. Thus, it has to be questioned whether or not this indicator is able to describe the differences in export advantage between the countries.

4.3.3 Innovation - friendly regulation

Consistent development of a lead market must also be supported by innovation-friendly regulation. However, there is no concept of how to measure this on an aggregate level for green technologies. Expert opinions about the innovation friendliness typically measure the hindering effect of regulation on innovation processes, e.g. with regard to bureaucratic procedures. However, green technologies clearly differ here from normal innovations. Due to the externality problem and the problem of monopolistic bottlenecks to innovation from the established suppliers that

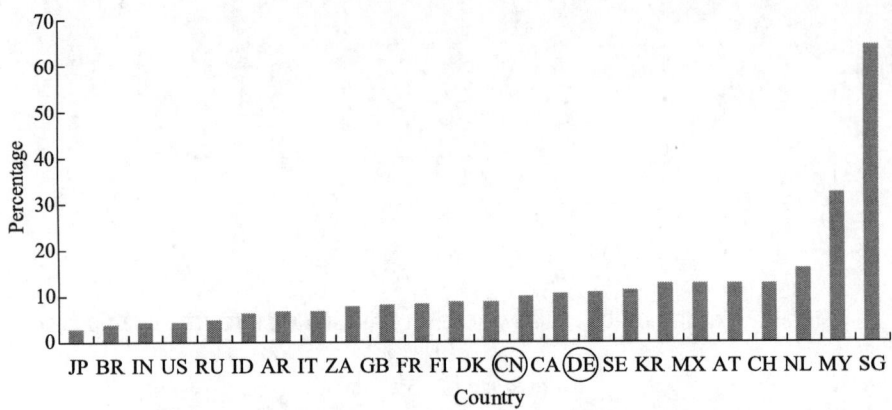

Figure 4.5 Percentage of high-tech exports at GDP
Source: Calculations of Fraunhofer ISI, based on UN-Comtrade data

constitute the regime, regulation becomes a key prerequisite for green technologies(see section 4.2). The paper by Walz et al. (2011) summarizes the empirical state-of-the-art on the role of regulation: Various case studies using a technological system of innovation approach have shown the importance of regulation. However, there seems to be no easy indication about what constitutes an innovation- friendly regulation. Soft context factors definitely play an important role. The results on the influence of policy instrument choice is rather inconclusive: Econometric estimations either indicate contradicting results depending on the technology or the innovation phase(Johnstone et al. ,2010), or point towards small and not very significant influence at all(Walz et al. ,2011). Clearly, however, innovation-friendly regulation has to be assessed on a technology specific level.

4.3.4 Technological capabilities

Measuring technological capabilities can draw on the experience with innovation indicators made over the last two decades(Freeman and Soete, 2009). Among the different innovation indicators, patents are among the most widely used when it comes to indicators influencing the export structure. Recently, progress has been made in applying patent indicators also for green technologies(Walz and Marscheider-Weidemann, 2011). The analysis draws on patent applications at the World Intellectual Property Organization and thus transnational patents. In this way, a method of mapping international patents is employed which does not target individual markets but is much more transnational in character. The patents identified in this way reveal those segments in which patent applicants are already taking a broader international perspective. The latest year available is 2007, the years 2003 – 2007 were chosen as the period of study so that a statistically more reliable population is achieved in which random fluctuations in individual years are evened out.

There are various aspects how the technological capability can be measured by patents. If one looks at the overall technological capability within the field, the share of patents can be used. Clearly big countries have an advantage here over small ones. In order to make the different countries comparable, patent intensities can be used. Figure 4.6 shows the results. Germany is among the top with regard to this indicator. China shows currently lower values, but is increasing her patent numbers quickly in the last years. Furthermore, the specialization within a country is important. If a country is specializing on a technology, it can be assumed that it is easier for this technology to attract capital and the best human resources. Thus, the specialization also gives some indication about the future prospects. Typically the RPA is used as an indicator to measure patent specialization. Additional calculations show that Germany is specializing on green technologies, with China showing average specialization.

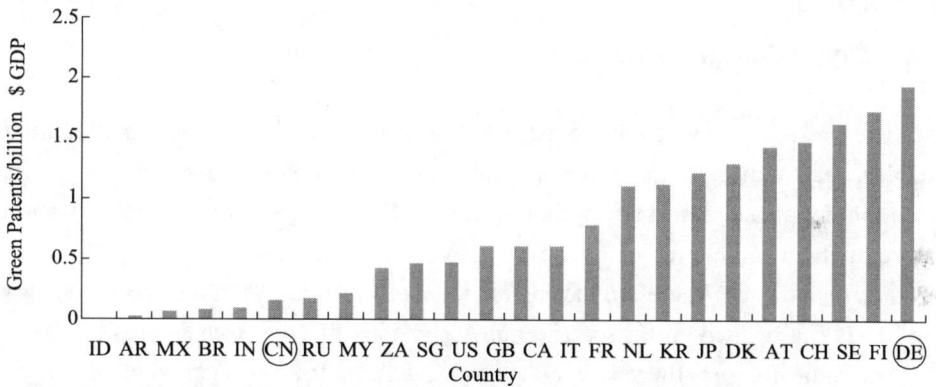

Figure 4.6 Patent intensity for green technologies
Source: Calculations of Fraunhofer ISI

4.3.5 Complementary sectors

It is widely held that innovation and economic success also depend on how a specific technology is embedded into other relevant industry clusters. In order to give an overview about the empirical situation, the RCA of R & D -intensive goods was used. The numbers indicate from a top-down perspective which countries have advantages (Figure 4.7) with regard to the inter-linkage of green technologies to complementary sectors. Germany is in the midfield and China is among the countries with lower values with regard to this indicator.

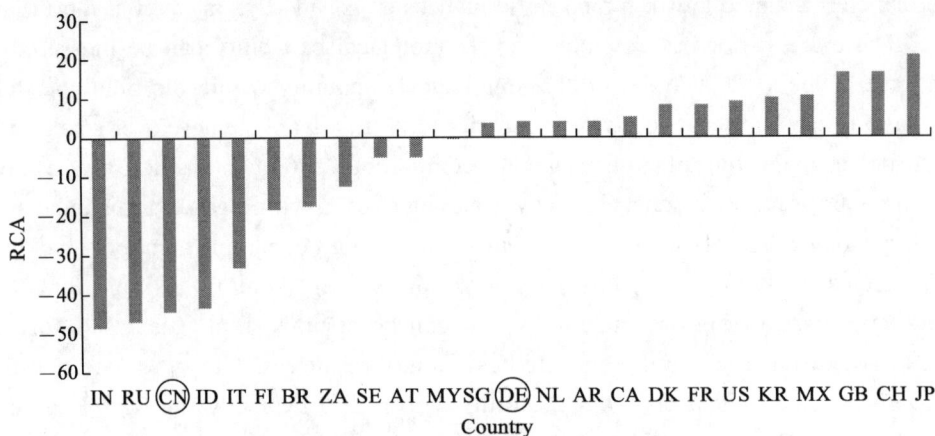

Figure 4.7 RCA of high technology
Source: Calculations of Fraunhofer ISI, based on UN-Comtrade data

4.4 Discussion and summary

The previous sections have presented the factors which influence the potential to establish lead markets, and an empirical top-down perspective on available proxy indicators for these factors. A methodological reflection about the availability and the nature of the available indicators reveals three different cases.

For some factors, there are indicators available which are valid on a more aggregated level. They can be used in this specification for various different technologies.

For some factors, there are indicators available for the aggregate of all green technologies. However, it can be foreseen that the respective indicator values fluctuate substantially between the different technologies. By and large, these kinds of indicators must be analyzed on a technology specific level.

For some factors, no indicators are available. They can only be analyzed on a very technology specific case.

The lack of availability of indicators for some factors and the early stage of methodological discussion about the choice and use of indicators, do not permit a robust empirical conclusion on the data. Nevertheless, it allows a first glimpse of which countries seem to enjoy relatively favorable starting conditions for establishing lead markets in green technologies. The results still show that traditional OECD countries seem to have the best starting points for developing lead markets in the field of green technologies, with Germany, Switzerland and Japan being among the top players.

However, there are some interesting results: First of all, the U. S. does not show up as one of the leading countries. Even more interesting, however, is that some of the Newly Industrializing Countries seem to make inroads. In this context, the dynamic of change in indicator values is important. Even though China does not show up among the leaders yet, it has been improving in some of the areas which are measured by the indicators recently.

Nevertheless, it has to be kept in mind that not all factors can be assessed from such a top-down perspective. Especially the factors of regulation, which is linked to the environmental policy making, and the existence of economic players are missing. Thus, the results presented here are only an intermediate step. Furthermore, some indicators can only be assessed on a technology specific basis. Thus, there is a need to move the analysis towards a more disaggregated level. Future challenges will be to quantify the export opportunities which are related to improving the countries' position with regard to the various indicators. Indeed, the opportunities for Germany and China become more obvious on such a technology specific level. China, for example, is highly successful in PV cell exports, and Germany is a key exporter of wind turbines. A comprehensive analysis on such a disaggregated level will identify more areas in which both countries will be able to play lead roles in the future.

Such an analysis will be also important for other reasons: Under globalization, value chains will become more and more international, and it will be less likely that one country alone will dominate a value chain. Thus, an analysis showing complementary strengths along a value chain will be necessary for identifying areas for cooperation between countries. Given the positioning of Germany and the dynamics of China towards becoming an important exporter of green technologies, it can be assumed that such an analysis will reveal that green technologies offer a wide array of fruitful technological partnership between the two countries.

References

Archibugi, D. , Pietrobelli, C. 2004. The globalization of technology and its implications for developing countries—windows of opportunity or further burden? *Technological Forecasting and Social Change*, 70, 861-883.
Amable, B. , Verspagen, B. 1995. The role of technology in market shares dynamics. *Applied Economics*, 27(2): 197-204.
Beise, M. , Cleff, T. 2004. Assessing the lead market potential of countries for innovation projects. *Journal of International Management*, 10(4), 453-477.
Beise, M. 2004. Lead markets: country specific drivers of the global diffusion of innovations.

Research Policy, 33, 997-1028.

Blind, K. 2001. The impacts of innovations and standards on trade of measurement and testing products: empirical results of Switzerland's bilateral trade flows with Germany, France and the UK. *Information Economics and Policy*, 13, 439-460.

Dosi, G., Pavitt, K., Soete, L. 1990. *The Economics of Technical Change and International Trade*. New York: Pinter

Fagerberg, J. 1995. Technology and Competitiveness. *Oxford Review of Economic* Policy, 12 (3), 39-51.

Freeman, C., Soete, L. 2009. Developing science and technology indicators: what can we learn from the past? *Research Policy*, 38(4), 583-589.

Greenaway, D., Sousa, N., Wakelin, K. 2004. Do domestic firms learn to export from multinationals? *European Journal of Political Economy*, 20, 1027-1043.

Griliches, Z. 1991. The search for R&D spillovers. Working Paper No. 3768. Cambridge: National Bureau of Economic Research.

Grossman, G. M., Helpman, E. 1991a. Quality ladders and product cycles. *Quarterly Journal of Economics*, 106, 557-586.

Grossman, G. M., Helpman, E. 1991b. Trade, knowledge spillovers, and growth. *European Economic Review*, 35, 517-526.

Jamasb, T., Köhler, J. 2008. Learning curves for energy technologies: a critical assessment. In: Grubb, M., et al. (Eds.), *Delivering a Low-carbon Electricity System*. Cambridge, 314-332.

Johnstone, N., Haščič, I., Popp, D. 2010. Renewable energy policies and technological innovation: Evidence based on patent counts. *Environmental and Resource Economics*, 45(1), 133-155.

Krugman, P. 1979. A model of innovation, technology transfer, and the world distribution of income. *Journal of Political Economy*, 87, 253-266.

Lachenmaier, S., Wössmann, L. 2006. Does innovation cause exports? Evidence from exogenous innovation impulses and obstacles using German micro data. Oxford Economic Papers, 58, 317-350.

Linder, S. B. 1961. *An Essay on Trade and Transformation*. New York: Wiley.

Lundvall, B. A. 1985. *Product Innovation and User-producer Interaction*. Aalborg: Aalborg University Press.

Madsen, J. B. 2008. Innovations and manufacturing export performance in the OECD countries. *Oxford Economic Papers*, 60, 143-167.

Magnier, A., Toujas-Bernate, J. 1994. Technology and trade: empirical evidences for the major five industrialized countries. *Weltwirtschaftliches Archiv*, 130(3): 494-520.

Pain, N., Wakelin, K. 2004. Export performance and the role of foreign direct investment. *The Manchester School*, 66, 62-88.

Pan, H., Köhler, J. 2007. Technological change in energy systems: learning curves, logistic curves, and input-output coefficiencts. *Ecological Economics*, 63, 749-758.

Peuckert, J. 2011. Assessment of the social capabilities for catching-up through sustainability innovations. *International Journal Technology and Globalization*, 5(3/4), 190-211.

Porter, M. E. 1990. *The competitive advantage of nations*. Harvard Business Review.

Porter, M. E., van der Linde, C. 1995. Toward a new conception of the environment-competitiveness relationship. *Journal of Economic Perspectives*, 9(4), 97-118.

Sanyal, P. 2004. The role of innovation and opportunity in bilateral OECD trade performance. *Review of World Economics*, 140(4), 634-664.

Soete, L. L. G. 1981. A general test of technological gap trade theory. *Weltwirtschaftliches Archiv*, 117(4): 638-660.

Vernon, R. 1966. International investment and international trade in the product cycle. *Quarterly Review of Economics*, 88, 190-207.

von Hippel, E. 1988. Sources of Innovation. New York: Oxford University Press.

Wagner, J. 2007. Exports and productivity: a survey of the evidence from firm-level data. *The World Economy*, 30, 817-838.

Walz, R., et al. 2011. Regulation, innovation and wind power technologies—an empirical analysis for OECD countries. Paper presented at the DIME Final Conference, Maastricht.

Walz, R., et al. 2008. Zukunftsmärkte Umwelt—Innovative Umweltpolitik in Wichtigen Handlungsfeldern. Berlin: Reihe Umwelt, Innovation, Beschäftigung of the German Environment Ministry.

Walz, R., Helfrich, N., Enzmann, A. 2009. A system dynamics approach for modelling a lead-market-based export potential. Working Papers Sustainability and Innovation, Karlsruhe.

Walz, R. 2006. Increasing renewable energy in Europe—impacts on competitiveness and lead markets. *Energy & Environment*, 17(6), 951-975.

Walz, R., Marscheider-Weidemann, F. 2011. Technology-specific absorptive capacities for green technologies in newly industrializing countries. *International Journal of Technology and Globalization*, 5(3/4), 212-229.

Walz, R., Meyer-Krahmer, F. 2003. Innovation and sustainability in economic development. Global Network on Economics of Learning, Innovation and Competence Building Systems (Globelics) First Conference on "Innovation Systems and Development Strategies for the Third Milennium", Rio de Janeiro.

Walz, R. 2007. The role of regulation for sustainable infrastructure innovations: the case of wind energy. *International Journal of Public Policy*, 2(1/2), 57-88.

Wei Y. Q., Liu XM, Wang, C. 2008. Mutual productivity spillovers between foreign and local firms in China. *Cambridge Journal of Economics*, 32, 609-631.

Acknowledgement

The research for this paper has been performed within the project "Lead Market

Strategies: First Mover, Early Follower, Late Follower". The financial contribution of the German BMBF is acknowledged.

Author

Priv. -Doz. Dr. Rainer Walz is head of the Competence Center Sustainability and Infrastructure Systems at the Fraunhofer Institute for Systems and Innovation Research(ISI) in Karlsruhe. He studied economics and political science at the University of Freiburg and at Brock University in Canada. Ph. D. and "habilitation" in economics. In 1992, he received the Friedrich-August-von-Hayek Price from the University of Freiburg. In 1991, Dr. Walz joined the FhG-ISI. His prior employment includes the University of Wisconsin and the Enquête Commission "Protecting the Earth's Atmosphere" of the German Bundestag. He is now teaching at the University of Karlsruhe and is a guest professor at the Institute of Policy and Management of Chinese Academy of Sciences.

An Evaluation on Driving Forces for Green Innovation in China

Su Liyang, Chen Shaofeng

The green growth, which is regarded as a win-win approach to coordinate economic development and environmental and climate protection, is a response to multiple challenges, such as climate change, environmental degeneration, resources shortage and financial crisis. Currently, the pursing for green growth has become more and more popular all over the world. For example, Korean has released the *Framework Act on Low Carbon, Green Growth*; China has also integrated green and low carbon development into its 12th Five-Year Plan for Economic and Social Development, which is the most important guideline for the following 5 years' economic development. While for a transition to green growth, green innovation is at the core for realizing such kind of goals. The implementation of green innovation will effectively reconstruct the impetus for economic growth. Thus, an analysis of green innovation, especially its driving force is rather important for green development.

5.1 Green innovation: definition and driving forces

5.1.1 Definition of green innovation

The concept of innovation emerged one hundred years ago when Schumpeter (1990) defined the innovation. But only until the 1990s, along with the growing popularity of the concept of sustainable development, more and more attention was directed toward the connection of innovation and sustainability. Several concepts have been proposed, including environmental innovation(Beisea and Rennings,2005;Kemp et al. ,2001;Klemmer et al. , 1999), eco-innovation (Rennings, 2000), sustainability innovation(Horbach, 2005),innovation for sustainability(Weaver, 2005),and system innovation(Elzen et al. , 2004;Bruijin et al. , 2004). There is not much difference among these concepts or ideas in essence. Basically they can be labeled as sustainable innovation or green innovation.

Innovation is a dynamic process for the introduction of new production factors or production conditions into the production system and thus the productivity improves (Schumpeter, 1990). While for green innovation, which is a combination of sustainability and innovation, there is no universal definition for green innovation until now. At micro level, green innovation consists of new and modified processes, equipment, products, techniques and management systems that avoid or reduce harmful environmental impact (Kemp, 2001). Whether green innovation succeed depends on whether we obtain the same instrumental value with less environmental impact or gain more instrumental value with the same environmental impact. At macro level,green innovation refers to all the creative activities that contribute to the coordinated development of environment and economic growth, and thus helps to decouple economic growth and environmental impact.

5.1.2 The driving forces of green innovation: technology pushed, market pulled and policy driven

According to Rennings(2000), the driving forces of green innovation could be classified into three types: technology pushed, such as the development of green technologies;market pulled,such as the sustainable consumer demand; and regulation driven,such as the implement of environmental standards(Figure 5.1).

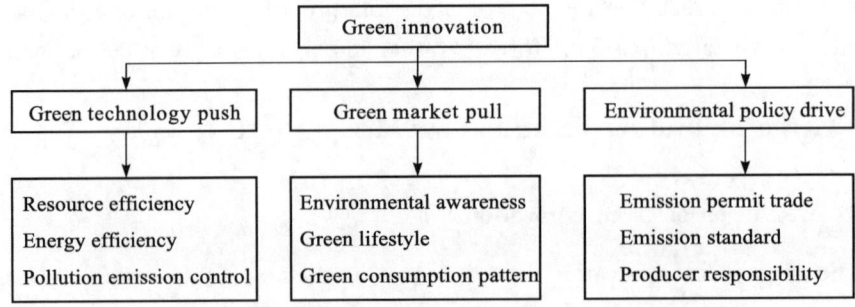

Figure 5.1 Three driving forces of green innovation
Source: Adapted from Rennings(2000)

The green technology pushed type includes the progress of technology for the improvement of energy efficiency and material efficiency and the reduction of pollution emission when producing the same output. This is quite different from the traditional technology R&D, which tries to improve labor productivity and capital utilization. The green technology pushed type not only refers to the technologies for production process, but also relates to the products for the consumers.

The green market pulled type is the change in lifestyle and consumption pattern, which is more sustainable than before. The impact of green market on green innovation is as follow: One is the change in lifestyle that directly reduces the use of water, energy and so on; the other is the change in consumption pattern that influences the product structure. This is also quite different from the traditional one, which focuses on price and quality.

What should be highlighted is the role of environmental regulation in promoting green innovation. A feature of green innovation is its double-externality problem, which reduces incentives for firms to invest in environmental innovations(Beisea and Rennings, 2005). The double-externality problem of green innovations is that they bring positive spillovers in both the innovation and the diffusion phases(Rennings, 2000). On the one hand, there is spillover in the diffusion process of green technology as the cost of imitation is much lower than the innovation's cost. On the other hand, when the innovator creates or adopts a new process, product or organizational measure which improves the quality of the environment, he has to cover the costs by himself while the benefit doesn't belong to him exclusively. In this situation, the motive to promote green innovation might be weak. And thus, the environmental policies such as environmental subsidies, the trade of emission permit, market access, performance standard, product standard, product ban, producer responsibility, information disclosure, voluntary agreement, and so on, may have a strong impact on green innovation in a way of tackling externality.

5.2 The green innovation in China: highly rely on policy driven and technology pushed

Over the past few decades, great efforts have been made in China to promote green innovation. Our environmental policies are much better than before, our investment in green technology R&D is substantial, and the consumers' environmental awareness is also improving. However, it is safe to say that China's green innovation over the past few decades is characterized as policy driven and technology pushed. The three driving forces are actually not in balance.

5.2.1 Policy driven: a formation of comprehensive policy framework for green innovation in China

A series of policies promoting green innovation both at national level and local level are developed in China. The policy framework on China's green innovation consists of national strategy, scientific & technological special plans, sectoral policy and local action plan (Figure 5.2). The national strategies relate to the green innovation mainly include China's sustainable development strategy, strategy of developing our country by relying on science and education, comprehensive working plan on China's energy saving & emission reduction in the "11th Five Years" and "12th Five Years", and so on. At the legislation level, China's *Renewable Energy Law*, *Energy Conservation Law*, *Pollution Prevention and Control Law*, and so on have some articles on investment in R&D and creating green market. What should be highlighted is the *National Outline for Medium- and Long-term Program for Science & Technology Development* (2006 - 2020), which lists energy and environment as 2 of the 11 main areas. In addition to the national programs and laws, the provincial authorities have also paid attention to promoting green innovations.

One feature of China's policy framework for promoting green innovation is that control and command policies are highly emphasized. This is rather suitable for China's top-down political system and imperfect market. Especially, in the "11th Five Years", with the decomposition of energy-saving and pollution reduction goal, the green technology is taken seriously all over the nation and great domestic demand for green technology is created, which promotes the green innovation.

5.2.2 Technology pushed: great improvement in green technology in China

China's capacity of technology pushed for green innovation is enhanced dramatically and acts as one of the most important driving forces for China's green innovation.

First of all, the investment of R&D in green innovation in China increases greatly. In the "10th Five-Year" period, China invested around RMB 2.5 billion yuan in climate-related and low-carbon technology R&D. It is estimated that the total amount of investment in climate-related R&D activities will reach RMB 10 billion yuan in the "11th Five-Year" period[①] through Key Technologies R&D Program, the

---

① http://www.chinanews.com.cn/gn/news/2009/09-30/1895463.shtml.

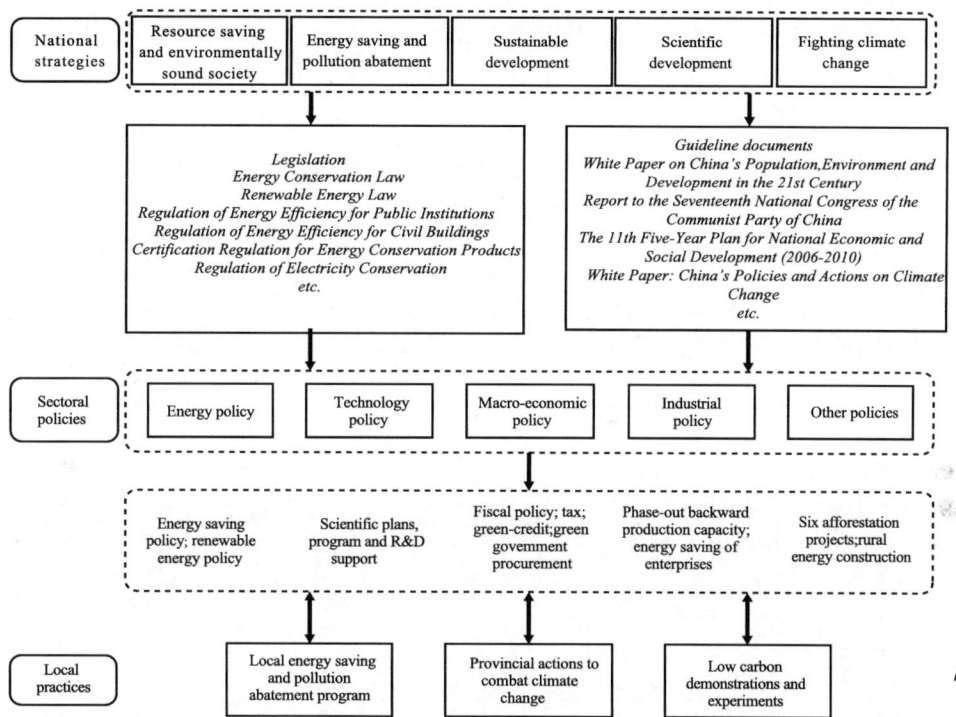

Figure 5.2 China's policy framework for green innovation
Source: UNDP(2010)

National High-tech Research and Development Program ("863" Program) and the National Basic Research Program ("973" Program).

Secondly, lots of green technologies are gone through a fast development and commercialization processes in China (Table 5.1). Taking wind energy for example, China's installed wind power exceeded 6 GW in 2011—the world No.1 installed wind power. Besides, the development of electric vehicles, including electric bicycles and electro-tricycle, is also exciting in China, which could not only contribute to solving the problem of mobility in rural areas, but also reduce pollution emission and oil use compared with the gasoline vehicles.

Table 5.1 Renewable energy technologies and the stage of their development in China

Technology	Development stage			
	R&D	Prototype	Small scale application	Commercialization
Small hydropower plant				◆
Solar power water heater				◆

Continued

Technology	Development stage			
	R&D	Prototype	Small scale application	Commer-cialization
Passive solar house				◆
Solar cooker				◆
Solar dryer		◆		
Solar cell			◆	
Large scale wind power grid operating system			◆	
Small scale and mini wind power grid operating system			◆	
Geothermal power generation technology				◆
Geothermal heating technology				◆
Traditional biomass power technology				◆
Miniature biogas pool				◆
Large and middle biogas technology			◆	
Urban organic waste power generation technology		◆		
Biomass gasification technology		◆		
Tidal power generation technology			◆	

Sources: OECD(2009)

Thirdly, the green technology gap between China and the world is narrowing. In 2007, China's comprehensive energy efficiency gap of 14 products from 8 major sectors from the international advanced level has been reduced to 20% from 40% in 2000(Feng and Wang, 2009). Currently, China is in the lead position all over the world in many key technologies, such as solar water heater, small hydropower and so on. Some experts even argue that if China adheres to the energy conservation & emission reduction strategy, China's green technology will catch up with the international advanced level(Wang et al. ,2009). Besides, more enterprises conduct R&D activities of green technology and become competent in the international market.

5. 2. 3 Market-pulled: China's lifestyle and consumption pattern are following developed countries' pattern

Along with the increase of income in China, China's lifestyle and consumption pattern are following developed countries' pattern. Over the past three decades, China's consumption expenditure and life quality are improved quickly and in 2008 the per capita consumption expenditure are 8 times more than 1978's. Especially, since 2003 when China's per capita GDP reached to 1000 dollars, people's demand is changing from food and clothes to housing and vehicles. More and more people are buying automobiles,which leads China running to "Auto Society".

On the other hand, China's consumer's awareness is still very weak compared with the people in developed countries. Chinese people have the ideas of buying expensive and luxurious products, which might result in resource waste and pollution emission.

Thus, the contribution of change in taste is not positive for green innovation.

5.3 Challenges for China's green innovation

A transition to green innovation is a process for system revolution, and it faces the challenges from technical, organizational, institutional, and cultural barriers. This part tries to discuss some challenges in China for green innovation.

5.3.1 Compared with developed countries, the technology gap is still large

Firstly, the R&D investment in green technology is low compared with developed countries(Liu et al. ,2010). Taking the energy sector for example, Japan's energy R&D intensity is more than 0.8‰, and the United States, France and Canada are about 0.2‰- 0.5‰. Most of the investment is spent on nuclear power(if the country has nuclear power),energy efficient and renewable energy. However, China's energy R&D intensity is only 0.068‰ (Ma et al. ,2003) and most of which has been used in the traditional energy, for example, China's investment in energy efficient R&D only accounted for 10.6% of the total energy R&D investment in 2004 (Energy R&D Research Team,2007).

Secondly, for the key green technology, there is a big gap between domestic company and international advanced level, and the core technology is still subject to foreign companies. From Table 5.2, we can find that China's 20 key green technologies have lagged behind the world's advanced level by at least 7 years. As a result, China is at the low level of the industrial chain in some industries. Taking China's PV industry for example, 90% of raw materials and equipment are imported from other countries[①].

---

① http://www.sipo.gov.cn/sipo2008/ztzl/ywzt/zlsd/200904/t20090408_449666.html.

Table 5.2 China's technological gaps in key green technology

Serial number	Green technologies	The gap with foreign countries
1	Million-kilowatt-class nuclear power technology	9 years
2	Marine oil and gas development technology	9 years
3	Coal gasification-based poly-generation technology	8 years
4	Renewable resources and comprehensive utilization of waste	10 years
5	Coal liquefaction technology	8 years
6	Large scale network security and scheduling technology	7 years
7	Efficient power generation technology of coal	10 years
8	Oil and gas exploration and development technology	8 years
9	High voltage electric inverter technology	8 years
10	Energy crops and fuel fabrication technology	8 years
11	Green lighting technology	7 years
12	Superconducting transmission, extra-high voltage technology to improve transmission capacity	8 years
13	New generation of advanced nuclear power technology	9 years
14	Hydrogen and fuel cell technology	9 years
15	Wind, solar, biomass and other new energy technologies	9 years
16	Building energy conservation and energy transmission and distribution system	8 years
17	Environmental protection and new energy efficient cars car design and manufacturing technology	9 years
18	Pulverized coal power generation flue gas treatment technology	9 years
19	Process industry equipment manufacturing technology	8 years
20	Green design and manufacturing technology	10 years

Source: Qian(2008)

5.3.2 China's imperfect environmental policy system

First of all, there is no effective coordination mechanism among different ministries. Thus, there is not only no coordination between environmental policy and innovation policy, but also no coordination among different environmental policies. Taking water resource management for example, there are some conflicts between the Ministry of Environmental Protection, who is in charge of water quality, and the Ministry of Water Resources, who takes charge of water quantity. This will of course affect green innovation.

Secondly, the market-based instruments in China are not very popular and effective. The fiscal, tax and subsidy policies are not as perfect as required. This is mainly due to our imperfect market economy, within which some market-based instruments are not suitable or the effectiveness are not quite good.

Thirdly, China's monitoring system for energy consumption, CO_2 emission and pollution emission fails to reach the requirement of employing control and command policies. Thus the effectiveness of some control and command policies is not good.

5.3.3 The pursuing for high quality life continues

There is no doubt that China's economic growth will continue in the next 20 – 30 years. According to HSBC(2011), China's growth rate of GDP will be 6.7% annually from 2010 to 2020, and it will decrease to 5.5% from 2020 to 2030. This is still a very high speed compared with other countries. With the increase of GDP, Chinese people will continue to pursue a high quality life. This creates the great market for green technology, but also for traditional technology, which might result in lock-in of energy and pollution insensitive industry.

5.4 Policy recommendation on promoting green innovation in China

In order to address the major challenges faced in china, it is necessary to re-orient the national innovation system to green existing dominant technology system and transform the current economic development pattern, production mode and consumption pattern to a more sustainable way. From the view of macro-level, green development in China needs to focus on strengthening and coordinating of the following four aspects.

5.4.1 Developing the road map of China's green technology

It is necessary for Chinese government to assess the current reports, such as *Energy Science & Technology in China: a Road map to 2050* and *China's Crucial Technologies and Its Road map for Energy-saving and Emission-reduction*, and set the green technology road map as the national strategy.

5.4.2 Increase the investment in green technology innovation

Firstly, government should establish the national green technology innovation programme to make use of financial resources for key technologies. Secondly, the principles of openness, transparency and impartiality should be enforced in national scientific management. Thirdly, the scientific and technological resources should be shared fairly and accessed across different regions and sectors.

5.4.3 Developing market-based environmental policy

Different policies have different impact on green innovation (Table 5.3). Both of market-based policy and command and control policy have their own advantages and disadvantages in practice and stimulate the green technology innovation in different ways. However, normally, the market-based policy, such as emission trading system and carbon tax which has been used in the northern European countries, is much more suitable for inspiring green innovation. China should try to emphasize the use of market-based policy in promoting green innovation. First of all, establish the emission trading system in some area. Along with the establishment of China Beijing Environment Exchange and Tianjin Climate Exchange, the government should enhance the supporting policy and develop the pilot programs. Secondly, conduct the research on the enforcement of carbon tax. Relevant studies show that carbon tax with low taxation rate will not damage China's economic growth remarkably, but its effect on carbon emission reduction and promotion of green technology innovation is significant.

Table 5.3 Climate policy and its advantages, disadvantages and impact on innovation

Classification	Instrument	Advantage	Disadvantage	Impact on green technology innovation
Market-based policy	Emission trading system	The carbon price will be determined by market Companies can reduce the carbon emission at a low cost Private sectors are able to participate in reducing the emission Participants can be connected by the market	The carbon price will fluctuate and result in the gamble behaviors International carbon leakage may happen Transaction cost might be high	The emission trading system might promote the green technology innovation well on the condition that the emission permit is rationally allocated and the transaction takes place at the fair and open circumstance
	Carbon tax	It provides a clear price signal It can mobilize public sectors' resources. It can promote the carbon emission reduction	The tax policy is only authorized in the host country The amount of reduced carbon emission is uncertain It has no political appeal	The carbon tax policy is able to promote the green technology innovation cost effectively

Continued

Classification	Instrument	Advantage	Disadvantage	Impact on green technology innovation
Command and control policy	Standard	Set up the targets for a certain behaviour. The implementation and monitoring process is direct	The effectiveness might not be so significant and the cost might be higher compared with the market-based mechanism	The incentive for green technology innovation will be insufficient. It might be suitable for the technology having the potential of commercialization
	Clean technology subsidy	It is able to promote the industrial investment effectively. The implementation and monitoring is relatively simple	The effectiveness might not be so significant and the cost might be higher compared with the market-based mechanism	It is able to promote the diffusion of green technology. It is suitable for the technology which is relatively mature or economic
	R&D investment	It is of help to address market failure	Effectiveness might appear slowly, however it might be a promising way and the cost might be higher compared with the market-based mechanism	It can accelerate the development of new technologies

Source: Zhou(2010)

5.4.4 Creating market and demand for green innovation

First of all, the government should guide consumers' lifestyle and consumption pattern to a more sustainable way. For example, government should promote people to take public transportation instead of private vehicles, and so on. Secondly, we should build government procurement institution for green technology. The government should work out the standards, products list and guidance for green products purchase clearly and rationally to manage green products purchase.

References

Beisea, M., Rennings, K. 2005. Lead markets and regulation: a framework for analyzing the international diffusion of environmental innovations. *Ecological Economics*, (52), 5-17.

Bruijin, et al. 2004. *Creating System Innovation*. London: Taylor & Francis Group.

Elzen, B. , Geels, F. W. , Green, K. 2004. *System Innovation and the Transition to Sustainability*. Cheltenham: Edward Elgar Publishing.

Energy Strategy Research Team, Chinese Academy of Sciences. 2009. *The Energy Science and Technology Development Roadmap by 2050 (in Chinese)*. Beijing: Science Press.

Ernest, B. , David, W. 1994. Regulation as a means for the social control of technology. *Technology Analysis and Strategic Management*, 6(3), 259-273.

Feng, F. , Wang, J. Z. 2009. The medium assessment on energy conservation and emission reduction in the 11th Five-Year period (in Chinese). *Green Leaf*, (4), 113-118.

Horbach, J. 2005. *Indicator Systems for Sustainable Innovation*. Heidelberg: Phisica-verlag.

Ward, K. 2011. *The World in 2050: Quantifying the Shift in the Global Economy*. London: HSBC.

Kemp, R. , et al. 2001. Survey indicators for environmental innovation. Paper for the International Conference "Towards Environmental Innovation Systems", Garmisch-Partenkirchen.

Klemmer, P. , Lehr, U. , Löbbe, K. 1999. Environmental innovation. Volume 3 of publications from a Joint Project on Innovation Impacts of Environmental Policy Instruments, Synthesis Report of a project commissioned by the German Ministry of Research and Technology (BMBF), Analytica-Verlag, Berlin.

Liu, Y. , Yu, J. , Wu, C. H. 2010. Technology development road map of low carbon innovation. In: Sustainable Development Strategy Study Group, CAS (Eds.), *China Sustainable Development Strategy Report* 2010. Beijing: Science Press, 3-40.

Ma, C. , et al. 2003. China's R&D investment (in Chinese). *Energy Research and Utilization*, (3), 3-6.

OECD. 2009. Eco-innovation policies in the People's Republic of China. Environment Directorate, OECD.

Qian, Z. 2008. The key technology and road map for China's energy-saving and pollution-reduction (in Chinese). *Innovation S&T*, (8), 54, 55.

Rennings, K. 2000. Redefining innovation—eco-innovation research and the contribution from ecological economics. *Ecological Economics*, (32), 319-332.

Schumpeter. 1990. *Economic Development Theory (in Chinese)*. Translated by He, W. , et al. Beijing: Commercial Press.

UNDP. 2010. *China and a Sustainable Future: Towards a Low Carbon Economy & Society*. Beijing: China Translation and Publishing Corporation.

Wang, Y. , Chen, S. F. , Su, L. Y. 2009. Respect the history and rules to select the rational carbon intensity indicator (in Chinese). http://www.cas.cn/zt/sszt/gbhg/200912/t20091216_2709713.shtml[2012-01-01].

Weaver, P. M. 2005. National systems of innovation. In: Hargroves, K. C. , Smith, M. H. (Eds.), *The Natural Advantage of Nations: Business Opportunities, Innovation and Governance in the 21st Century*. London: Earthscan Publication Ltd.

Zhou, H. C. 2010. Policy evaluation and recommendation for China's S&T innovation (in Chinese). In: Sutainable Development Strategy Study Group, CAS (Eds.), *China Sustainable Development Strategy Report* 2010. Beijing: Science Press.

Author

Su Liyang is a Ph. D. candidate at the Institute of Policy and Management of Chinese Academy of Sciences. His main fields of research are sustainability innovation, energy and climate policy analysis, and low carbon technology diffusion. He has authored or co-authored 6 books and 10 scientific articles.

Dr. Chen Shaofeng is an associate professor of the Institute of Policy and Management of Chinese Academy of Sciences. He received his Master Degree from the Institute of Policy and Management of Chinese Academy of Sciences and Ph. D. from the University of Science and Technology of China. His main fields of research are sustainability theory and assessment, sustainable development strategy and policies, and governance for sustainable development. He has authored or co-authored 12 books and more than 60 scientific articles.

Will the European Emission Trading Scheme Promote Green Innovation in the European Industry?

Karoline Rogge, Wolfgang Eichhammer

6.1 Introduction

Despite the setback in Copenhagen(UNFCCC,2009) and the very limited progress in Durban(UNFCCC,2011), the delicate global negotiations for a successor of the *Kyoto Protocol* (UNFCCC,1997) as well as the implementation of a variety of climate policies around the world(IEA,2009a) reveal an increasing political will to limit climate change(UNFCCC,1992). In a pioneering move, in 2005 the European Union(EU) introduced the world's largest multi-country greenhouse gas emission trading system, the EU Emissions Trading System(ETS), representing the cornerstone of its climate policy(EU,2003). The main advantage of this cap-and-trade scheme going back to the seminal work of Dales(1968) is its static efficiency: By establishing a price for greenhouse gas(GHG) emissions and granting participating companies flexibility in their choice of compliance strategies, the instrument promises the cost-minimal achievement of its emission cap(Tietenberg,1985; Baumol and Oates,1988). In addition, by establishing a price for carbon such a trading scheme is expected to generate dynamic incentives for the development and diffusion of low carbon technologies(for an overview, see Fischer, 2005). In line with this theory-based economic reasoning regarding the superiority of economic instruments for spurring innovation(Jaffe et al., 2002; Requate, 2005; Vollebergh, 2007; Popp et al., 2009), a number of other countries are in the process of implementing their own emission trading schemes. However, the actual implementation of the EU ETS has cast doubts over its capacity for triggering innovation, although this may be its most important property for achieving the required deep greenhouse gas emission cuts(IPCC,2007b). Therefore, this article sets out to improve the understanding of the innovation impact of the EU ETS.

The existing literature on the innovation impact of the EU ETS can be differentiated into those studies trying to anticipate the scheme's impact and those conducting ex-post evaluations. Regarding the former, based on theoretical and empirical evidence from US trading schemes for SO_2, NO_x and lead (for an overview, see Hansjürgens, 2006), Gagelmann and Frondel(2005) conclude that the innovation impact of the EU ETS in its pilot phase from 2005 – 2007 is likely to be limited. As main reasons for this they identify the generous initial allocation of EU ETS allowances as well as the linking with the project-based Kyoto Mechanisms Joint Implementation(JI) and Clean Development Mechanism(CDM) without upper limits(EU,2004), and the distribution of allowances free-of-charge. Schleich and Betz(2005) arrive at a similar conclusion by discussing the potential innovation relevance of EU ETS design choices. These innovation-specific studies are complemented by broader analyses on the economic implications of the design of the EU ETS(Egenhofer et al.,2006; Ellerman and Joskow, 2008). For example, two innovation-relevant aspects of the EU ETS having been analyzed are the distortionary incentives arising from the treatment of new entrants and closures as well as the short trading phases and resulting investment uncertainties (Neuhoff et al., 2006; Ahman et al., 2007; Ellermann, 2008; Hoffmann et al., 2008). It thus comes as no surprise that the rare ex-post evidence indicates a rather limited actual innovation impact of the EU ETS, particularly on research and development and long-term portfolio decisions (Hoffmann, 2007; Cames, 2008). However, these early studies do not cover all aspects relevant for such an analysis (del Río González,2009) and do not consider the more stringent second trading phase(2008 – 2012) and the ambitious revision of the EU ETS post-2012(Schleich et al.,2009).

Against this background, it is the aim of this paper to provide a comprehensive analysis of how the EU ETS has impacted innovation and whether it does so at a level adequate for reaching the long-term political targets required for a decarbonization of the economy. In doing so, we address several of the research recommendations brought forward for studying the determinants of environmental technological change(del Río González,2009). We build our research framework on environmental economics and innovation studies(Fagerberg and Verspagen,2009) and extend the existing studies in four respects: First, we distinguish innovation into the three dimensions of research, development and demonstration(RD&D), adoption, and organizational change, and address interactions between them. Second, we include not only regulated entities in our analysis, but also corporate actors from other value chain positions relevant for innovation outcomes(Pavitt,1984). Third, we specifically address firm heterogeneity to understand how the innovation impact of the EU ETS differs according to firm characteristics, such as a firm's technology portfolio. Fourth, we also explicitly address the role of context factors to account for the multitude of determinants of corporate innovation activities(del Río González,2005;Horbach,2008;OECD,2007).

We limit our study to the power sector because it constitutes by far the largest share of CO_2 emissions covered by the scheme(EU,2005). The power sector is also the largest contributor to CO_2 emissions in the rest of the world and thus plays a key role in future innovation and emission reductions(IEA,2009b). Furthermore, we confine our analysis to Germany as it exhibits a fairly diversified mix of power generation technologies and is characterized by significant capacity renewal needs(IEA,2007;Platts,2008). We base our analysis on multiple company case studies because such a methodological approach enables us to uncover the complex effects and causal links relevant for corporate innovation decision making(Yin,2002).

This paper is organized as follows: section 6.2 presents the main features of the EU ETS, section 6.3 presents the research framework, section 6.4 describes the case study methodology, section 6.5 presents our findings on the impact of the EU ETS on RD&D, adoption, and organizational change. And finally, section 6.6 concludes with research and policy recommendations.

6.2 Main features of the EU ETS

Launched in 2005, the EU ETS works on the cap- and-trade principle. This means there is a "cap", or limit, on the total amount of certain greenhouse gases that can be emitted by the factories, power plants and other installations in the system. Within this "cap", companies receive emission allowances which they can sell to or buy from one another as needed. The limit on the total number of allowances available ensures that they have a value. At the end of each year each company must surrender enough allowances to cover all its emissions, otherwise heavy fines are imposed. If a company reduces its emissions, it can keep the spare allowances to cover its future needs or else sell them to another company that is short of allowances. The flexibility that trading brings ensures that emissions are cut where it costs least to do so. The number of allowances is reduced over time so that total emissions fall. In 2020 emissions will be 21% lower than in 2005.

The three different phases of the EU ETS and their main allocation principles are shown in Figure 6.1[1].

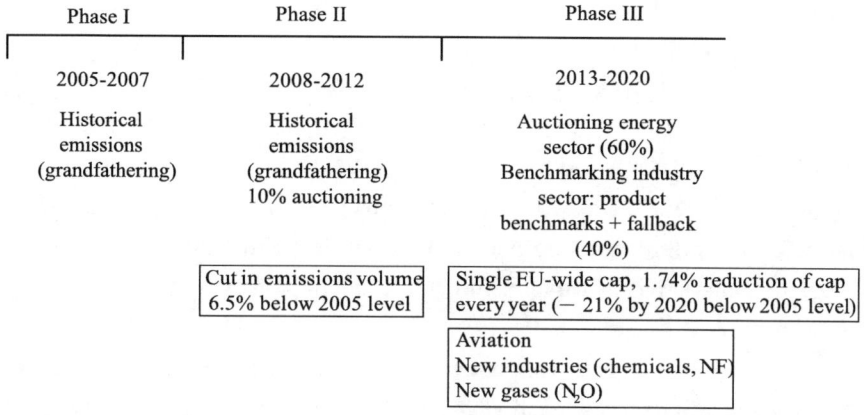

Figure 6.1 The three phases of the EU ETS

The EU ETS "cap" is the total amount of emission allowances to be issued for a given year. Since each allowance represents the right to emit one tonne of CO_2—or an amount of another greenhouse gas giving the same contribution to global warming as one tonne of CO_2—the total number of allowances, i.e. the "cap", determines the maximum amount of emissions possible under the EU ETS. In July 2010, the Commission adopted a first decision that determined the "cap" for 2013 based on the current scope of the EU ETS, i.e. the installations covered in the 2008–2012 period. The second decision, adopted in October 2010, takes into account the extended scope of the

---

[1] The main legislative texts that regulate the EU ETS are the following:
(1) Consolidated version of Directive 2003/87/EC of the European Parliament and of the Council of 13 October 2003 establishing a scheme for greenhouse gas emission allowance trading within the Community.
(2) Directive 2009/29/EC of the European Parliament and of the Council of 23 April 2009 amending Directive 2003/87/EC so as to improve and extend the greenhouse gas emission allowance trading scheme of the Community.
(3) Directive 2008/101/EC of the European Parliament and of the Council amending Directive 2003/87/EC so as to include aviation activities in the scheme for greenhouse gas emission allowance trading within the Community(19 November 2008).
(4) Directive 2004/101/EC of the European Parliament and of the Council of 27 October 2004 amending Directive 2003/87/EC establishing a scheme for greenhouse gas emission allowance trading within the Community, in respect of the *Kyoto Protocol's* project mechanisms.
(5) Directive 2003/87/EC of the European Parliament and of the Council establishing a scheme for greenhouse gas emission allowance trading within the Community and amending Council Directive 96/61/EC(13 October 2003).

EU ETS as from 2013. Since its launch in 2005 the EU ETS has covered power stations and other combustion plants, oil refineries, coke ovens, iron and steel plants and installations producing cement, glass, lime, bricks, ceramics, pulp, paper and board. As for the greenhouse gas, it currently covers only CO_2 emissions. As from 2013, the scope of the EU ETS will be extended to include other sectors and greenhouse gases. More CO_2 emissions from installations producing bulk organic chemicals, hydrogen, ammonia and aluminium will be included, as will N_2O emissions from the production of nitric, adipic and glyoxylic acid production and perfluorocarbon from the aluminium sector. Installations performing activities which result in these emissions will be included in the EU ETS as from 2013.

The "cap" for the year 2013 has been determined at around 2.04 billion allowances. The "cap" will decrease each year by 1.74% of the average annual total quantity of allowances issued by the Member States in 2008 – 2012. In absolute terms this means the number of allowances will be reduced annually by 37.4 million allowances. This annual reduction will continue beyond 2020 but may be subject to revision not later than 2025.

6.3 Research framework for studying the innovation impact of the EU ETS

Figure 6.2 summarizes our research framework for investigating the innovation impact of the EU ETS subject to the influence of context factors and the varying characteristics of firms.

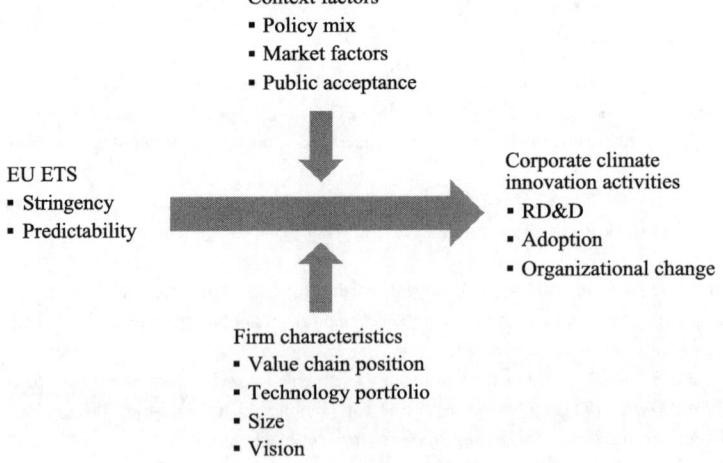

Figure 6.2 Research framework for studying the innovation impact of the EU ETS

We build our conceptualization of innovation on the *Oslo Manual* and focus on innovations new to the firm(OECD,2005). In line with neoclassical(Requate,2005) and evolutionary studies(Oltra and Saint Jean,2005), we differentiate innovation into research and adoption and add organizational change as third innovation dimension (Christensen and Rosenbloom,1995; Edquist,1997; Armbruster et al.,2008).

Regarding *research, development, and demonstration* (RD&D), "research" stands for basic laboratory research, "development" consists of testing the new technology at a small scale in pilot projects, and "demonstration" refers to the first larger-scale implementation of the technology.

We conceptualize *adoption* as companies' investments in state-of-the-art technologies. It encompasses both investments in new installations and retrofits of existing ones, thereby determining the diffusion of commercially available technologies.

Finally, *organizational change* consists of procedural change, structural change, and vision change. We are particularly interested in activities contributing to a reduction of GHG emissions and refer to them as *corporate climate innovation activities*.

Since the recent literature has pointed out that a policy's design features may be more influential for innovation than the instrument type(Kemp and Pontoglio,2008; Vollebergh,2007), we do not merely consider the EU ETS' carbon price and thus its nature as a market-based instrument. Instead, we focus on two design features that have previously been identified as important: stringency(Frondel et al.,2007;2008) and predictability(Jänicke et al.,2000;Hoffmann et al.,2008).

Stringency measures the necessary monetary effort in a given firm for complying with the environmental requirements of the policy instrument EU ETS(Bernauer et al.,2006). One element of the stringency of the EU ETS is its "cap" and the corresponding market price for CO_2. In addition, its specific policy details, such as the share of auctioning, the rules governing the allocation of allowances free of charge, or the share of CDM/JI credits allowed for compliance, also determine its overall stringency (Betz et al.,2006).

Predictability captures the degree of certainty associated with a policy instrument and its future development. This concerns the instrument's overall direction, detailed rules, and timing. Since the first two phases of the EU ETS operated in relatively short trading phases(3 and 5 years) with specific policy details as elaborated in the National Allocation Plans of Member States(Schleich et al.,2009), the scheme is associated with large regulatory uncertainty(Hoffmann et al.,2008; Hoffmann et al., 2009). This was one of the reasons to extend the third phase to eight years. Predictability is particularly relevant for sectors with long-lived capital-intensive investments, such as the power sector.

Since corporate innovation activities depend on a variety of firm-external and firm-internal factors(Rehfeld et al. ,2007; del Río González,2009), we also include context factors and firm characteristics in our research framework.

Context factors cover, first, the *policy mix*, which is constituted by the main policies other than the one under investigation. In our research case, important other policies include renewable resources support schemes(particularly the German feed-in tariffs), the nuclear phase-out law, and R&D subsidies(IEA,2007). The policy mix also incorporates long-term climate policy targets at the UN, EU, and national level, as well as the project-based Kyoto Mechanisms CDM and JI. Second, *context factors* include *market factors* such as prices, market structure, and demand as established innovation determinants(Newell et al. ,1999). For the power sector, these market factors include, for example, equipment prices, fuel prices and security of supply concerns, particularly for gas. Finally, *public acceptance* of technologies and thus their legitimacy can be an influential context factor(Hekkert et al. ,2007).

By including *firm characteristics*, we explicitly acknowledge the heterogeneity of corporate actors and their strategies(Barney, 1991). First, as the power sector is a supplier-dominated sector(Pavitt, 1984) we pay particular attention to firms' *value chain position* (Mazzanti and Zoboli,2006). We thus study both power generators as actors directly regulated by the EU ETS and technology providers. Second, we follow Christensen and Rosenbloom(1995)by including a company's *technology portfolio* because the type and share of technologies in a company's portfolio determines its technological capabilities and its exposure to the EU ETS. Third, we take account of company *size*, which may predetermine a company's scope and patterns of action. Finally, our framework encompasses a company's general strategic proactivity and its capability of establishing a shared long-term *vision* (Hart,1995). Vision also alludes to the recognition that collective frames may have to be broken in order to do things fundamentally differently(Kaplan and Tripsas,2008).

6.4 Methodology

In order to empirically analyze how companies are changing their innovation activities in response to the EU ETS, we chose a multiple case study approach as it is particularly appropriate for studying complex contemporary phenomena(Eisenhardt, 1989; Yin,2002). In selecting our cases, the goal was not to design a statistically representative sample, but to allow for analytic generalizations about the innovation impact of the EU ETS. Such an analytic generalization of findings requires their literal and theoretical *replication*, which is facilitated by the application of theoretical sampling(Yin,2002). This implies that, on the one hand, our theoretical sample includes at least two comparable companies so as to ensure the ability of finding similar results with different cases, i.e. *literal replication*. For example, we choose at least two technology providers with comparable firm characteristics, such as their technology portfolio and size(third column of Table 6.1). On the other hand, by choosing firms with different firm characteristics we allow for *theoretical replication*, i.e. the identification of contrasting results but for predict able reasons. For example, we interviewed both diversified and specialized technology providers(second column in Table 6.1).

Table 6.1 Overview of case studies

Value chain position	Other characteristics	Cases	Interviews
Power generator(PG)	Large	3	34
	Medium-sized	4	
Technology provider(TP)	Large (with varying degrees of diversification)	3	20
	Chemical process technology (for CCS)	3	
	Biogas	2	
	Wind	2	
Project developer(PD)	Diversified incumbents	2	7
Total		19	61

In order to generate a broad sample with a high level of variation, we incorporated both large incumbents and smaller corporate actors. We also included companies active in established(e.g. coal, gas) as well as in emerging power generation technologies(e.g. wind, biogas). These differences in firm characteristics are an important attribute of our sample as this allows the capturing of the diversity and heterogeneity of corporate innovation responses to the EU ETS. Finally, in order to triangulate our findings we also enclosed two project developers, leading to a total of 19 companies. Depending on the organizational setup of companies, we conducted between 1 and 7 interviews to cover all functions relevant for innovation technology, strategy, sales, and climate policy. This led to a total of 61 interviewed experts, or approximately 3 interviewees per case.

6.5 Results

Below, we present the EU ETS' main effects on the three innovation dimensions

RD&D, adoption, and organizational change, and explain the influence of the most important context factors and firm characteristics.

6.5.1 Impact on research, development, and demonstration

We concentrate the analysis of impacts on three main technology groups: CO_2 capture technologies, efficient coal technologies and renewable resources (in particular wind).

6.5.1.1 RD&D on CO_2 capture technologies

We find that the EU ETS has led to a significant intensification of RD&D activities on CO_2 capture technologies (CCS). While laboratory research on CCS had already been conducted by large diversified technology providers in the nineties, the introduction of the EU ETS triggered a strong increase in corporate CCS research, demonstrated by the initiation of pilot projects and plans for demonstration projects. As a consequence, private funding of CCS RD&D has risen significantly, with the largest share originating from large power generators. While companies pinpoint their initial spike in engagement to the EU ETS, the prospect of its continuation is what maintains it at a high level. Additionally, the prospect of full auctioning in the EU ETS from 2013 onwards seems to have further facilitated power generators' interest.

Apart from the EU ETS, a number of *context factors* seem important for the observed developments. First and foremost, the prospects of stringent long-term climate policy and debates about the introduction of command and control measures, such as performance standards for thermal power plants, are further spurring EU ETS triggered large-scale corporate RD&D activities as they indicate that CCS will be a must-have technology. Furthermore, RD&D on CCS is supported by public research funds which have also recently increased. The lack of public acceptance for coal is another driver, yet companies are also struggling with potential public resistance against CCS. Thus despite this uncertainty incumbents are pursuing CCS RD&D to be able to further rely on coal as their core business. By now, these research activities are taken very seriously as they are seen as important for ensuring companies' future competitiveness. However, more recently, the *context factors* have been degrading for CCS in Germany and to a large degree generally in Europe: regulatory uncertainty for the disposal of CO_2 in soils; the decision to prolong the use of nuclear which stopped coal investments on the supplier side despite the fact that Fukushima reversed this decision once again; increasing recognition on the investor side that acceptance for the technology is low; and low carbon prices in the ETS.

Regarding *firm characteristics*, companies' choice of which technological CCS routes to pursue at which intensity is influenced by their technology portfolio, i.e. the underlying core strategies and competencies[①]. For example, power generators' RD&D intensities appear especially large if the replacement need and thus the age of their coal plants and share of coal in their portfolio is high. Yet regardless of their portfolio composition, post-combustion appeals to all coal-based power generators alike due to its suitability for retrofitting and its flexibility. While the efforts of power generators are to a large extent driven by the EU ETS, technology providers' increased RD&D activities are typically driven by their customers' needs, illustrating the trickle-down effect of the EU ETS through the value chain. For them, core strategies and competencies again determine their choice of CCS routes. Finally, the involvement of power generators in CCS RD&D partnerships with technology providers appears more intense than is usually the case. Moreover, for all three technological CCS routes new RD&D cooperations have been formed with technology providers of the chemical industry.

6.5.1.2 RD&D on coal efficiency

Our case studies reveal that the EU ETS has accelerated previously ongoing incremental RD&D activities focusing on new materials to increase the energy efficiency of new coal plants up to 50% and beyond("50 + "). The first main reason for this acceleration is the CO_2 price, while the second is the efficiency losses that would occur if CCS was installed in the future.

That is, regarding *context factors*, fuel prices and corresponding fuel cost savings remain a prime motivation for RD&D on coal efficiency, but are now supplemented. In addition, the lack of public acceptance for new coal plants appears to further augment the coal efficiency RD&D engagement of large incumbents, as well as the perceived security of supply of coal. Of course, this line of research has also been benefiting from public RD&D funding, particularly at early stages. As for CCS, the *context factors* have been degrading more recently for coal efficiency projects for similar reasons.

Regarding *firm characteristics*, all large power generators, as well as technology providers with a big share of coal technologies in their portfolio, have been active in coal efficiency RD&D. Firm-internal reasons for an investment in "50 + " RD&D also include the German engineering mentality to strive for the best technological solutions.

6.5.1.3 RD&D on gas efficiency

The EU ETS' impact on incremental RD&D activities on gas technologies that aim for higher efficiency appears to be positive but relatively small. This strikingly

---

[①] The three main routes are postcombustion, integrated gasification combined cycle(IGCC), and oxyfuel.

low importance of the EU ETS can be explained by the high share of the fuel price relative to the CO_2 price.

This means that *context factors*, and here in particular the relatively high gas prices dominate gas efficiency RD&D. In addition, technology providers continue to invest large amounts of money into this line of research due to fierce competition, as gas turbines represent a high value core product.

Regarding *firm characteristics*, the players active in gas efficiency RD&D are again predominantly large incumbents with gas technologies in their core portfolio. The major share of investment continues to be made by technology providers.

6.5.1.4 RD&D on wind turbines

Our analysis shows that the EU ETS has a very limited and only indirect impact on the ongoing rapid incremental innovation activities for wind power[1], resulting from learning effects due to the increased adoption of wind turbines. The EU ETS contributes to this with the outlook that wind energy is on the verge of becoming competitive through rising electricity prices and decreased attractiveness of investments in fossil-based power generation.

However, currently this does not seem to affect wind RD&D, that is, *context factors* are clearly the most relevant drivers for RD&D on wind turbines. Here, public support mechanisms for renewable resources such as the German feed-in law with its degressive tariff structure and comparable policies in other countries continue to be the underlying prime motivation for wind RD&D because they result in a large demand for wind turbines and stable market growth. These RD&D activities are further supported by high public acceptance rates and long-term climate policy prospects.

Finally, there is no general pattern of *firm characteristics* which further explains the negligible innovation impact of the EU ETS for wind RD&D[2].

6.5.2 Impact on adoption

We investigate adoption of new coal or gas power plants, retrofit of existing cola plants and shift in the generation portfolio towards more renewable resources.

6.5.2.1 Adoption of new coal power plants

Regarding the adoption of new coal plants, the role of the EU ETS has changed

---

[1] Currently, wind RD&D activities are primarily aiming at output maximization, cost minimization, reliability improvement, grid management and offshore commercialization.

[2] By and large, this low indirect impact of the EU ETS on wind RD&D is exemplary for RD&D activities for other renewable resources. A similar argument also holds for nuclear power generation technologies.

significantly due to the switch from very favourable gratis allocation rules to full auctioning of EU allowances beginning in 2013. Initially, the generous coal benchmarks and standard load factors have functioned as quasi-subsidy leading to a temporary increase in planned coal plants(Ellermann, 2008). This attractiveness of new coal even improved further due to the "guaranteed" free-of-charge allocation for 14 years, leading to a rush of getting plants operational by 2012①. However, with the announcement of full auctioning in 2008 these subsidy effects vanished, making coal less profitable and intensifying site-specific engineering efforts.

The main reasons for the ongoing cancellations of some planned coal plants seem to be *context factors*. The prime cancellation reason appears to be market factors, particularly the significant increase of equipment prices, rendering some projects unprofitable. Another important withdrawal reason is the lack of public acceptance for coal plants in Germany. In addition, these anti-coal protests and resulting image problems together with the EU ETS support the planning of new coal plants as capture-ready, a trend that is also driven by restrictive governmental approval conditions. However, the perceived security of supply and the favourable coal-to-gas price ratio remain strong drivers for preferring new coal over new gas plants.

Regarding *firm characteristics*, we find that companies with large shares of coal in their portfolio tend to stick to their core competency. In contrast, power generators with gas-dominated or gas-only portfolios—being driven by regulatory and market uncertainties—favour investments in coal so as to diversify their portfolio.

6.5.2.2 Adoption of new gas power plants

We find that the incentives the EU ETS generates seem hitherto often insufficient for ultimately deciding in favor of new gas plants.

The main reason for this smaller than expected impact of the EU ETS on new gas plants lies in the domain of *context factors*. Compared to the relatively moderate CO_2 prices, high gas prices combined with security of supply concerns are often perceived as more important. In more recent time the expectation of low full time hours for gas-fired plants in electricity systems largely penetrated by renewable resources hampers investments making the discussion around capacity incentives more virulent.

Regarding *firm characteristics*, we only find that power generators with decentralized generation and low-carbon visions are less reluctant to invest in new gas.

---

① The EU Commission prohibited the application of the so-called 14-year rule in its decision on Germany's second allocation plan on November 29, 2006(EU, 2006).

6.5.2.3 Adoption of coal plant retrofits

We find that the EU ETS contributes to an increase in retrofit activities, particularly for older coal plants which can be traced back to CO_2 prices and specific allocation rules.

However, *context factors* such as fuel costs and electricity prices remain very relevant for retrofits. Further motivations for lifetime extensions are the current lack of public acceptance for constructing new coal plants, regulatory uncertainties of the EU ETS, and the political and technological uncertainties associated with CCS.

We did not notice striking differences due to *firm characteristics* aside from the straightforward relevance of power plant portfolios.

6.5.2.4 Portfolio shift towards renewable resources

While its overall impact on individual projects has so far been limited as other factors tend to be more important, the EU ETS is contributing to a strategic adjustment of power generators' target portfolios towards diversification and more specifically towards renewable resources.

However, this portfolio shift towards renewable resources would not have occurred if there were no public support for renewable resources making investments in renewable resources profitable and low risk. Closely connected to this key *context factor* are the tremendous market growth prospects for renewable resources, particularly for wind. The lack of public acceptance for coal and nuclear further supports this shift.

Regarding *firm characteristics*, almost all power generators reported an increase in portfolio thinking and renewable resources investment. The choice of renewable power generation technologies is mainly determined by geographic constraints, with smaller power generators being more bound to "*regional availabilities*". Leadership and vision were mentioned as very important for going forward with these investments.

6.5.3 Impact on organizational change

As the impact of the EU ETS on organizational change mainly differs between value chain positions, in presenting our findings we distinguish between power generators and technology providers, by investigating procedural changes, changes in vision and structural changes.

6.5.3.1 Procedural change

We find that the EU ETS has a strong impact on the business procedures of *power generators* but also on those of some *technology providers*, and as such has been changing companies' CO_2 culture. Companies have quickly integrated the new cost factor CO_2 in their routines, such as into investment appraisals or even employee suggestion systems. We also find increased top management attention to CO_2 issues, particularly for *power generators*. Finally, while the procedural change started with operational issues, it has been continuously moving towards strategic issues. *Power generators* have decentrally integrated the EU ETS in relevant business procedures. In contrast, for *technology providers* the business procedures most impacted by the EU ETS are those associated with sales, particularly for large diversified technology providers.

6.5.3.2 Vision change

We observe a change in companies' visions driven by long-term climate policy targets, including for renewable resources. However, the EU ETS and the support schemes for renewable resources as the operationlization of these targets are also contributing to these corporate vision changes. As a consequence, many *power generators* set long-term targets for renewable resources, CO_2 emission reductions, and energy efficiency improvements. These are typically oriented towards the EU's 2020 goals(EU, 2008b)[1], but are also driven by the feed-in law and the public climate discussion in general. That is, for such vision changes the EU ETS is just one aspect embedded in the larger landscape changes associated with climate change.

Regarding *technology providers*, we find that the extent of climate policy triggered vision changes depends—even more so than for *power generators*—on the carbon-intensity and diversification of their technology portfolio. For renewable resources, large diversified *technology providers* foresee these technologies as becoming equally important as their current fossil core business. This is best exemplified by wind power, for which the large players attempt to join the specialized technology providers in exploiting the booming market, while for wind specialists climate policy only further enhances their market visions. In contrast, for biogas specialists climate policy in the form of the CDM has influenced entry into new geographical markets. Finally, *technology providers* with CCS related know-how envisage a potential new market. Yet, for coal specialists we find that climate policy in its current form does not break the existing mental frame. Instead, these actors are driven by the growing coal business around the world.

6.5.3.3 Structural change

The impact of the EU ETS on structural change falls into two categories: the set-up of

---

[1] A 20% reduction of CO_2 emissions, an increase in the share of renewable energies to 20%, and a 20% improvement of energy efficiency.

CDM/JI sourcing units, and the indirect contribution to the establishment of new business units for renewable resources resulting from climate policy triggered vision changes. *For power generators*, the first structural change concerns all large *power generators*, and also a single medium-sized one, who established new business units for the sourcing of credits from the CDM/JI to reduce EU ETS compliance costs. Second, *power generators* which changed their vision regarding renewable resources have been adjusting their organizational structure accordingly by establishing new business units for renewable resources in which new competencies are being developed. These units are characterized by their own subculture and equipped with relatively large investment budgets. Large diversified *technology providers* whose vision changed towards renewable resources have also adjusted their organizational structures to reflect the ever increasing market potential of renewable resources. This can go so far as positioning renewable resources on the same organizational level as conventional *power generation* technologies.

6.6 Conclusions

We conclude that, in principle, the regulatory demand-pull of the EU ETS works, meaning that the trading scheme contributes to a change in corporate climate innovation activities across major parts of the value chain. We thus confirm that due to its establishment of a carbon price the EU ETS can serve as basic element in a climate policy portfolio(Fischer and Newell, 2008). However, while the introduction of full auctioning will generate undistorted carbon signals and the EU ETS' phase 3 "cap" will significantly contribute to the EU's efforts in reaching its 2020 targets, the EU ETS by itself is highly unlikely to lead to RD&D and adoption decisions in line with reaching the EU's proposed 2050 targets. Two examples supporting this are the limited impact of the EU ETS on renewable resources and demand-side energy savings. Here, complementary policies are needed to create attractive markets for renewable resources, particularly for technologies not yet competitive with conventional power generation technologies and for assisting companies in inventing viable business models promoting reductions in power consumption. More generally speaking, there is a need for complementing the pure carbon price incentives with long-term scenario-building efforts in order to start changing established mindsets of incumbents and create new corporate visions of the future.

Furthermore, we argue that through the EU ETS triggered changes in corporate routines companies in the power sector are better prepared for a tightening of climate policy in line with the 2°C target(UNFCCC, 2009). Nevertheless, while large incumbents are finally embracing the growing renewable resources market, thereby being faced with an internal clash of cultures, the majority of their investment is still earmarked to conventional technologies. It is therefore questionable whether the big players are moving quickly and proactively enough to become agents of change for the needed decarbonization of the power sector. Thus, keeping markets open and attracting new dynamic and innovative entrants seem to be essential.

Finally, if the EU ETS' stringency were further tightened to reflect the deep emission cuts indicated by climate science(IPCC, 2007b) we expect its innovation impact would increase. In such circumstances, the EU ETS as the cornerstone of EU climate policy, complemented by other policies, may ultimately live up to its potential of guiding the decarbonization of the European power sector. As stressed before, a precondition for this may be the passing of an ambitious and credible long-term global climate treaty because cap-and-trade can be understood as the operationlization of these overarching mitigation targets. Such a treaty would increase the overall predictability for innovators. Furthermore, as technology providers innovate for the global market such an international agreement should cover all major power markets as these other regions would then be likely to follow suit in establishing markets for CO_2 reductions and thus raise the gains from RD&D activities.

Our results on the innovation impact of the EU ETS shed some light on what may be expected from emission trading schemes being negotiated in the rest of the world. Most prominently, the trading scheme being developed in the US based on the Waxman-Markey Bill(ACES Act, 2009), while including some commendable features such as the foreseen long-term reduction path and high level of auctioning, is likely to have a relatively moderate impact on corporate climate innovation activities in the power sector. This is mainly because the foreseen inflow of CO_2 price reducing offset credits is too lenient for the scheme to ultimately have a decisive impact on adoption as well as RD&D decisions leading to the called for decarbonizing of the US power sector. Similarly, based on our analysis of the EU ETS, it is also unlikely that the proposed Australian carbon pollution reduction scheme(CPRS Bill, 2009) will be sufficient in promoting technological change up to levels required for a low carbon transformation of the Australian power sector due to the combination of a potentially lenient target, unlimited offsetting, and a rather low price cap.

Our study is not without limitations, however, and thus warrants future research. As we focused our analysis on the power sector, other studies will have to identify whether and how the innovation impact of the EU ETS differs across sectors. Additionally, all of our case companies were based in Germany—though often with international operations—so it might be useful to check whether companies with other home markets have reacted similarly to the EU ETS. Moreover, of the actors relevant for innovation in the power sector we only included power generators, technology providers, and project developers. While this value chain approach goes well beyond the standard of addressing the regulated entities only, the analysis could be extended to other actors, particularly to final power consumers, start-ups, and venture capitalists. Finally, while our qualitative approach enabled us to study the complex causal links and feedback loops of innovation processes in the power sector and how the EU ETS is impacting them, innovation surveys allowing for statistical generalizations should complement this analysis.

References

ACES Act. 2009. *American Clean Energy and Security Act of* 2009(H. R. 2454). Passed by the House of Representatives(Waxman-Markey).

Ahman, M., Burtraw, D., Kruger, J. et al. 2007. A Ten-Year Rule to guide the allocation of EU emission allowances. *Energy Policy*, 35(3), 1718-1730.

Armbruster, H., Bikfalvi, A., Kinkel, S., et al. 2008. Organizational innovation: the challenge of measuring non-technical innovation in large-scale surveys. *Technovation*, 28(10), 644-657.

Barney, J. B. 1991. Firm resources and sustained competitive advantage. *Journal of Management*, 17(1), 99-120.

Baumol, W. J., Oates, W. E. 1988. *The Theory of Environmental Policy*. Cambridge: Cambridge UP.

Bernauer, T., Daniel, S. E., Seijas, J., et al. 2006. *Explaining Green Innovation—Ten Years after Porter's Win-Win Proposition: How to Study the Effects of Regulation on Corporate Environmental Innovation?* Zürich: ETH Zürich.

Betz, R., Rogge, K., Schleich, J. 2006. EU emissions trading: an early analysis of national allocation plans for 2008 – 2012. Climate Policy, 6(4), 361-394.

Cames, M. 2008. Emissions trading and innovation in the German electricity industry. *Berlin's Energy Days*. Berlin: Öko-Institut e. V.

Christensen, C. M., Rosenbloom, R. S. 1995. Explaining the attackers advantage technological paradigms, organizational dynamics, and the value network. *Research Policy*, 24(2), 233-257.

CPRS Bill. 2009. Carbon Pollution Reduction Scheme—a Bill for an Act to reduce pollution caused by emissions of carbon dioxide and other greenhouse gases, and for other purposes. The Parliament of the Commonwealth of Australia, House of Representatives, Canberra.

Dales, J. H. 1968. *Pollution, Property and Prices: an Essay in Policy-making and Economics*. Toronto: University of Toronto Press.

del Río González, P. 2005. Analysing the factors influencing clean technology adoption: a study of the

Spanish pulp and paper industry. *Business Strategy and the Environment*, 14(1), 20-37.

del Río González, P. 2009. The empirical analysis of the determinants for environmental technological change: a research agenda. *Ecological Economics*, 68(13), 861-878.

Edquist, C. 1997. Systems of innovation approaches their emergence and characteristics. In: Edquist, C. (Ed.), *Systems of Innovation: Technologies, Institutions and Characteristics*. London: Washington, 1-35.

Egenhofer, C., Fujiwara, N., Ahman, M., et al. 2006. *The EU Emissions Trading Scheme: Taking Stock and Looking Ahead*. In: Climate Change, European Climate Platform Reports, Centre for European Policy Studies CEPS.

Eisenhardt, K. M. 1989. Building theories from case study research. *Academy of Management Review*, 14(4), 532-550.

Ellerman, D., Joskow, P. 2008. The European Union's Emissions Trading System in perspective. Report prepared for the Pew Center on Global Climate Change. Massachusetts Institute of Technology MIT, 2008.

Ellermann, A. D. 2008. New entrant and closure provisions: how do they distort? *The Energy Journal*, 29(Special Issue), 63-76.

EU. 2003. Directive 2003/87/EC of the European Parliament and the Council of 13 October 2003 establishing a scheme for greenhouse gas emission allowance trading within the Community and amending Council Directive 96/61/EC, *Official Journal of the European Communities*, L275, 32-46.

EU. 2004. Directive 2004/101/EC of the European Parliament and the Council of 27 October 2004 amending Directive 2003/87/EC establishing a scheme for greenhouse gas emission allowance trading within the Community, in respect of the Kyoto Protocol's project mechanisms, 18-23.

EU. 2005. EU action against climate change: EU emission trading—an open scheme promoting global innovation. *European Community*, Brussels.

EU. 2006. Communication from the Commission to the Council and to the European Parliament on the assessment of national allocation plans for the allocation of greenhouse gas emission allowances in the second period of the EU Emissions Trading Scheme accompanying Commission Decisions of 29 November 2006 on the national allocation plans of Germany, Greece, Ireland, Latvia, Lithuania, Luxembourg, Malta, Slovakia, Sweden and the *United* Kingdom in accordance with Directive 2003/87/EC, Brussels.

EU. 2008a. Directive of the European Parliament and of the council amending Directive 2003/87/EC so as to improve and extend the greenhouse gas emission allowance trading system of the Community, 1-73.

EU. 2008b. Energy and climate change—elements of the final compromise. European Union, Brussels.

EU. 2008c. Proposal for a Directive of the European Parliament and of the Council amending Directive 2003/87/EC so as to improve and extend the greenhouse gas emission allowance trading system of the Community. Commission of the European Communities, Brussels.

Fagerberg, J., Verspagen, B. 2009. Innovation studies—the emerging structure of a new scientific field. *Research Policy*, 38(2), 218-233.

Fischer, C., Newell, R. G. 2008. Environmental and technology policies for climate mitigation. *Journal of Environmental Economics and Management*, 55(2), 142-162.

Fischer, C. 2005. Technical innovation and design choices for emissions trading and other climate policies. In: Hansjürgens, B. (Ed.), *Emissions Trading for Climate Policy—U. S. and European Perspectives*. Cambridge: Cambridge University Press.

Frondel, M., Horbach, J., Rennings, K. 2007. End-of-pipe or cleaner production? An empirical comparison of environmental innovation decisions across OECD countries. *Business Strategy and the Environment*, 16(8), 571-584.

Frondel, M., Horbach, J., Rennings, K. 2008. What triggers environmental management and innovation? Empirical evidence for Germany. *Ecological Economics*, 66(1), 153-160.

Gagelmann, F., Frondel, M. 2005. The impact of emission trading on innovation science fiction or reality? *European Environment*, 15(4), 203-211.

Hansjürgens, B. 2006. *Emissions Trading for Climate Policy—U. S. and European Perspectives*. Cambridge: Cambridge University Press.

Hart, S. L. 1995. A natural-resource-based view of the firm. *Academy of Management Review*, 20(4), 986-1014.

Hekkert, M. P., Suurs, R. A. A., Negro, S. O., et al. 2007. Functions of innovation systems: a new approach for analysing technological change. *Technological Forecasting and Social Change*, 74(4), 413-432.

Hoffmann, V. H., Trautmann, T., Hamprecht, J. 2009. Regulatory uncertainty: a reason to postpone investments? Not necessarily. *Journal of Management Studies*, 46(7), 1227-1253.

Hoffmann, V. H., Trautmann, T., Schneider, M. 2008. A taxonomy for regulatory uncertainty—application to the European Emission Trading Scheme. *Environmental Science & Policy*, 11(8), 712-722.

Hoffmann, V. H. 2007. EU ETS and investment decisions: the case of the German electricity industry. *European Management Journal*, 25(6), 464-474.

Horbach, J. 2008. Determinants of environmental innovation—new evidence from German panel data sources. *Research Policy*, 37(1), 163-173.

IEA. 2007. *Energy Policies of IEA Countries: Germany 2007 Review*. Paris: OECD/IEA.

IEA. 2009a. Addressing climate change—policies and measures. http://www.iea.org/Textbase/pm/index_clim.html[2011-09-20].

IEA. 2009b. World Energy Outlook 2008. Paris: IEA.

IPCC. 2007a. *Climate Change 2007—Synthesis Report*. Valencia: IPCC.

IPCC. 2007b. *Climate Change 2007 Mitigation*. Cambridge and New York: Cambridge University Press.

Jaffe, A. B., Newell, R. G., Stavins, R. N. 2002. Environmental policy and technological change. *Environmental & Resource Economics*, 22(1/2), 41-69.

Jänicke, M., Blazejczak, J., Edler, D., et al. 2000. Environmental policy and innovation: an international comparison of policy frameworks and innovation effects. In: Hemmelskamp, J., Rennings, K., Leone, F. (Eds.), *Innovation-oriented Environmental Regulation: Theoretical Approach and Empirical Analysis*. Heidelberg: Springer Verlag.

Kaplan, S., Tripsas, M. 2008. Thinking about technology: applying a cognitive lens to technical change. *Research Policy*, 37(5), 790-805.

Kemp, R., Pontoglio, S. 2008. The innovation effects of environmental policy instruments—a typical case of the blind men and the elephant. Paper for DIME WP 2.5 Workshop on Empirical Analyses of Environmental Innovations, Fraunhofer ISI, Karlsruhe.

Mazzanti, M., Zoboli, R. 2006. Economic instruments and induced innovation: the European policies on end-of-life vehicles. *Ecological Economics*, 58(2), 318-337.

Neuhoff, K., Martinez, K. K., Sato, M. 2006. Allocation, incentives and distortions: the impact of EU ETS emissions allowance allocations to the electricity sector. *Climate Policy*, 6(1), 73-91.

Newell, R. G., Jaffe, A. B., Stavins, R. N. 1999. The induced innovation hypothesis and energy-saving technological change. *Quarterly Journal of Economics*, 114(3), 941-975.

OECD. 2005. *Oslo Manual: Guidelines for Collecting and Interpreting Innovation Data*. 3rd ed. Paris: OECD.

OECD. 2007. *Environmental Policy and Corporate Behaviour*. Cheltenham and Northampton: Edward Elgar Publishing.

Oltra, V., Saint Jean, M. 2005. Environmental innovation and clean technology: an evolutionary framework. *International Journal of Sustainable Development*, 8(3), 153-172.

Pavitt, K. 1984. Sectoral patterns of technical change: towards a taxonomy and a theory. *Research Policy*, 13(6), 343-373.

Platts. 2008. *Platts Database*. London: The McGraw-Hill Company.

Popp, D., Newell, R. G., Jaffe, A. B. 2009. *Energy, the Environment, and Technological Change*. Cambridge: NBER.

Rehfeld, K. M., Rennings, K., Ziegler, A. 2007. Integrated product policy and environmental product innovations: an empirical analysis. *Ecological Economics*, 61(1), 91-100.

Requate, T. 2005. Dynamic incentives by environmental policy instruments—a survey. *Ecological Economics*, 54(2/3), 175-195.

Schleich, J., Betz, R. 2005. Incentives for energy efficiency and innovation in the European Emission Trading System. ECEE 2005 Summer Study—What works & who delivers?—Panel 7 New economic instruments, 1495, 1495-1506.

Schleich, J., Rogge, K., Betz, R. 2009. Incentives for energy efficiency in the EU Emissions Trading Scheme. *Energy Efficiency*, 2(1), 37-67.

Tietenberg, T. H. 1985. *Emissions Trading: an Exercise in Reforming Pollution Policy*. Washington D.C.: Resources for the Future.

UNFCCC. 1992. *United Nations Framework Convention on Climate Change*. New York: UN.

UNFCCC. 1997. *Kyoto Protocol to the United Nations Framework Convention on Climate Change*. New York: UN.

United Nations Framework Convention on Climate Change. 2009. Copenhagen Accord. http://unfccc. int/resource/docs/2009/cop15/eng/107. pdf[2011-09-25].

United Nations Framework Convention on Climate Change. 2011. http://unfccc. int/meetings/durban_nov-2011/meeting/6245/php/view/reports. php[2013-09-21].

Vollebergh, H. 2007. *Impacts of Environmental Policy Instruments on Technological Change*. Paris: OECD.

Yin, R. K. 2002. *Case Study Research: Design and Methods*. London: Sage Publications.

Author

Dr. Karoline Rogge graduated in Economics with specialization in Environmental and Ecological Economics, Public Choice, and Public Finance. PhD from ETH Zurich in 2010, in which she empirically analyzed the innovation impact of the EU emission trading system in the power sector. Since September 2004 researcher at the Fraunhofer Institute for Systems and Innovation Research ISI in the Competence Center Energy Policy and Energy Markets. Prior to joining the Fraunhofer ISI, consultant at the World Bank Institute in Washington, DC, USA. Work focus: Design, implementation and evaluation of environmental policy instruments, with a focus on the empiricial analysis of the innovation impact of climate policy instruments (particularly the EU ETS).

Dr. Wolfgang Eichhammer is Head of the Competence Center Energy Policy and Energy Markets of the Fraunhofer Institute for Systems and Innovation Research (Fraunhofer ISI)...

Physicist with professional experience in various countries of the European Union in the fields of design and evaluation of energy efficiency and renewable resources policies as well as climate policies. Extended knowledge in the systematic, technical and economic assessment of conventional and future energy systems, especially in energy intensive industries. Project co-ordinator of various international studies on the modelling and simulation of future potentials of the impacts of climate protection measures, energy conservation and renewable energy policies.

Part 2

Innovation Policies for Green Growth

Innovation Policy for Green Growth in China

Mu Rongping

7.1 Introduction

China had experienced a fast economic growth from 1978 to 2010, with an average GDP annual growth rate of 9.8%, and is facing increasingly great challenges and pressures related to limited natural resources and serious environmental problems and high demands for improving life quality of more than one billion people. The concept of development in China has also experienced the changes from emphasizing economic development, to economic and natural development, to economic, natural and societal development, and to emphasizing the integration of economic, natural, societal and human development. Therefore, Chinese government has raised a series of development goals during the past ten years, including: New Way for Industrialization in 2002, Scientific Outlook on Development in 2003, Recycling Economy and Resource-saving & Environment-friendly Society in 2004, Harmonious Society in 2005, Energy Conservation and Emission Reduction in 2006, Innovation-driven Country by 2020 in 2006, Ecological Civilization in 2007, Green and Low Carbon Economy in 2009, Transformation of Economic Development Pattern in 2010.

A series of global issues such as the global climate change and world financial crisis have drawn great attention from both academia and policymakers, which have profound impacts on the world development. Especially, the transformation of economic development pattern has become increasingly more important than ever in the policymaking agenda of catching-up countries and emerging economies.

UNEP defines a green economy as one that results in improved human well-being and social equity, while significantly reducing environmental risks and ecological scarcities (UNEP, 2011). UNEP put forward the initiative of development for "green economy" in October 2008 with a view to achieving green recovery from the global financial crisis. There is a growing recognition that it is necessary to take collective efforts of all nations to realize global sustainable development. In June 2009, ministers from 34 countries signed a *Green Growth Declaration*, which emphasized that "Strengthen their efforts to pursue green growth strategies as part of their responses to the crisis and beyond, acknowledging that green and growth can go hand-in-hand" (OECD, 2009). *Green growth means fostering economic growth and development, while ensuring that natural assets continue to provide the resources and environmental services on which our well-being relies* (OECD, 2011a).

The current "green growth" debate is taking place in an oversimplified setting, largely disregarding the innovation factor. Technologies to mitigate climate change are being treated as given, or as emerging spontaneously, ignoring the fact that the portfolio of technologies available tomorrow depends on what is done today (Aghion et al., 2009). Innovation for green growth needs the supports from both public intervention and private initiative. Business is the driver of green innovation. However, several well-known market failures provide the rationale for government action to shape the environment for green innovation (OECD, 2011b): (1) negative externalities associated with environmental challenges; (2) market failures specific to the market for innovation; (3) the prevalence of dominant designs, technologies and systems in energy and transport markets.

In order to monitor the progress towards green innovation, OECD proposed indicators about green growth embedded in a conceptual framework, including the sphere of production, evolution of natural assets, environmental quality of life, opportunities arising from environmental considerations(OECD, 2011c). Under this conceptual framework, four inter-related groups of indicators are explored: (1) the environmental and resource productivity of the economy; (2) the natural asset base; (3) the environmental dimension of quality of life; (4) economic opportunities and policy responses, and the last is social and economic context and characteristics of growth. Each of the indicator groups includes detail topics, which can describe the features of green growth. So far, OECD has already have data statistics of green growth, including 22 detailed indicators①. Therefore, innovation as the driver of green growth should be taken into policy-making agenda which implies that government's intervention should be indispensable for green growth.

This paper introduces the international experiences concerning innovation policy for green growth and the innovation policies for green growth in China, and provides some policy recommendations, based on international experiences, for Chinese government.

7.2 Innovation policies for green growth: international experiences

Lots of countries' international organizations have paid great attention to green growth. OECD has released policy instruments which can foster innovation for green growth with a combination of demand-side and supply-side. The possible policies include 9 policy challenges, and each of them has the corresponding policy options.② The policy challenges highlight the entire innovation chain including innovation demand, innovation capability, finance, innovation adoption, technology transfer, etc. Korea, Japan and UK have accumulated a lot of experiences in making innovation policies and strategies for green growth in order to accelerate the pace of green transformation.

7.2.1 Green growth policies in Korea

Numerous challenges have threatened the sustainable development of South Korea, such as the economic recession in 2008, the energy import dependence, increasing carbon emissions, the significant pressure on environment because of rapid industrialization and urbanization, etc. These challenges have prompted South Korea to seek a new paradigm to shift the economic development from "quantitative growth" to "qualitative growth". In August 2008, President Lee Myung-Bak announced a "low-carbon, green growth" strategy as a new vision to guide the nation's long-term development. Thereafter, Korea government successively released a series

---

① http://stats.oecd.org/Index.aspx? DataSetCode=GREEN_GROWTH.

② OECD. 2011. Fostering Innovation for Green Growth. OECD Green Growth Studies. OECD Publishing. http://dx.doi.org/10.1787/9789264119925-en.

of policies and action plans to foster a favorable environment for green growth.

Korea government launched "Green New Deal" in January 2009, which includes nine key projects: revive four rivers, build green transport, build integrated national land information system, rain discharge facilities and small-/medium-sized dams, supply green car and clean energy, recycle wastes, green forestation, green home and green school and eco-river. The stimulus package amounted to a total of 38.1 billion dollars. During 2009-2012, about 80% of the total stimulus will be allocated to environmental themes such as renewable energies, energy-efficient buildings, low carbon vehicles, railways and water and waste management (UNEP, 2010). Korea government issued a *Five-Year Plan for Green Growth in 2009-2013* in July 2009, with a view to accelerating the pace of the strategic transformation and implementing a low carbon green growth strategy. The five-year plan introduced three strategies: (1) measuring climate change and securing energy independence; (2) creating national growth engines; (3) improving the quality of life and strengthening the status of the country, focusing on ten directions to realize the above three strategies. The government will invest a total of 83.6 billion dollars during 2009-2013 to induce production worth of 141.7 billion to 160.3 billion dollars and create green jobs of 1.56 million to 1.81 million people in the next five years. Korea government intends to take intensive efforts to develop 27 core technologies covering five categories defined by National Science & Technology Council. The share of green technology R&D in gross R&D expenditure will be increased from 16% in 2009 to 20% in 2012 (Jones, 2011).

The five-year plan has explicit goals of the development stages of green growth with progressive milestones both in the mid-term and long-term. The target is to build infrastructure for green growth in 2010, to become dominant in green technology and green industry via expanding exports of green technology and industry and creating jobs in 2013, to become top seven green countries in the world in 2020, and to become top five green countries in the world in 2050.

A significant feature of the Korean green growth strategy is to formulate relevant laws about green growth. In January 2010, the government passed *The Basic Act on Low Carbon Green Growth* to back up green growth with legal bases. The act consisted of 7 chapters and 64 articles, with a comprehensive scope including the legislation on climate change, energy efficiency, natural resources, greening industry, green livelihood and the responsibility of central and local governments [1]. The Presidential

---

[1] 〈Act No. 9931, Jan. 13, 2010〉, Framework Act on Low Carbon Green Growth. Ministry of Government Legislation.

Committee on Green Growth was established in February 2009 according to the act, which consists of 47 members including relevant government ministers and representatives from stakeholders and has the mandate to discuss all subjects relevant to pursuing green growth as well as coordinating government works on this area [1]. In addition, Korea established Global Green Growth Institute (GGGI) to publicize Korea's "low carbon, green growth" strategy in order to provide experiences for developing countries to formulate their own green strategy.

7.2.2 Green growth policies in Japan

The Council for Science and Technology Policy (CSTP) of Japan put forward the *Low Carbon Technology Plan*[2] in May 2008, including two strategies: (1) technological strategy of Japan for realizing a low carbon society, which identified the technologies required for short-medium term (until around 2030) and medium-long term (after 2030) as well as the deployment measures for society and revolution of social system; (2) promotion strategy for developing innovative environment and energy technologies, focusing on R&D investment in innovative technology development and R&D structure. The plan also takes concerns on international GHG emission reduction by using a variety of approaches, increasing use of the environment and energy technologies, and through the diffusion and transfer of technologies to developing countries, as well as promoting international standardization (energy saving standards, emission assessment criteria, etc.) and cooperation in R&D.

Japan Cabinet released the *Act Plan for Achieving a Low-carbon Society*[3] in July 2008, which aims to realize the national long-term goal of reducing 60%-80% GHG emission in 2050. The plan set three targets including: (1) building agreement on a fair, equitable, and effective post-2012 framework; (2) setting quantified national targets; (3) support for other countries' efforts. It also put out specific innovation policy measures focusing on the dissemination of innovative technologies and existing advanced technologies.

There are three measures for the development of innovative technologies, namely: (1) steady enforcement of the road map to innovative technology development; (2) upgrading coal use with the development of clean combustion technology and carbon capture and storage (CCS) technology; (3) bringing about an

---

[1] Progress Report 2008-2009, Presidential Committee on Green Growth, Republic of Korea.
[2] http://www8.cao.go.jp/cstp/english/doc/low_carbon_tec_plan/low_carbon_tech_plan.pdf.
[3] http://www.kantei.go.jp/foreign/policy/ondanka/final080729.pdf.

international partnership for environment and energy. There are nine measures for dissemination of existing advanced technologies, namely: (1) increasing in the installation of solar power generation facilities with the target of increasing the amount of installations 10-fold by 2020 and 40-fold by 2030; (2) raising the proportion of zero-emission energy sources over 50% by 2020; (3) introducing next-generation vehicles with the target of one in every two next-generation vehicle sales by 2020; (4) changing from incandescent light bulbs to low-energy lamps around 2012; (5) accelerating the introduction of energy-efficient televisions, water heaters, air-conditioning, and refrigerators; (6) promoting energy-efficient housing and office buildings; (7) promoting nuclear power; (8) providing outstanding nuclear power safety technology and expertise to the world; (9) implementing Japan's own initiatives.

Japan launched a new growth strategy in June 2010, focusing on demand-led growth and innovation in order to prosper its economy and resolve the problems arising from climate change and population aging. The strategy includes 7 growth engines and 21 strategic projects. The seven growth engines include green innovation, life innovation, Asian economic integration, tourism and local revitalization, science, technology and IT, employment and human resources, and financial sector. The target of this strategy is to stimulate a potential growth rate to 2% in real terms in next decades and a nominal GDP growth rate of 3%.

As one of the seven growth engines, the objective of green innovation to 2020 is to generate market value of over 50 trillion yen and 1.4 million jobs in environment-related areas as well as to reduce global GHG emissions by at least 1300Mt CO_2eq by promoting Japanese technology worldwide(Capozza, I., 2011). In order to achieve this objective, the strategy issued comprehensive policy package, including regulatory reforms and the green tax system. In 2008, Japan launched a trial Emission Trading System(ETS) with about 600 participants by 2010. In addition, Japan has expanded tax benefits and subsidies on environment-friendly products instead of raising environment-related taxes(OECD, 2011d). In order to accelerate implementation of the strategy, the New Growth Strategy Realization Promotion Council was established in September 2010, chaired by the prime minister.

7.2.3 Green growth policies in UK

The development of low carbon economy is a primary goal of green economic policies in the UK. In 2008, the government delivered the *Climate Change Act* in order to provide legal bases for GHG emission reduction targets. In accordance with the *Climate Change Act*, the government set three carbon budgetary periods in 2008-2012, 2013-2017, 2018-2022, and committed to achieving at least 34% reduction in GHG emissions in 2020 and 80% in 2050, compared to 1990 levels ①.

In July 2009, the United Kingdom released the *Low-Carbon Transition Plan* which is presented to Parliament pursuant to sections 12 and 14 of the *Climate Change Act* 2008. The *Low-Carbon Transition Plan* includes five transformations, including: (1) power sectors; (2) homes and communities; (3) workplaces and jobs; (4) transport; (5) farming and the sustainable management of land and waste. The plan develops a road map to 2050 for all the areas related above. For the first time, all major UK government departments have been allocated their own budget and must produce their own plan ②.

For the transformation in power sectors, 40% electricity will come from low carbon sources by 2020. The plan will secure power supplies and cut emissions from power and heavy industry together by 22% on 2008 levels by 2020. Besides the EU Emission Trading System, the government provides additional supports for the transition: (1) launching the Office for Renewable Energy Deployment to secure the increase in renewable electricity around 30% by 2020; (2) planning for new nuclear power stations; (3) setting a mechanism to support four demonstrations for carbon capture and storage as well as smart electricity grid.

For the transformation in homes and communities, the emissions from homes need to be almost zero by using energy more efficiently and using more low carbon energy. The plan will cut emissions from homes by 29% on 2008 levels in 2020. To realize this goal, the government is : (1) increasing the obligation on energy suppliers to help households reduce emissions and save energy; (2) introducing a community-based approach to delivering significant energy efficiency treatments to 90,000 homes in low-income areas; (3) piloting a move from upfront payment to "pay as you save" models to help people make house greener and a community-based approach to delivering green homes in low-income areas ; (4) introducing "clean energy cash-back" schemes so that people, businesses and communities will be paid if they use low carbon sources to generate heat or electricity.

For the transformation in workplaces and jobs, all the workplaces need use less energy and make use of clean energy to reduce GHG emissions. The plan will cut

---

① Climate Change Act 2008 (c. 27) CHAPTER 27:Part 1-Carbon Target and Budgeting.
② The UK Low Carbon Transition Plan, National strategy for climate and energy, Presented to Parliament pursuant to sections 12 and 14 of the *Climate Change Act* 2008, July 2009, http://centralcontent.fco.gov.uk/central-content/campaigns/act-on-copenhagen/resources/en/pdf/DECC-Low-Carbon-Transition-Plan.

emissions from workplaces by 13% on 2008 levels in 2020. To realize the green transition, the government will invest up to £120 million in offshore wind and £60 million in marine energy and develop the South West of England as the UK's first Low Carbon Economic Area.

For the transformation in transport, the plan will cut emissions from transport by 14% on 2008 levels by 2020. The first step is to improve the fuel efficiency of new conventional vehicles. The government is: (1) cutting average CO_2 emissions from new cars across the EU to 95g/km by 2020, a 40% reduction from 2007 levels; (2) pressing the EU to require new vans to be more efficient; (3) investing up to £30 million over the next two years to deliver several hundred low carbon buses; (4) demonstrating 340 new electric and low-carbon cars on the UK's roads; (5) providing help worth about £2,000 to £5,000 per vehicle towards reducing the price of ultra-low carbon cars from 2011, and £30 million to support the installation of electric vehicle charging infrastructure in six or so cities.

For the transformation in farming and managing land and waste sustainably, the plan will cut emissions from farming and waste by 6% on 2008 levels in 2020 through: (1) encouraging English farmers to take action themselves to reduce emissions to at least 6% lower than currently predicted by 2020; (2) supporting for anaerobic digestion, a technology that turns waste and manure into renewable energy; (3) reducing the amount of waste sent to landfills, and better capture of landfill emissions.

In order to foster the innovation for low carbon transition, the UK government established Low Carbon Innovation Group (LCIG), consisting of major public sectors such as DECC[1], BIS[2], TSB[3], ETI[4], and UKRC[5] to ensure that support for innovation is coordinated and targeted to best effect. Besides, the government cooperated with private sectors on the transition to a low carbon economy. The UK government set up the Green Economy Council in February 2011 by bringing together ministers from BIS, DECC and DEFRA[6] with business leaders from a cross-section of industries. The Council will discuss green growth policies affecting infrastructure, innovation, investment and regulation.

The EU released the *Renewable Energy Directive* (*2009/28/EC*) in April 2009,

---

[1] Department of Energy & Climate Change
[2] Department for Business, Innovation & Skills
[3] Technology Strategy Board
[4] Energy Technologies Institute
[5] UK Research Council
[6] Department for Environment, Food and Rural Affairs

which set a target for the UK to achieve 15% of its energy consumption from renewable sources by 2020. The UK government presented the *Renewable Energy Strategy* in July 2009, and *National Renewable Energy Action Plan* for the United Kingdom in 2010. The *Renewable Energy Strategy* ensured that the renewable energy sources will be accounted for 15% of the share in the energy supply, and more than 30% of the electricity, 12% of the heat supply and 10% of the transport energy are generated from renewable energy sources in 2020[1]. The action plan is required by Article 4 of the *Renewable Energy Directive* (*2009/28/EC*).

7.3 Innovation policies for green growth in China

The Outline of National 11th Five-Year Plan for Social and Economic Development has raised the mandatory targets of energy efficiency and pollution reduction, while the Outline of National 12th Five-Year Plan for Social and Economic Development has given very high priority to S&T progress and innovation in supporting transformation of the economic development pattern. The innovation policies for green growth in China consist of laws, regulations and policy documents, including the *Environmental Protection Law*[2], the specific laws for pollution control[3] and environment resources[4], and the administrative regulations[5].

7.3.1 Related laws for green growth

China has issued several laws for promoting sustainable development during past

---

[1] The UK Renewable Energy Strategy, Presented to Parliament by the Secretary of State for Energy and Climate Change by command of Her Majesty, July 2009, http://www.decc.gov.uk/assets/decc/what%20we%20do/uk%20energy%20supply/energy%20mix/renewable%20energy/renewable%20energy%20strategy/1_20090717120647_e_@@_theukrenewableenergystrategy2009.pdf.

[2] The law was issued by the Standing Committee of National People's Congress.

[3] Law of the People's Republic of China on the Prevention and Control of Water Pollution, Law of the People's Republic of China on the Prevention and Control of Air pollution, Law of the People's Republic of China on Prevention of Environmental Pollution Caused by Solid Waste, Law of the People's Republic of China on the Prevention and Control of Environmental Noise Pollution, Marine Environment Protection Law of the People's Republic of China, etc. are all issued by the Standing Committee of National People's Congress.

[4] Water Law of the People's Republic of China, Forest Law of the People's Republic of China, Mineral Resources Law of the People's Republic of China, Land Administration Law of the People's Republic of China, Grassland Law of the People's Republic of China, Fisheries Law of the People's Republic of China, Law of the People's Republic of China on Water and Soil Conservation, etc. are all issued by the Standing Committee of National People's Congress.

[5] Administrative Regulation of Environment Standards, Environmental Administrative Punishment Procedures, Administrative Measures for the Qualified Environmental Protection Products, etc.

ten years. The *Environmental Protection Law* requires that the environmental protection plan must be incorporated into national economic and social development plan, and the government should adopt environmental-friendly policies for economic and social development. The *Circular Economy Promotion Law* came into effect in January 2009, which provides policy provisions for energy conservation and industrial structure adjustment, including eight support policy documents[①] made for implementing the law, namely: (1) the *National Circular Economy Development Plan* made by the State Council and the regional plans in local governments; (2) special funds for promoting circular economy; (3) mandatory recycling catalogs of products and packaging; (4) measures for the supervision and administration of key-water-using unit; (5) the list of prohibiting the use of toxic and hazardous substances in electrical and electronic products; (6) the catalog and restrictive tax and export measures for restricting the production and sales of disposable consumer goods; (7) administrative regulations on waste electrical and electronic equipment (WEEE) dismantling and recycling; (8) tax preference for industrial activities promoting circular economy and some taxation measures for encouraging energy-saving products imports and limiting high energy-consuming products export.

The *Energy Conservation Law* was revised in 2007 and came into effect in April 2008, which gives high priority to conservation in the energy development strategy, and focusing on nine issues [②]: (1) the State Council and the local governments at or above the county level shall incorporate energy conservation in the plans for economic and social development and annual plans; (2) the performance of energy conservation shall be included in the assessment of the performance of local governments and their leaders; (3) governments should apply industrial policies to facilitate energy conservation and environment protection; (4) the government's agency for standardization should formulate and modify national and industrial standards for energy conservation and set up a system for energy conservation standards, to encourage enterprises to establish more rigorous standards for energy conservation; (5) to apply an elimination system for the outdated products, equipment and production techniques which consume excessive quantities of energy. The government's agency for energy conservation shall compile and release the eliminating

---

① Including Article 12, Article 15, Article 16, Article 19, Article 28, Article 38, Article 42 and Article 44.

② Including Article 5, Article 6, Article 7, Article 13, Article 16, Article 56, Article 57, Article58, Article60 and Article61.

catalogue of the energy-using products, equipment and production techniques; (6) both the central government and the provincial governments shall allocate special funds for financing energy conservation technologies R&D, demonstration and promotion of energy conservation technology and products, construction of key energy conservation projects, dissemination and training of energy conservation knowledge, provision of information consultation and rewarding for energy conservation; (7) the government's agency for energy conservation in conjunction with the ministry of S&T shall publish the policy outline on energy conservation technologies to provide guidance in the R&D and wide application of energy-saving technologies; (8) the governments at or above the county level shall put priority to energy-saving technologies in S&T investment; (9) the government's agency for energy conservation should compile and release a catalogue of energy-saving technologies and products, which will be supported by preferable tax policies in manufacturing and using process. However, there are only two support documents[1] to guarantee the implementation of the law.

The *Renewable Energy Law* was formulated in 2005 and revised in 2009. The law focused on non-fossil energy including wind power, solar energy, hydraulic power, biomass energy, geothermal energy and ocean energy. The law includes the development and utilization plan of renewable energy, technical support, technology dissemination and application, price management and cost compensation, economic incentives and supervision measures, with great attention to following five issues [2]: (1) The medium and long-term targets for the development and utilization of renewable energy as well as the *National Development and Utilization Plan of Renewable Energy*. (2) A guidance catalog for renewable energy industrial development. Finance discount and tax preference will be made for the projects included in the catalog. (3) National standards on renewable energy power grid-connected, renewable energy technologies and products. (4) S&T research of renewable energy should be included in the national science and technology development plan and high-tech industry development plan. (5) Special funds for renewable energy development.

7.3.2 National 12th five-year plan related to green growth

Chinese government has proposed many plans to provide an innovation-friendly environment for green growth, including: the *Outline of the 12th Five-Year Plan for*

---

[1] Energy-saving Regulations of Civil Building and Energy-saving Regulations of Public Institutions.
[2] Including Article 7, Article 8, Article 10, Article 11, Article 12, Article 24, Article 25, Article 26.

National Economic & Social Development, the *National 12th Five-Year Plan for Strategic Emerging Industries Development*, the *National 12th Five-Year Plan for Innovation-capacity Building*, the *National 12th Five-Year Plan for Science and Technology Development*, and the *National 12th Five-Year Plan of Environment Protection*.

The *Outline of the 12th Five-Year Plan for National Economic & Social Development* (12th FYP) aims to build a resource-saving and environment-friendly society by green development. During the 11th Five-Year period, the government took energy consumption intensity and the total discharge of major pollutants as the mandatory targets for national economic and social development for the first time. The 12th FYP has formulated new mandatory targets to impel green growth, namely: (1) the energy consumption and the CO_2 emissions per GDP will reduce by 16% and 17% perspectively; (2) non-fossil fuels in primary energy consumption is about to reach 11.4%; (3) water consumption per unit of industrial value-added will reduce by 30%; (4) the total discharge of major pollutants will decrease significantly, COD and SO_2 emissions reduced by 8%, ammonia and nitrogen oxide emissions reduced 10%.

The *National 12th Five-Year Plan for Strategic Emerging Industries Development* has given three industries high priority, such as energy conservation, environmental protection and new energy. The *National 12th Five-Year Plan for S&T Development of Environment Protection* is to enhance the environmental innovation capacity, especially the technology areas: water pollution prevention, air pollution prevention, soil pollution prevention, ecological protection, environment and human health, nuclear and radiation safety and some global environmental issues such as climate change, biodiversity, ozone layer protection and persistent organic pollutants.

7.3.3 National action plans for green growth

Chinese government has taken a series of measures to implement the laws and Five-Year Plans with a view to promoting green growth based on the innovation, including: (1) *National Climate Change Program of China*; (2) *China's S&T Initiative on Climate Change* [①]; (3) *Renewable Energy and New Energy International Science and Technology Cooperation Program*; (4) supportive policies and detailed policy

---

[①] Jointly Issued by MOST, NDRC (National Development and Reform Commission), MOFA (Ministry of Foreign Affairs), MOE (Ministry of Education), MOF (Ministry of Finance), MOWR (Ministry of Water Resources), MOA (Ministry of Agriculture), SEPA (MOEP), SFA (State Forestry Administration), CAS (Chinese Academy of Sciences), CMA (China Meteorological Administration), NNSFC (National Natural Science Foundation of China), SOA (State Ocean Administration), CAST (Chinese Academy of Science and Technology) in June, 2007.

documents for innovation.

Chinese government has issued the *China's National Climate Change Program* in June 2007, which has introduced the climate change and corresponding efforts in China, the impacts and challenges of climate change on China, the guidelines, the principles and the objectives of China on climate change. The program emphasizes the principle relying on the S&T progress and innovation, namely to develop new energy, renewable energy and energy saving technology as well as carbon absorption technologies with a view to providing S&T supports for upgrading of sustainable development capacity. Thereafter, Chinese government issued *China's S&T Action Plans on Climate Change* in 2007 with a view to implementing the *China's National Climate Change Program*.

China's S&T Action Plans on Climate Change has raised six policy measures, including: (1) to strengthen the leadership and coordination so as to jointly promote S&T progress on climate change; (2) to increase S&T investment and provide more financial support for scientific research and technological development on climate change; (3) to strengthen human resources development and the recruitment of overseas talents as well as disciplinary building in the field of climate change; (4) to build S&T basic infrastructures/platforms so as to support S&T development on climate change; (5) to strengthen the popularization of scientific knowledge and to improve public awareness of science on climate change; (6) to promote international S&T cooperation and technology transfer so as to develop global resources.

NDRC and MOST jointly issued *Renewal Energy and New Energy International Science and Technology Cooperation Program* in November 2007, which supports research on basic science and applied technologies in the following fields: (1) solar power and integrated solar energy building; (2) biomass fuels and biomass power generation; (3) wind power generation; (4) hydrogen energy and fuel cells; (5) natural gas hydrate development. Public funds for the program have attracted financial support from foreign governments, international organizations, and private capital, and the investment from the business sector especially the international energy giants would stimulate international S&T cooperation in the field of new and renewable energy.

7.4 Major conclusion and recommendations

China has made great progress in establishing and optimizing the innovation laws and policies for green growth during past ten years. Chinese government issued the

Outline of Medium and Long Term Plan for National Science and Technology Development (2006—2020) (MLP) and related supportive policies in 2006, incorporated 60 articles involving in S&T investment, preferential tax treatment, financial support, procurement, foreign technology absorption, IPR protection, talent, education and popularization of sciences, science and technology bases and platforms, overall coordination and others. Besides, Chinese government has released 78 detailed policy documents to implement the supportive policy by 2009, which have profound impact on green development.

Korea's green growth strategy has clearly defined goals with supportive policies and laws as well as implementing organizations. Korea government released comprehensive plans for green growth with a series of legal and policy documents such as the *Basic Law on Low Carbon Green Growth*, the *Green New Deal* and the *Five-Year Plan for Green Growth*. The green growth strategy in Korea has three characteristics: (1) to clearly define the targets of green growth strategy by introducing short, medium and long-term goals for green development; (2) to invest public funds in R&D of key green technologies; (3) to set up special organizations for promoting green growth strategy.

Japan's green growth strategy emphasize both the development of new technologies and the diffusion of existing advanced technologies, and the social system reform for promoting green growth. The green growth strategy in Japan has three characteristics: (1) to reduce the dependence on imported energy by means of the green transformation; (2) to encourage green innovation and investments by means of market mechanism; (3) to assure the government R&D investment in energy saving technologies and emission-deduction technology.

The low carbon strategy in UK has clear objectives with support of comprehensive policy and law system. UK government released the *Climate Change Act* to promote low carbon transition in 2008 and formulated a series of policies related to low carbon so as to effectively implement the act and to meet the EU's emission reduction targets. The low carbon strategy in UK has three characteristics: (1) to clearly define the emission reduction targets; (2) to request all government departments to propose plans for mitigating carbon emission; (3) to make a comprehensive plan for emission reduction covering all areas of social and economic development.

China is facing great challenges in the period of green economic transformation. Therefore, it is necessary to learn from the experiences in promoting green growth in Korea, Japan and UK, and is highly recommended to take three points into policy-making process in China: (1) To formulate the basic law for green development, which consists of the *Energy Conservation Law*, *Renewable Energy Law* and *Circular Economy Promotion Law*, and other laws related to social aspects of green development, and provide the legal basis for the green development strategy. (2) To develop the green development plan to implement the strategy in the social and economic development both at national and provincial level, with national long-term strategic targets, technology road maps and policy measures. (3) To promote the development and deployment of green technologies, and give higher priority to the deployment of existing advanced technologies.

References

Aghion, P., Hemous, D., Veugelers, R. 2009. Bruegel policy brief: no green growth without innovation. http://www.gmfus.org/doc/Bruegel-GMF%20event%20COP15%20invite%20with%20map.pdf.

Capozza, I. 2011. Greening growth in Japan. OECD Environment Working Papers, No. 28, OECD Publishing. http://dx.doi.org/10.1787/5kggc0rpw55l-en.

Jones, R. S., Yoo, B. 2011. Korea's green growth strategy: mitigating climate change and developing new growth engines. OECD Economics Department Working Papers, No. 798, OECD Publishing. http://dx.doi.org/10.1787/5kmbhk4gh1ns-en.

OECD. 2009. Declaration on green Growth: adopted at the meeting of the council at ministerial level on June 2009 [C/MIN(2009)5/ADD1/FINAL]. http://www.oecd.org/env/44077822.pdf.

OECD. 2011a. Towards green growth: a summary for policy makers. *OECD Green Growth Studies*, http://www.oecd.org/greengrowth/48012345.pdf.

OECD. 2011b. Fostering innovation for green growth. *OECD Green Growth Studies*, OECD Publishing. http://dx.doi.org/10.1787/9789264119925-en.

OECD. 2011c. Towards green growth: monitoring progress. OECD Indicators. http://www.oecd.org/greengrowth/48224574.pdf.

OECD. 2011d. OECD economic surveys: Japan 2011, Publishing. http://dx.doi.org/10.17871/eco_surveys-jpn-2011-en.

UNEP. 2010. Overview of the Republic of Korea's National Strategy for Green Growth. Prepared by the United Nations Environment Programme as part of its Green Economy Initiative.

UNEP. 2011. Towards a green economy: pathways to sustainable development and poverty eradication-a synthesis for policymakers. http://www.unep.org/greeneconomy.

Author

Prf. Dr. Mu Rongping, received his B. S. (1983) and M. S. degree(1990) from the University of Science and Technology in China, and his Ph. D. (2001) from Technische Universität Berlin in Germany. Dr. Mu is now director-general and professor of the Institute of Policy and Management(IPM) of Chinese Academy of Sciences(CAS), director-general of the CAS Center for Innovation and Development, editor-in-chief of the Journal of Science Research Management(an academic bimonthly). Besides, he is also collaborating editor of Science Technology & Society(bi-annually, published by SAGE), vice-president and secretary-general of the China High-tech Industry Promotion Society(CHIPS), vice-president of the Chinese Association for Science of Science and S&T Policy Research.

Dr. Mu has published more than 30 papers in peer-reviewed journals and international conferences, and drafted some documents concerning the National Innovation Policies and the 12th Five-Year Plan for National Basic Capacity-building for Innovation. He has published one book with the title "Technology Transfer from Germany to China: Case Studies on Chinese Carmakers and Parts Suppliers" in English, and some books concerning technology foresight towards 2020 in China, China innovation report. He has led more than 30 research projects entrusted or financed by National Development and Reform Commission(NDRC), Ministry of Science and Technology, National Natural Science Foundation of China(NSFC), CAS, and EU Commission. His research interests include S&T & innovation policy, technology foresight, R&D management, and competitiveness of high-tech industry.

Governance of Innovation Alliances in Green Industries

Ricarda Bouncken

8.1 Introduction

Firms in green industries need to constantly learn and improve their structures and products to bring forward sustainability and to succeed in the growingly competitive markets. Alliances serve as an important vehicle to acquire knowledge from other firms (Mowery et al., 1996). In alliances, firms carry out a project or work in a specific business area by coordinating the required skills and resources rather than by operating alone (Dussage et al., 2000). Firms in green industries can improve competitive performance through the combination of complementary resources provided by alliances. Further, alliances' performance potential is largely rooted in the leveraging effects of combination and learning. Successful firms in green industries create knowledge both internally and by exposing themselves to a variety of knowledge from the outside that encourages an extension and the development of their competencies. As such, learning in alliances has been a persistent theme in organization theory and innovation management and provides strong benefits for firms in green industries (Hagedoorn and Schakenraad, 1994; Hoang and Rothaermel, 2005; Kotabe and Swan, 1995; Shan et al., 1994).

This paper aims to research the performance implications of two different classes of relational learning across alliance partners in a green industry: learning from the partner, and mutual learning with the partner. Alliance performance is a broad concept that includes financial and relational dimensions. Therefore we investigate how four different performance dimensions are influenced by the two learning classes.

Our research focuses on innovation alliances on a project basis in a specific green industry, the solar energy generation. Project-based alliances allow their members advantages through complementary specialization (Sydow, 2006). The flexible combination of specialized capabilities in project-alliances is particularly beneficial for industries in which they allow firms to experience a reduction in the technology barriers industry entry and/or facilitate ongoing changes to the innovative product. The fast moving and innovative solar energy industry is such a setting.

This paper investigates the intermediary role of the learning classes on the relationship between project management and the performance dimensions in project-based alliances. We further specify prior work by classifying two components of project management. We assume that content and schedule orientated components of project management will have different relationships to performance and learning in alliances. In essence, this paper will research how firms in the green solar industry can improve alliance performance by two components of project management and two classes of relational learning. Results are derived by a survey study in the green solar industry of 149 alliances. The testing approach we will apply is Structural Equation Modelling with mediator analysis.

8.2 Theory

8.2.1 Alliances in the solar industry

This study selected the solar industry due to its environmental impact, innovativeness, and its strong reliance on innovation alliances. Since the beginning of industrialization the energy sector has been of increasing importance within national economies due to the fact that energy is an essential input factor in industrial processes. With the *Kyoto Protocol* from 1997 the industrialized nations committed themselves to reduce their combined emissions of greenhouse gases. In December 2008, the EU governments agreed on a guideline to increase the ratio of renewable energy to all energy consumption. It was agreed that 20% of energy consumption is to be derived from renewable energy sources by the year 2020, versus 8.5% in 2005(EU Guideline). Germany committed to a reduction of 21% (BMU *Kyoto Protocol*, 2008) and aims to maintain its lead in the international green industry. Finite fossil energy reserves, such as oil, coal, and natural gas and the growing awareness of the economic damage due to the global warming, along with increasing energy consumption levels and the unbounded dismantling of raw materials has also set ground for the German government to emphasize on green management matters. Renewable energy subsumes all energy sources derived by sustainable regeneration of natural processes. Thus, wind and solar energy, hydropower, geothermal energy and bio-energy are the main playgrounds of the renewable energy industry. An industry far from mainstream and high on the political agenda is expected to experience above average growth.

The renewable energy industry has grown to a € 25 bn. turnover business in Germany in 2007, representing an increase of 10% vs. the previous year. By 2007 the industry has created approximately 250,000 jobs, representing a growth of 55% compared to 2004 (Böhme and Dürrschmidt, 2008). Technical innovations and expanding markets are the solar industry (photovoltaic plants) to become increasingly cost-effective. The solar industry is the most dynamically developing sub-sector in growth terms and is the second largest after the bio-energy. These dynamics have been the argument for us to select the solar industry as the research objective of our study.

The highly specialized and innovative firms in the solar industry strongly operate on the basis of project alliances. Project-based alliances create complementary specialization upon their members' advantages (Sydow, 2006). In each project firms develop, readjust, or bundle their specific components to sell complete products for specific clients or for a growing mass market. Firms often form repeated collaborative projects. The recurring projects deliver an increased level of trust and performance through economies of repetition. Decisions in the actual project are then also influenced by resource allocations for the sake of subsequent projects. Firms have to consider further joint projects and economies of repetition that base upon learning. Learning results can be stored typical actions and procedures and then be used for further projects. Operating in a project alliance allows firms to establish typical project practices. Practices, e.g. project management procedures and guidelines may change but can provide a frame for the progressing inter-firm project management. Project practices have to cope with uncertainties and risks such as and inability to assess future innovations that base on the combination of technologies' potential and market's expectations (Bhattacharya et al., 1998). Specific forms of inter-firm project management or typical components of project management developed for internal project management might contribute to improve alliance performance for a single project but also for repeated collaboration.

8.2.2 Project management in project alliances

Project management has become a key activity within industries and is widely used for new product development (Ayas, 1996). Project management allows organizations to enlarge their knowledge transfer and relational learning capacity, which in turn positively affects a company's overall performance(Ayas,1996). Project management is set up to deliver formalized processes and structures for the necessary activities in advance(Shepherd and Ahmed,2000).

Positive effects of project management were particularly articulated in innovation management by the well-spread diffusion of the "stage-gate" approach (Cooper, 1990), which separates project work into a sequence of consecutive steps of research and development activities, each of them leading to pre-defined interim results. Prior studies indicate that a formal approach to project management has positive effects on performance in innovation management.

Project management can be applied to project-based alliances. In alliance project management, key elements of structures, processes and desired outcomes are articulated, codified, and mutually agreed upon in advance. Ireland et al. (2002) demonstrate that project management in co-operations leads to competitive advantages. The planning and formality of project management in alliances can limit the threats of opportunistic behavior of alliance partners and ensures balanced benefits as a precondition for collaborative behavior. Bouncken et al. (2007) and Lewis et al. (2002) substantiate that the deployment of project management supports sustainable market success and performance.

We argue that project management activities can be classified in content directed and more schedule directed. Formalized procedures set up by content orientated project management to achieve the goal and content of the project alliance allow a detection and resolution of potential problems that was found to reduce time and work effort(Tatikonda and Rosenthal,2000). If partners are involved in the planning and conceptualization of the project management, they will articulate their goals and competencies. This allows them to avoid making costly and difficult changes to the specifications of components that would more likely appear later in the project alliance innovation process. Formality can assist the development of a project-focus and a collective orientation of project personnel facilitating the accomplishment of the project's goals (Tatikonda and Rosenthal, 2000). This is important for the distributed and joint work in alliance projects. If targets are made explicit, agreed and set up, there is a lower risk of misunderstanding across allying partners. Moreover, the greater interaction during the conceptualization of the project management allows the different partners to make certain that they will be able to deliver the required components, and to invest in equipment, tools, and training when necessary. The joint conceptualization of the project management e. g. about product design and customer needs further reduces the risk of design errors, and the danger that partners will have to make costly changes downstream the distributed and cooperative innovation process. In sum, we argue that partners who define and control the target of the alliance by content orientated project components will improve the project effectiveness and the pursuit of innovation targets in project alliances. By enhanced understanding and predictability of the content additionally the soft dimension of alliance performance, the relational performance, will advance. We hypothesize:

Hypothesis 1: Content directed project management improves alliance performance.

Partners set up a schedule directed project management to harmonize the timing of the development and to merge the distributed production processes in time. The formal schedule states how operations should be performed with stages, controls, and sequences to reduce ambiguity for the project's participants(Gilson et al., 2005). The formulation of deadlines and milestones will assist each allying partners' planning process. The improved planning and greater interaction during the conceptualization of the schedule allows the allying partners to make certain that they will be able to supply the required components, and to invest in equipment, tools, and training in time. They feel less uncertain about the delivery dates and the supply of components required for their own development. Components are finalized in a timely manner. This improves the efficiency of the project alliance. If firms do not have to wait for their required input of their partners due to schedule directed project management, they will be more satisfied with the collaboration and regard to the project alliance as less risky. This improves the soft dimension of alliance performance. We hypothesize(for the model see Figure 8.1 and Figure 8.2):

Hypothesis 2: Schedule directed project management improves project efficiency and the soft dimension alliance performance.

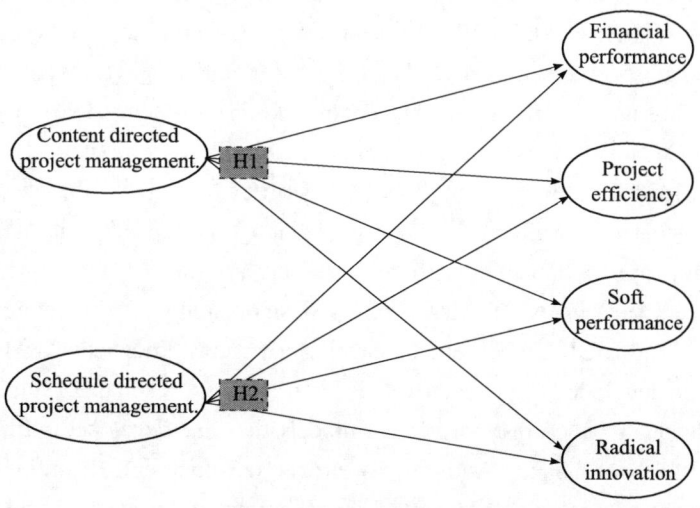

Figure 8.1 Small model

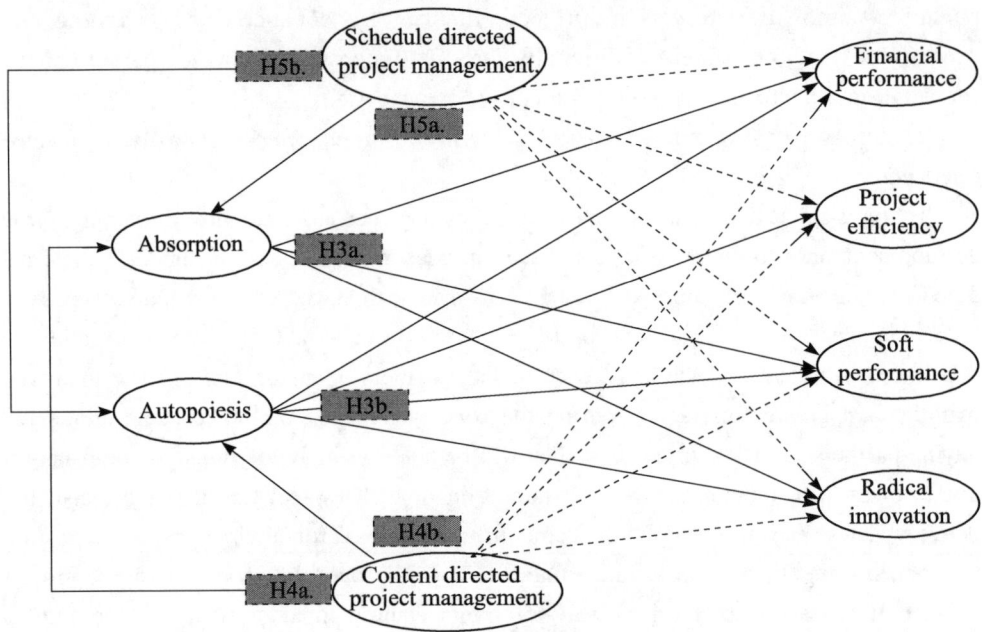

Figure 8.2　Full model

8.2.3　Relational learning in project alliances

A number of studies ascertain that firms' success is supported by learning and knowledge sharing within networks and co-operations(Kale and Singh, 2007; Lane et al., 2001; Williams, 2007). The literature on learning in alliances has strongly focused on single partners that learn from each other through the transfer of explicit knowledge(Dussage et al., 2000; Hagedoorn, 1993; Inkpen, 1996; Inkpen, 1998; Simonin, 2004). Nevertheless, there is more than the mere combination of explicit and implicit knowledge and the learning from one firm of the other—the absorption of the partner's knowledge—in alliances. We argue that firms can also mutually learn with each other in project alliances. We thereby develop an inter-organizational level of the learning process through which firms jointly develop mutually shared new knowledge and learn relationally. The mutual learning of new knowledge, which we call autopoiesis, is developed and manifested by a web of exchanges and interactions between individuals which distinct mental models that are developed with reference to the firms and the alliance. Autopoiesis directs development of mutual knowledge between alliance partners on the basis of contributions of the partners and their frame of reference within their firm and environment. Herein social processes influence the reflection and adjustment of mental models of the allying firms.

Alliances can achieve positive effects by newly created knowledge. Specifically, absorption in project alliances will improve the knowledge bases of partners as they transfer knowledge and learn from the absorption and application of new knowledge. The reflection of the transferred knowledge will induce improvements in the brains of employees, teams, interaction routines, technologies, artificial memories as well as creative processes of the knowledge-receiving partner that improves performance and innovativeness. However, absorption might be associated with the risks of asymmetrical and/or unintended knowledge spillover. Furthermore, partners may spend too much time in the absorption of unnecessary knowledge which decreases project efficiency. Considering the total effects, we argue that absorption increases the effectiveness, financial performance, radical innovation, and the soft factors of project alliance performance.

Hypothesis 3a: Absorption improves performance in project alliances.

Alliances can achieve positive effects by newly and jointly created knowledge. Synergies are more likely when partners develop new knowledge jointly. With autopoiesis partners have a fundamental win-win situation as they jointly develop mutual knowledge that even can achieve common benefits. The development of new knowledge will induce improvements in the brains of employees, teams, interaction routines, technologies and artificial memories improving performance and innovativeness. The collective birth of new knowledge—learning—arises from mental sorting, grouping, matching, and melding where the interplay of individuals has a notable influence (Leonard and Sensiper, 1998). Autopoiesis covers the development—the collective birth—of new knowledge across alliance partners. This birth brings about new insights and will largely increase radical innovations.

Hypothesis 3b: Autopoiesis improves performance in project alliances.

8.2.4 Mediating role of relational learning

Partners set up project management to improve performance of their project alliances. Yet, the formal aspects of content and schedule directed project management might limit project alliance performance. We argue that the positive performance effects, content and schedule directed project management, only occur if allying firms do learn relationally during the alliance's progress.

When proceeding, project alliances always require adjustments and re-adjustments that include direct communication between partners (Doz, 1996).

These informal exchanges and changes are not automatically included in formal project management. Instead, the formal project management per se limits the spontaneous reaction of partners. The high formalization of project management reduces openness, which discourages new ideas and behaviors(Pierce and Delbecq, 1977). It is necessary to improve project efficiency, innovativeness, and the soft dimension of project performance. Furthermore, the existence of uncertainties related to innovation projects and different allying partners in project alliances can hardly be integrated by complete formalized project management standards. Furthermore, new pooling of knowledge does not necessarily create the same joint knowledge. New issues have to make sense to the participating actors in the allying firms and be understood in order to enable the application of the new insights in the project. Sensemaking and meaning improves by more direct, intense, and flexible interrelation between allying partners. High degrees of formality might reduce this openness in flexibility in project alliances. Moreover, formality can be very time-consuming, detracting from the accomplishment of components, i. e. prototype development or product-design(Tatikonda and Rosenthal, 2000). At last, high formality of content and imposition of constraints can signal distrust of the partner and initiate opportunistic behavior that reduces relational learning and alliance performance.

As such, we argue that in spite of the product and relational uncertainty associated in highly innovative and uncertain environment in the solar industry, e. g. the lack of knowing the exact requirements of the final product to satisfy the clients, and the lack of complete knowledge of the partners' behaviour and capabilities, formal project management is only beneficial when partners maintain relational learning processes. Specifically, we posit that content and schedule directed project management will only achieve project efficiency and soft performance effects when firms maintain absorption or autopoiesis in project alliances.

Hypothesis 4a: *Content directed project management improves project efficiency only when alliance partners achieve absorption.*

Hypothesis 4b: *Content directed project management improves project efficiency only when alliance partners achieve autopoiesis.*

Hypothesis 5a: *Schedule directed project management improves project efficiency only when alliance partners achieve absorption.*

Hypothesis 5b: *Schedule directed project management improves project efficiency only when alliance partners achieve autopoiesis.*

8.3 Method

8.3.1 Survey and setting

We selected German solar firms for our study. German firms are understood to be highly innovative and effective in a worldwide comparison(Wiese, 2007). A survey was sent out to firms that were selected by a database in June 2007. From June 21st to 23rd, 2007, we further directly contacted firms' representatives in charge of alliances at the Intersolar 2007, which is Europe's largest solar technology trade fair. With more than 630 exhibitors presenting their products and services the venue was expected to provide a valid and reliable representation of the industry structure. We achieved 151 responses in total.

We verified our hypotheses by Structural Equation Modelling(SEM). Figure 8.1 and Figure 8.2 present our hypothesized model to examine our postulated hypotheses that are in the standard shape of LISREL models by Joreskog and Sorbom(1996). We tested the effects by content and schedule directed project management on performance and the direct and mediating effects by the two relational learning types. We therefore provide a small model(Figure 8.1) that only includes the effects through project management on performance and a large model(Figure 8.2) that shows all effects including the mediating effects. We checked the measurement model by a confirmatory factor analysis. The global fit of our measurement model was estimated to be good with CMIN value of 389.835, degrees of freedom 296, p-value of 0.000 (Bentler and Bonett, 1980) and comparative fit index of 0.938, above the threshold of 0.90 and RMSEA value of 0.046 better than the required threshold of $<$ 0.06(Hu and Bentler, 1998).

8.3.2 Measures

We used a multi-measure approach for the constructs. All responses were provided on five-point Likert-type scales. Our measures of performance are mostly based on the scale developed by Arino(2003). For validity and reliability see Table 8.1. All local fit measures were acceptable according to standards(DeVellis, 1991; Nunnally and Bernstein, 1994). Composite reliability of the latent variables always reached the necessary condition of $\geqslant 0.6$. Average Variance Explained AVE $\geqslant 0.4$ threshold was always accomplished(Hair et al., 1998).

Table 8.1 Local fit, convergent, and discriminant reliability

Construct	Item	Stand. factor-loading	Indicator reliability	α	Composite reliability	AVE	Fornell larcker
Absorption	We do learn from our alliance partner	0.645	0.416	0.869	0.834	0.460	1.172
	Due to the knowledge learned from our alliance partner we are able to progress tasks more quickly	0.792	0.628				
	Our partner's knowledge helps us to develop ideas, products or services	0.635	0.404				
	By accessing our partner's knowledge we learn to solve problems more quickly	0.789	0.623				
	By learning from our partner we are able to progress projects more quickly	0.826	0.682				
	Having a project finalized it becomes clear that we do have learned novelties from our partner	0.655	0.429				
Autopoiesis	We are skilled to transpose knowledge with our partner and to combine it in a manner that new ideas, products or services evolve	0.775	0.600	0.736	0.782	0.551	0.979
	We share and combine our knowledge with our partner to manage new projects for success	0.732	0.536				
	New ideas develop by shared thinking and reflecting with our partner	0.530	0.280				

Continued

Construct	Item	Stand. factor-loading	Indicator reliability	α	Composite reliability	AVE	Fornell larcker
Content directed project management	Our partner delivers on the promises granted	0.785	0.616	0.838	0.861	0.674	0.799
	Our partner is honestly interested in the success of our business	0.846	0.716				
	Our partner considers the well-being of our firm when important decisions are made	0.769	0.591				
Schedule directed project management	During project execution we assure that milestones are met on schedule	0.799	0.638	0.845	0.855	0.663	0.813
	We strive to meet sub-ordinate targets on schedule	0.800	0.640				
	We strive to meet sub-ordinate targets precisely with agreed quality standard	0.812	0.659				
Overall performance	Satisfaction with entire project achievement	0.797	0.636	0.769	0.813	0.593	0.908
	Satisfaction of alliance partner with entire project achievement	0.785	0.616				
	Achievement of economic and fiscal result	0.642	0.412				
Project efficiency	Adherence to cost budget	0.704	0.496	0.772	0.835	0.635	0.848
	Adherence to time schedule	0.802	0.644				
	Adherence to objectives is standard practice	0.720	0.518				
Soft performance	To overcome interpersonal barriers	0.556	0.300	0.696	0.827	0.621	0.868
	Sound problem solving	0.873	0.762				
	Smart cooperation with alliance partner	0.639	0.408				

Continued

Construct	Item	Stand. factor-loading	Indicator reliability	α	Composite reliability	AVE	Fornell larcker
Radical innovation	Provides advantages new to the customer	0.655	0.428	0.749	0.809	0.601	0.896
	Provides product attributes/functionality new/inimitable to the customer	0.938	0.880				
	Provides radical improvements on product attributes/functions	0.595	0.354				

8.4 Results

This paper started with an analysis of performance implications by two components of project management on project alliances. Afterwards, the results of relational learning on performance were explored. At last, the study investigated in the mediating role of relational learning on the relationship between project management components and project alliance performance. For this purpose we started with the small model(Figure 8.1) that contains the direct effects of the project management components on alliance performance(hypotheses 1 and 2). We then accomplished a second the full model(Figure 8.2) that contained project management components, relational learning types, and the performance dimensions. This large model allows us to simultaneously estimate the direct effects of relational learning on performance, and the mediating effect of relational learning on the relationship between project management components and project alliance (hypotheses 3a,3b,4a,4b,5a,5b). Table 8.2 shows all estimated items and the T values for all dimensions of alliance performance. Table 8.3 shows the estimates for the path coefficients required for the testing of the hypotheses.

Table 8.2 Standardized coefficients and T values of the small model

Performances	Path	Project management component	Estimate	S.E.	C.R.	P
Financial performance	<—	Content directed project management	0.480	0.112	4.444	0.000***
Project effectiveness	<—	Content directed project management	0.205	0.123	2.011	0.044
Soft performance	<—	Content directed project management	0.226	0.095	2.098	0.036
Radical innovation	<—	Content directed project management	0.034	0.090	0.373	0.709
Project effectiveness	<—	Schedule directed project management	0.390	0.115	3.530	0.000***
Financial performance	<—	Schedule directed project management	0.104	0.086	1.082	0.279
Soft performance	<—	Schedule directed project management	0.223	0.081	2.071	0.038
Radical innovation	<—	Schedule directed project management	−0.074	0.078	−0.789	0.430

Table 8.3 Standardized coefficients and *T* values of the full model

Performances	Path	Project management component	Estimate	S.E.	C.R.	P
Project effectiveness	<—	Absorption	0.223	0.137	2.238	0.025
Financial performance	<—	Absorption	0.265	0.107	2.807	0.005
Soft performance	<—	Absorption	0.292	0.107	2.661	0.008
Radical innovation	<—	Absorption	0.088	0.121	0.862	0.389
Project effectiveness	<—	Autopoiesis	0.423	0.136	3.465	0.000 ***
Financial performance	<—	Autopoiesis	0.482	0.107	4.137	0.000 ***
Soft performance	<—	Autopoiesis	0.458	0.109	3.319	0.000 ***
Radical innovation	<—	Autopoiesis	0.231	0.116	1.908	0.056
Absorption	<—	Content directed project management	−0.018	0.085	−0.191	0.848
Absorption	<—	Schedule directed project management	0.277	0.078	2.720	0.007
Autopoiesis	<—	Content directed project management	−0.020	0.113	−0.199	0.842
Autopoiesis	<—	Schedule directed project management	0.381	0.105	3.425	0.000 ***
Financial performance	<—	Content directed project management	0.538	0.103	5.269	0.000 ***
Project effectiveness	<—	Content directed project management	0.225	0.118	2.336	0.020
Soft performance	<—	Content directed project management	0.243	0.088	2.386	0.017
Radical innovation	<—	Content directed project management	0.032	0.103	0.326	0.744
Soft performance	<—	Schedule directed project management	−0.015	0.080	−0.137	0.891
Project effectiveness	<—	Schedule directed project management	0.144	0.114	1.319	0.187
Financial performance	<—	Schedule directed project management	−0.192	0.090	−1.847	0.065

*** indicates the result is statistically meaningful.

Hypothesis 1 stated a positive effect through content directed project management on alliance performance. We find significant and positive effects on three dimensions of alliance performance. The corresponding standardized path coefficients are 0.480 on financial performance; 0.205 on project effectiveness, and 0.226 on soft (relational) performance. The effect of content directed project management on radical innovation was not sufficient (path coefficient 0.034). Overall, hypothesis 1, stating a positive effect through content directed project management is supported.

Hypothesis 2 stated effects of schedule directed project management on project effectiveness, financial performance, and the soft dimension alliance performance. We found that this component of project management has positive effects on project effectiveness (standardized coefficient 0.390) and soft performance(standardized coefficient 0.223). However, we were not able to identify a positive effect on financial performance(standardized coefficient 0.104). Hypothesis 2 as such partially supported for project effectiveness and soft performance.

The next hypotheses were tested in the large model. The direct effects of relational learning are as follows. We find that absorption improves different dimensions of performance in project alliances: project effectiveness(0.223), financial performance(0.265), and soft performance(0.292). We did not find a significant effect on radical innovation. As such hypothesis 3a is largely accepted. Hypothesis 3b that directed the performance effects of autopoiesis in project alliances is instead completely accepted. Autopoiesis improves project effectiveness (0.423), financial performance(0.482), soft performance(0.458), and additionally on radical innovation (0.231).

Hypotheses 4 and 5 included mediating effects of relational learning. The examination of mediating effects in path models requires a three-step approach. First there has to be proven a significant correlation between the antecedents (project management) and the consequence (alliance performance). Therefore we have to check the effect of antecedents(project management) and the consequence(alliance performance)in the small model. We can use the results discussed for hypotheses 1 and 2, stated above. Content directed project management has positive effects on financial performance, project effectiveness, and soft performance that could be mediated. Schedule directed project management has significant effects on project effectiveness and soft performance that could be mediated.

The next step has to verify that the mediators(relational learning)have positive relationships to the both, the antecedents(project management) and the consequences (alliance performance). For this step a complete model with antecedents, mediators, and consequences is required. We again can use the results stated above. Absorption is positively associated with the following consequences: financial performance, project effectiveness, and soft performance. Autopoiesis has positive effects on all consequences. We find that only the schedule directed project management has positive relationship with absorption (standardized coefficient 0.277) and with autopoiesis (standardized coefficient 0.381). Consequently only schedule directed project management could be mediated by learning on the two consequences: project effectiveness and soft performance.

The last step of the mediating analysis requires that the direct paths between the antecedents (here: schedule directed project management) and the consequences (here: Project effectiveness and soft performance) are no longer significant when the mediators (relational learning) is integrated into the model. We here need again the estimations of the full model. We identify a change from significance (small model) to insignificance (full model) of schedule directed project management on project effectiveness and soft performance when relational learning is integrated in the model. The corresponding path coefficients are 0.144 (project effectiveness) and -0.015 (soft performance). Consequently, relational learning might mediate the relationship between schedule directed project management on project effectiveness and on soft performance.

We have to reject hypothesis 4. It stated that content directed project management improves project efficiency only when alliance partners achieve relational learning. Different to this, we can accept hypothesis 5: Schedule directed project management improves project performance in terms of project effectiveness and soft performance only when alliance partners achieve relational learning. This means that schedule directed project management only improves project effectiveness and soft performance, when project partners do achieve relational learning.

8.5 Discussion

This study was set up to clarify the effects of relational learning on performance and its relationship to two components of project management, schedule, and content orientated. We use a new classification of project management that is highly relevant for alliance coordination: components of content and schedule directed project management. Innovation alliances, specifically those operating on a project basis have to coordinate a distributed innovation process. As such they have two major activities. Partners have to ensure that the alliance fulfils its targets in terms of content, which concentrates on the development of novel and coherent components to a new product. Moreover, partners have to ensure that components are supplied in time. As such, content and schedule directed components of project management are of main importance. This classification has so far been neglected in studies of project management and innovation project management.

At a first glance one would believe that content and schedule directed project management are very close concepts that might have identical performance effects. Our results question this. We find that content directed project management covers activities which improve project effectiveness as well as financial and soft performance of alliances. Schedule orientated activities do only increase project effectiveness and soft performance. Surprisingly, our results indicate that both project management components do not directly improve radical innovations.

The divergence between both components becomes highly visible when we research the mediating effects by relational learning. Content directed project management has positive performance effects on project effectiveness as well as financial and soft performance, regardless if firms achieve relational learning or not. On the opposite, the positive performance effects of schedule directed project management are rooted in the relational learning across firms. As such, partners have to ensure that firms follow learning procedures in project alliances. If not, partners will fail to meet project targets and to achieve good relationships with their partners that build social capital and improve future collaboration.

Further, we find that the two forms of relational learning have partly different performance outcomes. Absorption that covers the learning from the partner, improves alliance performance in three dimensions. However, learning from the partner, absorption, does not improve the generation of radical innovation. Autopoiesis is distinctive. It improves all four categories of alliance performance including radical innovation. Autopoiesis covers the development—the collective birth—of new knowledge across alliance partners. This birth brings about new insights and will increase radical innovations. Moreover, autopoiesis generates a win-win situation for both firms. We therefore can confirm the assumptions by Scarbrough et al. (2004) who make a call for learning by reflection.

We extend and specify the work by Lewis et al. (2002) who differentiate different styles and aspects of project management aspects but have neglected the schedule and content directed components of project management. We also extend and specify the research by proponents of a formal style of project management. Those have assumed and proofed that formalization in project management and innovation projects increases performance (Tatikonda and Rosenthal, 2000). However, the mediating effect by relational learning on the relationship between schedule orientated project management and alliance performance gives a fundament for proponents of an emergent style of project management who stress the limitations of formalization (Lewis et al., 2002). The control of milestones and deadlines outlined by the schedule orientated project management is according to our results not sufficient for the achievement of performance.

As all studies, ours has some drawbacks. A study on mutual learning in alliance could use a dyadic analysis. Still, the issue of learning requires a survey study and is confronted with low response rates. The implementation of a survey on dyads then will be confronted with serious respondent barriers.

What we further do not provide is what other antecedents exist of relational learning and which structures and routines alliance partners can implement to improve relational learning. The establishment of direct communication or a learning climate across firms might trigger the relational learning. Thus, with the largely unexplored issue of mutual learning in alliances, there is room for further research. The influences stated above and others could be explored in subsequent studies. We recommend studies that explore antecedents of mutual learning and interaction effects between project management and those antecedents. Inter-firm teams and communication are furthermore potential classes of antecedents of relational, and specifically of mutual learning in alliances. Moreover, leadership styles might influence the relational and mutual learning. The study of leadership e. g. transactive vs. transformational (Bass, 1990) might bring across novel insights about fine-grained issues and the "climate" of relational learning in alliances. So we suggest further research of leadership styles on the project management, relational learning, and performance nexus. Studies could gain insights about the actual or ideal or perceived leadership style of the internal project leader by the project members. The internal project management must also be knowledgeable of the external project managers' styles. Interesting results might also result from a study of both managers' differential or similarity of leadership styles on relational learning and performance of the allying firms.

For business practice it is necessary to raise the level of awareness about the different project management styles and the differences in the relational knowledge learning methods with their multiple effects on alliance performance. There is no single on fits all solution to increase output. Management should be aware that different project management styles do have dissimilar impact. E. g. our results show that schedule directed project management does not positively impact radical innovation, but content driven project management style does have a positive effect on radical innovation in alliances. For circumstances management needs to steer projects within a frame of milestones, sub-ordinate targets, and time schedules, so to say in a schedule driven project management style, it is useful to consider that the alliance is designed to enable relational learning. Thus the emphasis in business operation must be to balance, if not merge the needs for both relational learning and schedule driven project management.

8.6 Conclusion

Especially in fast moving industries, as the Solar Energy innovation project-alliances offer the chance to leverage the advantages of flexible combination of complementary competences of partner firms, striving for common innovation targets in alliances is strongly influenced by relational learning performance which itself is influenced by the manner(content or schedule directed components) the projects are managed. With our empirical study we could show evidence for the different effects of content and schedule directed project management on alliance performance. By incorporating mediating effects of relational learning classes into our research model the differences became even more visible. Particularly the schedule orientated component of project management requires relational learning to achieve performance in project alliances. With our findings we hope to have contributed to the knowledge management research and provided basis for future research on mutual learning and their managerial antecedents.

References

Arino, A. 2003. Measures of strategic alliance performance: an analysis of construct validity. *Journal of International Business Studies*, 34, 66-79.

Ayas, K. 1996. Professional project management: a shift towards learning and a knowledge creating structure. *International Journal of Project Management*, 14(3), 131-136.

Bass, B. M. 1990. From transactional to transformational leadership—learning to share the vision. *Organizational Dynamics*, 18(3), 19-31.

Bentler, P. M., Bonett, D. G. 1980. Significance tests and goodness of fit in the analysis of covariance-structures. *Psychological Bulletin*, 88(3), 588-606.

Bhattacharya, R., Devinney, T. M., Pillutla, M. M. 1998. A formal model of trust based on outcomes. *Academy of Management Review*, 23(3), 459-472.

Böhme, D., Dürrschmidt, W. 2008. Renewable Energy Sources in Figures—National and International Development. Berlin: Federal Ministry for the Environment, Nature Conservation and Nuclear Safety.

Bouncken, R. B., Koch, M., Teichert, T. 2007. Innovation strategy explored: innovation orientation's strategy preconditions and market performance outcomes. *Zeitschrift für Betriebswirtschaft*, 2(Special Issue), 71-94.

Cooper, R. G. 1990. Stage-gate systems: a new tool for managing new products. Business Horizons, (May-June), 44-54.

DeVellis, R. F. 1991. *Scale Development*. Newbury Park: Sage Publications.

Doz, Y. 1996. The evolution of cooperation in strategic alliances: initial conditions or learning processes. *Strategic Management Journal*, 17(Summer Special Issue), 55-83.

Dussage, P., Garette, B., Mitchell, W. 2000. Learning from competing partners: outcomes and durations of scale and link alliances in Europe, North America and Asia. Strategic Management Journal, 21(2), 99-126.

Gilson, L. I., Mathieu, J. E., Shalley, C. E., et al. 2005. Creativity and standardization: complementary or conflicting drivers of team effectiveness? *Academy of Management Journal*, 48(3), 521-531.

Hagedoorn, J., Schakenraad, J. 1994. The effects of strategic technology alliances on company performance. *Strategic Management Journal*, 15(4), 291-309.

Hagedoorn, J. 1993. Understanding the rationale of strategic technology partnering—interorganizational modes of cooperation and sectoral differences. *Strategic Management Journal*, 14(5), 371-385.

Hair, J. F., Anderson, R. E., Tatham, R. L., et al. 1998. *Multivariate Data Analysis*. 5th ed. New York: Upper Saddle River.

Hoang, H., Rothaermel, F. T. 2005. The effect of general and partner-specific alliance experience on joint R&D project performance. *Academy of Management Journal*, 48(2), 332-345.

Hu, L. T., Bentler, P. M. 1998. Fit indices in covariance structure modeling: sensitivity to underparameterized model misspecification. *Psychological Methods*, 3(4), 424-453.

Inkpen, A. 1996. Creating knowledge through collaboration. *California Management Review*, 39(1), 123-140.

Inkpen, A. 1998. Learning, knowledge acquisition and strategic alliances. *European Management Journal*, 16(2), 223-229.

Ireland, R. D., Hitt, M. A., Vaidyanath, D. 2002. Alliance management as a source of competitive advantage. *Journal of Management*, 28(3), 413-446.

Joreskog, K. G., Sorbom, D. 1996. *LISREL 8: User's Reference Guide*. Chicago: Scientific Software International, Inc.

Kale, P., Singh, H. 2007. Building firm capabilities through learning: the role of the alliance learning process in alliance capability and firm-level alliance success. *Strategic Management Journal*, 28(10), 981-1000.

Kotabe, M., Swan, K. S. 1995. The role of strategic alliances in high-technology new product development. *Strategic Management Journal*, 16(8), 621-636.

Lane, P. J., Salk, J. E., Lyles, M. A. 2001. Absorptive capacity, learning, and performance in international joint ventures. *Strategic Management Journal*, 22(12), 1139-1162.

Leonard, D., Sensiper, S. 1998. The role of tacit knowledge in group innovation. *California Management Review*, 40(3), 112-128.

Lewis, M., Dehler, G., Green, S. 2002. Product development tensions: exploring contrasting styles of project management. *Academy of Management Journal*, 45, 546-564.

Mowery, D. C., Oxley, J. E., Silverman, B. S. 1996. Strategic alliances and interfirm knowledge transfer. *Strategic Management Journal*, 17(Winter Special Issue), 77-91.

Nunnally, J. C., Bernstein, I. H. 1994. *Psychometric Theory*. 3rd ed. New York: McGraw-Hill, Inc.

Pierce, J., Delbecq, A. L. 1977. Organizational structure, individual attitudes, and innovation. *Academy of Management Review*, 2, 26-37.

Scarbrough, H., Bresnen, M., Edelman, L. F., et al. 2004. The processes of project-based learning—an exploratory study. *Management Learning*, 35(4), 491-506.

Shan, W., Walker, G., Kogut, B. 1994. Interfirm cooperation and start-up innovation in the biotechnology industry. *Strategic Management Journal*, 25, 387-394.

Shepherd, C., Ahmed, P. K. 2000. NPD frameworks: a holistic examination. *European Journal of Innovation Management*, 3(3), 160-173.

Simonin, B. L. 2004. An empirical investigation of the process of knowledge transfer in international strategic alliances. *Journal of International Business Studies*, 35(5), 407-427.

Sydow, J. 2006. Managing projects in network contexts: a structuration perspective. In: Hodgson, D., Cicmik, S. (Eds.), *Making Projects Critical*. Houndmills, Basingstoke, Hampshire and New York: Gower, 252-264.

Tatikonda, M. V., Rosenthal, S. R. 2000. Successful execution of product development projects: balancing firmness and flexibility in product innovation. *Journal of Operations Management*, 18(4), 401-425.

Wiese, R. 2007. Status of solar energy in Germany and framework conditions for the market development abroad. Karachi: Bundesverband Solarwirtschaft (BSW) e. V.

Williams, C. 2007. Transfer in context: replication and adaptation in knowledge transfer relationships. *Strategic Management Journal*, 28, 867-889.

Author

Prof. Dr. Ricarda Bouncken has been a chair professor of the Strategic Management and Organization at the University of Bayreuth, Germany, since 2009, before she was the chair professor at the University of Greifswald, Germany. Until the end of 2004 she held the chair of Planning and Innovation Management at the Brandenburg Institute of Technology, TU Cottbus. In 2002, she achieved her Habilitation at the University of Lueneburg, Germany. She received her Ph. D. from the University of St. Gall, Switzerland. Ricarda Bouncken is the author of more than 130 journal publications and books.

Her research focuses on firm strategies, their organization and innovation, particularly in alliances and supply chains. Her strong interest is on the effects of knowledge transfer across alliances partners and the projects management, as well as on diversity effects in and across organizations e. g. of employees' age and cultural diversity on firms' strategies and innovation.

The Regional Innovation Capacity Construction for Green Growth: An Essential Way to be an Innovative Country

Song Hefa

9.1 Introduction

In recent years, more and more countries pay attention to the regional innovation capacity construction. In 2007, Japan issued a report of *Innovation 25: Creating the Future, Challenging Unlimited Possibilities* and required to enhance the regional ecosystems construction from basic research to markets. It also required to implement policies that invigorate regional communities, especially through a larger regional system. In January, 2010, after issuing the *American Competition Initiative*, the *Competition Act* and the *Recovery Act* and so on, USA issued a *Strategy for American Innovation: Securing Our Economic Growth and Prosperity* to enhance the innovation capacity construction. In order to improve the environment of the Silicon Valley and to enhance its regional innovation capacity, California revised its public policy and regional innovation system(Cluver and Shelley, 1997). In 2010, European Union issued a report of *Europe 2020: Innovation, Green growth and Jobs* and listed knowledge, innovation, green growth as the core of regional and national competence. The report also put forward 5 reform goals for the member countries and regions. In *Innovating for Sustainable Growth: a Bioeconomy for Europe*, Europe put forward a bio-economy strategy which contributed significantly to the objectives of the *Europe 2020 Flagship Initiatives Innovation Union* and *A Resource Efficient Europe*. Many other countries like South Korea,

India also issued innovation strategies or plans to promote regional innovation. Now, the Silicon Valley (USA), Tsukuba (Japan), Oxford (UK), Bangalore (India), Zhongguancun (China), Datian (South Korea) have become models of the regional innovation capacity construction in the world.

China has laid down an ambitious objective to be an innovative country in 2020. To be an innovative country, China has to achieve to some standards. The R&D investment ratio of GDP shall be more than 2%, the scientific and technological progress contribution rate to GDP shall be more than 70%, the dependence degree on foreign technology shall be less than 30% and so on. From now, there is only 8 years left for China to achieve the objective, but there is still a huge gap between the current situation and the objective. The regional innovation capacity is still weak and imbalanced. The regional innovation system still has many deficiencies and problems and can't be adapted to the requirement of the objective. China is still in industrialization phase with excessive resources consumption and heavy pollution. It can be said that China is now in tackling stage and critical period to be an innovative country.

The national innovation capacity construction for green growth is a very important and effective way for China's future innovation and sustainable development. The national innovation capacity construction shall finally be implemented through construction of the regional innovation capacity. This paper will review situation of China's regional innovation capacity, study its main problems and put forward some policy recommendations for China's regional innovation capacity construction for green growth.

9.2 Literature review

The regional innovation system is an useful analytical framework for advancing understanding of the innovation capacity and process in regional economies (Asheim et al., 2003). The concept of regional innovation systems was firstly introduced by Philip Cooke in 1992, and refers to a normative and descriptive approach aiming at capturing how technological development takes place within a territory (Cooke, 2001). Asheim and Coenen (2005) defined the regional innovation system as the institutional infrastructure supporting innovation within the production structure of a region. Doloreux (2003) considered that the regional innovation system should be understood to be an interacting set of private and public interests, formal institutions, and other organizations that function according to organizational and institutional arrangements and relationships conducive to the generation, utilization, and dissemination of knowledge.

In recent years, study on the regional innovation capacity is one of the important issues of academic research. Cooke et al. (1997) advocated to strengthen regional level capacities for promoting both systemic learning and interactive innovation. The innovation capacity is the ability to create and commercialize new technologies based on innovation restructures (Furman et al., 2002). The innovation capacity is the systematic potential for sustainable interaction innovation (Hu and Mathews, 2005). OECD(1997) established an innovation capacity evaluation system including 4 major categories factors and compared the developed countries' innovation capacity. Carlos (2009) and many other scholars completed an innovation development report including 60 indicators of innovation capacity and measured 131 countries' innovation capacity. The Center for Regional Development of Purdue University and the Indiana Business Research Center(2009) developed an innovation capacity index system and compared the regional innovation capacity index of all states of U. S. A. Fraunhofer for Innovation Systems Institute and the United Nations University (Schubert et al., 2011), INSEAD Business School and the Confederation of Indian Industry (2009), United States Information Technology and Innovation Foundation and the Ewing Marion Kauffman Foundation (Informationtendogy and Innovation Foundation 2012) also issued their innovation capacity evaluation systems and compared some countries' and regions' innovation capacity.

It is a very important issue for the regional innovation capacity construction facing the green growth. Weitzman (1976) studied the usual net domestic product (NDP) income measure of the traditional national accounts system, and his study was the foundation for green GDP or economy growth. Talberth and Bohara (2006) developed models of green GDP growth and calculated the gap between traditional and green GDP by using a panel data set from eight countries spanning 30 – 50 years. And now, more and more scholars began to study the green GDP through innovation or innovation for sustainable economic growth.

Every year, the Chinese Academy of Science and Technology Development Strategy (CASTAD, 2006) issues the *Regional Innovation Capacity Report of China* and puts forward a regional innovation capacity evaluation index system including knowledge creation, knowledge acquisition, business innovation, technological innovation environment and management, innovation economic results. In 2010, the Center for Innovation and Development of Chinese Academy of Sciences(CID, 2010) issued the *2009 Innovation and Development Report of China* and put forward a regional innovation capacity evaluation system which included innovation input, innovation output, innovation condition (infrastructure), innovation promoting economic and social development from 2 dimensions of innovation strength and innovation efficiency. All these two reports include indicators of environment protection and natural resource utilization.

Now, the most important problem of China's regional innovation system was the weak linkage among the players(Chen and Guan,2011). There is still a long distance for the regional economy of China to become a real innovation-driven economy, the western region is still in the factor-driven stage(Xue,2009). Although many scholars have studied the regional innovation system, the regional innovation capacity and the green GDP, they seldom studied the policy of the regional innovation capacity construction, especially for green growth. Some innovation capacity evaluation system is not perfect, especially the GDP isn't the result of innovation.

9.3 China's regional innovation capacity construction

From the foundation of the new China, China began to construct her innovation system following with Soviet Union. But the real beginning of the innovation system is in 1998 twenty years after the reform and opening up in 1978. In December 1997, Chinese Academy of Sciences came up with a report named *Welcoming the Era of Knowledge Economy and Constructing the National Innovation System* for the central government of China. In June 9,1998, the central government approved the report and required Chinese Academy of Sciences to implement the knowledge innovation project as a pilot unit for construction of the national innovation system. From then on, China began to construct her regional innovation system with characteristics and strengths through a lot of national and regional development strategies or plans.

In 1992, in order to enhance the economic cooperation, 14 cities around Yangtze Delta launched a joint conference. In 2010, the State Council officially approved the implementation of the Yangtze River Delta Regional Plan. On the basis of regional development strategies or plans of Yangtze River Delta, Pearl River Delta, China recently issued nearly 20 regional development plans on national level. China now has formed a regional development framework of 18 key regions, 9 economic circles or zones and 10 groups of cities. Each strategy or plan emphasized on consummating the regional innovation system, lifting the regional innovation capacity, saving resources and protecting the environment. Till now, China has established 64 national high-tech industrial development zones, and many local high-tech industrial zones. In 2010, the Sate Council approved the development plan of Zhongguancun(Beijing) and required

Zhongguancun science and technology zone transformed to the national self-dominant innovation demonstration zone. From then on, Zhangjiang(Shanghai) High-tech zone, East Lake(Wuhan) High-tech Zone and Hefei-Wuhu-Bengbu District also began to be transformed to the national self-dominant innovation demonstration zones or districts. These three zones were permitted to adopt new policies especially permitting the service inventor to had a percentage of stock right and net profit dividend right of the company implementing the service invention to promote technology transfer and application.

In 2006, in *National Outline for Medium and Long Term S&T Development Plan*, China clearly demanded to establish regional innovation systems with diverse characteristics and strengths, the regional innovation system planning and associated innovation capacity construction shall be made in a unified and coordinated manner, and taken into account the characteristics and strengths of the regional economic and social development. In 2011, the *National Economy and Social Development 12th Five-Year Plan* also called to speed up transformation of economic development mode and create a new situation of scientific development, and called to accelerate building a resource-saving and environment-friendly society lifting the level of ecological civilization. The *National Innovation Capacity Construction 12th Five-Year Plan* which will be issued soon requires the regional innovation capacity construction from three aspects. The first is to optimize the innovation resources deployment for construction of the regional innovation capacity. The second is to establish and develop the innovation and service platforms across the regions. The third is to promote key regions to play roles of piloting and demonstrations in regional innovation capacity construction.

The innovative city construction is an effective way for the construction of the regional innovation capacity for green growth. On January 6, 2010, the *National Development and Reform Commission* approved 16 cities including Dalian, Qingdao, Xiamen, Shenyang, Xi'an, Guangzhou, Chengdu, Nanjing, Hangzhou, Jinan, Hefei, Zhengzhou, Changsha, Suzhou, Wuxi, and Yantai to be the national innovative cities. And on January 10, 2010, the Ministry of Science and Technology named Beijing (Haidian Distict), Tianjin(Binhai New Area), Tangshan, Baotou, Harbin, Shanghai (Yangpu District), Nanjing, Ningbo, Jiaxing, Hefei, Xiamen, Jinan, Luoyang, Wuhan, Changsha, Guangzhou, Chongqing(Shapingba District), Chengdu, Xi'an, and Lanzhou to be the national innovative cities or districts. All the two ministries support the regional innovation system construction by increasing investment of innovation facilities, arranging more R&D projects and enhancing industrial innovation and so on.

9.4 Problems for China's regional innovation capacity construction

The fist of the most important problems of China's regional innovation capacity construction are deficient government ability leading the regional innovation capacity for green growth from shortage of innovative capacity infrastructures, weak innovation dynamic and vitality of enterprises, weak capacity of innovation supporting economic and social development and environment protection. On the one hand, although there are many government departments responsible for innovation, the innovation functions of local government are weak in fact. The government functions of innovation are overlapping, co-existing, or even missing. Many regional governments haven't met the demand of the statutory growth of R&D input to financial expenditure. There are no effective coordination system and mechanism among governmental departments of science and technology, industry and economy, social development. Their functions are divided from each other. The innovation activity was mainly dominated by government and not the market. On the other hand, many regional governments only pay attention to GDP growth. In some regions, they import many heavy chemical industries and the pollution becomes more and more heavy. Orally, they pay attention to environment protection and sustainable development, but they pay less in fact.

The second is the weak innovation foundation capacity(infrastructure), especially the engineering, inspection and testing platforms. The investment in innovation infrastructures such as large scientific facilities, big scientific engineering as well as key laboratories and engineering research centers, comprehensive data and information centers are inadequate (Song and Mu, 2012). Most engineering (technology) research centers and various types of laboratories were built in universities and institutes and not in enterprises. The co-construction, co-utilization and social openness of information centers, science and technology museum and other service facilities are short of seriousness. Their operation mechanism is not active. Most of them are lack of operating funds, and their supporting capacity for regional innovation capacity construction has declined in recent years.

The third is the innovation resources distribution. The innovation resources in central government and local investment level no matter S&T infrastructures, innovation bases or R&D funds are distributed more to eastern districts, coastal regions and major cities, and less to the medium and west regions(Song et al, 2012). It results in a larger gap between the eastern and medium and west regions, the coastal and inner land regions, the major cities and little cities than ever. From the evaluation index system of the regional innovation capacity of China(CID,2010), it can be found that the less developed regions' regional innovation capacity fell behind much with the developed regions and the gaps between them was widened gradually. Innovation resources were distributed unevenly, more to the east and less to west regions. The central and west regions increase very quickly in innovation efficiency, but their efficiency of the innovation promoting economic and social development is far low. From the study of Song and Mu(2012), it can be found that the total entropy changes of most central and west regional innovation system were more than 0, showing they were in disordered state, the total entropy changes of Hebei, Fujian, Heilongjiang, Jiangxi,Jilin, Yunnan, Guangxi, Neimenggu, Xinjiang, Guizhou, Ningxia, Qinghai and so on were increasing.

The fourth is that the orientation of the innovation output is deformed. The current assessment system of science, technology and innovation focus mainly on the academic articles, patents application number and GDP. Because articles and patents have a long distance to the market, China's regional innovation efficiency is not high. There is some waste of innovation resources. China's GDP is a comprehensive calculation method. But about 80% of the high-tech industry output value was created by foreign-funded enterprises. So, simply calculating the profits of enterprises and GDP in the evaluation system of the regional innovation capacity is not reasonable. This orientation will inevitably result in low efficiency of innovation to promote economic and social development.

The fifth is the weak innovation dynamic and vitality of enterprises. The enterprises' main player position of innovation in China is far from being established. They aren't the real innovation main player in self-dominant innovation in particular decision-making, governmental resources investment and the use of high-end creative talents. The industries of real estate, entertainment, monopoly and other lucrative industries affect enterprises' innovation and development orientation. The actual existence of bureaucratic culture, counterfeiting culture and impetuous culture seriously block the innovation dynamic and vitality. Because of the gap with the universities and research institutes in innovation capacity, as well as less national and regional innovation resources allocated to enterprises, the enterprises often invest less in edge-cutting technologies and pay insufficient attention to capacity construction for long-term development.

The sixth is the weak capacity of innovation promoting economic and social development. China's science, technology and innovation promoting role to regional economic and social development has not fully brought into play. China's economic growth relies largely on investment and export, not mainly on innovation. The social undertakings in China are relatively less developed. There are serious rural-urban divide and regional disparities in education, medical and health services. There is a big gap between food safety, environmental safety, and production safety with people's need. Reducing differences between urban and rural areas, resolving problems of natural resources depletion and environmental pollution, and minifying imbalance of the social development needs innovative ideas, innovative approaches and innovation policies.

9.5 Factors of the regional innovation capacity construction for green growth

In general, the green growth should mainly include the following three aspects: resources economization and utilization, environment protection and social development. Resources economization and utilization further includes effective utilization of land resources, effective utilization of water resources, effective utilization of fossil energy and low carbon dioxide emissions. The assessment indicator can be the unit GDP energy consumption (carbon emissions) and forest cover rate. Environment protection includes chemical oxygen demand, sulfur dioxide emissions, ammonia, and nitrogen oxide emissions. The assessment indicators can be the unit GDP waste water, waste gas and waste emissions. Social development includes development of science, technology, education development, health care, social safety, food and drinking water safety, and environment safety in a coordinated, equal and integrated way.

So, the regional innovation capacity for green growth should refer to the capacity by which problems of resources economization and utilization, environment protection and social development can be mainly resolved by innovation in specific geographical regions. It is the regional capacity generating innovative ideas, engaging R&D and engineering, achieving commercialization and production scale, applying the innovative achievements in social development, and getting the economic returns and other kinds of value for the overall economic and social sustainable development with low energy and resource depletion and low pollution. It is also the ability to form the regional capacity of scientific research, capacity of technology development, capacity of innovation investment, capacity of commercialization, capacity of applying innovative achievements to social development, and capacity of the innovation management in high efficiency.

From the definition, there are 7 factors influencing the regional innovation capacity construction for green growth. In this paper, we proposed a 7 factors model to describe how to conduct the regional innovation capacity construction. It can be showed in Figure 9.1. The first is regional development strategy or plan. On June 12, 2010, the State Council issued the Main Functional Area Plan and divided the homeland into 4 types of regions. They are the optimized development regions, the key development regions, the restricted development regions and the prohibited development regions. Each of China's regional development strategy or plan emphasized on enhancement of self-dominant innovation capacity construction, optimization and upgrading of industrial structure, promotion of economic and social sustainable development. The construction of the regional innovation capacity is needed to be in accordance with the requirements of the main functional areas and regional development strategy or plan.

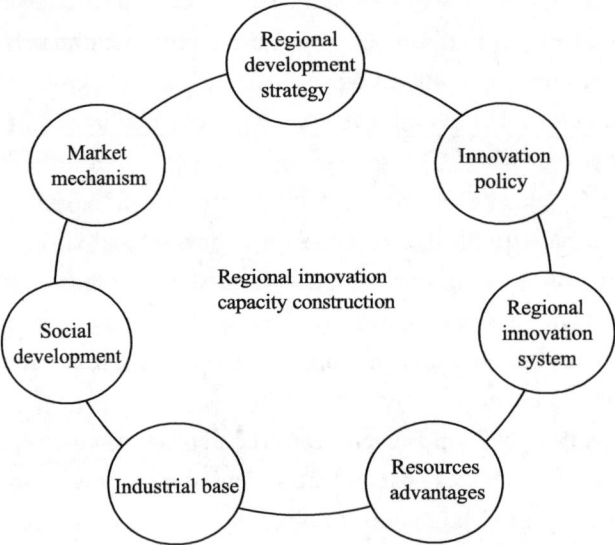

Figure 9.1 The 7 factors model influencing the regional innovation capacity construction

The second is the innovation policy. The most important national innovation policies are the 60 supplemented policies to put the outline of the *National Medium and Long Term Plan for Science and Technology Development* issued in 2006 into practice. In national level, the mainly policy instruments of the regional innovation capacity for green growth are as follows: Supportive policy such as the National S&T Plan, the Plan of the State Key Laboratories, the National Engineering Laboratories, the National Certified Enterprises' Technological Centers, the State Engineering (Technology) Research Centers, the National High-tech Industrialization Base Plan, the Industry Investment Guidance Fund, and the Venture Capital Investment Guidance Fund, and the S&T Innovation Fund for SMEs. In order to promote the regional innovation capacity construction, the local government shall set down appropriate implementing measures, especially those ensuring the statutory growth of investment in science and technology, shall simplify the technology development expenditure deduction policy in corporate income taxable at 150%, and shall develop vigorously the investment and financing for innovation.

The third is the regional innovation system. The regional innovation system is a learning system in which a company and other organizations interact through the institutional environment (Cooke, 1998). It has been an important and effective analysis tool for the national innovation system construction. The innovation system is a comprehensive analysis framework for cooperation among academia/universities, industry and state/government (Etzkowitz and Leydesdorff, 2000), media-based and culture-based public and the civil society (Carayannis and Campbell, 2009) and natural environments of society (Carayannis and Campbell, 2010). Besides putting the national level strategies or plans of the innovation regional capacity construction into practice, it is needed to bring up a number of key regional innovation players, especially institutes and enterprises with strong innovation capacity for new product development, to deploy construction of a number of regional innovation-oriented cities, to implement a group of technical innovation projects oriented to cooperation among academia, universities and industry, and to construct a high level innovation service intermediary network.

The fourth is the regional advantages. Regional advantages include not only natural resources advantages but also human and education advantages and science and technology advantages. At present, human and education, science and technology resources are real advantages for the regional innovation capacity. When transform the natural resources advantages into innovation advantages, the human and education advantages and science and technology advantages must be had, otherwise it will be unsustainable. The key of the regional innovation capacity construction is to release the potential advantages of human and education, science and technology and transform it to be advantages of innovation capacity.

The fifth is the industrial bases. The regional industrial base is the basis of the regional innovation capacity construction, and is the focus of the regional innovation capacity construction policy. Each region can optimize its own industrial layout and forming new competitive industries. The emphasis of the key industries is on enhancement of research and development capabilities, promotion of the product upgrading and the supporting capacity. The emphasis of the strategic emerging industries is on promoting breakthroughs of key technologies and having self-dominant intellectual property rights, on strengthening innovation infrastructure construction, and on promoting innovation achievements commercialization. The emphasis of the modern service industry is on improving the policy and cultural environment of the regional innovation capacity construction and on enhancing the service capabilities for production and life.

The sixth is the social innovation and development demand. The social innovation and development is an indispensable part of the regional innovation capacity construction. It mainly covers undertakings of science and technology, education, culture, health, sports, and public safety, as well as resources conservation and comprehensive utilization, environmental protection. The social innovation and development refers not only to the technological innovation for social development itself, but also refers to the innovation arrangement from social demand and lifting the social welfare through innovation. On the one hand, the social innovation is innovation in social undertakings such as IT technology research and development of distance education which can promote equity in education resources distribution. On the other hand, it is application of the innovation achievements for social undertaking and is promotion activities of social development through wholly and rapidly applying the innovation achievements. Its goal is to promote the coordinated, integrated and equal development between urban and rural areas, workers and farmers, mental and physical labors and build up a harmonious society.

The seventh is the market mechanism. The role of government and the role of market for regional innovation capacity construction are not actually the same and their boundary is very vague. So, government failure and market failure often exist at the same time. Even in developed countries, government promotion for innovation capacity construction is an indispensable factor. Even in developing countries, market competition still plays a fundamental role for innovation capacity construction. As for the regional innovation capacity construction, it is needed to play the government's promoting role and market's basic role.

9.6 Conclusion and future directions

This paper studies the history and state of art of China's regional innovation capacity construction, and extracts 6 problems China now faces. To achieve the innovative country objective for China, it proposed a 7 factors model to form the future policy framework for the regional innovation capacity construction. In the end, it brings forward some detailed policy recommendations from six aspects. The first is optimization of the distribution of innovation resources. It is necessary to support the eastern regions agglomerated high-end innovative elements including technologies, capital and talents, and encourage them to transfer talents, technologies and industries to the central and west regions. It is necessary to support the central regions to enhance construction of industrial technology innovation and innovative service platforms to accelerate the industrial innovation. It is necessary to support the western regions to play affluence resources advantages, improve characteristic technology innovation platforms, extend the industrial chain and increase the added value. It is necessary to support the northwestern regions to develop high-end manufactures and upgrade the traditional industries.

The second is to enhance the regional innovation foundation capacity. It is needed to build up national and local level public technological service platforms and research institutes of water resources, agriculture development, environmental protection, and quality inspection. It is needed to tilt policies of national and local engineering research centers, engineering labs, enterprise technology centers, and public technological service platforms to the west and central regions, and impel them to upgrade innovation efficiency. It is needed to strengthen collaboration among the regional innovation platforms focusing on data collection, research and experiments, monitoring and early warning and other needs in agriculture, transportation, water and other key industries, and establish a number of widely distributed and efficient collaboration platforms for cross-regional innovation network.

The third is to strengthen management of regional innovation capacity construction. The local governments shall promote close integration of scientific research and education, innovation and economy. The local governments shall change their functions to promoting security and development of livelihood, social justice, public safety and other social undertakings based on innovation. The Local governments shall change functions to pushing forward energy saving, employment, and safeguarding life safety of food, water and so on.

The fourth is to strongly enhance the regional industrial innovation capacity construction. One is focusing on high-tech breakthroughs and application of power generation, industrial energy economization, energy-efficient consumer products, transportation, and building energy saving fields. Two is promoting the use of advanced industrial boilers, furnaces and insulation, and other techniques. Three is laying down industrial policies to adapt to more stringent energy efficiency standards, low-carbon commodity standards and a carbon tax policy. Four is developing safety power including hydropower, and natural gas even nuclear as a strong pillar of green low-carbon energy.

The fifth is to optimize the national, regional innovation zones. It is needed to create a number of regional innovation centers through establishing national innovation demonstration districts and upgrading high-tech industrial development zones, to build up a number of national and regional innovative cities and innovative city groups based on the existing cities, and to promote the economic development zones to be innovative zones through improving their innovation conditions, cultivating innovation-friendly environment, strengthening innovation services and developing high-end industries.

The sixth is to promote social innovation vigorously. Developing financial and insurance industries, business and exhibition industries, modern logistics industries, service outsourcing industries, information services, cultural and creative industries are good measures. Improving application of the scientific knowledge and technological innovation achievements in fields of science and technology, education, health, culture, sports and public security and others is necessary. Facing the significant demands of social development, undertaking technological innovation and enlarging new applications of innovation to promote coordination, equalization and integration of public services is also necessary.

References

Asheim, B. , Coenen, L. 2005. Knowledge bases and regional innovation system: comparing Nordic Clusters. *Rearch Policy*, (34), 1173-1190.

Asheim, B. , Isaksen, A. Nanwelaers, C. and Totdling. 2003. Regional innovation policy for small media enterprises. Cheltenham, UK and Lyme, US: Edward Elgar.

Carayamis, E. , Campbell, D. 2009. "Mode3" and "Quadruple helix": toward a 21st century fractal innovation eco-system. *International Technology Management*, 46, 201-234.

Carayamis, E. , Campbell, D. 2010. Triple Helix, Quadruple Helix and Quintuple Helix and how do knowledge, innovation and enviroment relate to each other? A proposal framework for a trans-disiplinary analysis of sustainable development and social ecology. *Internation Journal of Social And Sustainable Development*, 1, 4169.

Center for Innovation and Development of Chinese Academy of Sciences. 2010. China Innovation and Development Report . Beijing: Science Press.

Center for Regional Development, Purdue University, Indiana Business Research Center, etc. 2009. Crossing the next regional frontier: information and analytics linking regional competitiveness to investment in a knowledge-based economy.

Chen, K. ,Guan, J. 2011. Mapping the functionality of China's regional innovation systems: A structural approach. China Economic Review, (22), 11-27.

Claros, L. 2009. The Innovation for Development Report 2009-2010: Strengthening Innovation for Prosperity of Nations. London: Palgrave MacmiLlan.

Cluver, J. H. , Shelley, L. L. 1997. Politics and Public Policies in California. Newyork: the Mcgraw-Hill Company Inc. Press.

Cooke, P. 1998. In troduction: origins of the concept. In: Braczy K, H. , Cooke P. and Heidenreich(edt.). *Regional Innovation System*. London: UCL Press.

Cooke, P. 2001. Regional innovation system, cluster, and the knowledge economy. Industrial and Corperate Change, (10), 945-973.

Cooke, P. ,Uranga M. and Etxebarria G. 1997. Regional innovation systems: Institutional and organizational dimensions. Research Policy, (26), 475-491.

Doloreux, D. 2010. China academy of science and technology development. The regional capacity development report. Technology in Society ,(24)24, 243-263.

Doloreux, D. 2003. Reghional innovation system in the periphery : the case of the Beauce in Quebec (Canada). International Journal of the Innovation Management,(7),67-94.

Dutta, S. , INSEAD. 2012. The global innovation index 2011: accelerating growth and development. http://www. globalinnovationindex. org/gii/main/fullreport/index. html Etzkowitz, H. , Leydesdorff, L. 2000. The dynamics of innovation: from national systems and "mode 2" to a triple helix of university-industry-government relations. Research Policy, (29),109-123.

Europe Union. 2010. *Summary of Document: Europe* 2020 *Flagship Initiative -Innovation Union*.

Furman J. , Porter, M. , Stern, S. 2002. The determinants of national innovative capacity. *Research Policy*, (31), 99-933.

Hu, C. ,Mathews, A. 2005. National innovative capacity in east Asia. Research Policy, (9), 1322-1349.

Information ,Technology and Innovation Foundation, and the Cauffman Foundation. 2012. *The Global Innovation Index*.

INSEAD Bussiness School, Conference of Indian Industries. 2009. *The Global Innovation Index* 2008-2009.

OECD. 1992. *Oslo Manual: The Measurement of Scientific and Technological Activities, Proposed Guidelines for Collecting and Interpreting Technological Innovation Data*. Paris: OECD Publishing.

OECD. 1997. *Science , Technology and Industry: Score Board of Indicators*. Paris: OECD Publishing.

Schubert, T. ,Neuhäusler, P. , Frietsch, R. , et al. 2011. Innovation Indicator Methodology Report,15-20.

Song, H. 2013. China's national innovation system toward an innovative country. In Carayamis, E. Campbell, D. (edt). *Springer Encyclopedia on Creativity, Invention, Innovation, and Entrepreneurship*. London: Springer press.

Song, H.; MU, R., REN, Z. 2012. Thinking on policies for regional innovation capacity building basing on the Entropy model, *Science of Science Study*, 30(3), 372-379.

Talberth, J., Bohara, K. 2006. Economic openness and green GDP. *Ecological Economics, Elsevier*, 58(4), 743-758.

Weitzman, L. 1976. On the welfare significance of national product in a dynamic economy. *The Quarterly Journal of Economics*, 90(1), 156-162.

Xue, P. 2009. Study on the regional innovation capacity evaluation and it's enhancement mechanisms. *Harbin Institute of Technology, Doctoral Thesis*.

Author

Dr. Song Hefa is an associate professor of the Institute of Policy and Management of Chinese Academy of Sciences. He received his Ph. D. degree from the Institute of Policy and Management of the Chinese Academy of Sciences in 2007 and his master degree from school of public and policy management of Tsinghua University in 2004. His research areas include innovation policy and intellectual property right. He has been a Chinese patent attorney for more than 15 years focusing on software and communication technologies.

Dr. Song has completed lots of innovation and intellectual property right projects for SIPO and CAS. He also participated the 12th five-year plan for innovation capacity construction and strategic emerging industries development and some key research projects of innovation policy. Dr. Song has published more than 30 papers in peer-reviewed journals and important conferences. He has published one book with the title "the Self-Dominated Innovation Capacity Construction and the Intellectual Property Right Development: from the view of Chinese hi-tech industry".

10

Are Regional Clusters Necessary for Innovation? Case of German Wind Turbine Innovation Clusters

Zou Xiuping, Frank Marscheider-Weidemannb

10.1 Introduction

The fourth *Assessment Report of the United Nations' Intergovernmental Panel on Climate Change* confirmed that the Earth's climate is changing as a result of human activities, particularly from fossil energy use(IPCC,2007). There is a range of climate-friendly energy options that could be implemented over the next 20 years to help reduce greenhouse gas(GHG)emissions. Significant global business opportunities will result from the near term potential for energy efficiency and renewable energy and related new industries, their business earning capacity, and their high employment potential(Sims,2004). Among the climate-friendly technologies, especially renewable energy technologies are receiving high interest as a new business opportunity and as backbone of a sustainable energy system. Governments around the world are placing considerable faith in these technologies as important technologies for reducing energy related environmental problems, particularly CO_2 emissions (Gross et al., 2003). Among the renewable energy technologies, wind energy technologies have remarkably been experiencing fast expansion worldwide. According to the data from World Wind Energy Association(WWEA), in the year 2010, the wind capacity reached worldwide 196,630 MW, after 159,050 MW in 2009, 120,903 MW in 2008, and 93,930 MW in 2007(Figure 10.1). The turnover of the wind sector worldwide reached € 40 billion

($ 55 billion) in 2010, after € 50 billion ($ 70 billion) in the year 2009. By the end of the year 2010, about 670,000 persons were employed worldwide directly and indirectly in the various branches of the wind sector. Within five years, the number of jobs almost tripled, from 235,000 in 2005. There is an increasing demand for a very broad range of jobs, from engineers, skilled workers to mangers, financial, environmental and legal experts(WWEA, 2011).

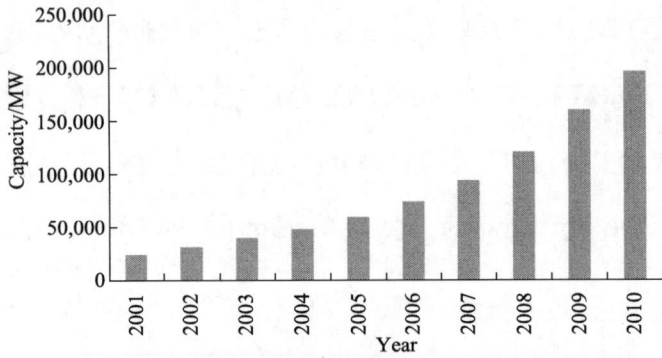

Figure 10.1 World total installed capacity since 2001
Source: WWEA(2011)

With the background of global rapid development and utilization of wind energy, the technologies of wind energy experienced fast upgrading and showed strong dynamic of innovation. The patent of wind turbine technology, for instance, has been impressive increasing since late 1990s(Figure 10.2).

Modern wind energy technology is thought originated from North America, but got fast catching up for European countries for example Germany, Denmark and so on (Figure 10. 3). The innovation-friendly policies and well-established regional innovation network was considered as key elements for such rapid development because innovation is increasingly accepted as a process of learning and interacting (Lundvall and Borrás, 1999). Innovation exhibits a very distinctive geographic distribution and widely observed the uneven spatial distribution(Fornahl and Brenner, 2009; Audretsch, 1998). Location and geographic space where knowledge created and diffused have become crucial factors in explaining the spatial distribute of innovation (Nijkamp et al. ,1999). Asheim and Gertler(2005) pointed out that one simply cannot understand innovation properly if one does not appreciate the central role of spatial proximity and concentration in this process.

This paper focuses on the spatial effects of innovative activities of wind turbine technology in Germany, and tries to identify the spatial distribution pattern of wind turbine technology innovative activities, to explore the mechanisms that contribute to

Part 2 Innovation Policies for Green Growth

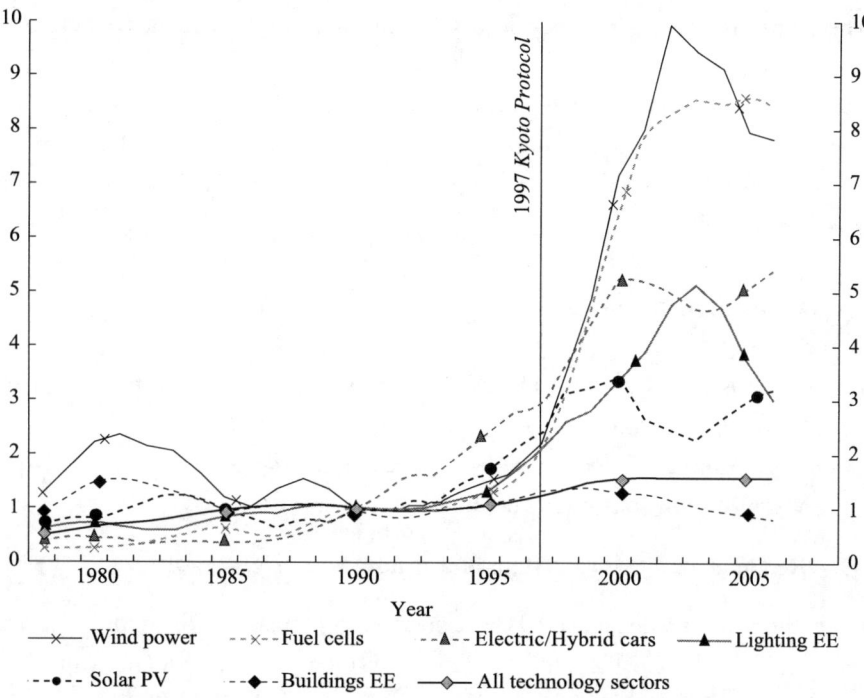

Figure 10.2 Innovation trend in climate change mitigation technologies
Source: OECD Project on Environmental Policy and Technological Innovation

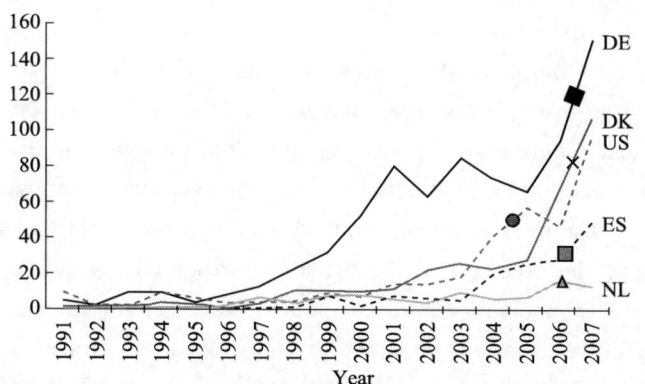

Figure 10.3 Patent dynamics of wind technology among most active nations (patent counts)
Source: Data from Fraunhofer ISI Lead Market Database

the spatial concentration of innovation activities and to discuss potential implications for policy makers who aim to foster clusters of innovation. It will provide a background for policy makers as they come to terms with understand the geographic characteristics of innovation.

The remainder of this paper is organized as follows. The next section is the theoretical background related to innovation and geographic location. In section 10.3 we introduce the data set and the methods which are employed to the analysis. Section 10.4 presents the empirical findings on the spatial clusters of the wind power technology and some explanations. Section 10.5 concludes and discusses future possible research issues.

10.2 Theoretical overview

Innovation is firstly defined by Josef Schumpeter as new combinations of new or existing knowledge, resources, equipment and so on (Schumpeter, 1934), and considered as a source of energy within the economic system which would of itself disrupt any equilibrium that might be attained.

10.2.1 Regional innovation system and innovation of geography

Over the past two decades, the most decisive contributions of innovation research that were considered are the introduction of systemic features in innovation models and the integration of non-firm actors, such as research organizations, technology transfer agents or innovation policy actors (Preissl, 2003). For example, local public research institution provides specific research and specialized training. Local industry associations may provide commercial research on foreign markets. Local governments often make much more contributions to industry-specific infrastructure. Local specialization often provides focal points for investments and new business activities. The geographical configuration of economic entities, social organizations, and government agencies plays a fundamental role in developing the innovative capabilities of innovators because innovation is produced though regional networks of innovators, local clusters and the cross-fertilizing effects of research institutions (Lundvall and Borrás, 1999). The innovation process tends to be highly localized because the networking and face-to-face interaction in the innovation process is critical to the innovation process. Even in the age of rapid communication and advanced information system, it appears that important forms of information are still best transmitted when the actors are more proximity (Enright, 2003). The informal and oral information sources are considered as the majority of the key communications about market need and technological possibilities that lead to innovation (Utterback, 1974). Moreover the specialist or industry specific information is subject to steep distance decay and that a geographically concentrated configuration allows for more interchange and exchange of such information(Goddard, 1978).

Feldman and Kogler(2010) summarized the stylized and commonly accepted facts of the importance of spatial proximity and geographic location to innovative activities from the perspective of the geography of innovation. Tacit knowledge is considered as a key determinant of the geography of innovation, which is difficult to exchange over long distance, and heavily imbued with meaning arising from the social and institutional context in which it is produced, this context-specific nature make it spatially sticky (Asheim and Gertler, 2005; Gertler, 2003). Since innovation is increasingly seen as the result of an interactive process of knowledge generation, diffusion and application(Todtling et al., 2009). Tacit knowledge was particularly emphasized in the process of innovation (Sternberg and Nigel, 2009; Asheim and Gertler, 2005; Koskinen and Vanharanta, 2002). Tacit knowledge is difficult to acquire and transfer because it is based on the experiences of individuals, resides in social relations, and is highly context and history dependent (Koskinen and Vanharanta, 2002). Action learning and informal face-to-face interaction and imitation are two ways to acquire and transfer tacit knowledge, which makes spatial proximity much more important.

10.2.2 Local clusters and knowledge spillover

Clusters were defined firstly by Michael Porter as geographically proximate group of interconnected companies and associated institutions in a particular field, linked by commonalities and complementarities(Porter, 1998). The approach of cluster is an important tool to study innovation from the perspective of spatial proximity of actors. There are a number of literatures discussing on the relationship between cluster and innovation. Regional cluster is regarded as kind of repositories for local specific knowledge stock and skills, which are of importance to the innovation. Over time, the knowledge accumulates, skills handed down from person to person, and the specific knowledge becomes common knowledge within the clusters. The geographic proximity of producers, suppliers and users can provide the short feedback loops for ideas and innovations(Enright, 2003). This is particularly important in sectors in which the interaction between the suppliers and users are crucial sources of new products or services. Regional clusters often attract sophisticated buyers from outside of the region that provide additional insights into advanced market demands, which is helpful to trace the dynamic of frontier market in order to find the right direction of innovation. Empirical studies also indicated that firms located within clusters are more innovative than firms from the same industry located elsewhere (Yang et al., 2009; Beaudry and Breschi, 2003; Baptista and Swann,1998).

Regional clusters also may give rise to knowledge spillovers and enhanced innovation (Audretsch et al., 2004; Beaudry and Breschi, 2003; Malmberg and Maskell,2002; Feldman,2000; Keeble and Wilkinson,2000). Knowledge spillovers are thought to be important to innovation by facilitating knowledge accumulation (Tappeiner et al., 2008; Bottazzi and Peri, 2003). Knowledge spillovers are intellectual gains through exchange of information without paying or less paying to the producer of the knowledge (Audretsch and Feldman, 1996; Feldman and Florida, 1994). Knowledge spillovers are geographically localized, nuanced, subtle, pervasive as well as not easily amenable to measurement (Feldman and Kogler, 2010; Fritsch and Franke,2004). Several possible mechanisms of knowledge transmission were discussed by scholars, for instance, the monitoring and imitation of competitors (Malmberg and Maskell,2002), the reading of patents or scientific articles (Jaffe et al., 1993), the setting up of spin-offs or the mobility of qualified labor (Keeble and Wilkinson,2000).

However, there is also criticism on the approach of cluster because of the vague definition of cluster. The lack of concrete definition makes it difficult to get comparable results from case to case. Therefore cluster oriented policies is not guaranteed to be success(Falck et al.,2010).

10.3 Methodology and data

In this section, both the geographical spatial model and statistic model were employed to analysis the clusters of innovation for German wind energy technologies. Here, we defined the wind energy technologies as the equipment production related to the wind electricity. Since patent is directly relevant with the technological innovation, patent data are used in this study.

10.3.1 Data sources

Patent data from German Patent and Trade Mark Office (DPMA) are used to measure the technological innovation capability in the field of wind energy in Germany. The reason for using the patents from the German Patent Office but from other patent organizations is twofold. Firstly, since inventors might file their patent at more than one patent office, selection patent data from one organization could avoid repeating. Secondly, different patent office reflects the different market which inventors want to protect their innovation or which is the most important one for them. In other words, inventors who applied to patents at the German Patent Office are affected by domestic policies much more than international ones. According to the concerns of the paper, we use the patent from DPMA. The dataset analyzed in this paper derived from Fraunhofer ISI Lead Market Database, which contains 1,019 patents granted for the 9-year period from 2000 to 2008.

The spatial analysis was conducted on the county level. There are 413 counties by the end of 2008 in Germany. While statistic analysis was conducted on the state level for the sake of the availability of related statistic data, of which there are 16 states in Germany.

10.3.2 Index of spatial concentration

There are numbers of indicators to capture the disparity among regions. The most popular indicators of course are Gini coefficient, Herfindahl index as well as Moran's I(Fornahl and Brenner, 2009; Davies, 1979). The three indicators are different in terms of spatial characteristics. Moran's I directly focuses on the effect of spatial adjacent to spatial distribution. While the Herfindahl index and Gini coefficient take regional difference into account.

10.3.2.1 Moran's I

Moran's I was developed by Moran (1950) to test the presence of spatial dependence, which is defined as follows(Anselin, 1995):

$$\text{Moran's I} = \frac{N \sum \sum W_{ij}(p_i - \bar{p})(p_j - \bar{p})}{W \sum (p_i - \bar{p})^2} \quad (i \neq j)$$

Where p_i is the patent for the region i (with the average for all regions is given by $\bar{p}$). N is the total number of regions. W_{ij} is a matrix of spatial weights that characterises geographic proximity between regions i and j (if geographic proximity, then $W_{ij} = 1$; if not, then $W_{ij} = 0$). W is the sum of the elements of matrix of the spatial weights. Moran's I ranges between -1 to 1. The larger is the absolute of Moran's I, the more activities are concentrated in a few nearby regions. Hence, a high Moran's I implies that activities are distributed across a number of regions, with these regions being located next to each other.

10.3.2.2 Gini coefficient

The Gini coefficient was first proposed by Italian statistician Gini(1955), which is a comprehensive indicator used to quantitatively analyze the income differences. Following on Wen(2004), the formula used in this study is as follows:

$$\text{Gini} = \frac{1}{2n^2 s} \sum_{r=1}^{n} \sum_{j=1}^{n} |s_j - s_r|$$

Where s_r denotes the share of patent in region r, s_j is the share of patent in region. The variable j, n is the number of regions($=413$) and $\bar{s}$ is the mean of patent shares. The Gini coefficient ranges between 0 and $1-1/n$. The more Gini coefficient closes to 0, the more equal the patents among regions are, on the contrary, it will be indicated that the more unequal among regions are.

10.3.2.3 Herfindahl-Hirschman index

The Herfindahl-Hirschman index(HHI) was developed by Herfindahl(1950) and Hirschman(1964), which is widely used to evaluate the characteristics of distribution among markets, firms and regions. In this paper, HHI is used to measure the concentration level of patents among counties. Herfindahl-Hirschman index is defined as follows:

$$\text{HHI} = \sum_{r=1}^{N} (p_r / \sum p_r)^2$$

Where p_r denotes the patents in a given region r, N is the total number of regions($=438$). The Herfindahl index ranges between 0 and 1. If HHI is close to 0, it means that there is low degree of concentration. Conversely, if it is close to 1, it means that there is high degree of concentration.

10.3.3 Hotspots detecting

Getis-Ord G_i^* is a multiplicative measure of overall spatial association of attributes which fall within a critical distance of each other. Spatial autocorrelation analysis consists of a set of statistics describing how a variable is autocorrelated through space(Hardy and Vekemans, 1999). Getis-Ord G_i^* is widely used to detect spatial clusters based on the fundamental concept of spatial autocorrelation. The following equation is used for general Getis-ord G_i^* test(Anselin, 1995).

$$G_i^* = \frac{\sum_{j=1}^{N} W_{ij} P_j - \bar{p} \sum_{j=1}^{N} W_{ij}}{\sqrt{\frac{\sum_{j=1}^{N} p_j^2 - (\bar{p})^2}{N}} \sqrt{N \sum_{j=1}^{N} W_{ij}^2 - \frac{(\sum_{j=1}^{N} W_{ij})^2}{N-1}}}$$

Where P_j is the patent for county j, W_{ij} is the spatial weight between county i and county j (if geographic proximity, then $W_{ij}=1$; if not, then $W_{ij}=0$), N is the total number of the counties. The general Getis-ord G_i^* only measures the spatial clusters and does not test the statistical significance of the obtained measurements. The Z-score of Getis-ord G_i^* provides an estimate of the statistical significance of G_i^*. For statistically significant positive Z-scores, the larger Z-score is, the more intense the clustering of high patents(hot spot), and for negative Z-scores, the smaller the Z-score is, the more intense the clustering of low patents(cold spot).

10.4 Results

10.4.1 Spatial distribution of innovative activities

The innovative activities of wind energy technology in geographic space showed two tendencies. On the one hand, the innovation activities appeared to spread on the whole country in the early sample time(Figure 10.4). On the other hand, the innovation tended to be concentrated mainly in the regions(Figure 10.5). The Lorenz Curves of patent shows the variation and inequality among counties over time. As we can see that 50 percent of counties had almost 30 percent of patents in 2002, 25 percent in 2005, and 20 percent in 2007. There is a clear spatial evolution trace that innovative activities tend to move to the center of regions such as Munich, Hamburg, Aurich, Berlin, Stuttgart and so forth, where relevant industry and institutions are well developed.

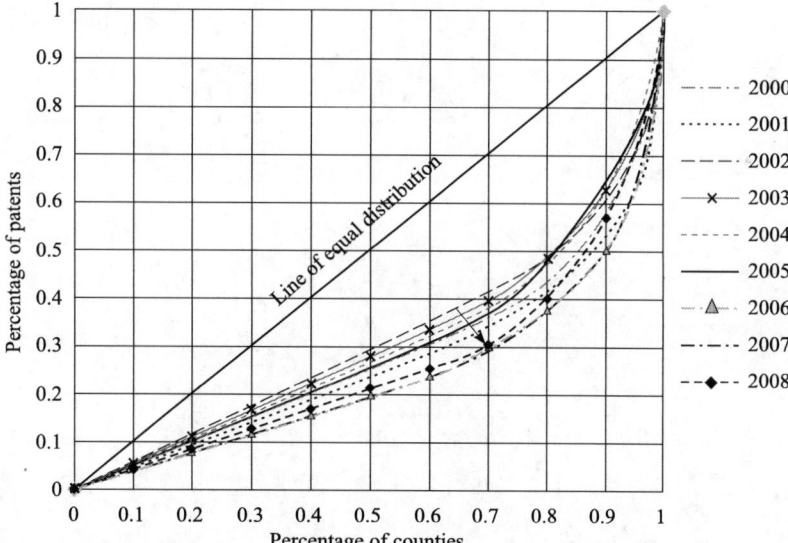

Figure 10.4　Spatial diffusion of patents of wind energy technology in German counties (Lorenz Curve)

The indexes of spatial concentration for innovation of German wind technology also show the significant concentration tendency, as showed in Table 10.1. Although there are some differences among the indexes, the similar direction of evolution was clear as showed by the indexed.

Innovation for Green Growth

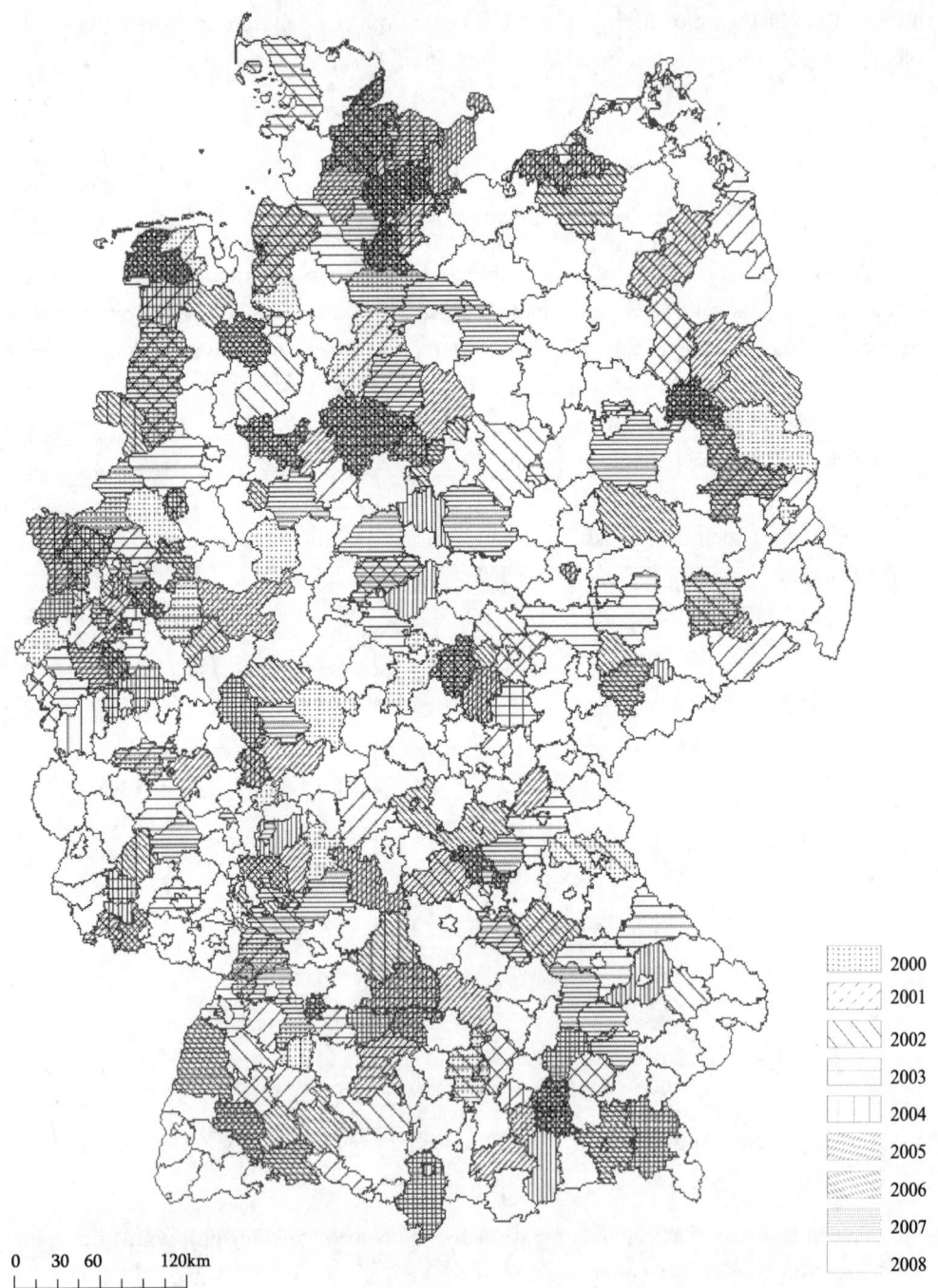

Figure 10.5 Patents for wind energy technology in 2000 to 2008

Table 10.1 The calculated concentration index at states level, 2000 to 2008

Index of concentration	2000	2001	2002	2003	2004	2005	2006	2007	2008
Moran's I	0.12	0.12	0.10	0.14	0.15	0.07	0.06	0.11	0.11
Z score	4.37	4.66	3.33	4.83	4.87	2.53	2.21	3.82	3.74
Gini coefficient	0.94	0.92	0.91	0.89	0.95	0.93	0.94	0.91	0.94
HHI	0.08	0.07	0.04	0.07	0.05	0.04	0.07	0.05	0.05

Figure 10.5 shows the spatial characteristics of patents of wind turbine technology from 2000 to 2008.

10.4.2 Clusters for innovation of wind energy technology

According to the analysis in section 10.3.3, we detected several local clusters of innovated activities, which showed in Figure 10.6. As we can see, four of six clusters were located in the north part of Germany, others were located in the south. The clusters have the clear tendency in accordance with the boundary of the states, which indicated the local interacting tends to be very important to the innovation of wind energy technology. Walz (2009) highlights that the strong production clusters in machinery have a particularly good starting point for developing renewable energy technologies because wind energy technologies generally have very close links to machinery. Indeed, the innovation activities of wind energy concentrated in the regions with strong machinery production such as Munich, Hamburg, as well as the regions with excellent special technical knowledge base and well developed technology transfer institutions such as Aurich, Berlin, Münster and Stuttgart (Figure 10.6).

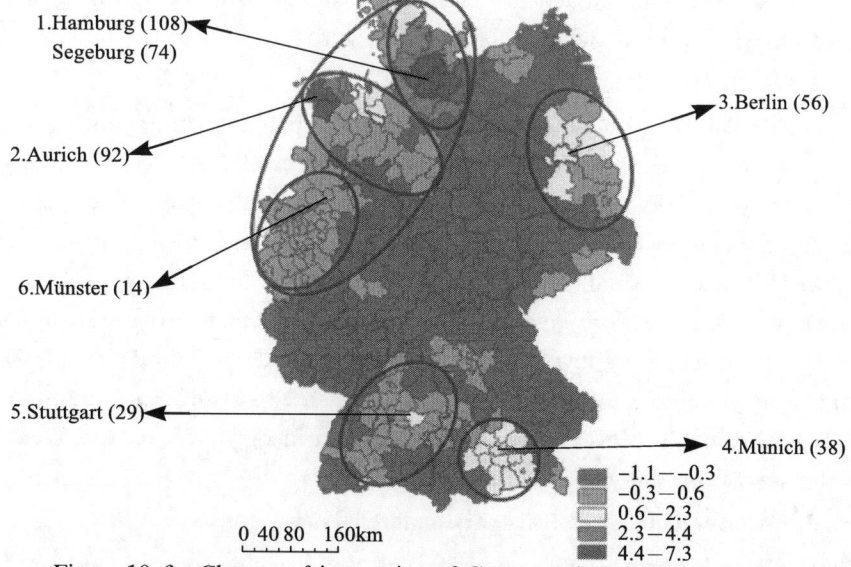

Figure 10.6 Clusters of innovation of German wind energy technology

10.4.3 The explanation for the innovation clusters

There are several factors influence innovation activities and further contribute to the clustering of innovation, which include policy and regulation framework for fostering innovation, R&D expenditure, technology diffusion and relevant industrial development. Five indicators which are selected as follows: (1) policy index by interview(5 grades and normalized); (2) accumulated wind energy generation (normalized with reported potential); (3) increase in wind energy capacity (normalized data with reported potential); (4) R&D expenditure of province on renewable resources/GDP of province(Euro/Mio Euro); (5)employees in wind energy industry in percent of all employees. Figure 10.7 shows the differences of the indicators among the states.

10.4.3.1 Policy for fostering renewable development

Development of wind energy in Europe was strongly supported by legal regulations(Michalak and Zimny, 2011). Wind energy is one of the six "European Industrial Initiatives" proposed by the European Commission to accelerate innovation and deployment of strategically important technology(Dubaric et al. ,2011). Germany has encouraged the use of wind energy since the 1970s. The major government instruments that led to the rapid diffusion of wind power capacity at the end of the 1980s consisted of: the 100/250 MW program, the feed-in law, the tax breaks, as well as the provision of low-interest loans. According to the survey made by IWR(2008), policies in Stuttgart and Munich are the best compare to other states, which could contribute to innovation of wind technologies(Figure 10.7).

10.4.3.2 R&D expenditure

R&D subsidies are one of the most common policy instruments to stimulate innovation from the technology providing side(Walz et al. 2011). In Germany, R&D support for wind energy started in 1974 with the Growian project, which later ended in 1987. With a new focus for wind energy in the mid 1980s, R&D support was resumed again. The progress of small wind turbines was proved to be more successful than large-scale ones as they were developed on the basis of engineering and shipbuilding knowledge. Knowledge spillovers did occur, in particular, small German windmill manufacturers were able to benefit from the Danish expertise(Ger Klaassen et al. , 2003). It is obvious that R&D and research program in the north part of Germany is above the average in the whole country(Figure 10.7).

10.4.3.3 Wind technology diffusion and industrial development

Lundvall and Borrás (1999) emphasized the learning process as the key to

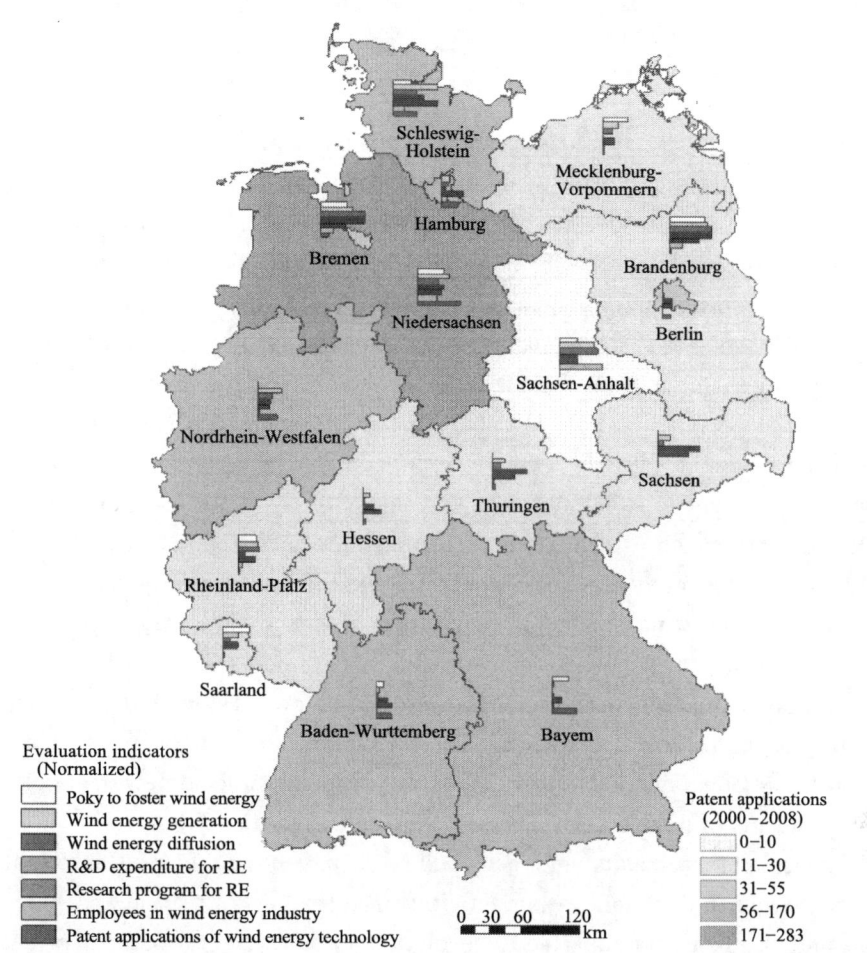

Figure 10.7 The explaining variables for clustering of wind energy technology innovation
Source: Data from IWR(2008)

successful economic and innovation. Kamp et al. (2004) investigated four types of learning processes in Denmark and Dutch, which are learning by searching, learning by doing, learning by using and learning by interacting, and argued that Denmark's success of wind turbine development benefits from learning by interacting. Just as Andersen and Lundvall (1988) pointed out that successful innovation is to a large degree dependent on close and persistent user-producer contacts. Innovation activities concentrated in Hamburg, Aurich and Berlin could be attributed to R&D programs and accumulated experience in producing and installing wind turbines(Figure 10.7).

10.5　Conclusion and discussion

In this study, we explored the innovative activities of wind energy technology in Germany and the empirical analysis indicated that innovative activities clearly concentrated on regions either with strong wind manufactures as well as wind farms such as Aurich, Hamburg or with well-established technological and regional innovation systems such as Munich, Stuttgart and Munster. We argue that policies for fostering renewable diffusion did play a crucial role on nurturing innovation in the south part of Germany as we can see from the differences of policy between the north and south part of Germany. Sternberg (1996) stated that government R&D spending generates unintended spatial effects which are far more consequential than the intended ones. In Germany, government R&D spending with implicitly spatial effects clearly outweighs the instruments, which explicitly pursue regional goals. The boundary similarity of the clusters and states imply that local interacting and knowledge spillover are important processing for the wind technology innovation. Klaassen (2003) argued that Germany benefited both from the basis of engineering and shipbuilding knowledge and sound policies gained the lead position in the innovation of wind energy technology. The nurturing of innovation clusters has become an important component of public policy both at the regional and local scale. To build and maintain local network could be one of the elements in policies that aim to nurturing the cluster of innovation.

Besides, patent counts and geo-coding of patent are helpful information to capture the dynamic of innovation activities in terms of both space and time. Patent data could also be used to analyze the evolution and the level of maturity of particular technology (Dubaric et al., 2011). Spatial autocorrelation of innovation indicator is interpreted as evidence of knowledge spillovers that spread from the place of origin to the adjacent locations and decay with distance (Tappeiner et al., 2008). Henderson (2007) pointed out that the developments in GIS and geo-coding of data have provided much better spatial information, and developments in spatial statistics and econometrics have contributed to thinking about how to specify spatial effects at different distance.

Acknowledgements

I would like to thank Prof. Rainer Walz for accepting me as a guest researcher and providing me with the appropriate and helpful guidance to conduct this study. Thanks to Dr. Christian Sartorius and Dr. Henning Kroll for helping me with the related data. Thanks also to Dr. Ulrike Tagscherer for the helpful comments.

References

Andersen, E. S., Lundvall, B. Å. 1988. Small National Systems of Innovation Facing Technological Revolutions: An Analytical Framework. London: Pinter, 9-36.

Anselin, L. 1995. Local indicators of spatial association—LISA. *Geographical Analysis*, 27(2), 93-115.

Asheim, B., Gertler, M. 2005. The Geography of Innovation. The Oxford Handbook of Innovation, 291-317.

Audretsch, D. B. 1998. Agglomeration and the location of innovative activity. *Oxford Review of Economic Policy*, 14(2), 18.

Audretsch, D. B., Feldman, M. P., et al. 2004. *Handbook of Regional and Urban Economics. Elsevier*, 4, 2713-2739.

Audretsch, D. B., Feldman, M. P. 1996. R&D spillovers and the geography of innovation and production. *The American Economic Review*, 86(3), 630-640.

Baptista, R., Swann, P. 1998. Do firms in clusters innovate more? *Research Policy*, 27(5), 525-540.

Beaudry, C., Breschi, S. 2003. Are firms in clusters really more innovative? *Economics of Innovation and New Technology*, 12(4), 325-342.

Bottazzi, L., Peri, G. 2003. Innovation and spillovers in regions: evidence from European patent data. *European Economic Review*, 47(4), 687-710.

Davies, S. 1979. Choosing between concentration indices: the iso-concentration curve. *Economica*, 67-75.

Dubaric, E., Giannoccaro, D., et al. 2011. Patent data as indicators of wind power technology development. *World Patent Information*, 33(2), 144-149.

Enright, M. J. 2003. Regional clusters: what we know and what we should know. // *Innovation Clusters and Interregional Competition*, Heidelberg: Springer 99-129.

Falck, O., Heblich, S., et al. 2010. Industrial innovation: direct evidence from a cluster-oriented policy. *Regional Science and Urban Economics*, 40(6), 574-582.

Feldman, M. P., Florida, R. 1994. The geographic sources of innovation: technological infrastructure and product innovation in the United States. *Annals of the Association of American Geographers*, 84(2), 210-229.

Feldman, M. P., Kogler, D. F. 2010. Handbook of the Economics of Innovation. *North Holland*, 1, 381-410.

Feldman, M. P. 2000. Location and innovation: the new economic geography of innovation, spillovers, and agglomeration. *The Oxford Handbook of Economic Geography*, 373-394.

Fornahl, D., Brenner, T. 2009. Geographic concentration of innovative activities in Germany. *Structural Change and Economic Dynamics*, 20(3), 163-182.

Fritsch, M., Franke, G. 2004. Innovation, regional knowledge spillovers and R&D cooperation. *Research Policy*, 33(2), 245-255.

Ger Klaassen, et al. 2003. Public R&D and innovation: the case of wind energy in Denmark, Germany and the United Kingdom. *Interim Report*.

Gertler, M. S. 2003. Tacit knowledge and the economic geography of context, or the undefinable tacitness of being (there). *Journal of Economic Geography*, 3(1), 75.

Gini, C. Ottaviani, Q, Mome, Ic. 1955. Memorie di metodologia statistica, *EV Veschi*.

Goddard, J. 1978. *Contemporary Industrialization*. London: Longman, 62-85.

Gross, R., Leach, M., et al. 2003. Progress in renewable energy. *Environment International*, 29 (1), 105-122.

Hardy, O. J., Vekemans, X. 1999. Isolation by distance in a continuous population: reconciliation between spatial autocorrelation analysis and population genetics models. *Heredity*, 83 (2), 145-154.

Herfindahl, O. C. 1950. *Concentration in the Steel Industry*. New York: Columbia University Press.

Hirschman, A. O. 1964. The paternity of an index. *The American Economic Review*, 54(5), 761-762.

IPCC. 2007. IPCC fourth assessment report. *The Physical Science Basis*.

Jaffe, A. B., Trajtenberg, M., et al. 1993. Geographic localization of knowledge spillovers as evidenced by patent citations. *The Quarterly Journal of Economics*, 108(3), 577.

Kamp, L. M., Smits, R. E. H. M., et al. 2004. Notions on learning applied to wind turbine development in the Netherlands and Denmark. *Energy Policy*, 32(14), 1625-1637.

Keeble, D., Wilkinson, F. 2000. *High-technology Clusters, Networking and Collective Learning in Europe*. Ashgate: Aldershot.

Kitchin, R., Nigel, T. 2009. *International Encyclopedia of Human Geography*. Oxford: Elsevier Science Ltd., 481-490.

Koskinen, K. U., Vanharanta, H. 2002. The role of tacit knowledge in innovation processes of small technology companies. *International Journal of Production Economics*, 80(1), 57-64.

Lundvall, B. A., Borrás, S. 1999. The globalising learning economy: implications for innovation policy. Office for Official Publications of the European Communities, 1-30.

Malmberg, A., Maskell, P. 2002. The elusive concept of localization economies: towards a knowledge-based theory of spatial clustering. *Environment and Planning A*, 34(3), 429-450.

Michalak, P., Zimny, J. 2011. Wind energy development in the world, Europe and Poland from 1995 to 2009; current status and future perspectives. *Renewable and Sustainable Energy Reviews*, 15(5), 2330-2341.

Moran, P. A. P. 1950. Notes on continuous stochastic phenomena. *Biometrika*, 37 (1/2), 17-23.

Nijkamp, P., Mills, E. S., Cheshire, P. C., et al. 1999. *Handbook of Regional and Urban Economics: Applied Urban Economics*. North Holland.

Porter, M. E. 1998. *Competitive Strategy: Techniques for Analyzing Industries and*

Competitors. Florence: Free Press.

Preissl, B. 2003. Innovation clusters: combining physical and virtual links. Discussion Papers of DIW Berlin.

Rolf, G. S. 1996. Government R&D expenditure and space: empirical evidence from five industrialized countries. *Research Policy*, 25(5), 741-758.

Schumpeter, J. A. 1934. *The Theory of Economic Development*. Cambridge: Harvard University Press, 65.

Sims, R. E. H. 2004. Renewable energy: a response to climate change. *Solar Energy*, 76(1-3), 9-17.

Tappeiner, G., Hauser, C., et al. 2008. Regional knowledge spillovers: fact or artifact? *Research Policy*, 37(5), 861-874.

Todtling, F., Lehner, P., et al. 2009. Do different types of innovation rely on specific kinds of knowledge interactions? Technovation, 29(1), 59-71.

Utterback, J. M. 1974. Innovation in industry and the diffusion of technology. Science, 183(4125), 658-662.

Vernon, H. J. 2007. Understanding knowledge spillovers. *Regional Science and Urban Economics*, 37(4), 497-508.

Walz, R. He Cfrich, N, Enzmann A. 2009. A system dynamics approach for modelling a lead-market-based export potential. Working Papers.

Walz, R., Schleich, J., Ragwitz, M., et al. 2011. *Regulation, Innovation and Wind Power Technologies—an Empirical Analysis for OECD Countries*.

Wen, M. 2004. Relocation and agglomeration of Chinese industry. *Journal of Development Economics*, 73(1), 329-347.

Yang, C. H., Motohashi, K., et al. 2009. Are new technology-based firms located on science parks really more innovative: evidence from Taiwan. *Research Policy*, 38(1), 77-85.

Author

Dr. Zou Xiuping studied the cartology and geographic information system in the Institute of Geographical Sciences and Natural Resource Research of Chinese Academy of Sciences and got her Ph. D. in 2006. Since then she has joined the Institute of Policy and Management of Chinese Academy of Sciences in the field of environmental sustainability research. In 2010, she won the Alexander von Humboldt international scholarship for climate protection, which enabled her to work as a guest researcher at the Fraunhofer Institute for System and Innovation Research in Karlsruhe. Her research focuses on environment, sustainable development, application of GIS&RS, and also on renewable energy industry clusters and technology transfer.

Part 3

Industrial Innovation for Green Growth

The Competitive Position of German and Chinese Photovoltaic Companies in International Markets

Reinhard Meckl

11.1 Introduction and research question

Renewable energies, whether photovoltaic, biomass, tidal waves or wind energy are generally regarded as high growth markets with a promising future development in technologies, revenues and hence profits. Looking at the life cycle of an industry, Photovoltaic (PV) is the most advanced one among the renewable energies. Due to a high volatility in public subsidies in lead markets like Germany or the US, the PV industry was going through several ups and downs in the last years. Nevertheless, numerous companies managed to establish a solid business model e. g. by specializing on different parts of the PV-value chain. In addition, a strong export activity from the leading players in the industry resulted in an intensive international exchange of products and investments. As a consequence a high volume international market for PV equipment was established in the last years.

Empirical evidence shows that companies especially from Germany and China were and are still playing a leading role in those international markets. Presently a consolidation in the main national markets for PV is under way mainly because of a decrease in public subsidies(e. g. in Germany) or a general surplus of capacities(e. g. in China). From a researcher's point of view it is interesting to see the way PV companies from both countries have been building up their competitive advantages and which strategies they have chosen for survival regarding the different present and upcoming conditions.

Taking that starting point the research questions for the project were based on the idea of taking a closer look at the present situation of the international PV-market with a focus on the positions of Chinese and German companies. The objective was to identify the most promising value chain allocations and strategies. This view was supposed to focus mainly on the international aspects of the business for many companies have taken significant steps to expand their activities abroad. The research question of the project consists of two parts:

(a) Which are the relevant competitive factors in PV industry and what is their status quo for German and Chinese companies?

(b) Which are the most promising internationalization strategies for German and Chinese PV companies for international markets?

Part(a) deals with the identification of the most important competitive forces in the PV market. It is mainly descriptive and explicative and is taking some aspects from the research results of comparable international product business. The focus on German and Chinese companies is supposed to reveal the competitive advantages of the leading corporations worldwide.

Part(b) is concerned with a basic objective of research in strategic management: Which (internationalization) strategies should be developed and implemented? This normative part has a strong predicting element and is supposed to reveal information and recommendations about optimal market development in the PV industry.

The project which is still work-in-progress is conducted at the chair for international management at the University of Bayreuth and was supported by Goetzpartners consultants in Munich.

11.2 The international market for PV-wafers and modules

For reaching a better understanding of the PV market it is first of all important to identify the value chain of the industry. Figure 11.1 gives an aggregate impression.

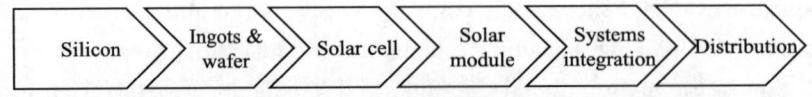

Figure 11.1 The aggregated value chain of the PV industry

The production of silicon requires quite special, more chemical knowledge. In addition, companies specializing on systems integration and distribution are not typical in their competitive forces and especially their knowledge for the PV industry but show a quite common base with other product markets. Engineering offices and trading houses are typical companies of these two value chain components. We focused on companies which are in the value chain components stretching from wafer production to producing complete solar modules.

Regarding the global market development of PV industry, an interesting constellation emerged in the last years. In 2000 – 2005 there was a first mover advantage of German photovoltaic companies with the feed-in program of the German government on the home market supplying revenues and cash for investments in production facilities and R&D paving the ground for a relatively fast internationalization of the companies. Companies from other European countries like Spain with better natural conditions for PV followed relatively slowly. The US PV companies were strongly focused on their home market with only First Solar which specialized on thin film gaining an international advantage in that technology. Relatively late but then with quite offensive strategies, Chinese newcomers to the international markets quickly reached leading positions with enormous investments in production volume and aggressive exports. Presently a global consolidation and shake out period in the industry with German and US companies suffering from a difficult strategic and cost position can be observed. Insolvencies, Mergers & Acquisitions and shut-downs are nowadays quite common in the industry.

Forecasts of PV market volumes are difficult due to the strong influence of (hardly predictable) political decisions. For example, the decision of the German federal government to strongly and quickly cut the feed-in tariffs of PV in March 2012 is probably limiting the growth of the sector in Germany in the next years. Nevertheless Figure 11.2 represents an estimation of the general development of PV regarding the regional distribution of PV in the past and the years coming.

Generally speaking, an ongoing growth of the industry is predicted being driven by both technological innovation and government sponsored increase of demand. Germany will lose relative strength as a market whereas North America and China are gaining. The crucial question will be at which time the PV-based production of energy will reach parity to the alternative production of energy e. g. by fossil or nuclear facilities. In addition, the development of other renewable resources like wind energy with their respective advantages/disadvantages to PV is a strongly influencing factor. Accordingly, the forecast of the growth rate of PV is burdened with high uncertainty.

With this background it is necessary to deeper elaborate on the development and status of companies from Germany and China in the international markets for PV in

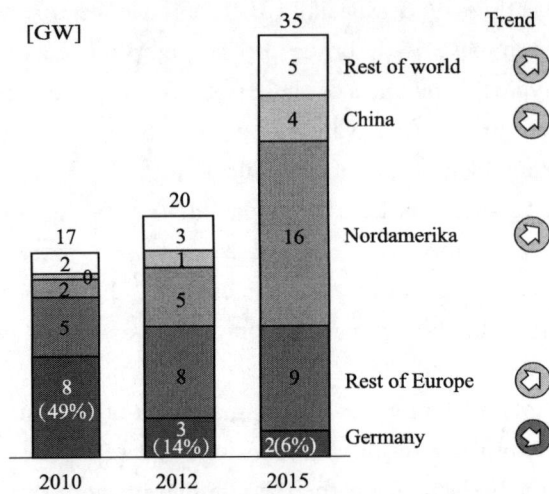

Figure 11.2 Forecast for renewable energy volume
Source: Goetzpartners renewable energy database

order to lay the basis for answering the research questions.

Until 2008 the renewable energy sector was characterized by over-proportional growth and surplus of demand. The photovoltaic sector attained a growth rate of over 45% (Fontaine et al., 2009). In most countries, demand was controlled by governments. Especially in Germany, subsidies, in the form of guaranteed feed-in tariffs, had a considerable effect. Under the umbrella of state pricing policy, German entrepreneurs very quickly emerged as providers of renewable energy systems. The PV sector, with its high growth rate, limited market risks and high profit margins, became an attractive object for capital investment.

The end of 2008 witnessed a change in these paradisiacal conditions. Due to the economic crisis, the demand for photovoltaic facilities sank in Germany and other countries. The huge capacity expansion in the PV sector in the years 2008 – 2010 led to overcapacity. Increasing competition by cheaper manufacturers in Asia heightened the competitive intensity. As a result, component prices fell. Since this meant increased yield at the operating facilities, politicians strove to reduce the guaranteed purchasing price (Mrusek, 2010; Murphy et al., 2010). Reducing the feed-in tariffs inevitably leads to a fall in demand. The PV sector was therefore moving over to a more challenging market with higher competitive intensity. With ongoing cuts in feed-in tariffs and their consequences on demand and prices, the difficult situation has prevailed up to now.

As a consequence future growth of PV will shift outside Germany to the USA and

Asia (Figure 11.2). The forthcoming subsidy cuts and market saturation tendency will mean that the PV sector in Germany will reach a below-average growth by international standards, growth most likely can be realized for German companies by foreign market expansion.

Against this background, future prospects for the German PV sector are indeed heterogeneous. Whereas many leading companies already have solid quotas abroad, small- and medium-sized companies operating in the PV industry serve foreign markets only sporadically or focus on fewer markets. The result is high economic dependency on a very few markets. Thus the turnover of many medium-sized photovoltaic companies, recently booming in the Spanish market, has fallen drastically as a result of the sudden subsidy caps. The risk issue is pushing several domestic companies further into internationalization to diminish dependency and spread the risks. Larger companies also reflect considerable shortcomings with regard to internationalization. Especially the cost position of those players may be a severe burden for entering foreign markets with view to compensating the decrease in volume in the German home market.

With this development in mind, the questions of which strategy to choose or whether the implemented internationalization strategies are able to cope with those problems are gaining a central importance. So it is to be verified whether the strategies of leading German PV companies, who in the past served the foreign market primarily as exporters, leaving the market potential untapped through a somewhat defensive internationalization policy, will have enough potential to further drive the international expansion. Others expanded considerably in a "one-fits-all" strategy by opening sales companies in most diverse countries. As a result of inadequate competencies and resources and inefficient market strategies, they withdrew from many foreign markets. With regard to the urgency for cost reducing off-shore production in Asia only few companies in the PV sector in Germany already have ventured this promising step.

Regarding the Chinese side, the investors, supported by regional state policy, built up new production facilities thus realizing economies of scale which they intended to use for further expanding their market share in the high volume PV markets like Germany. The production of wafers and modules is a typical example of standardized mass production. Thus this business is predestined for Chinese PV companies which were able to profit from their ability to realize economies of scale and provide competitive technology at prices which were lower than those of most foreign competitors. In addition the ample experience of Chinese companies in successfully accessing foreign markets via export led to a leading position of Chinese in the world PV markets. This success war realized although the expansion of PV-based energy production in China for quite a long time lagged behind the growth ratios of other countries for lack of extensive government subsidies. Nevertheless due to the strong dependence on the development of foreign markets the Chinese PV industry is also concerned by the stagnation e. g. in Europe and is also going through a consolidation period with a distinctly slower expansion of capacities and a shake-up of industry structures.

11.3　Conceptual framework of the study—the GAINS concept

11.3.1　Theoretical grounding: basics of the GAINS concept

For being able to answer the research questions (see section 11.1) it is necessary to employ a sound theoretical basis for the analysis. The Growth and Income Securities (GAINS) approach is suitable as a theoretical basis for the derivation of hypotheses with a view to developing international strategies. It presents a specification of the configuration theory in the field of international management research (Macharzina and Engelhard, 1991). Contrary to alternative theories, e. g. the situational theory or contingency theory, the configuration theory—and with it the GAINS approach—can be of considerable benefit with regard to methodology, content and conception. The weaknesses of the configuration system (Meckl, 2000; Henselek, 1996; Meyer et al., 1993; Miller and Friesen, 1984) are thus considerably compensated. The configuration system is particularly suitable for research into foreign marketing, since, by way of its multidimensional research design, it can embrace the multifarious complexity of internationalization, with the interaction of corporate environment, features and strategy (Meckl, 2000; Macharzina and Engelhard, 1991).

Defining the respective configurations is fundamental to establishing a configuration system. Configurations represent groups of homogeneous companies with common characteristics in both internal and external operations (Miller and Friesen, 1984; Miller, 1981). Configurations are defined as "any multidimensional constellation of conceptually distinct characteristics that commonly occur together. Numerous dimensions of environments, industries, processes, practices, beliefs, and outcomes have been said to cluster into configurations, archetypes or gestalts" (Meyer et al., 1993). The observed "sets" (Meckl, 2000), with typical configuration features, present a multidimensional, interdependent relationship which can change in due course(Scherer and Beyer, 1998; Doty and Glick, 1994; Miles and Snow, 1984). The objective for configuration theory is to find configurations which, by way of their main, coherent, external and internal features belong to the "fit" category(Doty et al., 1993). The search for fit constellations lies in the assumption that these are particularly successful (Meckl, 2000; Roth, 1992; Khandwalla, 1973; Lawrence and Lorsch, 1976). The complex configuration of a company, as a coordinated interaction of resources, competencies, strategies and environmental characteristics, can thus postulate a focal competitive advantage(Miller and Whitney, 1999; Black and Boal, 1994), which bears a far greater potential influence than individually observed competence and resource profiles(Miller and Whitney, 1999).

Macharzina und Engelhard have applied the configuration system, with use of the GAINS approach, at an international level(Macharzina and Engelhard, 1991). Many other authors have availed themselves of the GAINS approach and applied it to international management research (Strothe, 2006; Meckl, 2000; Bufka, 1997; Roth, 1992; Roth et al., 1991). Analogous to the general definition of configuration theory, with their application to the international environment and search for suitable internationalization strategies, the objective is to identify suitable configurations with matched corporate and environmental features. According to the underlying assumptions, a so-called "fit" is generally an indication that the success potential of an internationalization strategy is relatively high(Macharzina and Engelhard, 1991).

The basic question then is, how the "fit" is determined or in other words: Which internationalization strategy would be the most promising one for, in our case, a PV company. The ultimate result will be provided by the empirical research. Nevertheless it is necessary to develop hypotheses in the framework of the GAINS approach which will allow a verification/falsification of the respective statements. For the objective of this study, the competence-based view is suggested as an adequate tool.

11.3.2 The competence-based view

Corporate strategy decision-making is influenced by diverse factors. As a theoretical basis and creation of internal variables for strategic decision-making, the classical resource-based view is used(Barney, 1991; Grant, 1991 Prahalad and Hamel, 1990; Wernerfelt, 1984;). The competence-based view—a recent theory—evolved from the discussions governing the resource-based view, and, as a conceptional extension of the resource-based view, is thus preferred. Discussions concerning the resource-based view, with its strengths and weaknesses, are for example outlined by Foss(1997), Priem and Butler(2001), Lynch(2009) and Wolf(2008).

In the competence-based view, as already conceived in the resource-based view, competences present a special form of resources and are necessary for the efficient deployment of tangible and intangible assets(Burr et al.,2005;Hall,1993). The most significant distinguishing feature of the resource-based view lies in the causal chain of the competitive advantage rationale(Freiling,2004). The resource-based view requires that the tangible and intangible assets be distributed asymmetrically as resources for the development of competencies, which, by way of varying manifestations, imply performance variations(Grant,1991). In the competence-based view, on the other hand, competencies represent the first link in the causal chain of competitive advantage. Competencies represent goal-oriented, sustainable knowledge and empirically-based,mostly collective,handling potential,which,as market potentials, have to be strictly separated from resources(Freiling,2001). Competences are based on the individual knowledge of individual persons in a company, since the entire company is to be perceived as an interactive network of individuals(Hayek,1952). The learning process of the individual is important in the development of competences, since knowledge is generated through learning(Lierow,2006). The next stage is the integration of individual knowledge, important for collective competencies, whereby individual knowledge is fine-tuned and coordinated for the purpose of common usage(Grant,1991; Prahalad and Hamel,1990). Only when the company possesses relevant competencies, it is able to generate competitive advantages by means of refinement of market available inputs for company-specific resources (Lierow, 2006; Freiling, 2001). The underlying terminology governing the competence-based view is also different to that one used in the resource-based view. In the competence-based view, e.g. the word "resources" is not a collective term for the most varied assets of a company. Instead, resources may only be referred to as such, if they have a market potential in the form of sustainable competitive advantages (Freiling et al., 2005). Strategic decision-making is governed by competences and generated skills.

The competence-based view therefore presents a theory with an explanatory potential which focuses on the entire company levels(Lierow,2006). If the basic definition of the competence-based view is transferred to internationalization, then companies should orientate the internationalization according to type, scope and time towards the available competences and resulting skills. Therefore competences, and not resources, are first and foremost that ones which influence the form and subsequent success of internationalization. This can serve as a guideline for foreign market strategies in general and can be postulated for the PV sector as well.

11.4 Internationalization of PV companies and the GAINS-approach

As explained above, the basic idea is that the resource/competence-profile of a company in connection with the market constellation determines the probability of success of internationalization strategies. Figure 11.3 illustrates the conceptual idea of this study for the PV market.

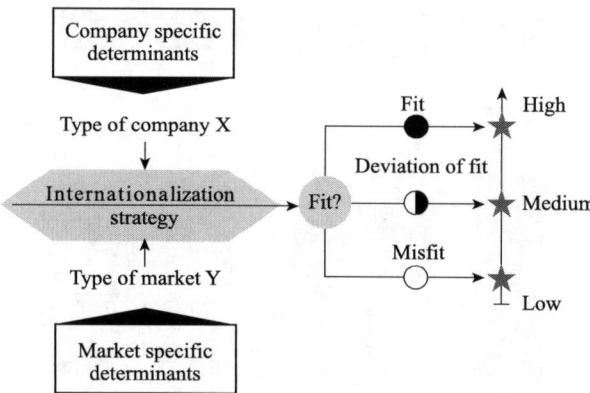

Figure 11.3 The "fit" between company specificities and the market

A "fit" would characterize the most promising strategies. A "misfit" shows that the competences are not adequate for the chosen strategy. The result "deviation of fit" would imply that adequate competences are basically present for a chosen strategy and they are partially employed but not used in their entire potential.

For deriving hypotheses, the next step would be to determine the competences and the market constellations in more detail. Regarding the competences, a useful approach is to define types of companies according to the specification of important influencing variables. These variables must be chosen with respect to the specificities of the international PV markets i. e. they must represent the relevant factors of competence of a PV firm. We selected the production capacity/location, the organizational maturity, the marketing/distribution and the technological/innovation capabilities(Meckl and Olbert,2011).

The production capacity/location is a representative mainly for the cost position of the PV companies. The main cost factors in the industry are the production costs which again are determined by labor costs and financing costs to a large extent. Both components are expected to give the Chinese firms a lead in that variable with cheap banking loans and labor at hand. The situation in this respect is more difficult for German firms. Their main production locations are situated in Germany which is not famous for low production costs in standardized mass production due to wages and regulations for production sites. German companies have been quite slow regarding the build-up of international production capacity. In the present consolidation they even close down such sites as Solarworld has done. As a consequence, German PV companies show a worse cost position in comparison to the Chinese competitors (Figure 11.4).

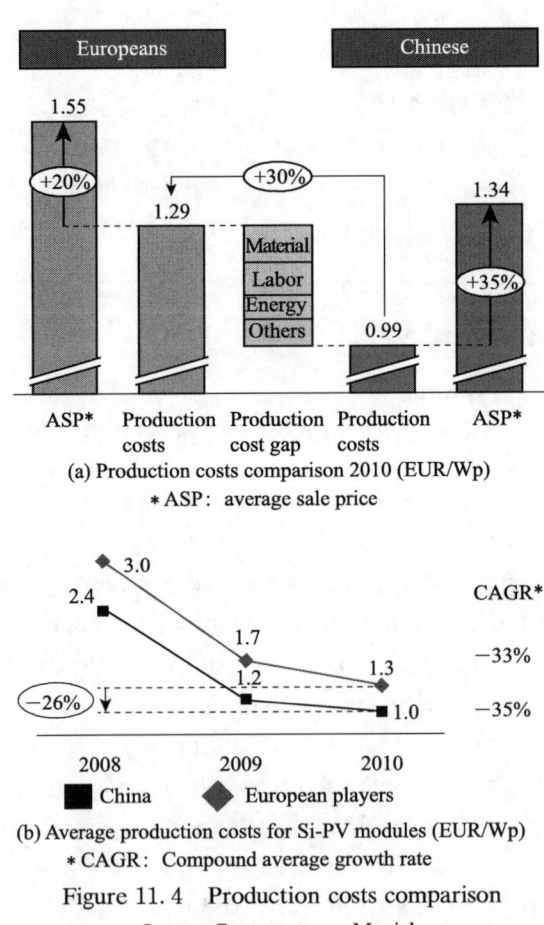

Figure 11.4 Production costs comparison

Source: Goetzpartners, Munich

The organizational maturity of a company is mainly determined by its abilities in managing the value chain and the organizational efficiency. Competitive pressure and learning effects in the life cycle of a company lead to an increase in process efficiency. E. g. a shorter time-to-market of new products or a higher degree of flexibility in production or distribution are the consequences which may be expected. Regarding the early entry into PV markets and the subsequent early mover advantages German companies tend to show quite a high level of organizational maturity with Chinese companies quickly catching up in this respect. Figure 11.5 illustrates the idea.

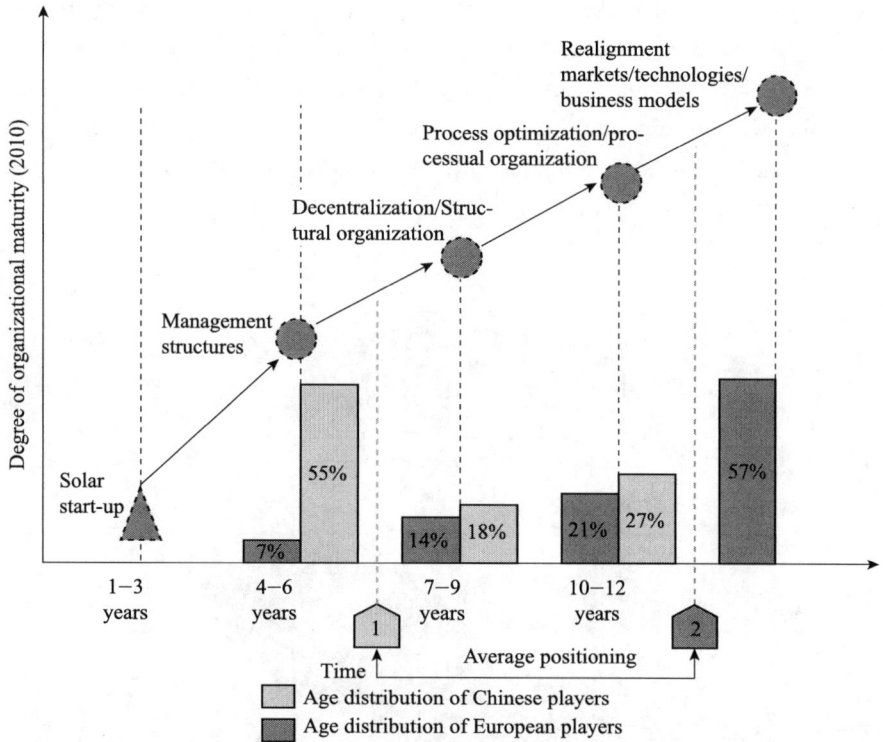

Figure 11.5　Organizational maturity of German and Chinese PV companies
Source: Goetzpartners, Munich

On the marketing/distribution side the relevant factors for the PV sector are heterogeneous. Very important in almost all product businesses is brand reputation. The quality/price-relationship being connected to a brand name is in foreign markets still more important than at home. German and Chinese companies have been able to establish a quite good reputation in that field. Especially Chinese suppliers managed to increase their brand awareness level and their reputation by strongly investing in marketing campaigns abroad. Besides brand reputation "classical" factors like customer service or the distance to the main regional markets are of importance(See Figure 11.6(a)). For larger PV projects the ability to plan, structure and implement such projects is of crucial importance for customers. Having numerous reference projects abroad German companies seem to have a lead in this factor(See Figure 11.6 (b)). One aspect which is often neglected is the "bankability". PV projects, especially the larger ones from investors, are normally leveraged for increasing the yield on equity. For that, a certain percentage of loans, which may be up to 80%, are acquired mainly from banks. Banks take the modules for securing their loans. It is important for banks to have a high probability of resale of the modules which also depends on the manufacturer of the modules. Generally banks tend to prefer local PV suppliers and for years this was an important argument for German PV companies for convincing potential customers. In the last years due to the market consolidation and the gain in reputation of the Chinese firms this seems to have changed.

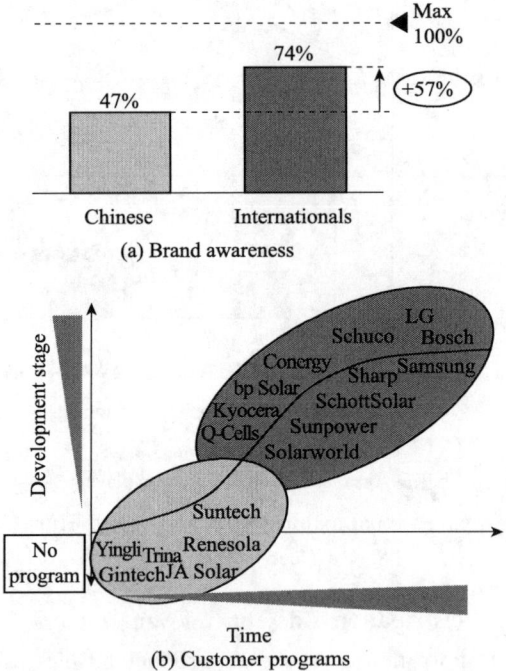

Figure 11.6　Marketing competence of German and Chinese companies

Source: Goetzpartners, Munich

A central objective for all suppliers, as mentioned above, is the reaching of parity with other energy sources. Driving down production costs of modules is one aspect which will probably not be enough to match the other sources. Inevitably, technological progress and innovation in the efficiency of energy being converted from sun by the modules must be drastically increased. So the innovative capabilities are central for PV companies for the long range survival. Since this is a dynamic development it is hard to say which companies are in the lead but the leading suppliers from both China and Germany are heavily investing in their R&D for reaching further technological breakthroughs.

Taking these factors we defined three different types of companies within the GAINS framework: the cost-leading, the technology-driven and the market-focused PV companies.

The second thing is to identify and categorize regional market types (Figure 11.3). We defined three categories: The "sleepers" are regional or national markets with basically advantageous natural conditions which are in PV markets of course the duration of sun hours in a given period of time. Despite these favorable conditions the installed base and especially the forecasted growth rate of the PV market are very low and usually demand is only generated by small-scale, private customers. The reason for this is mainly the lack of government sponsored programs for promoting PV.

The "potential markets" are also having favorable natural conditions. But in contrast to the sleepers government programs have been announced or have just been installed. High growth rates and demand also from large-scale investors are expected.

The last category is the "core markets". Government programs which are running for quite a long time have led to a large installed base and created a high volume market with large players from the supplier and the demand side being present on a differentiated market.

Figure 11.7 gives some hints on where which categories of markets will be located. USA and Japan will become core markets with China showing a high potential. Regarding the current development it would probably be a good idea to define a "post-peak" market, i.e. a regional market in which the volume is decreasing with government programs being cut back and the parity not being reached yet. But since the downsizing strategies in international markets follow quite different rules this category is not taken into account in this study. Another possibility would be to categorize markets according to the dominant customers which could be small privates, large investors or governments. But there is no evidence that the important players in the international markets have exclusively focused on specific customer groups so this aspect is given up in favor of the above mentioned categorization.

Having defined the sets of variables it is now possible to formulate the hypotheses for the successful internationalization strategies in PV industry. Figure 11.8 gives a graphical illustration of the hypotheses.

The types of strategies we used are taken from the basic possibilities of entering

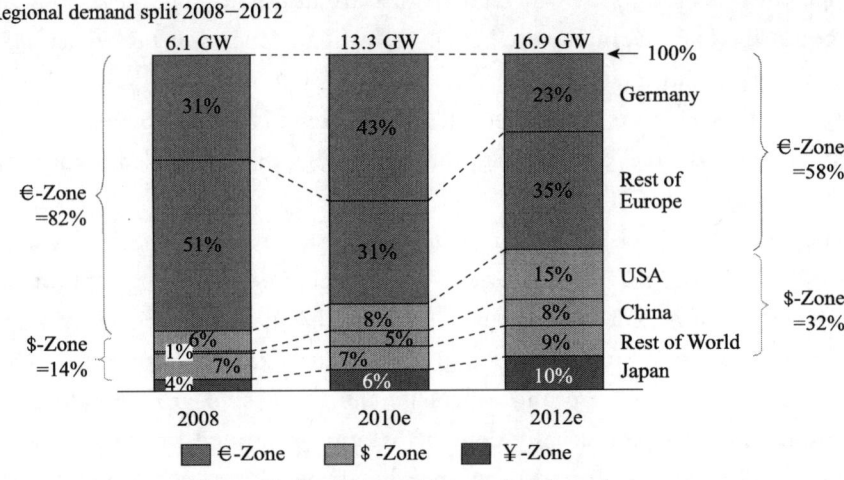

Figure 11.7 Categorizing regional markets
Source: Goetzpartners, Munich

Market types

		Sleepers	Potential markets	Core markets
Company types	Technology driven	Do-nothing	Do-nothing	Cooperation/JVs
	Cost leading	Export	Export cooperation	Greenfield/M&A
	Market oriented	Export	Greenfield (low scale)	Greenfield/M&A

Figure 11.8 Tentative "fit combinations" for internationalization strategies in PV industry

and working in a foreign market which are exports as the least committing strategy, cooperations with partners which also include joint ventures(JVs) and the do-it-alone strategies of greenfield investments or Mergers & Acquisitions (M&A) (for details concerning the entry modes see Meckl, 2010). Of course there is always the alternative to not work in a market which is represented by the do-nothing strategy.

The hypotheses are represented by the assignment of those basic internationalization strategies to combinations of company-market types. The hypotheses would for example read:

"A technology-driven PV company should work in a foreign core market with the help of cooperation or JVs for maximizing the probability of success in that market."

(compare the combination in the square top right in Figure 11.4)

Or another one would be:

"A market-oriented PV company should work in potential markets with a greenfield investment which is giving the possibility to quickly expand the processed volume in that market."(compare the combination in the middle square in lower row in Figure 11.4)

Where are the assignments taken from? Basically we used plausible argumentation from theoretical background and/or profited from empirical studies from other product businesses and their related internationalization strategies which had to be adapted to the PV constellation. This more or less heuristic approach is quite typical for GAINS-based studies for generating testable hypotheses. The reasoning for the two hypotheses formulated above is exemplified.

From a competence-based point of view a technology-driven company is strong in quickly innovating and developing new products with new technological features e.g. for specific customer groups or basic innovations. This internal capability is not matched by a fully developed and widespread distribution system and/or a highly developed brand name in the foreign markets. In extreme cases there may even be a lack of competences to establish such systems. In addition the cost aspect is not a central skill of a technology-driven company. Taking those strengths and weaknesses, the recommendable internationalization strategy would be a cooperation or JV. The main reason for that is the access to complementary competences of a potential partner company which is able to provide local marketing skills and distribution capacities as well as general knowledge about the market. This partner will normally come from the foreign market which is to be dealt with. A contract-based cooperation could include licenses and the transfer of know-how to the foreign partner. A JV is a vehicle with a higher degree of engagement due to the involvement of equity(a detailed discussion of the advantages and risks of cooperation and JVs can be found in Meckl,2010).

The recommendation for the market-oriented company for a potential market would be different. Basically this company is able to build up a distribution system abroad and capable of implementing a promising marketing strategy. Furthermore it is able to profit from a good brand reputation. Potential markets do not show high growth rates yet. So it is not yet necessary to invest large amounts of capital for the marketing and the distribution. The investment should enable the company to quickly react once the government programs would fan demand or other variables make the market grow. Since there is a good chance that the potential market would transform into a core market, a do-it-alone strategy would allow the company to build up and profit from a strong position in a high-volume market.

11.5 Preliminary empirical results and what is left to do

First results for German companies are already derived. Figure 11.9 is graphically illustrating the combinations we found for German PV companies.

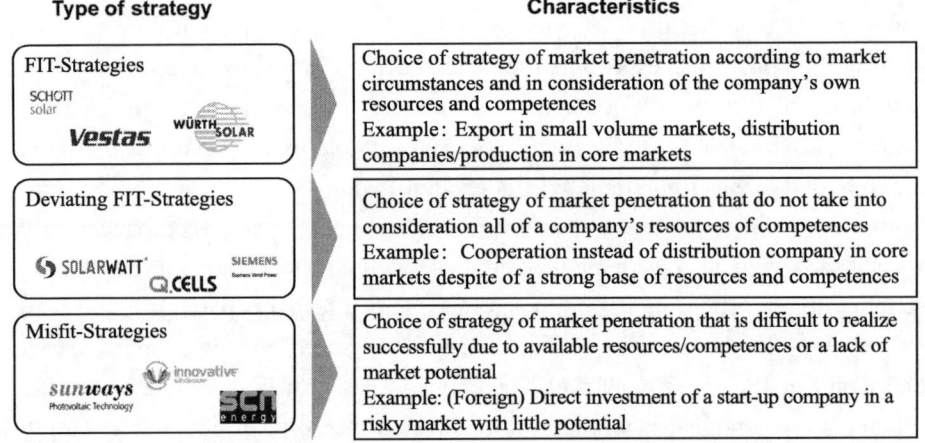

Figure 11.9 GAINS-based combinations: First empirical results

Sunways(see misfit-strategies) has recently been taken over by LDK Solar which is one of the leading Chinese PV suppliers. From the interviews and the data we collected we got the impression that many of the internationalization strategies were "emergent strategies" which means that no really planned moves were behind it but the management reacted quite spontaneously to opportunities they recognized. Building on these first results the next steps would be:

Generating of empirical data for markets and especially for Chinese players for also identifying the relevant combinations analogous to the German companies. Furthermore the data on the German companies has to be kept topical since the consolidation process may cause changes in the data.

Elaboration on statistical methods for evaluating the data and testing of the fit-hypotheses. In addition, a sharper formulation of the framework model and the GAINS derived hypotheses would give more accurate ways of interpretation.

Definition and measuring of a success related variable for being able to evaluate the empirically identified fit- and misfit-strategies with view to their financial success. An adequate measure and ratio for the success has to be determined and the respective data has to be generated.

Furthermore the wind energy market seems to be an equally interesting industry with also a consolidation going on with other players and different regional focus points. A study in this industry could also give interesting insights(see the position of Vestas in Figure 11. 9 as a first example).

The procedure should illuminate internationalization strategies of German and Chinese PV companies and allow the answering of the research questions.

References

Barney, J. 1991. Firm resources and sustained competitive advantage. *Journal of Management*, 17(1), 99-120.

Black, J. A. , Boal, K. 1994. Strategic resources: traits, configurations and paths to sustainable competitive advantage. *Strategic Management Journal*, 15(Summer Issue), 131-148.

Bufka, J. 1997. *Auslandsgesellschaften Internationaler Dienstleistungsgesellschaften*. Wiesbaden: Koordination-Kontext-Erfolg.

Burr, W. , Musil, A. , Stephan, M. , et al. 2005. *Unternehmensführung*. München: Vahlen Franz Gmbh.

Doty, D. H. , Glick, W. H. , Huber, G. 1993. Fit, equifinality, and organizational effectiveness: a test of two configurational theories. *Academy of Management Journal*, 36(6), 1196-1250.

Doty, D. H. , Glick, W. H. 1994. Typologies as a unique form of theory building: toward improved understanding and modeling. *Academy of Management Review*, 19(2), 230-251.

Fontaine, B. , Fraile, D. , Latour, M. , et al. 2009. *Global Market Outlook for Photovoltaics until 2013*. Brüssel: European Photovoltaic Industry Association.

Foss, N. J. 1997. The resource-based perspective: an assessment and diagnosis of problems. Druid Working Paper, 97(1), 1-38.

Freiling, J. 2004. A competence based theory of the firm. *Management Revue*, 15(1)27-52.

Freiling, J. , Gersch, M. , Goeke, C. 2005. Grundlagen einer "Competence-based Theory of the Firm". Arbeitsberichte des Instituts für Unternehmensführung, Ruhr-Universität Bochum, Arbeitspapier 100.

Freiling, J. 2001. *Resource-based View und Ökonomische Theorie*. Wiesbaden: Gabler Verlag.

Grant, R. M. 1991. The resource-based theory of competitive advantage: implications for strategy formulation. *California Management Review*, 33(3), 114-135.

Hall, R. 1993. A framework linking intangible resources and capabilities to sustainable competitive advantage. *Strategic Management Journal*, 14(8), 607-618.

Hayek, F. A. 1952. *Individualismus und Wirtschaftliche Ordnung*. Erlenbach-Zürich.

Henselek, H. F. 1996. *Das Management von Unternehmenskonfigurationen*. Wiesbaden: Gabler Verlag.

Khandwalla, P. N. 1973. Viable and effective organizational designs of firms. *Academy of Management Journal*, 16(3), 481-495.

Lawrence, P. R., Lorsch, J. W. 1976. *Organization and Environment: Managing Differentiation and Integration*. Boston: Harvard Business School Press.

Lierow, M. A. 2006. *Competence-Building und Internationalisierungserfolg*. Wiesbaden.

Lynch, R. 2009. *Strategic Management*. 5th ed. Harlow: Prentice Hall.

Macharzina, K., Engelhard, J. 1991. Paradigm shift in international business research: from partist and eclectic approaches to the GAINS paradigm. *Management International Review*, 31(Special Issue), 23-43.

Meckl, R. 2000. *Controlling im Internationalen Unternehmen*. München: Vahlen Verlag.

Meckl, R. 2010. *Internationales Management*. München.

Meckl, R., Olbert, S. 2011. *Strategische Erfolgsfaktoren: Vom heimischen Markt zur Internationalisierung*. Beitrag auf dem Business Forum Renewables, München: Vahlen Verlag.

Meyer, A., Tsui, A., Hinings, C. 1993. Configurational approaches to organizational analysis. *Academy of Management Journal*, 36(6), 1175-1195.

Miles, R. E., Snow, C. C. 1984. Fit, failure and the hall of fame. *California Management Review*, 26(3), 10-28.

Miller, D., Friesen, P. H. 1984. *Organizations: a Quantum View*. Englewood Cliffs: Prentice Hall.

Miller, D. 1981. Toward a new contingency approach: the search for organizational gestalts. *Journal of Management Studies*, 18(1), 1-26.

Miller, D., Whitney, J. O. 1999. Beyond strategy: configuration as a pillar of competitive advantage. *Business Horizon*, 42(3), 5-17.

Mrusek, K. 2010. Das ende der traumrenditen auf dem dach. *Frankfurter Allgemeine Zeitung*.

Murphy, M., Stratmann, K., Weishaupt, G. 2010. Minister Röttgen setzt Solarbranche zu. Handelsblatt.

Prahalad, H., Hamel, G. 1990. The core competence of the corporation. *Harvard Business Review*, 68(3), 79-91.

Priem, R. L., Butler, J. E. 2001. Is the resource-based "view" a useful perspective for strategic management research? *Academy of Management Review*, 26(1), 22-40.

Roth, K. 1992. International configuration and coordination archetypes for medium sized firms in global industries. *Journal of International Business Studies*, 23(3), 533-549.

Roth, K., Schweiger, D. M., Morrison, A. J. 1991. Global strategy implementation at the business unit level: operational capabilities and administrative mechanisms. *Journal of International Business Studies*, 22(3), 369-402.

Scherer, A. G., Beyer, R. 1998. Der konfigurationsansatz im strategischen management—rekonstruktion und kritik. *Die Betriebswirtschaft*, 58(3), 332-347.

Strothe, D. 2006. *Identifikation und Bewertung der Konfigurationen Internationaler Marktein- und Marktaustrittsentscheidungen junger Technologieunternehmen*. Frankfurt am Main: Peter Lang Verlag.

Wernerfelt, B. 1984. A resource-based view of the firm. *Strategic Management Journal*, 5(2), 171-180.

Wolf, J. 2008. *Organisation, Management, Unternehmensführung*. 3rd ed. Wiesbaden: Gabler Verlag.

Author

    Prof. Dr. Reinhard Meckl was born in August 1964, graduated from Regensburg University and majored in economics. He researches on internationalization strategies of corporations with a focus on knowledge management and acquisition strategies. When he was working for Siemens, he was among other fields in charge of planning and implementing the company's China strategy. By negotiating and founding joint ventures with Chinese partners he was involved early on in the problems of developing sustainable innovation and technology structures in the People's Republic of China (PRC). Therefore, he accumulated the experience of the cooperation between China and Germany. He was holding the chair of International Management at the Friedrich-Schiller-University Jena in Germany from 2000 – 2004. In November 2004 he accepted an offer from the University of Bayreuth to head the newly founded chair of International Management. In December 2004 he was elected member of the board of the German association for M&A. In November 2006 he was appointed the director of the Bavarian-Chinese centre for academic studies.

Role of Entrepreneurial Region in Development of Photovoltaic Industry of China[①]

Liu Xielin, Chen Ao, Gao Wei

12.1 Introduction

For a long time, traditional economic theories have emphasized the benefits of decentralization in the provision of public goods and services, such as education and health care. There are two related ideas. First, Hayek (1945) discusses the use of knowledge in society, emphasizing that local governments have better access to local information, which allows them to provide public goods and services that better match local preferences than the national government. Second, Tiebout (1956) introduces the inter-jurisdictional competition dimension and argues that such a competition provides a sorting mechanism to better match public goods and services with consumers' preferences. Competition rewards local governments who are friendly to markets as factors of production move to their regions, while it punishes heavily interventionist local governments as they lose valuable factors of production (Brennan and Buchanan, 1980).

[①] The paper is firstly presented in the Conference on the Political Economy of China's Technology and Innovation Policies, University of California, San Diego, La Jolla, California, June 27-28, 2011. Ms. Ying Zhang contributed a lot to the paper editing. The research was supported by the National Science Foundation of China (70932001).

In the literature of innovation studies, region is regarded as a very important resource for innovation(Porter, 1988). Region can distribute knowledge in arm's distance and spread tacit knowledge in traditional manufacturing clusters(Marshal, 1890) or high-tech science park such as Silicon Valley(Saxenian, 1994).

Firstly, innovation is the result of integration of new tacit and explicit knowledge (Polany and Pavitt, 2002). The explicit knowledge that can be coded is spread more easily in global environment. But the tacit knowledge which costs a lot of time to accumulate cannot be accessed directly through the rapid exchange (Maskell and Malmberg, 1999). This kind of knowledge needs geographical space as a media. It is considered that the tacit knowledge is difficult to exchange in long distance, because it is closely related to the special social and environmental, and this scenario makes it dependent and closely linked to geospatial(Gerler, 2003).

Lam(1998, 2000) pointed out that there is a high degree of spatial and temporal characteristics in collective learning process of the knowledge transfer. Interactive and collective learning are often based on consistent practice, implicit specification, and the hidden absorption mechanism of tacit knowledge. As the spatial proximity has a major impact on effective dissemination and sharing of the tacit knowledge, the importance of innovation cluster, district, role of region is also strengthened. These regions benefit from their special system endowment, and the endowment also can support and strengthen the superiority.

Secondly, researchers also found that different industries need different forms of new knowledge. Laestadius(1998) distinguishes two different types of knowledge base: analytical and synthetic. Synthetic knowledge base is common in the industries which need to compose existing knowledge and re-integrate innovation. The basis of these industries has the interaction problems that come from users and suppliers, such as specialized machinery, equipment installation engineering, and shipbuilding. The importance of R&D investment, as the form of applied research, is slightly lower in those industries relatively(von Hippel, 1988). The production and dissemination of tacit knowledge of these industries needed more specific know-how, skill, and practice. These forms of knowledge are supplied by professionals and technical institutions with ongoing training and face-to-face communication.

Thirdly, regionalization comes in parallel with globalization. There are various pipelines for the global knowledge flow, such as the FDI, trade, licensing, crossed authorization, and international cooperation. Local government is trying to change the technology-learning pattern and eliminate the licensing, specifically, encouraging cooperative R&D rather than simple licensing. In some new high-tech regions, international science communication and joint science projects have become quite common. When local knowledge supply cannot meet the enterprises' increasing demand, enterprises will have the motivation of seeking for other resources outside the region. In the past two decades, the global knowledge flow displays an accelerating tendency, which indicates that the internationalization of R&D capital expansion of MNCs is becoming increasingly significant: First, the complexity of technology and rising R&D cost determines the increasing demand of technology outsourcing, which accelerates the interaction among subjects who are geographically dispersed but have complementary knowledge; second, faster innovation motivates enterprises to find applying opportunities in specific regions; third, the increasingly intensive market competence in host countries compels better interaction between MNC and local partner for more market shares. Bathelt et al. (2004) considered that the innovation of companies in a special cluster not only relies on local knowledge network, but also needs to obtain non-localized sources of knowledge as a necessary complement.

In this paper, we proposed that there are entrepreneurial regions in China that serves as innovation drivers for strategic emerging industry. Firstly, since decentralization from the 1980s in China, regional innovation capability is widely distributed, some are worldly frontier, and some are lagging behind(Liu et al. ,2010). Secondly, as regions become more and more rich, the regional governments can make some strategies more ahead than the central government. Their competition provides the motivation for regions to innovate. Regions no longer are the servants to the central government, do what the central government tends to do. Rather, they have more autonomy to make strategy and policy for their regions to be more competitive. Thirdly, more and more research discovered that geographical space gives advantage in innovation as they provide more interactions among business, academy, and government(networking); this is also proved in China. Lastly, globalization gives regions more power to mobilize global resources for innovation in their regions.

So, there are four key elements for the growth of entrepreneurial regions: risk-taking characteristic of local government officials, local entrepreneurship, local industrial networking, and formation of global industry chain.

In this paper, we found that regional government can mobilize resources to strategic area beyond what the central government can do. They can use global resources to help local and new industry. This paper takes photovoltaic industry as the case industry to show the role of regions in innovation in these two emerging industry. We found that regional and global factors can be very important in the industrial innovation than what people expect.

12.2 The rapid growth of photovoltaic industry

China's photovoltaic industry has grown at an average annual rate of 49.5% in the past five years, and in 2007, it increased by 56.2%, China thus became the largest producer of solar energy in the world and took up 26.6% of the global (Zhao et al., 2008). In 2007, six of the top 16 solar cell companies in the world were from China. In addition, according to the statistics from China Solar Association, the output of solar cells produced in China in 2007 was 1,180 MW, while the output in Europe, Japan, and America was 1,062 MW, 920 MW, and 266 MW respectively, so China has truly become the largest producer of solar cells in the world (Table 12.1) (Zhao et al., 2008). However, the development of China's solar power market is rather slow. In 2007, the accumulative installed capacity was only 100 thousand kW, less than 1% of the global capacity (Zhao et al., 2008). According to our national plan at present, the accumulative installed capacity of China's photovoltaic industry reaches 300 MW by 2010, 1.8 GW by 2020 and 100 GW by 2050[①]. According to the prediction made by China Electric Power Research Institute, by the year 2050, the power installation of China's renewable energy will take up 25% of national power installation, of which photovoltaic installation will be 5% (Figure 12.1).

Table 12.1 Production and share of solar cell in different countries and regions in 2006 and 2007

Countries and regions	2006		2007	
	Output /MW	Share /%	Output /MW	Share /%
Japan	926.90	36.19	920.00	23.00
China	438.00	17.10	1088.00	27.20
German	508.00	19.83	810.00	20.25
Europe(others)	172.30	6.73	252.80	6.32
America	179.60	7.01	266.10	6.65
World(others)	166.90	6.52	295.15	7.38
Sum	2561.20	100.00	4000.05	100.00

Sources: PV News, Volume 27, Number 3, March 2008, Dec. 11.12, 2007, Wuxi, Frank Haugwitz, Photon International 2007

In the same time, Chinese photovoltaic companies have grown quickly and some are in the leading group of the world (Table 12.2).

[①] Long-term development plan for renewable energy, National Development and Reform Commission, 2007.

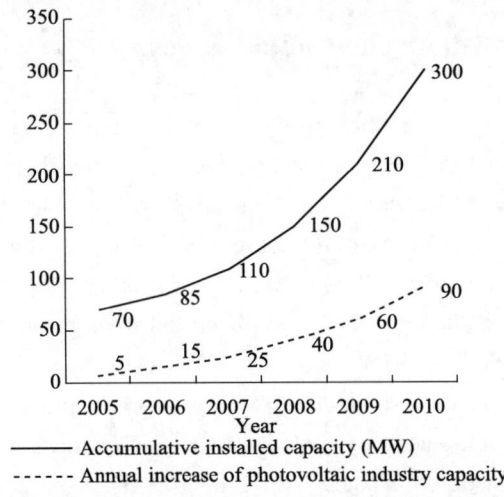

Figure 12.1 Installed capacity of solar energy in China

Source: Qian(2010), Zhao et al. (2008)

Table 12.2 The global ranking of China's main solar-cell manufacturers in the year of 2006 and 2007(MWP/Year)

Number	Corporations	2006		2007	
		Outputs/MWP	Ranking	Outputs/MWP	Ranking
1	Q-Cell(DE)	253.1	2	389.2	1
2	Sharp(JP)	434.4	1	363.0	2
3	Suntech(CH)	157.5	4	327.0	3
4	Kyocera(JP)	180.0	3	207.0	4
5	Firstsolar(US+DE)	60.0	13	207.0	4
6	Motech(TW)	102.0	7	196.0	5
7	Sanyo(JP)	155.0	5	165.0	6
8	SunPower(PH)	62.7	11	150.0	7
9	Yingli(CH)	35.0	17	142.5	8
10	Solar world(whole)	86.0	9	130.0	9

Source: Zhao et al, 2008. Chinese PV Industry Development Report(2). Solar Energy. 6:11-30.

If calculated by the standard that per megawatt of solar cells needs 10 to 11 tons of poly-silicon, China needed about 12 thousand tons of poly-silicon in the year 2007, while the amount of poly-silicon was less than 1,000 tons in China in 2007. The rate of self-sufficiency of raw material was less than 10% (Zhao et al. ,2008). Meanwhile, of 1,180MW solar cells produced in 2007, 1,000MW was exported (over 90%). At present, China's solar energy industry is featured by its dependence of raw material on the imports and production mainly dependent for the export. As the price of the imported poly-silicon is so high, this induced the establishment of large numbers of poly-silicon projects in 2008, which made this situation changed fundamentally.

Why did the photovoltaic industry grow so fast? Why did some regions play a more important role than central government here? In the following section we are trying to answer these two questions.

12.3 Regional innovation in Chinese photovoltaic industry

Region in China is used to act as a unit to implement the national plans. In the long traditional top-down system, regional agency is passive and limited.

But since the decentralization from 1980s, regions have become more and more important(Jin et al. 2005). Regional government officials not only follow the political mandates from the central government, but also play the role in entrepreneurship.

Firstly, local government can act as local entrepreneur to try both institutional and technological innovation. This is valued by the central government as experiment field and potential best practices for other regions. In fact, many social, managerial, and technological innovations came from the experiments by local regions. Secondly, as the region has the power to promote competitiveness of local industry, they have an advantage to contact the local business. They also embrace the advantage in having local market knowledge. Thirdly, regional capability and resource varies widely and some regions have the frontier technology even in the world. So, the demand for new industry is far more ahead than the other regions or even the central government. Fourthly, the resource of entrepreneurship also has regional feature such as appropriate infrastructure and human resources, the presence of FDI and domestic multinationals. All of these factors are able to make regions much more global so that the global innovation network stimulates the development of new industries. As the industry is very new to the regions, the approach by which they use to optimize global resources is critical to facilitate the development of industries. Lastly, forming cluster gives regions a special advantage. We found that there is a strong tendency for companies in different supply chains to locate near each other

12.3.1 Regional governments as entrepreneurship

12.3.1.1 Politician or entrepreneurship

Major policies in China, including policies in emerging industries, are all introduced by the central government, while local policies are mainly to execute specifically. Of course, this process itself also involves the enacting of local policies. This means that the local government, based on the central government's policies by taking local conditions into consideration, enacts specific industrial policies for local regions, which is also a process to implement the central government's industrial policies.

Since China is a country with a large territory and population, there is an imbalance in economic and social development and each region has its own conditions and situations. The policies made by the central government are usually in forms of general principles and regulations. Local industrial policies are the result of the implementation of such central policies and allowance of local conditions. Central policies are the premise of local policies, and regarded as the logical basis for local policies. Vice versa, central government will take bottom-up initiatives for national policy. So, a dynamic and interactive policy-making mechanism between the central government and local governments can be formed.

The local governments have two different choices to regulate the local economy. The first one is a traditional or conservative approach, which means local governments do what the central government tells. This is usually the case in north and west part of China. As a result of poor resources in their regions or risk aversion in politics, local governments from north and west China would stick to labor intensive industry by taking advantage of low-cost labor or comparative resources. The second approach is more entrepreneurial, by which local governments have great entrepreneurial enthusiasm to develop local economy or emerging industry. They take the risk and do what they thought would be good to the local regions. Local governments in this case play as the earlier bird in developing the new industry by finding the new growth sources. These provinces enthusiastically participate in developing emerging industries with a view of developing the general welfare of the governed area and political performance. The government officials (also called "political entrepreneurs") who have far-sight, the ability and insight, and willingness to pursue super-normal profit from innovation have broadened their view and brought in relevant technology and talents initiatively to create opportunities for the development of local emerging industries.

Though strategic emerging industry is right now a hot topic in China, we found it is the regional government who pushes the industry in their regions first ahead of the central government. For example, before the National Plan for Emerging Industries of Strategic Importance came out, eighteen provinces had put forward the idea to build new energy bases. Almost one hundred cities had started solar industry and wind power industry. The government from Wuxi City helped Suntech to start up the photovoltaic in 1990s, during which no other governments or ministry of central government ever regarded it as a green and strategic industry. But regional governments would echoed the central government quickly when the central government made the decision to develop "emerging industries of strategic importance" in 2009. The governments from some cities even proposed that they would carry out one hundred major projects related to emerging industries of strategic importance each year during the"12th Five-Year Plan"(Wu Xiaoqing, vice chairman of Central Committee of the China Democratic National Construction Association, deputy minister of the Ministry of Environmental Protection). To seize more opportunities in developing emerging industries of strategic importance, most local governments had accordingly executed and enacted corresponding policies one after another.

Qinghai is a poor province in China, and the local government tries to activate the local solar industry through local government subsidies. The reason behind is local government recognize the economic benefits of PV industry for the development of local regions. In 2011, Qinghai provincial government plans to allocate 13 billion subsidies in 800 MW photovoltaic project to join grid in the price of 1.5 yuan/kWh after the subsidy. It is an obvious advantaged subsidy, and will be much higher than that before (1.09 yuan/kWh as the PV concession biding). Qinghai's solar power generation installed capacity will be also accordingly expanded significantly[①]. This kind of local subsidy will set an example for other provinces and promote China's PV application market.

12.3.1.2 Regional capability

Since the 1980s, Chinese central government gradually adopted the policy of decentralization and allowed the regional government more and more active in innovation systems(Bo,2001). Though central government leads in policy-making, the implementation of the policy largely depends upon how regional governments respond. Each regional government has its own innovation system for its industrial development. Their motivation for promoting innovation ranges from gaining political capital by implementing policies from the central government to benefiting the local industry and economy. Regional governments, of course, may also choose to do nothing.

Today, the total amount of R&D investment by regional governments is larger than by the central government(MOST and NBS,2009); however, because innovation can be risky and requires huge capital investment, only governments from rich regions have the internal desire and capability to do so. Rich regions like Jiangsu, Shanghai,

---

① China Energy News. July 11, 2011.

Guangdong, Shandong, and Zhejiang Provinces are examples. They are more willing to push indigenous innovation and, in fact, they are the most innovative regions based on our research(Liu et al., 2010). The benefits of innovation for such regions include receiving subsidies from the central government and upgrading or renewing local industries. In fact, many of China's strategic emerging industries have been introduced initially by regional government rather than by the central government, especially in the southern China. For example, the photovoltaic industry originally emerged in Jiangsu(Suntech) in 2001 with no involvement from the central government. Now, more than 17 regions consider this industry as their key industry. Many regions also tried to capture a share of the wind power industry. In 2008, the National Development and Reform Commission (NDRC) established a program to limit industry capacity of 10 million kW by 2010, but the reality is that by that year, the real capacity had already reached 12.27 million kW.

In those regions, private enterprises dominate innovation activities. They are the main actors in the country's innovation system (Table 12.3). Usually, private enterprises innovate in areas that state owend enterprises (SOEs) do not pay attention to or in new areas that are relatively untouched in China. Capital-intensive sectors such as automobile, petroleum, banking, and utility industries are protected by the government, thus private enterprises find that there are high barriers to entry. However, for many other industries, including the IT sectors, machinery, light industry, garment and clothing, household electrical appliances, food and beverage, toys and other such industries, market competition drives private enterprises to be innovative as in other market economies.

Table 12.3 Funding for S&T activities in enterprises in top five regions(2008)

Region	Funding for S&T activities by state-controlled enterprises/billion RMB	Percentage	Funding for S&T activities by non-state-controlled enterprises/billion RMB	Percentage
National total	265.90	43.16	350.15	56.84
Jiangsu	13.67	14.07	83.47	85.93
Guangdong	14.86	21.15	55.41	78.85
Zhejiang	3.99	7.22	51.27	92.78
Shandong	27.08	41.20	38.64	58.80
Shanghai	22.66	69.31	10.03	30.69
Beijing	11.09	54.72	9.18	45.28

Source: China Statistical Yearbook on Science and Technology 2009

The regional governments have their own interests in the most of time. They have to make political commitments to economic decisions by the central government. This can help them get some investment from the central government, which controls most large investment for big projects. Therefore, when the central government lists the key industries such as the next generation of information technology, biology, new energy, etc. as national targets, most regional governments will take the initiative regardless of their capability and the corresponding development stage, even in poor western regions. Regional governments also have to make a decision based on their local comparative advantage. Usually, developed regions will make aggressive investments in innovation and new industry. For example, Jiangsu Province contributes more money than others to subsidizing enterprises for new industry and R&D. Jiangsu Province has many initiatives, such as special funding for innovation, global talent searching for new industries, money for attracting spin-offs, and the establishment of new joint research institutes(Liu et al., 2010).

12.3.2 Local entrepreneurship and industrial networking

Local entrepreneurship is the main source of entrepreneurial regions. In Jiangsu, Zhejiang and Guangdong regions, there are few SOEs and private business is the main ownership for enterprises. Many local managers are originally the farmers. They take light industry or new industry as their entering-mode to which SOEs do not pay attention. In Zhejiang, many cities evolved to specialize in the sectors of lighters, buttons, neckties, etc. Many private companies are the former township enterprises. In Jiangsu, multinationals and private stay with each other. We can see that many private companies are the spin-off of the large companies based in Shanghai(Liu et al., 2010).

Besides, the lack of credibility in local industry is still a fairly serious phenomenon in China(Xu, 2010), so the geographical guanxi plays the role of lubrication here. Entrepreneurs tend to invest in their own home where they have huge guanxi net. Meanwhile, in order to expand further relations and exploit network advantage, companies are willing to hire retired officers to coordinate the relationship between partners. In photovoltaic industry, overseas Chinese use their local "guanxi" to establish the network for their growth(Table 12.4).

Table 12.4 Network of local PV industry

Location	Enterprise	Whole show	Position	Native place	Experience
Jiangxi	LDK	Peng Xiaofeng	president	Jiangxi Anfu	Experience other industry inland
		Wan Yuepeng	CTO	Jiangxi Nanchang	Experience relevant industry overseas
Zhejiang	ReneSola	Li Xianshou	president	Zhejiang Yuhuan	Government sector experience
Jiangsu	Canadian Solar Inc.	Qu Xiaohua	president	Jiangsu Changshu	Experience relevant industry overseas
	Suntech	Shi Zhengrong	president	Jiangsu Yangzhong	Experience relevant industry overseas
	Trina Solar	Gao Jifan	president	Jiangsu Changzhou	Experience other industry inland
Hebei	Yingli Green Energy	Song Dengyuan	CTO	Hebei Zhangbei	Experience relevant industry overseas
		Miao Liansheng	president	Hebei Baoding	Demobilized soldier
	JA Solar	Jin Baofang	president	Hebei Ningjin	Government sector experience

Source: Authors' self-collecting based on the disclosure of the company

Taking solar photovoltaic industry as an example, localization of entrepreneurs and senior technical staff in this industry is an obvious feature. The staff can be divided into three groups. The first group consists of people who returned homeland after studying overseas, just like Shi Zhengrong in Suntech. The second group includes those who had established a business in other places before returning homeland, just like Peng Xiaofeng in LDK. The third group is made up by those who are fully localized in a certain region, just like Li Xianshou in ReneSola. Here, Chinese "guanxi" culture plays a significant role in the early stage of new industry which is very risky before the basic trust relationship is established.

12.3.3 Regions serve as part of global industrial network

12.3.3.1 Market

Finding the lead user is the key for the success of new industry. Usually, the high-end users are in the advanced countries, so, going global in a fast way is quite important to win the war.

Under globalization, it is of great importance to make full use of domestic market and foreign market to develop emerging industries. The market space for emerging industries is determined by the consumption capacity and prospect of corresponding products. The emerging and growing of a certain industry is closely related to its market returns. Only when the industry has enough market demands can it generate profits and can new industrial division be established.

12.3.3.2 Global financing

It is very interesting to see that the new industry got huge financial support from developed countries. In PV industry, most of the companies obtained a great deal of financing support from foreign financing market(Table 12.5).

Table 12.5 China's PV corporations listed overseas by 2007

Number	Corporations	Listing Time	Exchanges
1	Suntech, Jiangsu	Dec., 2005	NYSE, USA
2	Yuhui, Zhejiang	2005	LSE, UK
		July, 2007	NYSE, USA
3	ATS, Jiangsu	Nov., 2006	NASDAQ, USA
4	Linyang, Jiangsu	Dec., 2006	NASDAQ, USA
5	Trinasolar, Changzhou	Dec. 19, 2006	NASDAQ, USA
6	Jingao, Hebei	Dec., 2006	NASDAQ, USA
7	CEEG, Nanjing	Feb., 2007	NASDAQ, USA
8	Yingli, Hebei	April, 2007	NYSE, USA
9	Jetionsolar, Jiangsu	May, 2007	LSE, UK
10	LDK, Jiangxi	Aug., 2007	NYSE, USA

12.3.4 Learning by doing and technological innovation

China's photovoltaic industry has the following features: The raw material depends on import; products are mainly for export; and it is in the middle place in the international industrial chain. Recently, as a large number of poly-silicon projects with higher technological levels have been launched one after another, and foreign photovoltaic market is shrinking and the pattern of world photovoltaic industry has quietly changed, which provides a good opportunity for the fast development of China's photovoltaic industry. The development of China's wind power industry also follows the same law: starting from the machine assembly at the low-end of the industrial chain, and moved to the high-end manufacturing such as perfect blades, control system, and motor manufacturing.

Although there is a gap between high-purity silicon refining in manufacturing photovoltaic industry in China and the international advanced level, PV cell and module production in China have developed rapidly. Nowadays, China's level of production technology is close to the international advanced one. This is reflected in the capacity of the innovation of the industry in terms of patents. Since 2005, the number of patents granted to Chinese enterprises has been increasing in recent years (Table 12.6).

Table 12.6　Granted patents of leading companies of China

Year	Suntech	Yingli Green Energy	JA Solar	LinYang	Trina Solar	CSI	ReneSola	LDK
2005	1	0	0	0	1	0	0	0
2006	2	0	0	0	1	0	0	0
2007	1	0	0	0	1	0	5	0
2008	4	0	0	2	1	0	0	0
2009	11	2	8	2	27	5	1	9
2010	14	5	6	4	13	14	2	24
Deadline	8	5	4	3	38	7	4	6
Sum	41	12	18	11	82	26	12	39

Source: Author's calculation based on State Intellectual Property Office patent databases

12.3.5　Regional industry cluster and networking of solar energy

Regional cluster and networking are the characteristics of the new industry in China. The development of solar photovoltaic industry in Jiangsu Province started from the establishment of Suntech Power Holding Co. Ltd. in Wuxi in 2001. Within almost ten years' development, a relatively completed industrial chain has been formed. The industry has shown the features that upstream enterprises have gained some development, mid-stream enterprises become strong quickly and downstream enterprises emerge one after another. By the end of 2008, about 30 photovoltaic enterprises had gathered in Wuxi High-tech Zone with the achievement of 21.5 billion RMB sales revenue and more than 50% increase in the same field in China.

Later on, many regions in Jiangsu joined this industry. Of those companies, Suntech specializes on battery and usually imported poly-silicon material from abroad. Now, companies in Zhenjiang and Lianyungang City became the poly-silicon material suppliers for Suntech to reduce the cost. And companies in Changzhou become the main suppliers in Slicing(the technology for cutting the silicon). There are also some companies in the down-stream to play as an integrator for solar generators(Figure 12.2 and Figure 12.3).

Yingli, as another leading company in this industry, has the similar clustering story in Baoding City, Hebei Province, which we will not elaborate here.

12.4　Conclusions and implications

In China, there exists entrepreneurial regions. Local officials from there are ambitious to develop new industries. Local enterprises took the initiative to start the new business. Local industrial networking has been formed based on "guanxi".

Part 3 Industrial Innovation for Green Growth

High-puity silicon	Drawn and slices silicon	Batteries and components	Integrated system and equipment
Jiangsu Zhongneng Jiangsu Shunda Lianyungang Lottery Zhenjiang Daquan ...	Jiangsu Shunda Changzhou Trina Changzhou Yijing Jiangsu Huariyuan Zhenjiang RIMPAC Jiangyin Hairun ...	Wuxi Suntech Nanjing Power Suzhou Artes Changzhou Tuina Suzhou Best Solar ...	ET Solar Changshu Zhaofu NARI Central Engineering Nanjing Guanya Nicetown ...

	PV supporting industries	
	Tanglong Photoelectric Yangzhou Ups-huada ...	

Figure 12.2 Clustering of photovoltaic industry in Jiangsu Province

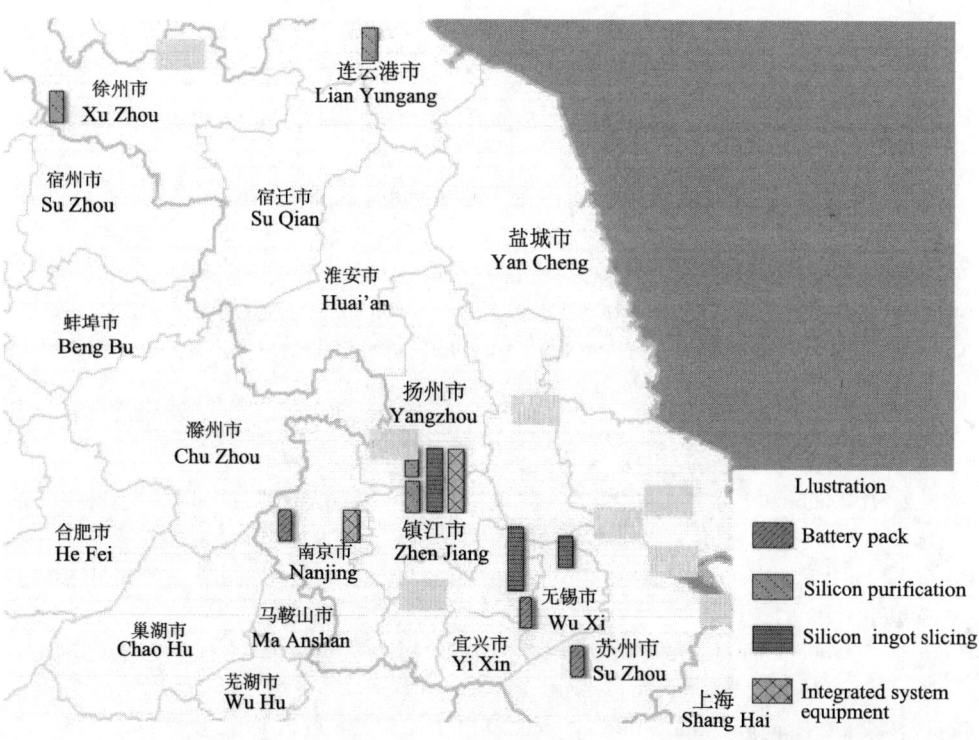

Figure 12.3 Distribution of PV industry in Jiangsu Province

Innovation follows the industry after learning by doing and leverage of global human resources. The industry tends to be global to break the national barriers such as lacks of earlier end users and financiers.

The industry still has many problems in their maturing up stage. In the photovoltaic industry, product sales and material resources heavily depend on foreign markets. There is also serious pollution. The photovoltaic is overheatedly invested though it is very young. Four conclusions are reached as follows:

(1) Regions have a large potential to be innovative; there are cornerstones of the national innovation system.

(2) Regional governments do have more advantages in marketing and incubating the new industry than central government.

(3) Only the regions with more entrepreneurial spirits and innovation capacity are able to play the role in leading strategic new industries.

(4) The regions aiming to be innovative in the new industry have to take globalization attitude to mobilize resources for the industry growth.

References

Alderman, N. 2004. *Mobility versus Embeddedness: The Role of Proximity in Major Capital Projects*. Aldershot: Ashgate.

Allen, J. 2000. Power/economic knowledge: symbolic and spatial formations. In: Bryson, J. R., Daniels, P., Henry, N., et al. (Eds.), *Knowledge, Space, Economy*. London: Routledge, 15-33.

Amin, A., Cohendet, P. 2004. *Architectures of Knowledge*. Oxford: Oxford University Press.

Amin, A. 2000. Organizational learning through communities of practice. Mrllennium Schum peter Conference. University of Manchester, 9-11.

Asheim, B. T., Herstad, S. J. 2003. Regional innovation systems and the globalizing world economy. *Economic Geography*, *Fac of Geography*, *Philipps-University*. 12.

Bathelt, H., Malmberg, A., Maskell, P. 2004. Clusters and knowledge: local buzz, global pipelines and the process of knowledge creation. *Progress in Human Geography*, 28(1), 31-56.

Bo, G. L. 2001. The re-adjustment of authority between central and local government. *Chinese Administration*, 7, 19-21.

Brennan, G., Buchanan. J. 1980. *The Power to Tax: Analytical Foundations of a Fiscal Constitution*. New York: Cambridge University Press.

Cooke, P. 2001. Regional innovation systems, clusters, and the knowledge economy. *Industrial and Corporate Change*, 10(4), 945-974.

Freeman, C. 2002. Continental, national and sub-national innovation systems-complementarily and economic growth. *Research Policy*, 31, 191-211.

Jin, H. H., Qian, Y. G., Weingast B. R. 2005. Regional decentralization and fiscal incentives: federalism, Chinese style. *Journal of Public Economics*, 89, 1719-1742.

Laestadius, S. 1998. Technology level, knowledge formation and industrial competence in paper manufacturing. In: Eliasson, G., et al. (Eds), *Micro Foundations of Economic Growth*. Ann Arbor: University of Michigan Press, 212-226.

Lam, A. 2000. Tacit knowledge, organizational learning and societal institutions: an integrated framework. *Organization Studies*, 21(3), 487-513.

Lam, A. 1998. The social embeddedness of knowledge: problems sharing and organizational learning in international high-technology ventures. DRUID Working Paper No 98 - 7.

Liu, X. L., Ping, L., et al. 2010. *For a Balanced Regional Innovation System (in Chinese)*. Beijing: Science Press.

Lundvall, B., Johnson, B. 1994. The learning economy. *Journal of Industry Studies*, 1, 23-42.

Marshal, A. 1890. *Principle of Economics*. London: Macmillan.

Maskell, P., Malmberg, A. 1999. Localized learning and industrial competitiveness. *Cambridge Journal of Economics*, 23, 167-186.

Narula, R. 2002. Innovation systems and "inertia" in R&D location: Norwegian firms and the role of systemic lock-in. *Research Policy*, 31(5), 795-816.

Pavitt, K. 2002. Knowledge about knowledge since Nelson and Winter: a mix record. Electronic working paper series paper No. 83, SPRU, University of Sussex, 6.

Porter, M. 1988. *On Competition*. Cambridge: Harvard University Press.

Qian, B. Z. 2010. World solar cell production got a new record in 2009 (in Chinese). *Solar Energy*, 10, 53.

Saxenian, A. 1994. *Regional Advantage*. Cambridge: Harvard University Press.

Tiebout, C. M. 1956. A pure theory of local expenditure. *Journal of Political Economy*, 64, 416-424.

von Hippel, E. 1988. *The Sources of Innovation*. New York: Oxford University Press.

Zhao, Y. W., Wu, D. C., Wang, S. C., et al. 2008. Chinese PV industry development report(1). *Solar Energy*, 6, 11-30.

Zucker, L. G., Darby, M. R. 1996. Star scientists and institutional transformation: patterns of invention and innovation in the formation of the biotechnology industry. *Proceedings of the National Academy of Science*, 93, 12709-12716.

Author

Liu XieLin, Professor and Associate Dean of School of Management, Director of Research Center of Management of Innovation, University of Chinese Academy of Sciences. Born in September 25, 1957, he got his BSc, Peking University, 1982; M. SC, Chinese Academy of Sciences; Ph. D, 1994, Tsinghua University. From February of

1995 to August of 1995, he was a visiting fellow in Sloan School of Management, MIT. From December of 2004 to February of 2005, he was a visiting professor in Hitochibashi University of Japan. From September to December of 2006, he was a visiting professor in Stockholm School of Economics. From April of 1994 to September of 1996, he was an assistant professor in Tsinghua University. From October 1996 to June of 2006, he was a professor in National Research Center for S&T for Development, Ministry of Science and Technology. He also acts as Vice-President of Chinese Association of Science of Science and S&T Policy.

His research areas mainly cover innovation policy, management of technology and innovation. He has published a lot of papers in *Research Policy*, *Technovation*, *Journal of Management Studies* and *International Journal of Technology Management*. He has written eight books in the last ten years.

13

Innovations for Electro-mobility and Renewable Energies: Prospects for Chinese and German Firms

Dirk Holtbrügge, Corinna Dögl

13.1 The relevance of electro-mobility and renewable energies in China and Germany

Corporate environmental responsibility (CER) is assumed to be one of the major instruments to resist the global ecological crisis strained by growing world population, massive pollution and depletion of natural resources. According to Huckle (2008), CER is the obligation of decision-makers to take actions that protect and improve the environment as a whole, along with their own interests. Many firms actively seek to implement CER practices in order to meet the growing stakeholder demand towards environmental responsibility. These may include green products, employee commitment, communication and products.

Green production can be generally described as investments in environmentally friendly and resource-saving production plants, equipment or technologies. A production process is considered green when a firm proactively and voluntarily exceeds governmental environmental regulations and emission targets (Lo et al., 2008). Green employee commitment contains all measures that are designed at motivating employees for environmental improvement (Govindarajulu and Daily, 2004). Green communication with stakeholders completes a firm's CER practices along the value chain, e.g. by issuing a formal report regarding corporate environmental performance or communicating environmental goals(Jensen and Berg,2012;Darnall et al. ,2008). Green products are built with reusable and renewable resources or components and can be recycled in an environmentally friendly way(Sharma,2000). Examples range from simple products such as reusable thermo cups to high-tech developments like electro-vehicles or renewable energies,i. e. the two industries which will be in the focus of this study.

Both, renewable energies and electro-mobility are particularly important and fast growing sectors in Germany and China. Because many technologies in these two areas are not efficient in economic terms by now, governmental support is crucial in both countries. In China, around € 17 bn are provided by the government for developing electro-mobility, and in Germany around € 1. 7 bn will be spent in the next few years. Thereby the German government focuses on R&D and market preparation which we can consider as supply-side support. It relies on a national development plan for electro-mobility which is intended to become a lead market by 2020(Arnold et al. , 2010). The Chinese government, on the other hand, supports customers by buying electrical vehicles for up to € 7,000 and efficient drive technologies in ten pilot areas (AMS, 2010; Arnold et al. , 2010). In an international comparison, Germany and China are also international leaders with regard to renewable energies (REN21, 2010). A comparison of promotion policies for renewable energies shows that Germany and China rank among the top five countries worldwide(Figure 13. 1).

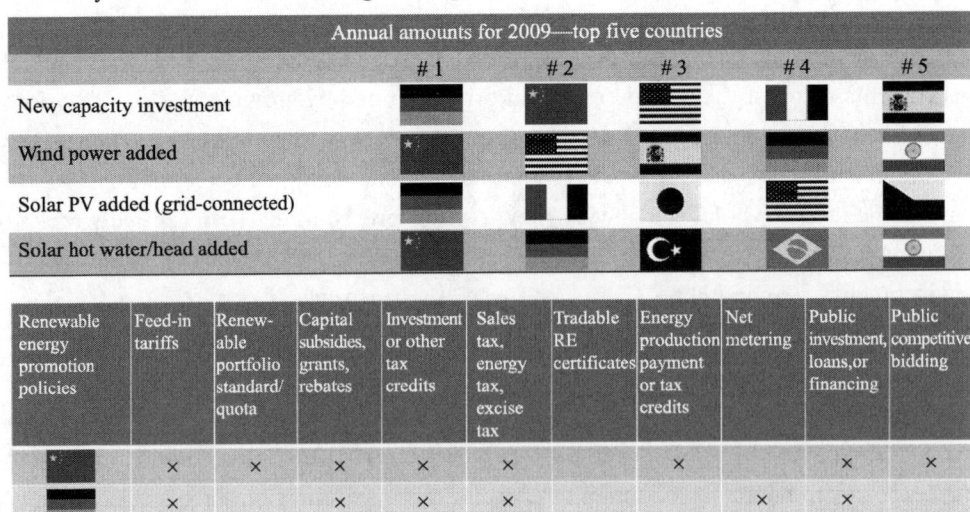

Figure 13. 1   International comparison of investment in renewable energy technologies and promotion policies

Sources:REN21(2010),OECD/IEA(2010)

13.2 Emerging fields of electro-mobility and renewable energies

From a managerial perspective, electro-mobility and renewable energy represent emerging fields that are characterized by disruptive innovations as well as the need for cross-boundary and cross-border cooperation(Figure 13.2).

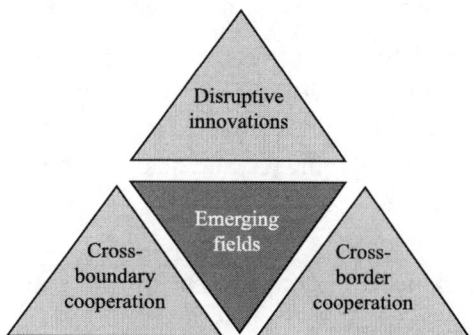

Figure 13.2　Emerging fields: disruptive innovations, cross-boundary and cross-border cooperation

Technologies for electro-mobility require disruptive innovations in several areas as many components of cars are dropped and substituted by new parts. For example, the combustion engine is replaced by four hub motors. Also, no starter and exhaust system is required anymore. Instead the batteries—a minor part in traditional cars—become a key component of electric vehicles. The need for disruptive innovations has far-reaching consequences for car manufacturers and their suppliers and requires new forms of collaboration.

Cross-boundary cooperation in the field of electro-mobility involves car manufacturers, car suppliers and utility firms. An example is the cooperation between the car manufacturer BMW and energy supplier RWE. On September 15, 2011, both firms signed an agreement to create a large-scale-zero emissions individual transport and travel system in Germany with the objective to make electric vehicles attractive for German customers. Another example is the cross-boundary cooperation by Siemens that is providing the infrastructure for public and private charging stations, the Stadtwerke München(Munich Municipal Utility Corporation) and BMW(Siemens, 2010). Siemens is also active in cross-boundary cooperation in the renewable energy industry, for example in an alliance with the energy provider EON in the area of wind turbines(Manager Magazin Online, 2008).

Innovations in the field of electro-mobility do not only take place between firms from different industries, but may also include cross-border cooperation. For example, the German car manufacturer Audi cooperates with Tongji University in Shanghai in training students in the fields of research, instruction and services of electro-mobility. The development of an electrical Audi A6L is one of the first joint projects(Xiao, 2010). Another example is the alliance between the German car maker Daimler and the Chinese battery manufacturer BYD. Regarding renewable energies, Siemens and Suntech, the world's largest manufacturer of photovoltaic (PV), entered a framework agreement for PV panels in 2011 (Siemens and Suntech Power Holdings Co., Ltd., 2011). The aim of these forms of cross-border cooperation is often to combine technological and management know-how of German firms with cost advantages and scaling opportunities of firms from China.

13.3 Institutional conditions of electro-mobility and renewable energies in China and Germany

In both countries, innovations in electro-mobility and renewable energies are strongly supported by the government. While there are several empirical studies that analyze the impact of governmental policies on CER practices (for an overview, see Holtbrügge and Dögl, 2012), there is a lack of research in these two industries. Therefore it remains an open question whether the institutional conditions in China or Germany are more suitable for companies in the fields of electro-mobility and renewable energies. As both countries are characterized by severe differences of their political, financial, educational, cultural and ecological systems(Table 13.1), different impacts on firm practices in these two fields may also be expected.

Table 13.1 Institutional conditions in Germany and China

System	Item	Germany	China
Political system	Economic freedom index(EFI)	70,5(Rank 23)	53,2(Rank 123)
	Ease of doing business index 2011 (EDBI)	(Rank 19)	(Rank 91)
	Corruption perceptions index(CPI)	7.9(Rank 14)	3.6(Rank 72)
Financial system	GDP per capita 2009(USD)	34,800(Rank 24)	6,000(Rank 132)
	Income inequality(Gini index)2006/2009	27(Rank 128)	48(Rank 28)
Education system	Human development index(HDI) (UNDP,2010)	0.885(Rank 10)	0.663(Rank 89)

Continued

System	Item	Germany	China
Cultural system (Hofstede cultural values)	Power distance	35	80
	Individualism/collectivism	67	15
	Uncertainty avoidance	65	40
	Masculinity/femininity	66	50
	Long-term orientation	29	114
Ecological system	Environmental performance index 2012	66.91(Rank 11)	42.24(Rank 116)
	Environmental sustainability index(ESI) 2005	56.9(Rank 31)	38.6(Rank 133)

Sources: CIA, 2011; Heritage Foundation, 2011; Hofstede, 2001; Transparency International, 2011; World Bank, 2011; World Bank, 2012; Yale Center for Environment Law and Policy and Center for International Earth Science Information Network, 2005; Yale Center for Environment Law and Policy, 2012

Therefore, we conducted an empirical study in Germany and China in order to examine the impact of institutional influences on CER practices and business outcomes as well as the prospects for cross-country cooperation in the fields of electro-mobility and renewable energies. In particular we sought answers to the following questions: (1) How do institutional pressures and incentives influence the implementation of CER practices in renewable energy and electro-mobility firms? (2) Which CER practices are implemented in Germany and China? (3) To what extent do CER practices lead to positive business outcomes in both countries? (4) Is there a potential for cooperation between Chinese and German companies in the fields of renewable energy and electro-mobility?

13.4 Methodology

To answer these questions we conducted a cross-country survey among renewable energy firms and electro-mobility firms in Germany and China. We searched in several databases(e.g. www.firmdatabase.org, www.re-database.com, www.enf.cn, www.bem-ev.de) and identified around 300 – 400 firms from each country operating in the renewable energy and electro-mobility industry. The survey was designed in English and addressed to the department responsible for CER/CSR/Corporate Communication, if a specific contact person was known. Approximately three weeks after the first mailing in January 2011, a reminder was sent out to all firms in the sample. In total, we received 35 usable questionnaires, 16 from China and 19 from Germany, resulting in a response rate of approximately 5% (Figure 13.3). Given that the questionnaires were addressed to senior-level managers who are often reluctant to participate in academic surveys, this response rate is comparable to other mail surveys

(Cycyota and Harrison,2006;Baruch,1999).

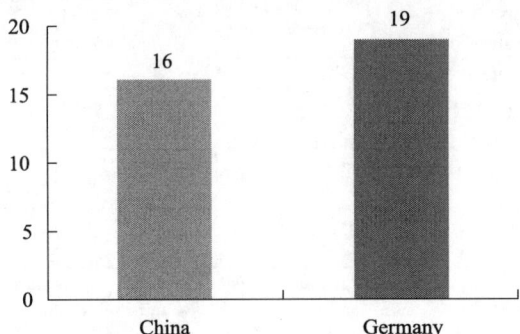

Figure 13.3　Sample distribution

Measures: Institutional pressures and incentives: We identified four dimensions (state incentives and pressures, market incentives and pressures, social incentives and pressures, ownership incentives and pressures) from established instruments of previous studies (Lo et al. , 2008; Kolk, 2003; Lu and Chiu, 2003; Maignan and Ferrell,2003;Melynk et al. ,2003;Orlitzky et al. ,2003;Margolis and Walsh,2001; Kaplan and Norton, 1993; Samiee and Roth, 1992). We asked respondents to indicate the influence of these pressures and incentives on their firm when considering environmental issues using a seven-point Likert scale (1 = very low influence and 7 = very strong influence).

CER practices: For measuring CER practices, we distinguished between green products, green production, green communication, and green employee commitment. We measured each practice with several items that we adopted from previous studies on a seven-point Likert scale(1 = very low influence and 7 = very strong influence)(He and Chen,2009;Egri and Ralston,2008;Sharma,2000).

Business outcomes: We measured the business outcomes with the balanced scorecard approach consisting of four dimensions—financial performance, innovation and learning perspective, customer perspective and internal business processes(Kaplan and Norton, 1993). Financial performance was measured with the four-item scale developed by Samiee and Roth(1992) and augmented with the item "growth in market share". Items for the innovation and learning perspective are based on Margolis and Walsh(2001), Orlitzky et al. (2003) and Lu and Chiu(2003) where participants were asked to rate the increase of technological competences for innovation leadership, new launch methods, the increase of patents, and the increase of new products. Customer perspective as well as internal business processes were measured with regard to Kaplan and Norton(1993). The internal reliability for all variables was very high with Cronbach's a well above the 0.8-level.

Cooperation potential: According to Das and Teng(2000), we distinguish between property-based resources and knowledge-based resources(Table 13.2). Property-based resources cannot be easily obtained and transferred to other firms as they are legally protected through property rights in the form of patents, licenses, or equipment. Knowledge-based resources refer to a firm's intangible know-how and skills. They cannot be imitated or copied easily, but they are more vulnerable to unintended transfers or leakage. We asked the respondents to rate their firms' most important resources in order to create competitive advantage on a five-point Likert scale(1 = very unimportant and 5 = very important). In addition, we asked them to rate the most important resources which they expect from potential alliance partners.

Table 13.2 Classification of property-based and knowledge-based resources

Property-based resources	Knowledge-based resources
Financial resources	Processes
Patents	Structures
Licenses	Culture
Buildings	Stakeholders
Equipment	Qualifications
	Skills
	Experience

13.5 Results and discussion

13.5.1 Institutional incentives and pressures

Figure 13.4 shows the relevance of institutional pressures and incentives in Germany and China. In general, all four institutional influences are perceived to be stronger in Chinese firms than in German. It is also remarkable that the differences between the four types of institutional pressures are relatively small. Thus, it can be assumed that innovations in the area of electro-mobility and renewable energies are complex phenomena that are characterized by multiple interests and the involvement of several stakeholder groups.

Interestingly, market pressures and incentives are the strongest in China. This may be explained by the fact that electro-mobility and renewable energies are

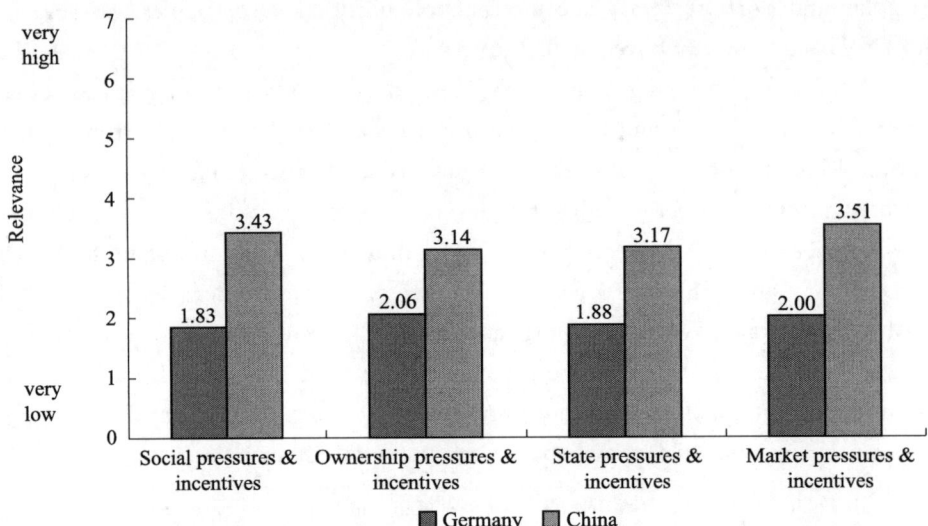

Figure 13.4　Relevance of institutional pressures and incentives—comparison of means

emerging fields that offer prosperous business opportunities. Moreover, the competition among a large number of Chinese firms in these two sectors is very high. The Chinese government follows a "survival of the fittest" strategy which means that only the strongest and most innovative firms survive.

Slightly less significant than market groups is the perceived strength of social groups. This is surprising because social groups generally do not play an important role in China and are often oppressed by the government. It may be assumed that they are tolerated in the fields of electro-mobility and renewable energy because they support the government's environmental objectives and policies.

Interestingly, state pressures and incentives are perceived as less relevant. This is surprising given the large financial support of electro-mobility and renewable energies by the Chinese government and the fact that electro-mobility is one of the most important objectives in the current Five-Year Plan.

Least important are ownership pressures and incentives. Chinese firms in the electro-mobility and renewable energies sectors are often state-owned or belong to private entrepreneurs(Anderson, 2010). As a consequence, shareholder pressures are perceived as less relevant.

In contrast to China, ownership pressures are the strongest in Germany. Many German electro-mobility and renewable energy firms are publicly listed. Their shareholders often have high expectations concerning profitability and the amortization of their capital. Market pressures are also regarded as relatively strong. This may be explained by the fact that the electro-mobility and renewable energy industries in Germany are highly competitive and characterized by several bankruptcies.

Finally, state pressures and incentives as well as social pressures and incentives play only a minor role. Thus, electro-mobility and renewable energies are predominantly perceived as business opportunities and less as social obligation.

13.5.2 CER practices

Although institutional pressures are perceived to be stronger in China than in Germany, the relevance of CER practices in the fields of electro-mobility and renewable energy are generally higher in Germany than in China (Figure 13.5). Thus, German firms either react more strongly to the perceived institutional pressures or implement CER practices more proactively.

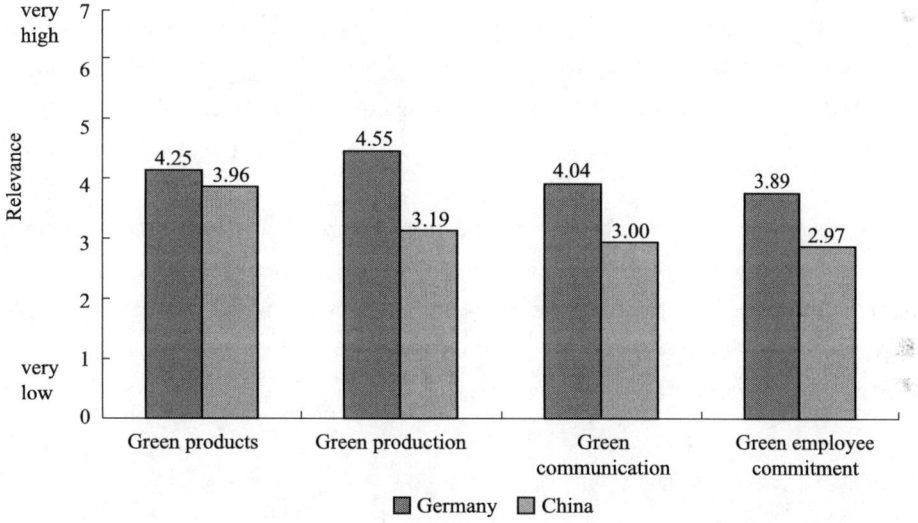

Figure 13.5 Relevance of CER practices—comparison of means

This is in contrast to the results of the literature review of Holtbrügge and Dögl (2012) that "external pressures appear to be the most effective method in forcing companies to implement CER practices (and that) communities and governments should implement strict regulations and other political incentives to push CER practices of firms". One explanation for this may be that electro-mobility and renewable energies, as emerging fields, require disruptive innovations which are less likely generated through external pressures than through entrepreneurial spirit.

Another explanation for the higher relevance of CER practices in Germany may be that German firms in these industries often follow a differentiation strategy while cost-leadership strategies are more typical in China. Thus, CER practices may be regarded as a differentiation factor by German firms while for their Chinese competitors cost efficiency is more important. Moreover, environmental responsibility has become a relevant factor in Germany over the last 30 years, while China is a latecomer and has just started to consider the importance of environmental issues (KPMG, 2008). This may lead to a generally higher relevance of CER practices in German firms than in Chinese.

A more detailed analysis shows that German firms are particularly active in greening their production processes. On the other hand, Chinese firms tend to focus more on inventing green products. Since customers are typically more interested in products than in internal processes, this reflects the high relevance of market pressures and incentives in China, which we discussed in the previous section.

In both countries, the least relevant CER practice is green employee commitment. Obviously, firms in China and Germany perceive employees of lesser importance for innovations in the fields of electro-mobility and renewable energy than customers and shareholders.

13.5.3 Business outcomes

With regard to our third research question, Figure 13.6 shows that German firms in the electro-mobility and renewable energy industries evaluate their business outcomes more positively than their Chinese counterparts. This applies to all four perspectives of the balanced scorecard. Obviously, CER practices are more valued by German stakeholders than by those in China.

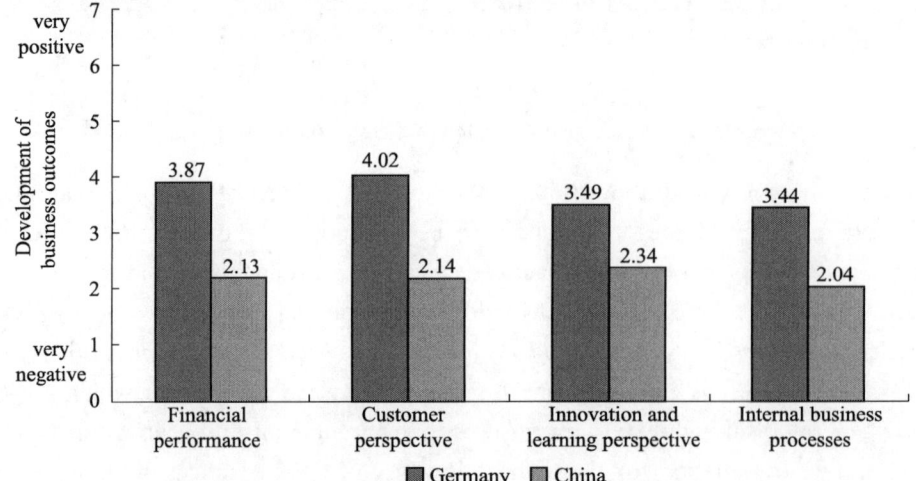

Figure 13.6 Business outcomes—comparison of means

The difference is particularly large for the customer perspective. While German firms regard their customer orientation as very high, this is perceived as least pronounced by Chinese firms. This can be explained by the eligibility of CER practices in the context of differentiation strategies which are—with regard to our previous considerations—often pursued by German firms. Chinese firms, on the other hand, are characterized by cost-efficiency strategies and have a stronger emphasis on learning and internal processes. This also reflects the general preference for imitating competitors and operating at low costs (Brouthers et al., 2000; Flannery, 2010). Consequently, the differences between Chinese and German firms for these two perspectives of the balanced scorecard are smaller than for the customer perspective and the financial performance perspective.

13.5.4 Relevance of firm resources for cross-border cooperation

In our last research question we tried to assess the potential for cooperation between Chinese and German companies in the fields of renewable energies and electro-mobility. Therefore, we asked the respondents to rate their own resources in order to create competitive advantage as well as the relevance of resources which they would like to obtain from potential alliance partners.

Figure 13.7 reveals that renewable energies and electro-mobility firms in both countries regard similar resources as relevant. On average, knowledge-based resources have a high priority, whereas property-based resources are considered as less important. Except for the two knowledge-based resources skills and experiences, Chinese firms rate all resources as more important than their German competitors. The most remarkable differences can be observed for buildings, equipment and financial resources. While German firms assess these resources at potential Chinese partners as insignificant, they are of high priority for Chinese partners. The perceived relevance of financial resources at potential German partners is even higher than that of all other resources.

With regard to different types of cooperation, German firms tend to link alliances, i.e. the combination of different strengths and weaknesses. For example, they consider themselves to possess considerable equipment and financial resources and expect skills and experience, in particular, from their Chinese partners...

On the other hand, Chinese firms have a tendency towards scale cooperation. This is illustrated by the fact that the differences between mean values of own resources and partner resources are smaller than for German firms. In China, economies of scale are important as often large quantities of the same products are produced. Thus they

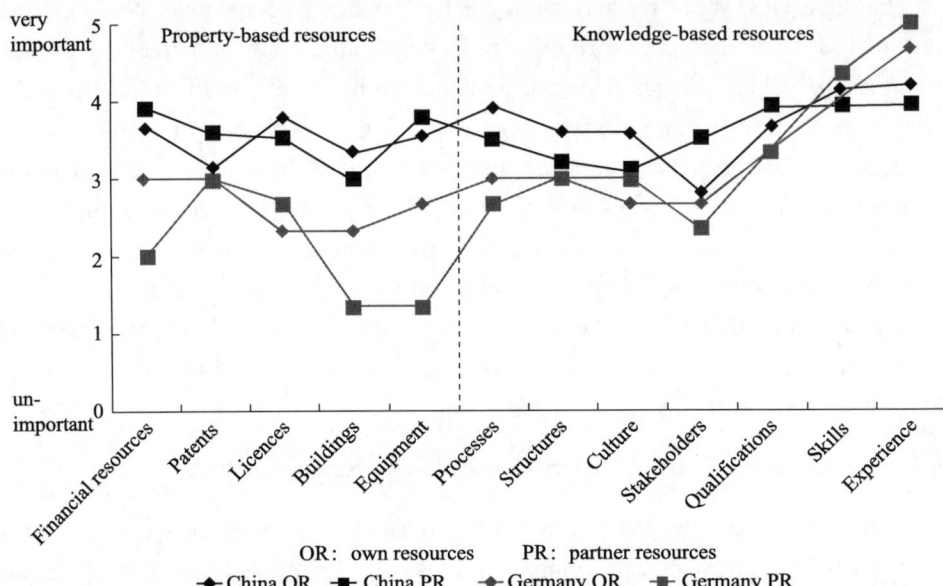

Figure 13.7 Relevance of firm resources for cross-border cooperation—comparison of means

seek cooperation partners with strengths in similar areas.

The different preferences for link vs. scale cooperation have several consequences for managing Sino-German alliances. For example, Chinese and German firms have different partner profiles and selection criteria. Moreover, empirical studies show that link alliances have a tendency towards dominant-parent structures while scale alliances are often characterized by shared-management structures (Holtbrügge, 2004). This may lead to conflicting attitudes about the governance of joint projects. It can be expected that those firms that succeed in integrating the advantage of both forms will be particularly successful, i.e. that pursue an outpacing strategy and exploit economies of scale and differentiation advantages simultaneously.

13.6 Conclusions, implications and limitations

The aim of the study was to explore the institutional pressures and incentives that are relevant for implementing CER practices and support positive business outcomes in the renewable energy and electro-mobility industries in Germany and China. Based on an empirical study of 16 Chinese firms and 19 German, we show that institutional influences are more intense in China; however the implementation of CER practices is higher and the evaluation of business outcomes is more positive in Germany. By considering the relevance of knowledge-based and property-based resources, remarkable differences between both countries have been established. We argue that cross-boundary and cross-border cooperation, that combine differentiation advantages of German firms and scaling opportunities of Chinese firms, are most likely to succeed. For example, several examples exist that integrate Chinese battery technology and German engineering know-how in the electrical drive engineering sector. Similarly, this strategy could be effective in the field of renewable energy. China produces cost-effective photovoltaic cells whilst Germany provides the appropriate engineering know-how that is needed to integrate this technology into electricity networks.

When interpreting our results, some limitations have to be considered. Our study relies exclusively on self-reported data. Therefore we have to consider the potential of common method bias. Social desirability in reporting a company's environmental practices may be one potential bias, despite the assurance of anonymity to respondents with regard to Podsakoff et al. (2003). Another limitation is the small sample size which limits our ability to generalize our findings. Thus, our interpretations are highly speculative and explorative. Nevertheless, we provide a first overview of an emerging and highly relevant field and of two countries that are expected to play an important role in this regard.

Our study may be regarded as a starting point for developing concrete research hypotheses and testing them on a larger sample. A prospective theoretical framework may be institutional theory which could be applied to conceptualize the relationships between international conditions, CER practices and business outcomes in a more detailed manner. The resource-based view could also be used to further analyze the potential of German and Chinese firms for cross-border cooperation. Finally, it may be useful to focus on existing examples of Sino-German cooperation in the fields of electro-mobility and renewable energies and to explore their governance structures and success factors.

Acknowledgements

We thank the Hans-Frisch-Foundation for the financial support of this study.

References

AMS. 2010. China auf dem weg zur marktführerschaft. http://www. auto-motor-und-sport. de/eco/elektroautos-in-china-so-foerdern-die-chinesen-die-e-mobilitaet-2780960. html[2011-12-01].

Anderson, G. 2010. The difference between the Chinese and the U. S. view of clean tech subsidies. http://www. renewableenergyworld. com/rea/blog/post/2010/08/the-difference-between-the-chinese-and-the-u-s-view-of-clean-tech-subsidies[2011-12-02].

Arnold, H. , Kuhnert, F. , Kurtz, R. , et al. 2010. Elektromobilität—Herausforderungen für Industrie und Öffentliche Hand. Price water house Coopers.

Baruch, Y. 1999. Response rate in academic studies: a comparative analysis. *Human Relations*, 52(4), 421-438.

Brouthers, L. E. , Werner, S. , Matulich, E. 2000. The influence of triad nations' environments on price-quality product strategies and MNC performance. *Journal of International Business Studies*, 31(1), 39-62.

CIA. 2011. The world factbook—distribution of family income—Gini index. https://www. cia. gov/library/publications/the-world-factbook/fields/2172. html[2012-06-01].

Cycyota, C. S. , Harrison, D. A. 2006. What (not) to expect when surveying executives: a meta-analysis of top manager response rates and techniques over time. *Organizational Research Methods*, V9(2), 133-160.

Darnall, N. , Henriques, I. , Sadorsky, P. 2008. Do environmental management systems improve business performance in an international setting? *Journal of International Management*, 14 (4), 364-376.

Das, T. K. , Teng, B. S. 2000. A resource-based theory of strategic alliances. *Journal of Management*, 26(1), 31-61.

Egri, C. P. , Ralston, D. A. 2008. Corporate responsibility: a review of international management research from 1998 to 2007. *Journal of International Management*, 14, 319-339.

Flannery, R. 2010. Why imitation bests innovation. http://www. forbes. com/2010/05/11/china-america-innovation-leadership-mangement-imitation-book. html[2012-06-20].

Govindarajulu, N. , Daily, B. F. 2004. Motivating employees for environmental improvement. *Industrial Management & Data Systems*, 104(4), 364-372.

He, M. , Chen, J. 2009. Sustainable development and corporate environmental responsibility: evidence from Chinese corporations. *Journal of Agricultural Environment Ethics*, 22(4), 323-339.

Heritage Foundation. 2011. Index of economic freedom world rankings. http://www. heritage. org/index/ranking.

Hofstede, G. 2001. *Cultures Consequences*. 2nd ed. Thousand Oaks: Sage Publications.

Holtbrügge, D. , Dögl, C. 2012. How international is corporate environmental responsibility? A literature review. *Journal of International Management*. 2011, 18(2), 180-195.

Holtbrügge, D. 2004. Management of international strategic business cooperation: situational conditions, performance criteria, and success factors. *Thunderbird International Business*

Review, 46(3), 255-274.

Huckle, J. 2008. Sustainable development. In: Arthur, J., Davies, I., Hahn, C. (Eds.), *The Sage Handbook of Education for Citizenship and Democracy*. London: Sage Publications, 342-354.

Jensen, J. C., Berg, N. 2012. Determinants of traditional sustainability reporting versus integrated reporting: an institutionalist approach. *Business Strategy and the Environment*.

Kaplan, R. S., Norton, D. P. 1993. Putting the balanced scorecard to work. *Harvard Business Review*, (9/10), 134-147.

Kolk, A. 2003. Trends in sustainability reporting by the Fortune Global 250. *Business Strategy and the Environment*, 12(5), 279-291.

KPMG. 2008. Climate change: is India Inc. prepared? http://business.outlookindia.com/pdf/ClimateChangereportfinal.pdf[2012-06-05].

Lo, C. W. H., Egri, C. P., Ralston, D. A. 2008. Commitment to corporate, social, and environmental responsibilities: an insight into contrasting perspectives in China and the US. *Organization Management Journal*, 5(2), 83-98.

Lu, H. L., Chiu, W. C. K. 2003. From corporate legal person to social citizen: social implications of corporate philanthropy. In: Lu, X., Enderle, G. (Eds.), *Developing Business Ethics in China (in Chinese)*. Shanghai: Shanghai Academy of Social Science Press, 202-214.

Maignan, I., Ferrell, O. C. 2003. Nature of corporate responsibilities: perspectives from American, French, and German consumers. *Journal of Business Research*, 56(1), 55-67.

Manager Magazin Online. 2010. Daimler baut elektroautos für China: Kooperation mit BYD. http://www.manager-magazin.de/unternehmen/artikel/0,2828,681100,00.html[2012-06-10].

Manager Magazin Online. 2008. Siemens und eon schmieden Bündnis. http://www.manager-magazin.de/unternehmen/artikel/0,2828,577146,00.html[2012-06-10].

Margolis, J. D., Walsh, J. P. 2001. *People and Profits? The Search for a Link between a Firm's Social and Financial Performance*. London: Psychology Press.

Melynk, S., Sroufe, R., Calatone, R. 2003. Assessing the impact of environmental management systems on corporate and environmental performance. *Journal of Operations Management*, 21, 329-351.

Miller, D., Shamsie, J. 1996. The resource-based view of the firm in two environments: the Hollywood film studios from 1936 to 1965. *Academy of Management Journal*, 39(3), 519-543.

OECD/IEA. 2010. Energy Technology Perspectives. Scenarios & Strategies to 2050.

Orlitzky, M., Schmidt, F. L., Rynes, S. L. 2003. Corporate social and financial performance: a meta-analysis. *Organization Studies*, 24(3). 403-411.

Podsakoff, P. M., MacKenzie, S. B., Lee, J. Y. 2003. Common method biases in behavioral research: a critical review of the literature and recommended remedies. *Journal of Applied Psychology*, 88(5), 879-903.

REN21. 2010. Global status report. http://www.ren21.net/Portals/97/documents/GSR/REN21_

GSR_2010_full_ revised%20Sept2010. pdf[2012-06-30].

Samiee,S. , Roth,K. 1992. The influence of global marketing standardization on performance. *Journal of Marketing*,56(2), 1-17.

Schröder, A. 2010. Staatliche Förderung der eMobilität im internationalen Vergleich. http://www. bem-ev. de/staatliche-forderung-der-emobilitat-im-internationalen-vergleich [2012-06-30].

Sharma, S. 2000. Managerial cognitions and organizational context as predictors of firm choice of environmental strategies. *Academy of Management Journal*,43(4), 681-697.

Siemens, A. G. 2010. Project model region electromobility Munich—drive eCharged. http://www. energy. siemens. com/hq/en/energy-topics/electromobility/practice[2012-06-30].

Siemens A. G. , Suntech Power Holdings Co. ,Ltd. 2011. Siemens and Suntech enter framework agreement for PV panels. http://www. siemens. com/press/en/pressrelease/? press = /en/pressrelease/2011/renewable_energy/ere201101036. htm[2012-06-30].

Transparency International. 2011. Corruption perception index 2010 results. http://earthtrends. wri. org[2012-06-30].

United Nations Development Programme. 2010. Human development report 2007/2008. Houndsmille, Basingstoke, Hampshire: Palgrave Macmillan. http://hdr. undp. org/en/reports/global/hdr2010[2012-06-30].

Wittmann, C. M. , Hunt, D. S. , Arnett, D. B. 2009. Explaining alliance success: competences, resources, relational factors, and resource-advantage theory. *Industrial Marketing Management*,38(7),743-756.

World Bank. 2011. Ease of doing business ranking. http://www. doingbusiness. org/rankings.

World Bank. 2012. GDP per capita 2009. http://data. worldbank. org/indicator/NY. GDP. PCAP. CD[2012-06-10].

Xiao, X. 2010. Joint lab unveils Audi all-electric concept car. http://www. chinadaily. com. cn/bizchina/2010-11/08/content_11516618. htm[2012-06-10].

Yale Center for Environmental Law and Policy, Center for International Earth Science Information Network. 2005. 2005 Environmental Sustainability Index. New Haven: Yale Center for Environmental Law and Policy.

Yale Center for Environmental Law and Policy. 2012. 2012 environmental performance index. Table of main results country scores. http://epi. yale. edu/Countries[2012-06-10].

Authour

Professor Dr. Dirk Holtbrügge is professor of International Management(Head of Department)at the School of Business and Economics of the University of Erlangen-Nürnberg, Germany. He received his doctorate and his habilitation from the University of Dortmund, Germany. He occasionally holds lectures at universities in

China, India and Russia. His main research interests are in the areas of international management, human resources management, and management in emerging markets. He has published seven books, eight edited volumes and more than 70 articles in refereed journals such as *Academy of Management Learning & Education*, *Asian Business & Management*, *European Journal of International Management*, *European Management Journal*, *Human Resources Management*, *International Business Review*, *International Journal of Cross Cultural Management*, *International Journal of Emerging Markets*, *Journal of Business Ethics*, *Journal of East European Management Studies*, *Journal of International Business Studies*, *Journal of International Management*, *Management International Review*, and *Thunderbird International Business Review*. He is also a member of the editorial boards of *Journal for East-European Management Studies and Management International Review*.

Dipl. Kffr. Corinna Dögl is a senior research assistant at the Department of International Management of the University of Erlangen-Nürnberg, Germany, where she also completed her studies in business administration in 2008. Her research interest is in the area of corporate social and environmental responsibility with a special focus on renewable energies and electro-mobility. She has published several articles in refereed journals such as *International Journal of Emerging Markets*, *Journal of East European Management Studies*, and *Journal of International Management*.

14

Low Carbon Industrial Development in Chongqing: Automotive Industry as Example

Tan Xianchun

14.1 Introduction

14.1.1 Research background

Global climate change is the most significant environment and development challenge that human beings face together in the 21st century. From the United Nations Framework Convention on Climate Change to Kyoto Protocol, and to the post-Kyoto negotiations and the UN Conference in Copenhagen, countries are fully aware that global warming will have a long-term, significant impact on the future social and economic development and on the continuation of natural ecology. More and more countries in the world are recognizing and supporting the development of low-carbon economy as the primary approach to coordinate the social and economic development, to assure the energy security and to cope with climate change.

14.1.2 Research objectives

Chongqing, as a major national automotive production base, produced and sold out around 1.7 million vehicles by Chongqing's automotive companies (including the investments on the branches outside the Municipality), accounting for 12% nationwide; on the other hand, automotive industry is the first major pillar industry in

Chongqing, and its low-carbon transitions are of core importance for Chongqing's low-carbon developments. The automotive industry, of relatively strong representations and of certain practical significances, will be the entry point to the study of Chongqing's low-carbon transitions.

The Chongqing's automotive and motorcycle industry in this report mainly refers to the automotive and motorcycle manufacturing sector, different from the transport sector. In the context that the transport sector increasingly becomes the main source of emissions, the achievement of the city's low-carbon transitions is bound to develop environment-friendly vehicles. According to the data provided by the Ministry of Construction(2008), vehicle fuel consumption of the road transport is the main transport energy consumption, accounting for about 70% (by equivalent) of the total energy consumption of the transport sector.

In this report, the vehicle greenhouse gas emissions are divided into the stages of designing, manufacturing, using and recycling in accordance with the full life cycle, wherein the course of use occupies the main part over the vehicle's life cycle emissions. This report starts from the manufacturing stage to study the method and major measures to achieve low-carbon transitions in automotive and motorcycle manufacturing sectors with the main purpose of reducing the carbon emissions of the produced vehicles during use.

14.1.3 Research methodology

This report summarizes and reviews the status of low-carbon developments in related areas as well as the national and international advanced-experiences, analyzing the current developments of automotive industry in Chongqing and the efforts of dealing with the climate change, and investigating current status of carbon emissions of the three sectors, and analyzing the corresponding carbon emission characteristics and the barriers of the low-carbon transitions. On this basis, systematically considering the international development trend of the automotive industry, the national industrial policy guidance and strategic layout, the resource, energy and environment constraints in Chongqing, and the future development plans of the industry as well as the future technological development trends in related fields, using Scenario analysis to analyze the future CO_2 emissions change trends of the industry and the key factors impacting the low-carbon transitions in different scenarios, and further determining the focus on the development of low-carbon transitions, and proposing the realization approaches and policy advices on the low-carbon transitions of the industry in accordance with local conditions.

14.2 Current status of automotive industries in Chongqing

14.2.1 Development trend of national and international automotive industry

Since 1970s, governments initiated the development wave for low-carbon automotive industry from the points of improving the future competitiveness of the national automotive industry and maintaining the sustainable development of economy and society. The energy-savings and environmental-protections of the automotive-using energy and power systems are the core and primary issues of the sustainable development of the automotive industry, and the energy diversification, vehicles with energy-savings and lightweight, clean emissions, and electric powers will be the development trend of the automotive industry. By the formulation of national development strategies, the organization of large-scale government and enterprises partner program, and the implementation of supporting policies during market introduction phase and other measures, the R&D, promotions and applications of new energy vehicles and energy-saving technologies of conventional vehicles will be encouraged.

14.2.1.1 The aspect of technology

There is still a big gap between the national energy-saving technological level of the conventional vehicles and the international advanced level, and only Beijing is implementing the EURO IV standard in the car field. The average fuel consumptions per hundred kilometers of the passenger vehicles in 2008 were 8.13 liters, significantly higher than the corresponding fuel consumptions of 6.6 liters in Europe and 5.9 liters in Japan, and the fuel consumptions and CO_2 emissions will become the major obstacles for China's vehicles' going to the world, as seen in Figure 14.1.

The development of the international new energy vehicles follows the trend of hybrid vehicles as the short-term focus and pure electric vehicles and hydrogen fuel cell vehicles as the medium- and long-term focus. China is increasing the supporting efforts on the new energy automotive industry, and will invest 100 billion RMB by 2020(including the central government financial subsidies/local government financial subsidies, tax breaks, travel tax exemptions and purchase tax exemptions, etc.), supporting the industry alliance for the development of energy-saving and new energy vehicles as well as the development of parts enterprises, the plug-in hybrid as the short-term focus, pure electric vehicles as the major long-term direction, promoting the formation of the industrial chain, developing the consuming market of new energy vehicles, and accelerating the infrastructure constructions for new energy vehicles.

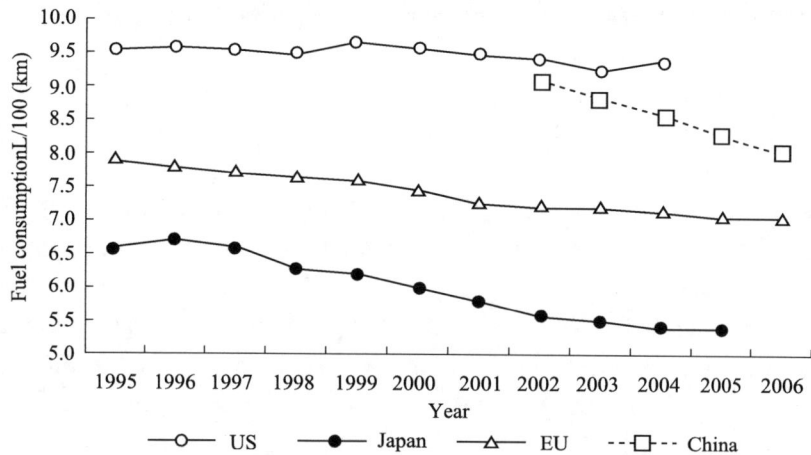

Figure 14.1 The trend comparison of the average fuel consumptions of China and foreign countries(2002 – 2006)

The alternative fuel vehicle industry in China is still in its starting stage, and there are many obstacles. Although with the dual national supports of policy and financial funding, some great breakthroughs in the R&D of certain technology fields have been achieved, however, there are still many challenges for the industrialization, such as low productions of biomass fuels, high cost of productions, urgent requirements for the optimization of alcohol fuel regulatory standards and emission standards, and urgent requirements for the upgrading of the vehicle technology for liquefied petroleum gas, natural gas and other fuel gas.

14.2.1.2 The aspect of policy

The developed countries in the automotive industry in the world ensured the improvement of the vehicle fuel economy mainly by levying fuel tax, increasing access standards and other measures, and encouraging the development and applications of energy-saving technologies by financial subsidies and other measures. Our country opened up the domestic energy-saving market mainly by the consumer subsidies and other incentives, and driving the improvement of the fuel economy of the automotive industry by consumption.

During the R&D, production and promotion stages of new energy vehicles, each country promotes the R&D and production and commercialization of new energy vehicles mainly by the formulation of government action plans and the increase of the R&D investment of new energy vehicles; and encouraging and guiding consumers to purchase energy-saving and new energy vehicles by the utilization of financial subsidies, and tax relief for the purchase tax, consumption tax and personal income tax and other measures.

Our country clearly proposed the implementation of national strategies for new energy vehicles, the formulation of government's action plans, the increase of R&D investment and the financial subsidy efforts, and the tax relief for the purchase tax, consumption tax, and personal income tax, and the promotion of the development, production and commercialization of new energy vehicles.

The biomass renewable energy vehicles have attracted wide attention and vigorous support from major automotive manufacturing countries, and the natural gas vehicles will continue to be promoted and utilized in special areas. Our country has established the overall development strategy for alternative energy as "with renewable energy as the alternative to fossil energy, with new energy as the alternative to conventional energy, with advantage energy as the alternative to scarce energy".

14.2.2 Current status of automotive industry in Chongqing

Automotive industry is the largest pillar industry in Chongqing. Chongqing's automotive industry completed a total of 258 billion RMB of industrial output value in 2009. The automotive industry output value accounted for 34.4% of the municipal total industrial output value, and the incremental amount contributed to 70% of the municipal total industrial incremental amount. The industrial output value of the enterprises above designated size of the automotive and motorcycle part industry was 92.8 billion RMB, of which automotive part industry achieved the industrial output value of 52.2 billion RMB.

In 2009, the city's automotive industry(excluding the investment in the branches outside the city) achieved a profit of 10.1 billion RMB, up 72.7% compared with last year; and the total profit and tax are 19.96 billion RMB, an increase of 58.7% compared with last year. The profits and taxes from each department of the municipal automotive industry(excluding the investment in the branches outside the city) in 2009 can be seen in Table 14.1.

Table 14.1 The profit and tax from different sectors of Chongqing's automotive industry

Item Department	Total profits /hundred million RMB	Growth/%	Tax /hundred million RMB	Growth/%
Chongqing's vehicle industry	101.0	72.7	199.6	58.7
Vehicle companies	36.0	120.6	102.4	91.8
Automotive parts companies	38.6	96.1	54.9	64.7
Motorcycle enterprises	8.0	0.7	13.6	4.8
Motorcycle parts enterprises	16.9	29.3	26.3	16.8

The gross industrial output value of the enterprises above designated size in the automotive and motorcycle parts industry in 2009 was 92.8 billion RMB, of which the automotive parts industry achieved 52.2 billion RMB of gross industrial output value.

By the end of 2009, there are 27 municipal manufacturing enterprises with national announcement that have formed a production capacity of 2 million cars. Chongqing is the national largest motorcycle production base.

In 2009, the cumulative productions and sales of automotives by Chongqing's enterprises (including the investment in the branches outside the city) were 1,698,000 and 1,676,000, respectively, and the sales accounted for 12.28% (Figure 14.2) of the national. The productions and sales of commercial vehicles were 507,000 and 497,000, respectively. The cumulative productions and sales of motorcycles were 9,518,000 and 9,561,000, respectively, and the sales accounted for 37.5% in the country.

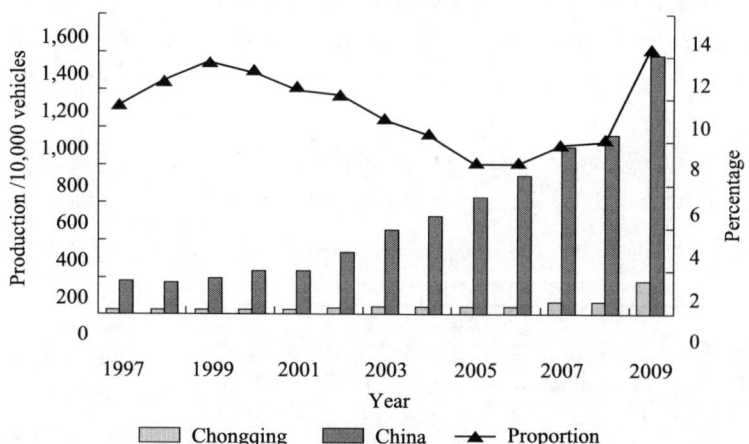

Figure 14.2 Chongqing's automotive output and national share (1997 – 2009)

In 2009, Chongqing totally exported 28,000 units of completed automotives, which was 51.5% lower than last year and earned $170 million foreign exchanges. The total exports of motorcycles were 2,160,000 and earned $820 million foreign exchanges.

In the field of conventional automotives, the automotive industry in Chongqing has always been committed to the development of small cars. In the lightweighting of the car, efficient the engine, advancing the transmission and other areas, Chongqing's automotive industry insists on the implementation of the R&D and applications of energy-saving and emission-reduction technologies. In the aspect of R&D of new energy vehicles, Chongqing's automotive industry is leading the country. However, the automotive industry in Chongqing is relatively weak in the aspect of R&D of supporting parts in electric vehicles. In the aspect of alternative-fuel vehicles, at present, the annual output value of Chongqing's natural gas vehicle industry is more than 1.8 billion RMB, forming the most completed chain of natural gas vehicle industry. In April 2009, some of municipal vehicles of Chongqing were in the first trial use of biodiesel refined from food-oil wastes.

14.2.3 Current status of automotive industry emission

According to the accounting method of the CO_2 emissions of automotive industry based on the whole life cycle, the total CO_2 emissions produced during use by the produced vehicles in Chongqing in 2008 were 1,855,000 tons, up 59% compared with 2005. The average CO_2 emissions per vehicle by the produced vehicles in Chongqing in 2008 were 178.8 g/km, down 5% compared with 2005.

The average CO_2 emissions per passenger vehicle in Chongqing in 2008 were 131.5g/km, down 5% compared with 2005; and the average CO_2 emissions per commercial vehicle were 183.7g/km, down 12.7% compared with 2005. The total CO_2 emissions during use and the average CO_2 emissions per vehicle generated by each vehicle model produced in Chongqing in 2008 can be seen from Table 14.2.

Table 14.2 The automotive production and CO_2 emissions of different type(by use) vehicles in Chongqing(2008)

Year Item	2005			2008		
	Passenger vehicle	Commercial vehicle	Total	Passenger vehicle	Commercial vehicle	Total
Production /10,000 units	46.9	18.2	65.1	76.0	32.4	109.0
CO_2 emissions per individual vehicles/g/km	136.6	203.6	188.4	131.8	184.0	178.8
CO_2 emissions /10,000 tons	608.7	557.1	1165.9	953.5	901.5	1855.0
Reduction ratio of CO_2 emissions per individual vehicles(compared to 2005)/%	—	—	—	4.9%	12.7%	5.0%

Notes: Accounting method—viewing the aforementioned introduction
Source: Production data from the *Report of Automotive Industry of Chongqing* 2008

The total CO_2 emissions of the conventional vehicles(excluding the new energy vehicles) during use in Chongqing in 2005 were 11,659,000 tons, of which the total CO_2 emissions of gasoline vehicles were 7,364,000 tons, accounting for 63.2%; the total CO_2 emissions of diesel vehicles were 4,295,000 tons, accounting for 36.8%. The total CO_2 emissions of the conventional vehicles(excluding the new energy vehicles) during use in Chongqing in 2009 were 18,485,000 tons, of which the total CO_2 emissions of gasoline vehicles were 11,007,000 tons, accounting for 59.5%; the total CO_2 emissions of diesel vehicles were 7,478,000 tons, accounting for 40.5% (Table 14.3).

Table 14.3 The automotive production and CO_2 emissions of different type(by fuel) vehicles in Chongqing(2008)

Year Item	2005		2008	
	Gasoline vehicle	Diesel vehicle	Gasoline vehicle	Diesel vehicle
Production/unit	503,258	148,293	800,878	285,662
Carbon Emissions per individual vehicle/g/km	149.3	295.5	140.2	267.1
Carbon emissions/10,000 tons	736.4	429.5	1100.7	747.8
Share/%	63.2	36.8	59.5	40.5

14.3 Research conclusions

14.3.1 The results of scenario analysis for the target formulations of the low-carbon transitions

The total carbon emissions and the growing rate of the whole life cycle of the automotive sector in Scenario Ⅰ, Scenario Ⅱ and Scenario Ⅲ between 2005 and 2020 are shown in Figure 14.3 and Table 14.4.

Table 14.4 The total CO_2 emissions of the vehicles produced in Chongqing during the whole life cycles   (Unit: 10,000 tons)

Year	Scenario Ⅰ	Scenario Ⅱ	Scenario Ⅲ
2015	4,415	3,863	3,596
2020	5,651.5	4,692	4,069

In 2020 the carbon emissions per vehicle of Chongqing's automotive industry in Scenario Ⅱ and Scenario Ⅲ will be reduced by 33% and 42%, respectively. Because of the development of energy-saving technology and new energy vehicles, in 2020 the carbon emissions during the whole life cycles of Chongqing's automotive industry in

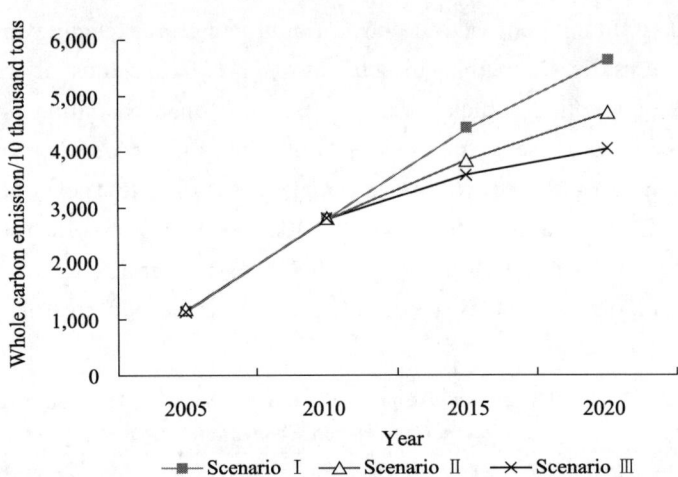

Figure 14.3　The total carbon emissions of the vehicles in Chongqing during use

Scenario Ⅱ and Scenario Ⅲ will be reduced by 17% and 28%, respectively, compared with Scenario Ⅰ. The carbon emissions per vehicle and the effects of emission-reductions of automotive sector in Scenario Ⅰ, Scenario Ⅱ and Scenario Ⅲ between 2005 and 2020 are shown in Table 14.5 and Figure 14.4.

Table 14.5　The scenario analysis of carbon emissions per vehicle produced in Chongqing　(Unit: %)

Year	The effect of average carbon emission-reductions per vehicle		
	Scenario Ⅰ	Scenario Ⅱ	Scenario Ⅲ
2015	16.88	27.28	32.30
2020	19.34	33.03	41.93

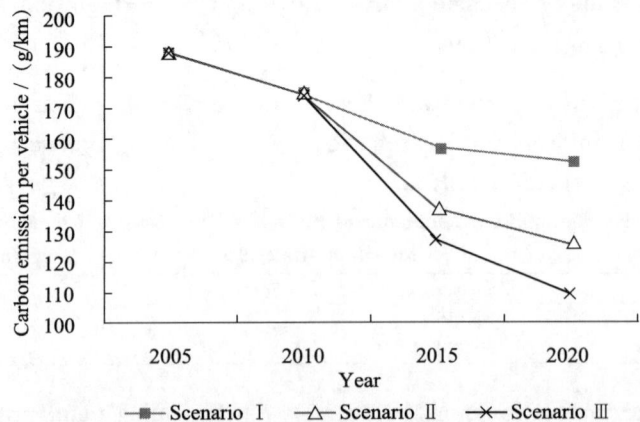

Figure 14.4　The carbon emissions per vehicle of Chongqing's automotive manufacturing industry

The main factors impacting on the carbon emissions level of Chongqing's automotive industry may be summarized as the product structure and technological progress and so on. The representative indicator of the product structure is the proportion of new energy vehicles in the automotive industry, and the representative indicator of the technological progress is the fuel economy at each time point. Next, the influence of the two main factors on the future carbon emissions level of Chongqing's automotive industry will be analyzed.

14.3.2 The target analysis of automotive industry

By the end of "12th-Five", the conventional energy-saving technology in the field of automotive manufacturing in Chongqing would be increased to the domestic advanced level, and be reaching the international advanced level in certain related field. The commercial production of hybrid vehicles will be 150,000 units and be accounted for 5% of the total automotive production. The production capacity of the pure electric vehicles will reach 300,000 units annually and be accounted for 10% of the total automotive production. The CNG automotives of 80 km/h and electric motorcycles would be encouraged and promoted with efforts and be trying to achieve the industrialization of pure motorcycles by 2015. The carbon-emissions per vehicle will be reduced by 27% compared with that in 2005. The production and sale of electric vehicles will reach 400,000 units, and the production and sale of hybrid vehicles and plug-in hybrid vehicles will reach 300,000 units. The target of reducing the carbon-emissions per vehicle by 33% compared with that in 2005 will be achieved.

14.3.3 Road map and policy advice

The government should be enhancing the planning guidance and assessment constraints on the low-carbon developments; setting the target constraints of total emissions; specifying the unit of emission standards of high emissions products; linking to the performance evaluations of the leaders of the districts and counties and departments; carrying out multi-levels and demonstrations using the experience of one point to lead the whole area; carrying out the pilot of automotive parts remanufacturing; strengthening the capacity building of the low-carbon developments; exploiting and developing the clean energy with efforts; expanding the development of the key technologies of new energy vehicles; providing the supporting policies on innovations; increasing the government procurement efforts; increasing the price subsidies and tax relief efforts for new energy; studying the carbon trading; and actively carrying out national and international exchanges and cooperation on the introduction of talents, project cooperation, investments on the low-carbon industries and other aspects. The road map of low carbon of Chongqing's automotive industry is shown in Figure 14.5.

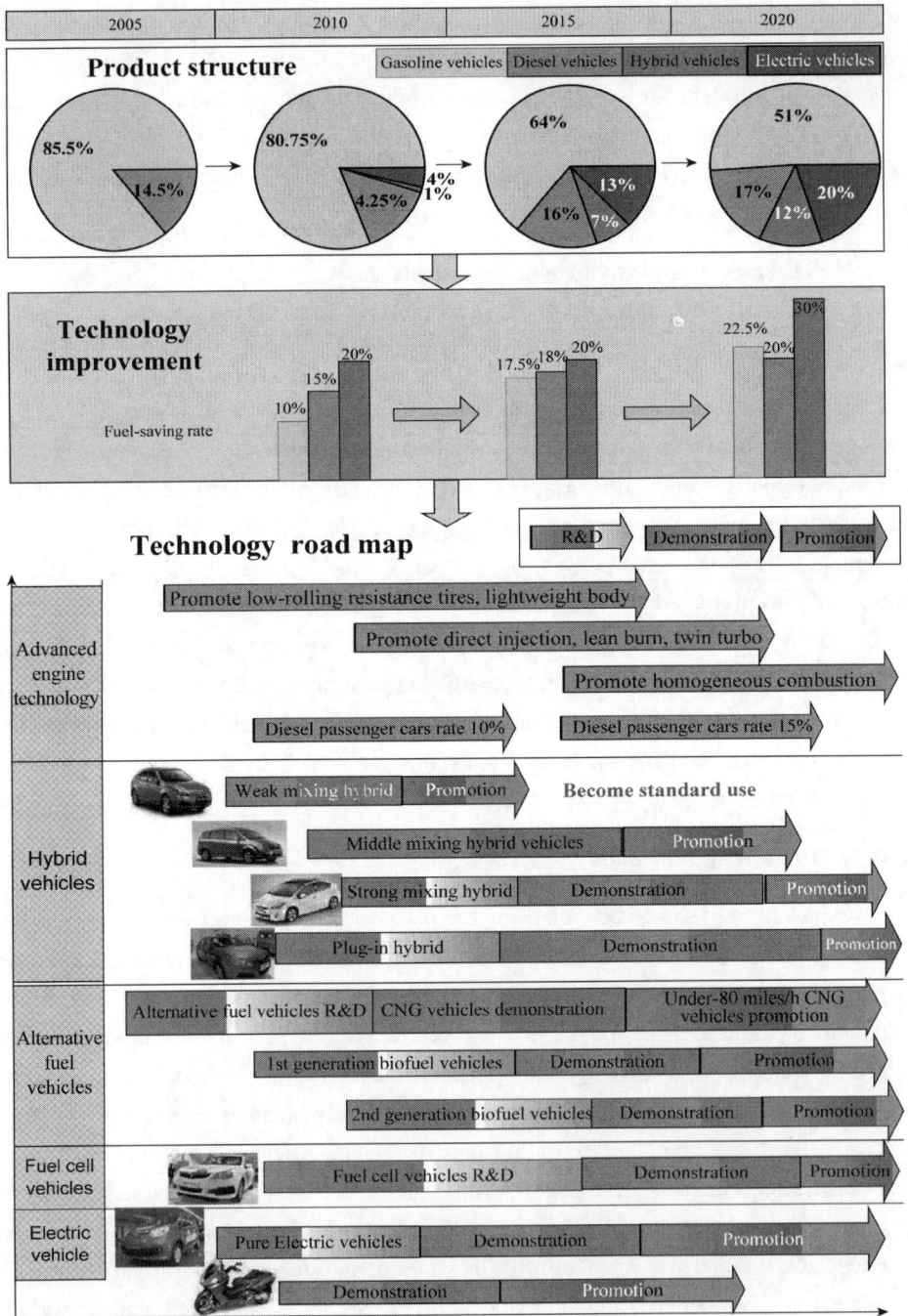

Figure 14.5 The road map of low carbon transitions of Chongqing's automotive manufacturing industry

References

Andress, D., Nguyen, D. T., Das, S., 2010. Low-carbon fuel standard-status and analytic issues. *Energy Policy*, 38(1), 580-591.

Barkenbus, J., 2009. Our electric automotive future: CO_2 savings through a disruptive technology. *Policy and Society*, 27(4), 399-410.

Bian, J. W., 2007. Direction and measures for emission reduction and energy saving of vehicles. traffic& transportation, 1, 55-56.

Chen, J. H., 2010. Several countermeasures for development of Chongqing new energy vehicles. *Technology and Market*, 17, 12.

Hekkert, M. P., Hendriks, F. H. J. F., Faaij, A. P. C., 2003. Natural gas as an alternative to crude oil in automotive fuel chains well-to-wheel analysis and transition strategy development. *Energy Policy*, 33(5), 579-594.

Hensher, D. A., 2008. Climate change, enhanced greenhouse gas emissions and passenger transport - What can we do to make a difference? *Transportation Research Part D: Transport and Environment*, 13(2), 95-111.

Hickmana, R., Ashirub, O., Banisterc D., 2010. Transport and climate change: Simulating the options for carbon reduction in London. *Transport Policy*, 17(2), 110-125.

Huang, Z. J., 2003. Model of Life Cycle Assessment of Vehicle Fuel. *Journal of Tongji University (Natural Science Edition)*, 31(12), 5.

McCollum, D., Yang, C., 2009. Achieving deep reductions in US transport greenhouse gas emissions: Scenario analysis and policy implications. *Energy Policy*, 37(12), 5580-5596.

Ou, X. M., Zhang, X. L., Chang, S. Y., 2010. Scenario analysis on alternative fuel/vehicle for China's future road transport: Life-cycle energy demand and GHG emissions. *Energy Policy*, 38(8), 3943-3956.

Prakash, R., Henham, A, Bhat, I. K., 2005. Gross carbon emissions from alternative transport fuels in India. *Energy for Sustainable Development*, Energy for Sustainable Development, 9(2), 10-16.

Tan, X. C., Mu, Z. K., Wang, S., et al. 2011. Study on whole-life cycle automotive manufacturing industry CO_2 emission accounting method and Application in Chongqing. *Procedia Environmental Sciences*. 5, 167-172.

Timilsina, G. R., Shrestha, A., 2009. Transport sector CO_2 emissions growth in Asia: Underlying factors and policy options. *Energy Policy*, 37(11), 4523-4539.

Xu, Y. Z., 2010. exploration for automobile industry how to put the national CO2 emission reduction strategy to practice. *Auto industry research*, 9, 12-14.

Author

Dr. Tan Xianchun is a professor of the Institute of Policy and Management of

Chinese Academy of Sciences (CAS). Her main fields of research are low carbon development, green manufacturing, and risk management. She has led many research projects, such as "Research on Low Carbon Transition for Heavy Industry of West China", "Chongqing: A Low Carbon Transition, with Case Studies in the Energy, Chemical, and Automotive Manufacturing Sectors", "Research on the Road map and Countermeasures of Low Carbon Development for Chongqing", and "Research on Risk Management Methodology Based on Process for Airline Companies".

Part 4

Enterprise Technology Innovation and Future Challenges for Green Growth

15

Green Technologies—Germany's and China's Activities in Renewable Energies

Rainer Frietsch

15.1 Introduction

China and Germany are the largest exporters of high-technology in the world. At the same time both countries are large importers of such technologies. This paper follows an empirical approach to assess the performance, the competitiveness, and the science and technology foundations of China and Germany in renewable energy technologies.

Renewable energies are defined by three categories, namely solar/photovoltaics, wind and hydro. For a patent and publication analysis also geothermal and biomass technologies are included. The first part of the paper addresses the question of export performance and comparative advantages in renewable energy technologies. The second part of the paper tries to shed some light on the scientific and technological foundations of these export activities. To assess the scientific foundations, scientific publications in the bibliometric database web of science by Thomson Reuters are used. The technological competitiveness, which mainly reflects the strengths and weaknesses of the industry system, is analyzed by using patent applications to the State Intellectual Property Office(SIPO) and on the transnational level(Frietsch and Schmoch, 2010) based on the EPO Worldwide Patent Statistical Database(PATSTAT)database. This chapter closes with a summary and some concluding remarks as well as a set of open questions for future research.

15.2 Methods

The trade theory argues, international exports contribute to productivity and high real income by specialization according to comparative advantages (Ricardo, 1996; Balassa, 1965). The two sides of this strategy are an efficient use of resources to increase the labor productivity and the import of relatively low-priced goods and commodities to meet the domestic demand instead of directly producing them. In consequence, an international division of labor is at play where countries are most successful with those goods and commodities, which they can produce more efficient (cheaper) or which cannot be produced by others at all or with at least the same quality. In this case the price is relative to the quality, which means that those goods and commodities are sold, which achieve a favorable cost-quality-ratio against the background of a given demand. For the analyses applied here in the context of renewable energy technologies, this idea can be reversed: If a country is specialized in certain technologies, this indicates relative strong positions in international trade and hence this country reaches positive cost-quality-ratios in producing the underlying goods, commodities or services. The data used here are exports of renewable energy goods, stemming from the UN database COMTRADE.

The scientific performance of a nation is the basis for its technological output. A major contribution of science to technological development—among others—is the results of scientific research. The link between science and technology is often indirect and less obvious, as in many cases a distinct time lag can be observed between activities in science and their effect on technology (Schmoch, 2006; Moed et al., 2004; van Raan, 1988). To measure the performance of science, publications in international journals are used. Scientific publications analyzed here refer to articles in journals included in the Science Citation Index (SCI). The bibliometric analyses of scientific publications have proved a meaningful and effective tool.

Patents are only applicable to technological innovations, where they can be interpreted as an output indicator of the R&D process. This study uses patent applications in renewable technology areas to measure the competitiveness of nations (Frietsch and Schmoch, 2010; Frietsch and Schmoch, 2006; Schmoch, 2004). From a simple legal perspective, patents give, for a limited period, the applicant an exclusive right of usage to secure monopolistic revenue. From the perspective of analyzing innovation systems, patents can be interpreted as an indicator of the codified knowledge of enterprises, and in a wider perspective, of countries. In this study, patent filings at two different levels are analyzed: Firstly, national applications to the SIPO, covering filings to the Chinese market. Secondly, patent applications to the European Patent Office(EPO) and via the so-called *Patent Cooperation Treaty* (PCT) route are used in an integrated perspective and they are referred to as "transnational patents". Any patent family that at least covering an EPO filing or a PCT application is included (Frietsch and Schmoch, 2010). This perspective allows a comparison beyond home bias effects and, at the same time, reflects to some extent patents of higher economic and technological importance.

The specialization index revealed literature advantage(RLA) for publications or revealed patent advantage (RPA) for patents is defined as:

$$RLA_{kj} = 100 \times \tanh \ln[(P_{kj}/\sum jP_{kj})/(\sum k P_{kj}/\sum kj P_{kj})].$$

With P_{kj} indicating the number of publications/patents of country k in the scientific/technological field j. Positive values point to the fact that the field has a higher weight in the portfolio of the country than its weight in the world. Negative values indicate specializations below the average, respectively. This indicator allows the assessment of the relative position of a field in a country beyond any size effects. Neither the size of the scientific/technological field nor the size of the country have an impact on the outcome of this indicator.

15.3 Exports from and to China

China's share of worldwide exports in renewable energy strongly increased since 2004 and reached a level well beyond 35% in 2010(Figure 15.1). This is well above China's total share of worldwide exports of finished goods, which was about 17% in 2010. The main driver of the Chinese renewable energy exports is the area of photovoltaics where China reached a level of more than 43% at the end of the observation period. While there was a slowing down between 2008 and 2009, an enormous growth can be seen between 2006 and 2008 and again between 2009 and 2010. It can also be seen that solar thermal energy is second in the list of renewable energy exports of China and its share is slightly above the total average of Chinese exports. Hydro energy products have recently gained some importance and were also growing since 2006. It is interesting to note that wind energy exports are the lowest for China and even decreased in 2010 compared to the previous years. In sum, China is very export oriented in photovoltaics and is almost not export oriented at all concerning wind.

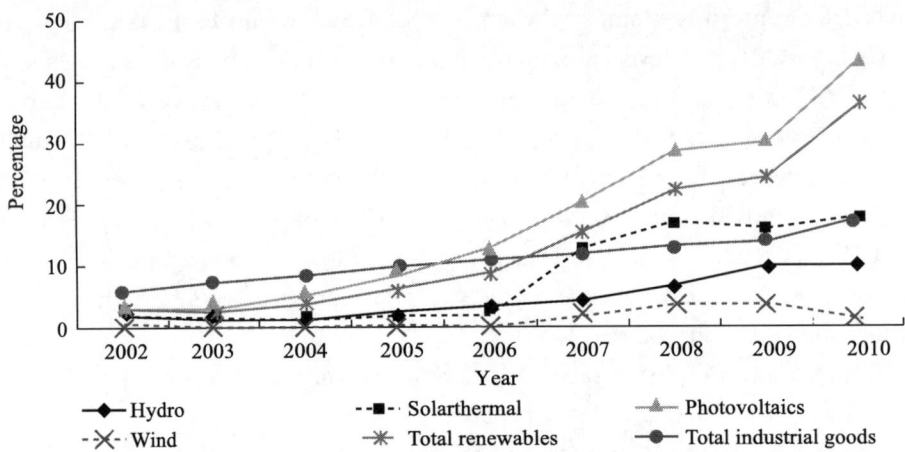

Figure 15.1 China's shares of worldwide exports in renewable energy and total

Source: UN—COMTRADE, Fraunhofer ISI calculations

When we compare China's and Germany's shares of worldwide exports in renewable energy in the period 2008 – 2010(Figure 15.2), this last statement is clearly to be stressed. The German profile, on the other hand, is somehow more balanced even though there is also one technology which is outstanding, namely wind. Almost one third of the worldwide exports in wind energy originate in Germany. It can also be seen that the share of total renewable exports is above the share of Germany's total industrial goods exports. However, only wind and also the small field of hydro are above this share whereas solar thermal and especially the large field of photovoltaics is slightly below the share of total renewable export of Germany. In sum, Germany is very export oriented in wind energy and also shows some activity in the other areas. In total, the German export profile contains considerable shares of renewable energy goods and commodities.

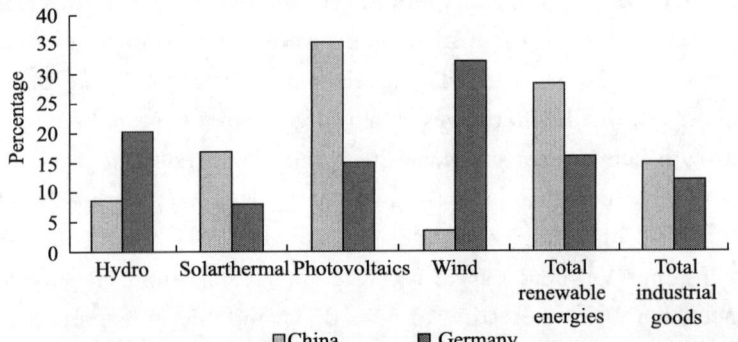

Figure 15.2 China's and Germany's shares of worldwide exports in renewable energy, 2008 – 2010

Source: UN—COMTRADE, Fraunhofer ISI calculations

What has been said so far based on worldwide shares of exports of the two countries under observation here, can be more clearly presented by using the export specialization profile in renewable energy as it is depicted in Figure 15.3. The specialization profile shows the revealed comparative advantage and can be interpreted in line with the argumentation formulated by Balassa(1965). Both countries have comparative advantages in the total area of renewable energy, with China ahead of Germany. This means that for both countries renewable energy goods and commodities play an outstanding role in their individual export profiles. It is very interesting to note that the two countries have—with the exception of photovoltaics—complementary profiles, which means that the strengths in one country is among the weaknesses in the other country and vice versa. Especially, wind exports belong to the German strengths, while they clearly belong to the Chinese weaknesses.

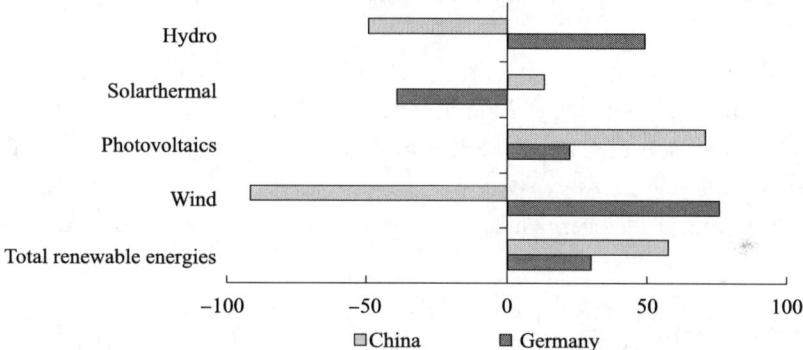

Figure 15.3 Export specialization of China and Germany in renewable energy, 2008 - 2010 Source: UN—COMTRADE, Fraunhofer ISI calculations

In the spirit of export theory and an international division of labor one would expect that Germany exports wind(and China imports wind), while China exports photovoltaics(and Germany, to some extent, imports these photovoltaics). When we look at Figure 15.4, we see that part of that story is true and is exactly what happens in reality. Almost 11% of China's worldwide exports in photovoltaics are going to Germany, which is almost one third of total Chinese exports in this area. However the German exports to China in the area of wind energy are limited to a level below 1%. As a reminder, Germany's total export share in wind goods and commodities was more than 32%. So, almost nothing of Germany's exports in wind goes to China so far.

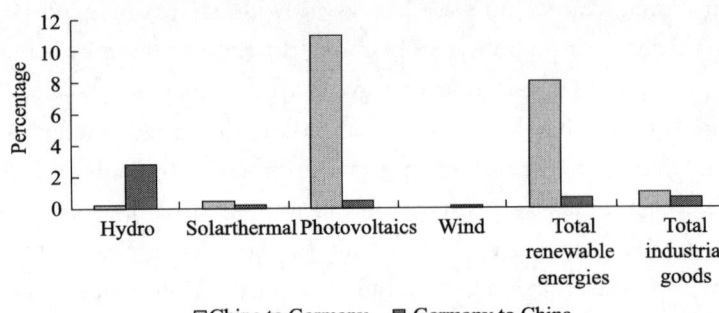

Figure 15.4 Bilateral exports of China and Germany in relation to worldwide exports, 2008 – 2010

Source: UN—COMTRADE, Fraunhofer ISI calculations

15.4 The science base—scientific publications in renewable energy

The absolute number of scientific publications in renewable energy was growing considerably since the beginning of the new century(Figure 15.5). It almost doubled every five years. In the case of Germany the growth was smoother, while China was growing steeply after 2002 and even accelerated in the recent years since 2008. More than 2,700 publications in renewable energy in 2010 are more than two times the number published by German authors(more than 1,200).

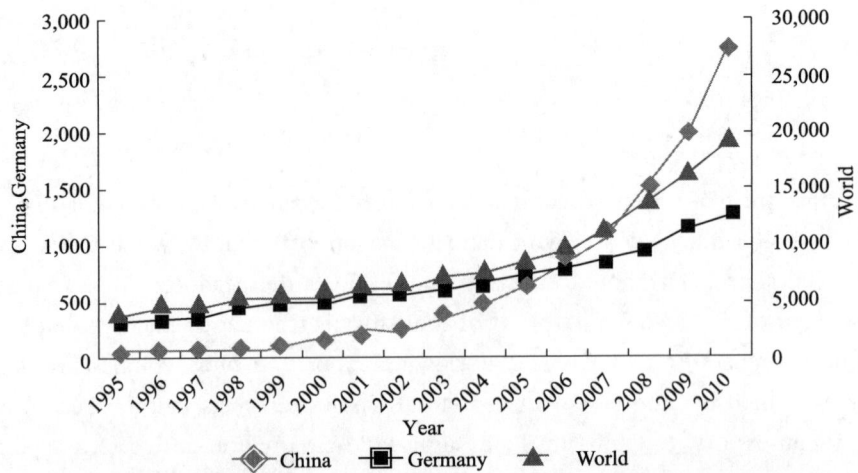

Figure 15.5 Absolute number of scientific publication in renewable energy

Source: ThomsonReuters—Science Citation Index, Fraunhofer ISI calculations

Germany's share(Figure 15. 6) in scientific publications slightly decreased in the last decade, recently reaching a level of about 8%, while it reached a level beyond 9% during the 1990s. Germany's share in renewable energy publications is on a similar level like the total share, but recently fell below the German average. China, on the other hand, permanently increased its worldwide share of scientific publications and recently reached a level of more than 15%. However, the share of renewable energy publications is clearly below the total shares, but recently caught up. This means that the role of renewable energy publications plays a smaller role in the scientific profile of China than it plays in the profile of Germany. It is interesting to note that both, photovoltaics and wind energy, reach equal shares in the case of China, while Germany has a much clearer scientific focus on wind energy sciences and only about half of their number is published in photovoltaics.

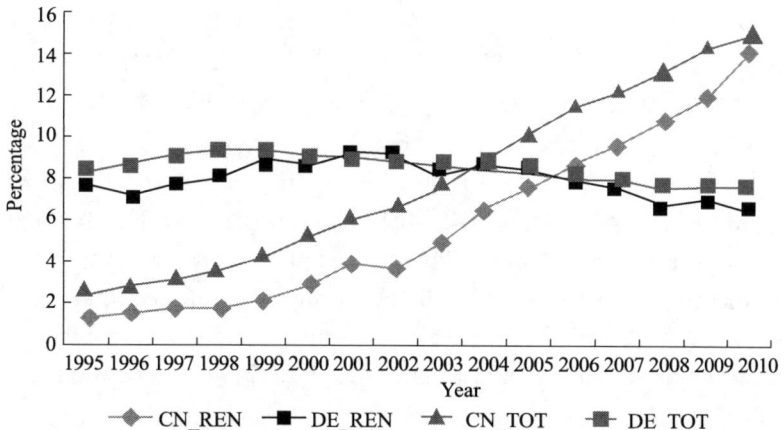

Figure 15. 6 China's and Germany's shares of scientific publication in renewable energy
Source: ThomsonReuters—Science Citation Index, Fraunhofer ISI calculations

15.5 The industry base in renewable energy

When comparing the patent applications in renewable energy at the SIPO of China(Figure 15. 7), covering the Chinese market, two main results are striking. First, for both countries positive long-term trends are visible, even with an accelerated increase after 2005. Second, China files 10 times more patents in renewable energy than Germany—at least in China. However, given the absolute number of patent filings in China, 1,100 patent applications in renewable energy in 2008 are not very much. China filed almost 150,000 patents in 2008, while Germany applied for 8,000 patents. This means renewable energy reached the share of about 0. 8% in the case of

China and about 1.8% in the case of Germany.

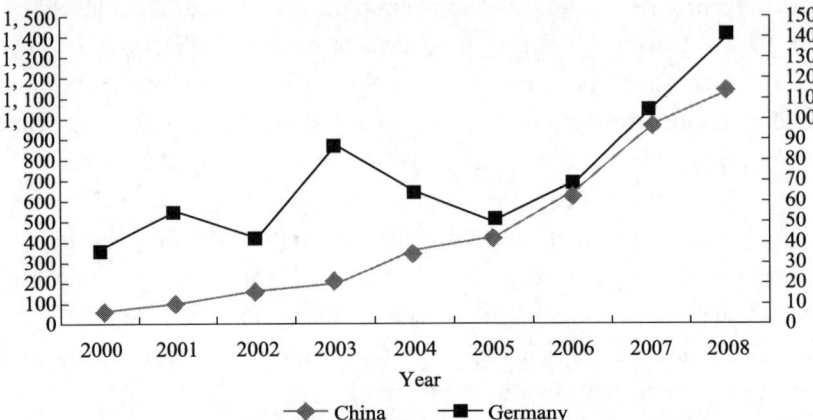

Figure 15.7 Patent applications in renewable energy technologies at SIPO—absolute numbers
Source:EPO-PATSTAT,SIPO,Fraunhofer ISI calculations

Figure 15.8 offers additional information. After 2004 the share of Chinese applications in China increased from about 40% to more than 70%. The shares in renewable energy technologies are slightly below that share and recently reached a level of about 65%. Germany, on the other hand, was responsible for about 5% of patent applications to the Chinese State intellectual property office, but even lost ground in the recent years after 2006. However, one can see that the shares of renewable energy technologies is above the German average which means that China is an attractive market for German technologies especially in renewable energy.

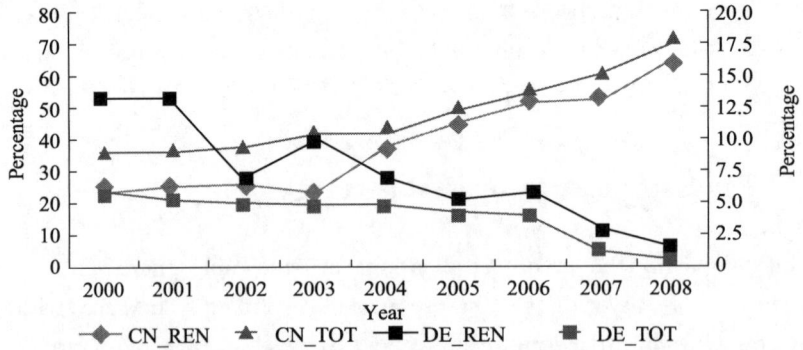

Figure 15.8 Patent applications in renewable energy technologies at SIPO—shares
Source:EPO-PATSTAT,SIPO,Fraunhofer ISI calculations

In the subfields of renewable energies considerable differences are depicted in Figure 15.9. China reaches only a level of about 50% of total photovoltaic patent applications in China, while it is responsible for 80% or more in the fields of thermal energy or biomass. In the case of wind China is responsible for almost 60% of the filings. Germany, on the other hand, almost only focuses on wind energy, where it reaches a share of about 9%, as well as photovoltaic where it reaches a level of about 6%. These two areas clearly belong to the technological strengths of Germany in China, where the Chinese market is attractive to German inventors.

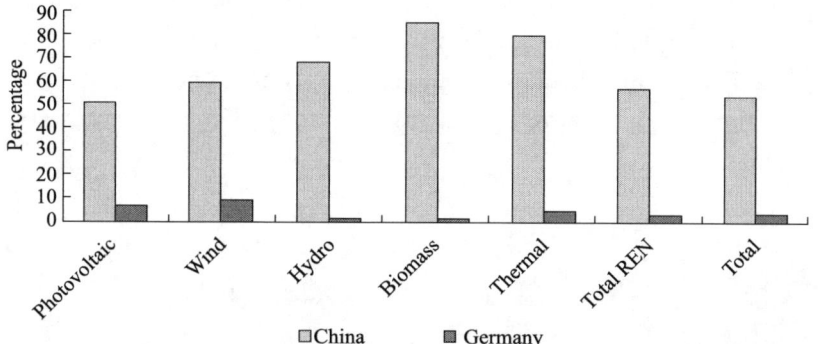

Figure 15.9 Shares of patent applications at SIPO by technology fields, 2006 - 2008
Source: EPO-PATSTAT, SIPO, Fraunhofer ISI calculations

The specialization profile in Figure 15.10 summarizes these findings and emphasizes the main results. The specialization profile is an index that compares national profiles beyond size effects. China has comparative advantages in total renewable energy, but especially in biomass and thermal energy as well as in hydro. Wind and especially photovoltaic do not belong to the technological strengths of China in their home market. Germany, on the other hand, clearly focuses on photovoltaic and wind technologies, but does not specialize in total renewable energies in China at all.

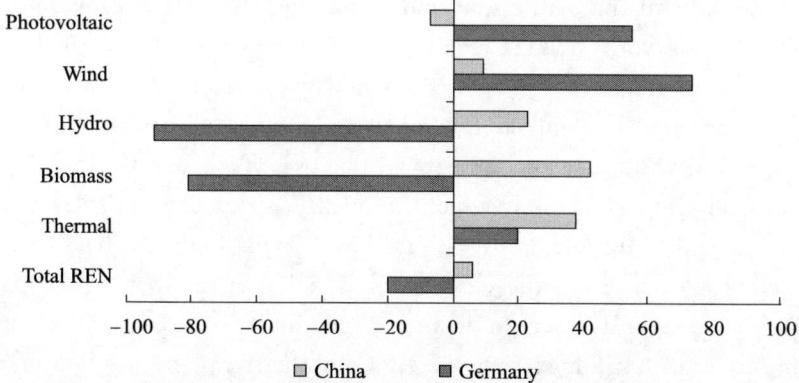

Figure 15.10 Specialization profile at SIPO, 2006 - 2008
Source: EPO-PATSTAT, SIPO, Fraunhofer ISI calculations

The regional differentiation of the Chinese patent applications in China reveals the well-known structures at first sight (Figure 15.11). It is Beijing, Shanghai and Jiangsu, but also Guangdong, who are at the top in absolute terms. However when we look at the map in Figure 15.12, which depicts the specialization profile within China, some other provinces are more prominent in renewable energy as well. As the specialization index always asks, what the role of renewable energy within the profile of the region is, the dark blue colored provinces are especially engaged in renewable energy. It is Beijing and Shanghai, but also Xinjiang, Inner Mongolia, Qinghai, Hebei, and Fujian, which have a relatively high engagement in renewable energy technologies.

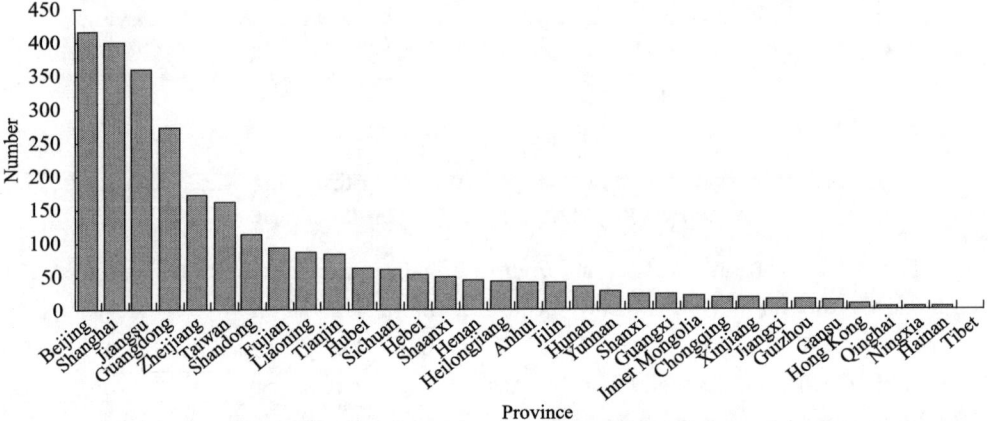

Figure 15.11 Absolute number of SIPO patents in renewable energy by provinces, 2006 – 2008
Source: EPO-PATSTAT, SIPO, Fraunhofer ISI calculations

When looking at the institutions and companies that file photovoltaic or wind patents in China, several striking results can be emphasized (Table 15.1). First, in the case of photovoltaic many universities and public research institutions are on the list. In consequence, only a few companies and enterprises can be found. Interestingly, not those are on the top of the list which are the main exporting companies, and also not so many which are clearly specialized in solar energy. For example, Xingzhe Multimedia or BYD have their main activity outside the renewable energy sector. In the case of wind, a larger number of companies are visible, but still several research institutes and universities can be found. It is interesting to note that Fangxia and Sewind are clearly at the top and many other companies only file smaller numbers of patents in the observation period from 2006 to 2008.

Part 4 Enterprise Technology Innovation and Future Challenges for Green Growth

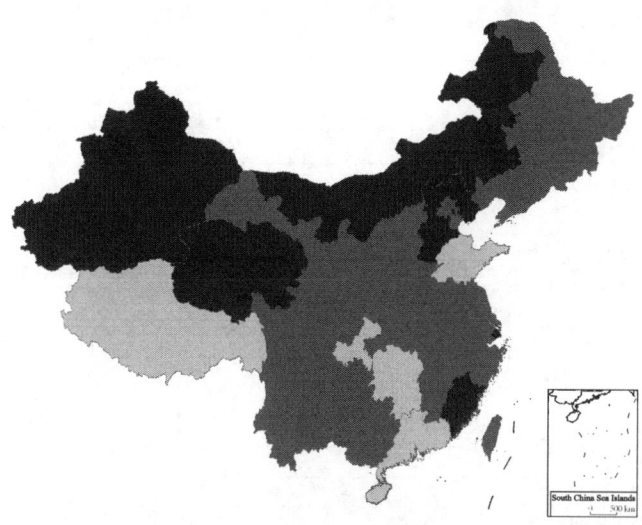

Figure 15.12 Regional specialization of Chinese inventors in renewable energy patents at SIPO, 2006 – 2008

Source: EPO-PATSTAT, SIPO, Fraunhofer ISI calculations

Table 15.1 Top Chinese applicants-structure of Chinese patent applicants at SIPO, 2006 – 2008

Photovoltaic/Solar	Number of Patent application
Beijing Xingzhe Multimedia Tec	35
Univ Nankai	32
Univ Beijing	29
Beijing Hikeen Technology Co L	27
Inst of Semiconductors Cas	23
Univ Shanghai	23
Hongfujin Prec Ind	20
Univ Nanjing	19
Univ Tsinghua	17
Ind Tech Res Inst	15
Univ Zhejiang	15
Shanghai Inst Tech Physics	13
Shanghai Tech Physics Inst	12
Chinese Acad Inst Chemistry	11
Shanghai Solar Energy S &	11
BYD Co Ltd	10
Changzhou Trina Solar Energy C	10
Inst Electrical Eng Cas	10
Univ Fudan	10
Univ Sichuan	10
Univ Tianjin	10

	Continued
Photovoltaic/Solar	Number of Patent application
Univ Xiamen	10
Wind	
Fangxia Entpr Inf Consult Co	25
Shanghai Sewind Co Ltd	21
Univ Shanghai	17
Shanghai Jiuneng Energy Techno	9
Suzhou Nanjifeng Energy Source	7
Beijing Xinxuanshiwei Technolo	6
Guangdong Mingyang Wind Electr	6
Suzhou Nanji Wind Energy Sourc	6
Univ Nanjing Aeronautics	6
Zhangjiagang Beier Machinery C	6
Inst Eng Thermophysics Cas	5
Shanghai Chifeng Mechanical An	5
Shanghai Electric Hydraulic Pn	5
Shanghai Qimou Energy Technolo	5
Univ Harbin Eng	5
Univ Xi An Jiaotong	5
Xinyuan Electrical Tech Co Ltd	5
Beijing Nego Automation Techno	4
Beijing Shuangfan Technology C	4
Delta Electronics Inc	4
Guangzhou Orient Yato Electric	4
Hongfujin Prec Ind	4
Sanyi Electric Co Ltd	4
Shanghai Inst Technology	4
Univ Tsinghua	4
Xinjiang Goldwind Science And	4

Source: EPO-PATSTAT, SIPO, Fraunhofer ISI calculations

When it comes to patent applications on the international level (Figure 15.13)—here we use the concept of transnational patent applications, which covers all patent families with at least an EPO or a PCT application—the comparison between Germany and China is completely different. Germany is responsible for about 15% of total transnational patent applications and recently for slightly more, namely about 18%, of the renewable patent applications targeting worldwide markets. China, on the other hand, although it shows clearly increasing shares of worldwide filings, only reaches a level of about 5% of total filings and even a smaller share of about 3% in renewable energy technologies. When we look at the absolute number of transnational patent applications in renewable energy (Figure 15.14), we can see that Germany files more than five times more patents than China. We can also see a large increase after 2005 in the case of

Germany, which we also found at the SIPO, also occurs on the transnational level. Furthermore, China was able to increase its filings especially after 2003 and reached a level of about 80 patents in 2008.

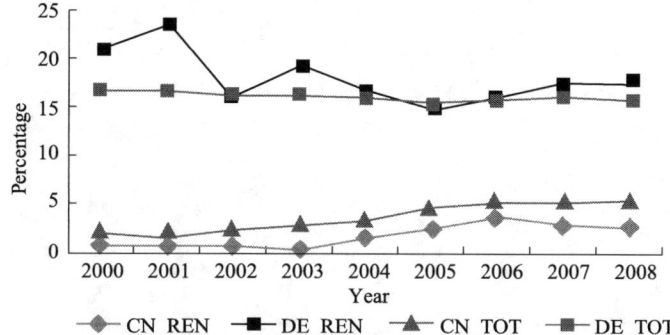

Figure 15.13 Patent applications in renewable energy technologies on a transnational level—shares

Source: EPO-PATSTAT, SIPO, Fraunhofer ISI calculations

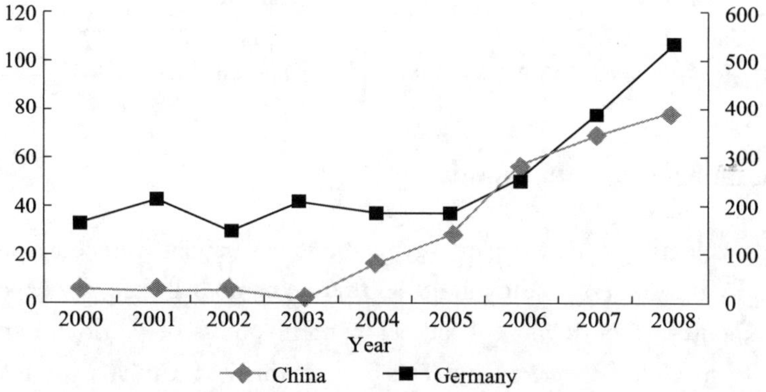

Figure 15.14 Patent applications in renewable energy technologies on a transnational level—absolute numbers

Source: EPO-PATSTAT, SIPO, Fraunhofer ISI calculations

The analysis of the subfields of renewable energy technologies reveals extraordinary shares in the small field of thermal energy for Germany, but also for wind, while photovoltaic and biomass reach an average level and hydro is clearly below that (Figure 15.15). It is interesting to note that also on the transnational level photovoltaic patents obviously do not belong to the strengths of Chinese companies. Hydro and especially wind are slightly above the total renewable energy shares, while the other subfields are below the total. One can say that international patent applications are one means to shape and to access international markets and to secure market shares. Above we have seen that China is the top exporter of photovoltaic and almost no export activities in wind could be found. Derived from the analysis of patent applications on the transnational level, we would say that the exports of photovoltaic are not backed by any technological competences. Furthermore, we would expect Chinese companies in accessing international wind technology markets in the present or future.

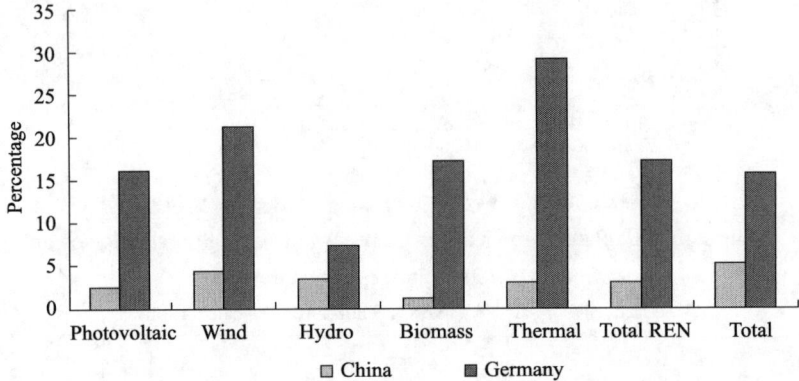

Figure 15.15 Shares of transnational patent applications, 2006 – 2008
Source: EPO-PATSTAT, SIPO, Fraunhofer ISI calculations

15.6 Summarizing conclusions

China's exports of renewable energy technologies have grown considerably almost only driven by the field of photovoltaic. So far, we can hardly see any exports of wind energy commodities from China. About 11 percent points of worldwide photovoltaic exports go from China to Germany. This is one third of China's total photovoltaic exports. Germany, on the other hand, holds about one third of the worldwide wind market in terms of exports. However, almost no exports go to China so far. When we compare the export profiles of the two countries, we can see that Germany and China seem to have a complementary profile on a worldwide scale, at least so far.

When we analyze the foundations of the Chinese photovoltaic export performance and also the national demand for wind energy technologies, the question arises if this is a solid and future oriented trend or if the performance of China almost only relies on price and scale effects. The science base of renewable energy in China is increasing over time—as it holds for almost any scientific field—but stays below the average of total publications. However, this also holds for Germany when we look at the total publications in renewable energy sciences. The conclusion of a weak foundation in the case of China is further supported by our analyses of patent applications. The number of patent applications to the SIPO was rising steeply in the recent past, but the structural differentiation reveals interesting patterns. It seems that wind is more important to Chinese applicants than photovoltaic. This holds for the home market as well as for the transnational market for technologies. However, Chinese hold slightly lower shares in renewable energy than in total patents in China which means that they are not strictly specialized in this area. Foreigners shape the technology market for renewable energy in China to a large extent. To put it in other words, the Chinese market for renewable energy technologies seems to be very attractive for foreign companies. This even more so, as the Chinese competitors do not seem to be able to compete on the quality or technological level, yet. We have seen that photovoltaic has a low science base and especially a very low technological foundation in China. And this is even more the case with respect to international markets. In wind technologies almost the opposite is true, as we see almost no activities on international markets in terms of exports, but some performance in terms of publications and patent applications on the transnational level.

So the question arises who owns the photovoltaic technologies, which Chinese companies sell on international markets? Obviously, Chinese companies license in and do not rely on their own R&D activities and technologies. It seems that they benefit from price and scale effects only. During the observation period of the data that are used here, the photovoltaic market in China almost did not exist at all. Recently this has clearly changed and it remains to be seen what Chinese companies are able to do in their home market in the present and the future. Once we have the statistical data we can conduct a similar analysis, which might uncover that Chinese companies were able to serve the demand in photovoltaic also in China, with some foreign companies participating in the market, either directly or indirectly via licensing of the technologies that they also secured at the SIPO.

The more interesting question is what happens when the Chinese market for wind technologies is growing slower or even becomes a saturated market? What happens when Chinese companies turn their attention to international markets? Based on the experiences in the photovoltaic field, one would expect that also price and scale effects offer them good opportunities on these international markets. In addition, it seems that at least to a larger extent than in the case of photovoltaic, a scientific and technological foundation is laid out also on an international level. So far, Germany dominates the international wind exports, but the competition with China in this area seems unavoidable. The conclusion that the German and Chinese technological as well as the export profile are complementary in large parts might then have to be revised.

References

Balassa, B. 1965. Trade liberalisation and revealed comparative advantage. *The Manchester School of Economics and Social Sciences*, 33, 99-123.

Frietsch, R., Schmoch, U. 2006. Technological structures and performance reflected by patent indicators. In: Schmoch, U., Rammer, C., Legler, H. (Eds.), *National Systems of Innovation in Comparison, Structure and Performance Indicators for Knowledge Societies*. Dordrecht: Springer.

Frietsch, R., Schmoch, U. 2010. Transnational patents and international markets. *Scientometrics*, 82, 185-200.

Moed, H. F., Glänzel, W., Schmoch, U. 2004. *Handbook of Quantitative Science and Technology Research. The Use of Publications and Patent Statistics in Studies of S&T Systems*. Dordrecht: Kluwer Academic Publisher.

Ricardo, D. 1996. Principles of Political Economy and Taxation. Amherst: Prometheus Books.

Schmoch, U. 2004. The utility of patent indicators for evaluation. *Plattform Forschungs—und Technologieevaluierung—fteval*, 22, 2-10.

Schmoch, U. 2006. Scientific performance in an international comparison. In: Schmoch, U., Rammer, C., Legler, H. (Eds.), *National Systems of Innovation in Comparison, Structure and Performance Indicators for Knowledge Societies*. Dordrecht: Springer, 69-88.

van Raan, A. 1988. *Handbook of Quantitative Studies of Science and Technology*. Amsterdam: North-Holland.

Author

Rainer Frietsch completed business training in wholesale and import/export trade. He studied social science at the University of Mannheim. Since October 2000 he has been employed at the Fraunhofer Institute for Systems and Innovation Research (ISI) in Karlsruhe. Rainer Frietsch is a deputy head of the department "Policy and Regions" and a coordinator of the business unit "Innovation Indicators". He is a visiting professor at the Institute of Policy and Management of the Chinese Academy of Sciences.

His current research activities involve patent statistics, bibliometrics, economic and social indicators, qualifications and education in the innovation process, and technology foresight, methodological foundations of empirical research.

Lead Market Potential for Phosphorus Recycling Technologies in Germany

Christian Sartorius

16.1 Introduction

The use of sewage sludge as a nutritious substrate in agriculture is a low-tech variation of phosphorous (P) recycling, which helps to replace the non-substitutable resource phosphorous essential for plant growth. Since the contamination of sewage sludge with heavy metals and toxic organic substances has increasingly discredited this type of sludge use, however, other technical approaches to recovering phosphorous from wastewater or sludge liquor are being sought. For this reason, a large number of different processes have been developed in the past decade especially in the programme "Recycling management of plant nutrients, in particular phosphorous", funded by the German Ministries for Education and Research and for the Environment, by means of which phosphate can be recovered from wastewater or sewage sludge to be subsequently used as a fertilizer for agricultural use.

In this context, this contribution[①] aims to identify the economic aspects of phosphorous recycling from wastewater, sludge liquor and sludge ash in Germany. We

---

① This contribution is a result of the Work Package 7 of the BMBF funded joint project "Phosphorous Recycling—Ecological and Economic Significance of Various Processes and Development of a Strategic Utilisation Concept for Germany" (PHOBE) (FKZ: 02WA0807). Funding is gratefully acknowledged by the author.

shall investigate with which methods and in which chronological sequence phosphorous recycling from wastewater can be introduced as cost-effectively and at the same time as comprehensively as possible (section 16.3) and which (framework) conditions are required so that the German economy as a technology provider can profit from this development (section 16.4). Preceding this (section 16.2) is a technology foresight which with a view to the year 2050 addresses the question, which drivers of this development can be considered favourable and which fundamental technical approaches are considered most promising. A summary (section 16.5) completes the paper.

16.2 Technology foresight for recycling phosphorous from wastewater

16.2.1 Meaning and context of phosphorous recycling

Long before science in the 19th century discovered that (in addition to other elements) phosphorous is essential for plant growth and thus for securing the food supply (i.e. non-replaceable), (farm and domestic) manure was collected and spread on the fields. This nutrient cycle threatened to be interrupted, above all in towns where excrement was collected in sewers and washed into the rivers. Only after municipal wastewater was increasingly collected and cleaned in sewage plants could a large part of the nutrients be collected in sewage liquor and thus re-utilised for agricultural purposes. This extended nutrient cycle threatens to be once again interrupted, as pollutants have recently been found to increasingly contaminate wastewater and sewage sludge, meaning that continued use in agriculture is no longer desirable. Even though sewage sludge utilisation is not yet forbidden in Germany, the regulations for sludge use are becoming increasingly strict so that the share which may be used for agricultural purposes threatens to shrink more and more.

The alternative, i.e. harvesting phosphate from fossil sources, is not threatened by exhausted resources, at least not in the short to mid term. However, it is obvious that, due to the increasing demand for food (for a growing population), animal feed and biomass (for climate and resource protection), the demand for phosphate will grow swiftly, while the accessibility of the resource is constantly deteriorating. In view of the widening gap between supply and demand, relying solely on rock phosphate as the phosphorous source does not appear to be a sustainable option.

Against this background, processes to reclaim phosphorous from domestic wastewater have been intensively researched, at least during the past 10 years. As will be shown in this paper, there are a number of methods to discharge the phosphorous content at different points in the wastewater disposal and treatment chain. Initially, the main task was to remove phosphate from the relevant material streams in order to avoid(after its elimination from the main wastewater stream) the deposition of phosphorous in the secondary stream or sludge, leading to various complications in operating wastewater treatment plants. Due to the (shrinking) resource problem, recycling has eventually increased in significance in the past years.

16.2.2 Results of a technology foresight exercise

In order to ascertain how the scarcity of the resource phosphorous is regarded by experts, which role will be attached to the agricultural utilisation of sewage sludge in the future, and which technology development paths are regarded as feasible in the area of phosphorous recovery from wastewater in the mid term, i. e. until the year 2030, we conducted a technology foresight exercise in the first half of 2010. A large number of experts who are actively involved in this area were invited to give their opinions about different, relevant aspects of phosphorous recycling. Altogether, 417 experts from 40 countries were contacted, who had either participated in May 2009 in the International Conference on Nutrient Recovery from Wastewater Streams in Vancouver(Canada) or in September 2009 in the "Baltic 21" in Berlin, or were addressees on the e-mail distribution list of the internet site"Phosphorous Recovery"of the IWAR Institute at the TU-Darmstadt (http://www.phosphorus-recovery.tu-darmstadt.de)or of the Centre Européen d'Études des Polyphosphates(CEEP).47%, i.e.197 experts from 31 countries answered at least a part of the questions.

Of the total results of this technology foresight exercise(Sartorius et al., 2011) we list the most important findings as follows.

The majority of experts is of the opinion that phosphorous recycling will have gained foot in industrialised countries by 2030 at the latest and that it will then be economically viable. In order to achieve this goal, the experts deem it necessary to support the introduction of phosphorous recovery processes by appropriate policy measures. They consider that applying phosphate by spreading sewage sludge on agricultural land will(further)decline in importance in the future.

For the introduction of a ubiquitous phosphorous recycling system, most experts in the introductory phase consider realizing simple methods in many (also smaller) locations more likely than implementing complex processes in central plants. phosphorous recycling from the liquid phase, above all from sludge liquor is assessed as a particularly relevant method in this context.

According to the experts, sludge incineration will become established in many industrialised countries at about the same time as phosphate recycling. In the course of this, phosphate recovery from ash (although a technically more complex procedure) will become increasingly important. In the comparison between recovery from digested sludge or ash, the latter seems to be preferred.

The votes of the experts are quite clear in the judgement that the quality of the products resulting from the process is always more important than the techno-economic aspects. In manufacturing fertilizer, as pure a product as possible with optimum plant availability is the goal.

Most experts also consider material flow separation and phosphate recycling from urine as future options, especially in areas with water shortages. In this context, the logistic problems are regarded as a critical issue, but also as a soluble one, above all by the professionals with great expertise. This technology will be more likely established in industrialised countries than in developing countries, say the experts.

Interestingly, according to the experts, the direct re-use of nutrients in many countries is made more difficult due to the increasing importance of trace element problems and this provides new market opportunities for nutrient recovery technologies.

16.3 Economic potentials of phosphorous recycling technologies

16.3.1 Promising technology approaches to phosphorous recycling

In Germany and in a number of other, mainly European countries, within the past decade a great variety of approaches were developed by which phosphorous (or phosphate), which arrives in the wastewater treatment plants, can be separated from the water or sludge liquor and recovered for further use e. g. in agriculture. Figure 16.1 lists most of the known processes and systematically differentiates them according to the material stream from which phosphorous comes, the principle of the recovery process and other parameters.

The following basic process principles can be differentiated.

The "easiest" in terms of process management is the precipitation or adsorption of phosphate from the plant effluent, as here almost all other impurities have already been removed and essentially phosphorous must only be enriched. The disadvantage is that the phosphate is very diluted and the yield rather low, which adversely affects the profitability of the process (e. g. P-ROC, RECYPHOS, PHOSIEDI).

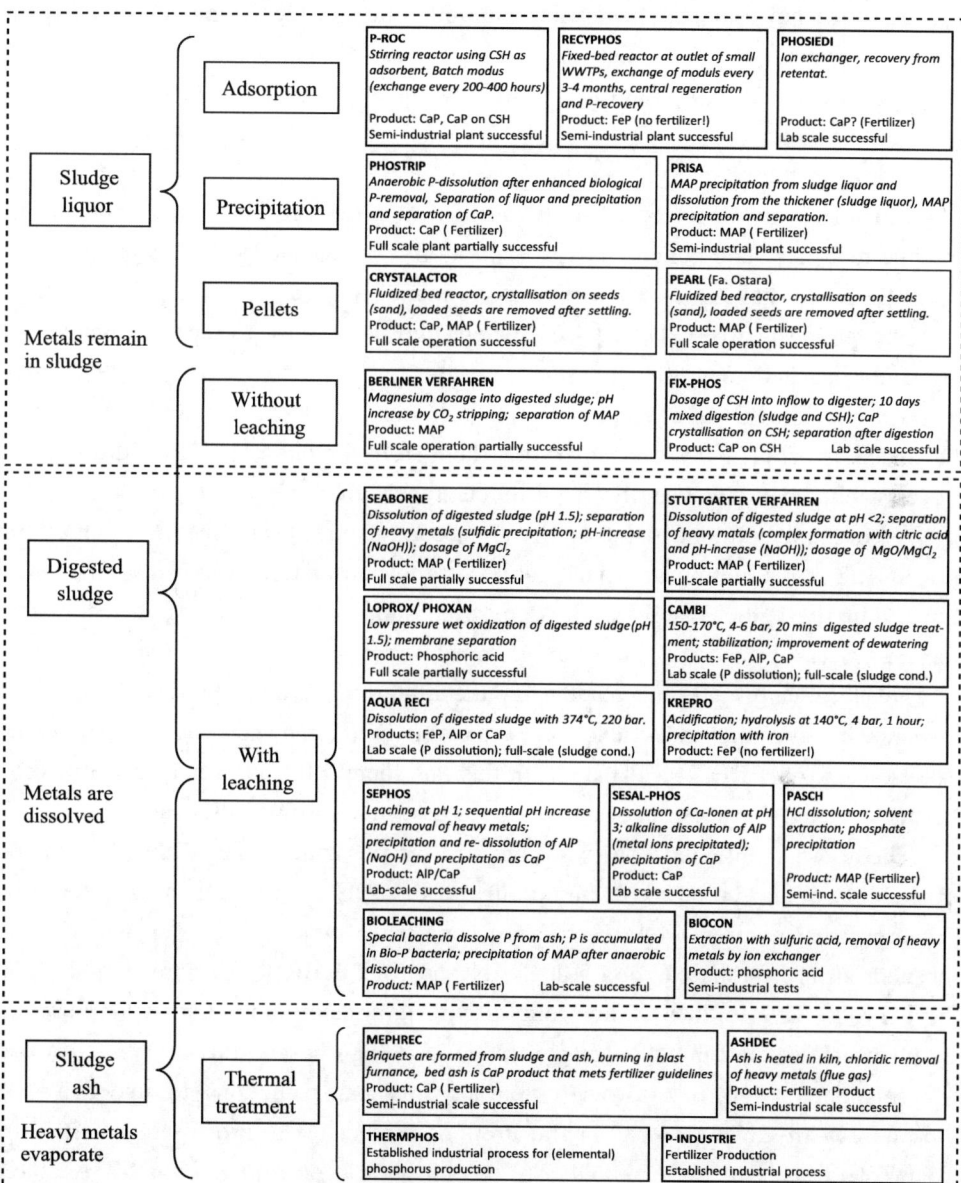

Figure 16.1 Systematic representation of known processes for recovering phosphorous from wastewater or sewage sludge

Source: Sartorius et al. (2011)

Phosphate is present in the sludge liquor in concentrated form, however, compared with the recycling from process(1), an additional effort is necessary to separate the sludge liquor from the remaining sludge. Heavy metals and organic pollutants remain in the sludge and do not need to be removed. The processes (e. g. PEARL, PRISA) are thus relatively inexpensive and have an average phosphorous yield.

Similar to the recovery from the sludge liquor(2) is the yield in the precipitation of phosphorous in sludge, preferably during or after its digestion. However, the precipitated phosphate pellets must be separated from the sludge in this process(e. g. AIRPREX, FIX-PHOS), which increases the input required.

The greatest effort is required when phosphate has to be chemically and physically leached out of the sludge prior to separation (e. g. PHOXNAN, SEABORNE). In this case, the undesirable pollutants are also typically leached out, so that much effort is involved in separating them from the phosphate. In addition to the process technology involved, the requisite chemicals are a cost driver.

As organic substances have already been removed during the incineration process, the re-dissolution and purification of the phosphate contained in the sludge ash(e. g. in the PASCH process) are somewhat simpler and require fewer chemicals than in process(4), but still considerable input is involved here.

Finally, attempts are being made to use the ash directly as a phosphorous source, but to previously remove the undesirable heavy metals via thermo-chemical or metallurgical processes(e. g. ASH DEC, MEPHREC). In this case there is the additional economic bonus that the depleted sludge ash must not be disposed of in a(costly) landfill site.

The above mentioned considerations are largely confirmed by the data on the profitability of the processes examined in the PHOBE project and in the literature. The processes in group (4) are the most expensive, where costs of over 11 €/kg phosphorous are estimated for PHOXNAN and for SEABORNE more than 14 €/kg phosphorous(Bayerle, 2009). The group(1) with its precipitation of phosphorous from the plant effluent lies in a similar cost range(12 €/kg phosphorous), whereby in very large plants (1 m p. e.) further potentials for cost reductions to under 5 €/kg phosphorous are given(P-ROC in the Prophos project). The processes described for group(5) are less expensive. About 8 €/kg phosphorous are quoted for SESALPHOS and a very favourable 4. 50 €/kg phosphorous for PASCH in large plants with an ash treatment capacity of 30,000 tonnes per annum, corresponding to 2. 9 million person equivalents(Pinnekamp et al. , 2011). The processes in groups (2) and (3) are of a similar dimension, whereby the costs greatly depend on the specific circumstances. They can amount to over 12 €/kg phosphorous under unfavourable circumstances, under suitable circumstances and using synergy effects in the existing plants, the costs can be reduced to 2 €/kg phosphorous(FIX-PHOS). All quoted cost figures must be seen in relation to a price of ca. 1.25 €/kg phosphorous which must presently(status January 2011)be paid for phosphate fertilizers from rock phosphate. The difference is thus no longer all that large. And in group(6), we even find processes which can be profitably operated at this price already, or will be profitable in the near future(ASH DEC, THERMPHOS, MEPHREC) (Sartorius et al., 2011; Scheidig et al., 2010). However, the profitability depends in part on certain framework conditions which are not always very favourable in Germany. We shall return to this issue later. Meanwhile, it can be stated that there are two fundamentally different approaches in the field of phosphorous recycling which appear to be especially promising in the short to mid term, above all for economic considerations: Precipitation or adsorption of phosphate from sludge liquor(after separation from the sludge or in the sludge)as well as the manufacturing of an effective phosphorous containing fertilizer from sludge ash.

16.3.2 Use and development potentials of recycling technologies

We can differentiate between medium-and longer-term application potentials for phosphorous recovery technologies. Among the medium-term potentials, we understand those which are realisable by the year 2020 or 2030; in other words, without essentially changing the existing framework conditions. This time horizon is also significant for the possible large-scale introduction of phosphorous recycling in German sewage treatment plants.

16.3.2.1 Phosphorous recycling from sludge liquor

The precipitation from the sludge liquor requires as high a concentration of dissolved or re-dissolved phosphate as possible in the sewage sludge, which is most likely the case after enhanced biological phosphorous removal(EBPR) in the main effluent stream. Water treatment plants with EBPR are also those which most frequently have to contend with problems caused by the release of previously biologically bound phosphate during and after the anaerobic sludge digestion and the accompanying spontaneous struvite incrustations. Accordingly, the processes PEARL, FIX-PHOS and AIRPREX start before, during and after the anaerobic digestion, in order to remove the phosphate selectively from the sludge stream before it can form incrustations in the pipes or cause other damage. The PEARL process made by the Ostara company can above all already today operate commercially on a large scale by utilizing a combination of reclaiming a fertilizer containing phosphorous (and N) (branded "Crystal Green") and by preventing operational difficulties.

The potential for the use of phosphorous recovery from the liquid phase of the sewage sludge liquor therefore encompasses all sewage treatment plants which already predominantly or exclusively eliminate phosphorous by means of the EBPR process. According to the DWA Sewage Survey for the year 2003 (DWA, 2005), this was the case for 37 percent of sewage treatment plants, which also treated 37 percent of the sewage of all residents connected to treatment plants. A change in this share is not to be expected without changes in the framework conditions that would increase the attractiveness of the EBPR process. In addition to the biological phosphorous share, in order to calculate the investments required (which at the same time mark out the market volume for relevant technology providers) in this phosphorous recycling approach, it must be taken into account that it only makes sense to remove phosphorous from the sludge liquor, if the remaining sludge liquor is subsequently neither used for mono-incineration (with subsequent phosphorous recovery from the sludge ash) nor for agricultural uses (fertilizer). Therefore only 48 percent of the sewage sludge is suitable for phosphorous recycling from sludge liquor.

In order to keep the costs for implementing phosphorous recycling low, the FIX-PHOS process (which was the one more closely examined in the PHOBE project) is primarily used in sewage treatment plants with anaerobic sludge digestion, having several digesters at their disposal and conducting EBPR. These will primarily be Class 5 sewage plants (>100,000 p.e.), 95 percent of which operate a digestion process (usually with several digesters). Taking the 37% share of EBPR and the availability of only 48 percent of the total amount of sewage sludge into account, it can be calculated that of the 252 sewage plants with a total designed capacity of 77 million p.e. which are presently classified in Germany as Class 5 (DeStatis, 2009), (0.95 × 0.37 × 0.48 × 252 =) 43 with a total treatment capacity of 13.2 million p.e. were equipped with the FIX-PHOS process, which corresponds to a total investment volume of (43/252 × 77 million p.e. × €70,000/100,000 p.e. =) €9.2 million. Since the required system components (sieves, pipes and pumps) do not have a high degree of innovation, in the first phase only low learning effects amounting to 5 percent are estimated, which however still reduce the required total investment sum to €7.3 million [1].

16.3.2.2 Phosphorous recycling from sludge ash

Phosphorous recycling from sludge ash presumes the prior incineration of the sewage sludge. Compared to simply dumping the sludge, this is associated with

---

[1] Direct landfilling of sewage sludge has been banned in Germany since 2005.

additional effort and costs and is accordingly mainly carried out if it is not possible to use the sewage sludge in agriculture or landscaping ①. In Germany, the share of sewage sludge disposed of via incineration increased from 12 percent in 1995 up to 53 percent in 2008 because of reservations among the population and politicians with regard to possible harmful effects of using the sludge agriculturally, and as yet this trend shows no signs of stopping(EUWID, 2010). However, only a proportion of the total volume of sewage sludge disposed of thermally is suitable to recover phosphorus. If the sludge is co-incinerated as an energy-rich fuel in power stations, cement works and waste incineration plants, the phosphorus contained in the sewage sludge is diluted to such an extent that it would be very difficult and costly to recover. Only a share of 44 percent of the sludge intended for thermal disposal, i. e. 23 percent of the total sewage sludge is burnt in mono-incineration plants and therefore has sufficient phosphorous content in the short term.

In the medium term until 2030, it can be expected that the share of thermally recycled sewage sludge will continue to increase. Studies assume that, in the future, about 40% to 80% of the sludge used agriculturally at present will not be able to comply with the strict threshold values of a revised Sewage Sludge Ordinance, which are currently being discussed. Including the 53% already being incinerated today, this would mean that 64 to 75 percent of the sludge would be incinerated by 2030. However, for operational reasons, it cannot be assumed that the share of co-incineration in power stations and cement works will increase significantly(EUWID, 2010). Even if the co-incineration share of 3 percent in waste incineration plants were to be doubled, the total share of mono-incineration that could be expected in the medium term would be about 37 percent②.

In order to recover phosphorus from 23% to 37% of the sewage sludge subjected to mono-incineration in Germany using the PASCH method, 7 to 11 PASCH plants would have to be constructed(corresponding to scenarios 3 and 4, respectively, in Pinnekamp et al., 2011), each with an annual capacity of 30. 000 tonnes of ash. As shown by Pinnekamp et al. (2011), on the basis of the currently existing mono-

---

① For Europe outside Germany, a significantly smaller potential can be assumed on the whole than in Germany, because of the lesser diffusion of nutrient elimination processes(EC, 2009) and a smaller share of the sophisticated bio-phosphorous process.

② Concerning the total potential of phosphorous recycling from sewage sludge ash in Europe, the situation is similar to the recycling from sludge liquor. In principle, the potential outside Germany is of a similar magnitude to that inside the country; at the moment, however, the existing incineration capacities are nowhere near as large as those already implemented in Germany.

incineration plants (corresponding to scenario 3), 8 locations actually make sense at which such PASCH plants could be operated economically. However, several of these plants would then have smaller annual capacities than the proposed 30,000 tonnes, or they would not be utilised to capacity, at least to start with. For the subsequent increase in the number of PASCH plants to 11 by the year 2030 (scenario 4), it is also indicated that, in reality, a larger number of smaller plants is more likely, which would then be slightly more expensive with regard to their specific investment costs. 7 to 11 PASCH plants each with an annual capacity of 30,000 tonnes of ash would correspond to a total investment of € 33 million to 52 million without considering the decline of marginal unit costs. If learning effects are included by assuming a learning coefficient of 0.85, the investment costs per plant could drop to around 60 percent of the initial value by the eleventh plant, which would mean a total investment volume of € 37 million by 2030. If it is assumed that there is the potential for the same number of plants again in the rest of Europe, then plant costs would drop further to € 2.3 million and the total investment volume would amount to € 64 million.

16.3.3 Cost development and profitability

16.3.3.1 Primary and secondary phosphates in comparison

At the present point in time (beginning of 2011), no process exists to recover phosphorus which is economical under normal conditions, i.e. in direct competition with the phosphoric acid recovered from rock phosphate and needed for chemical fertilizer production. The kilogram price for phosphoric acid now lies between € 1.20 and 1.30—with an upwards trend (Figure 16.2) after hovering around 0.5 €/kg phosphorous for many years and then climbing to more than 4 €/kg phosphorous during the recent crisis on the markets for raw materials. This current price is almost double the figure which was taken as a cost-based minimum price for phosphoric acid in AP1 of the PHOBE project (Horn and Sartorius, 2009). There are several reasons why the price is currently considerably higher than the costs: On the one hand, the strong utilisation or even over-utilisation of the existing mining capacities; and, on the other hand, the current speculation about further increases in the prices for raw materials—including phosphorus. Because the lower edge of the price band depicted in Figure 16.2 is not allowed to be crossed, this represents the reference price for all alternative processes of phosphorous recovery. On the other hand, based, among other things, on the phosphorus peak forecast for around 2035 by Cordell et al. (2009) no significant expansion of the effective mining capacities for rock phosphate is expected in the future. Because, in addition, it is likely that the demand for phosphorous sources will increase in the future, it cannot be assumed that the price for phosphoric acid will remain at the minimum level for long. Instead, it can rather be assumed that the phosphoric acid price will fluctuate between the upper and lower boundaries and on average will tend to move along the curve of the expected mean.

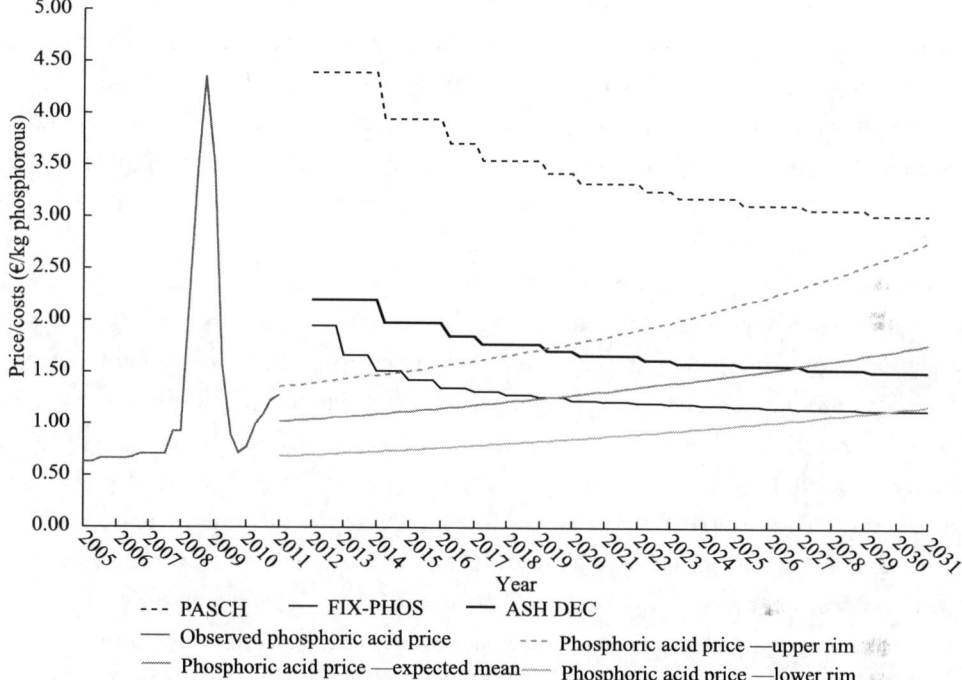

Figure 16.2　Cost degressions and break-even points for various more cost-effective phosphorous recovery processes

According to the discussion in section 16.3.1, the best processes of recovering phosphorous from municipal sewage treatment with regard to their costs, which are analysed in more detail in the following, are:

(1) FIX-PHOS in the cost-effective variant (drawing on existing digesters) with less than 2 €/kg phosphorous (for 1 million p. e. capacity);

(2) PASCH in a plant with an annual capacity of 30,000 tonnes ash (corresponds to almost 3 million p. e.) with 4.40 €/kg phosphorous, as well as the following process, which was not subject to a cost analysis in the PHOBE project:

(3) ASH DEC in incineration plants with an annual capacity of at least 25,000 tonnes ash with reported 2.20 €/kg P (Hermann 2010).

As well as the following process, which was not subject to a cost analysis in the PHOBE project:

ASH DEC in incineration plants with an annual capacity of at least 25,000 tonnes ash with reported 2.20 €/kg phosphorous (Hermann, 2010).

If these cost figures are to be compared with the reference price for phosphorous which can be used as a fertilizer, it has to be considered not only that the mining of rock phosphate as described in the previous section will become more expensive in the future due to increasing shortages or less accessible sources. In addition, the fact has to be taken into account that through the construction and operation of a larger number of phosphorous recovery plants, economies of scale and learning effects will be achieved. Economies of scale effects are caused by a larger number of plants being manufactured with standardized processes and employing machine tools, which enable a more efficient and therefore more cost-effective mode of production. Learning effects(also known under the phrase "learning by doing"), in contrast, tend to refer more to efficiency gains in operational procedures, i.e. more reliable routine operations, for example, with less need for monitoring and savings in operating materials and supplies. For every doubling of the cumulated installed plant capacities, depending on the level of innovation, a cost decrease of between 10 and 20 percent is usually assumed. For the phosphorous recovery plants, we assume a cost degression of 15 percent. The cost-effective variant of FIX-PHOS represents one exception to this, since this is assembled using standard technical components and therefore only justifies a cost degression of 5 percent. Because of their dependency on ever scarcer supplies of raw materials, we assume a general cost reduction of only 10 percent for operating the plants.

In Figure 16.2, the cost degression curves of the different processes of phosphorous recovery are compared with the expected price development of geogenic phosphorus.

Assuming that the systematic introduction of phosphorous recycling begins in 2012, a cost reduction of around one third to almost one half can be noted by 2030 for all processes. There are greater reductions to be made where a larger number of smaller plants are constructed(e.g. FIX-PHOS). As the most expensive process in this comparison, PASCH shows a decrease in its specific costs from 4.40 to 3.03 €/kg phosphorous and remains just above the upper boundary of the reference price corridor for geogenic phosphorous in 2030. ASH DEC und FIX-PHOS, which start in 2012 at 2.20 and 1.95 €/kg phosphorous, respectively, reach the upper boundary of the corridor as early as 2019 or 2015, and the mean expected price(= break-even)in the years 2027 and 2019, respectively. This means that, under these conditions, the more cost-effective processes can be expected to become profitable in less than a decade. It should be explicitly pointed out at this point that the cost reductions outlined above will only occur if a start is really made in 2012 to put the relevant recycling technologies into operation on the assumed scale.

16.3.3.2 Additional costs of phosphorous recycling

The additional or *differential* costs of the various phosphorous recovery processes are higher the farther the break-even point lies in the future. In order to quantify the differential costs incurred over time, it is necessary to explicitly include the aggregated plant capacities in the analysis in addition to the specific investment and operating costs. The results of these calculations for the three processes FIX-PHOS, ASH DEC und PASCH are presented in Table 16.1.

Table 16.1 Specific recovery costs and differential costs for various phosphorous recycling processes from 2012 until 2030

Year	Phosphorous reference costs * (€/kg phosphorous)	FIX-PHOS process		PASCH process		ASH DEC process	
		Specific recovery costs(€/kg phosphorous)	Total differential costs (€1,000)	Specific recovery costs(€/kg phosphorous)	Total differential costs (€1,000)	Specific recovery costs(€/kg phosphorous)	Total differential costs (€1,000)
2012	1.058	1.857	−104	4.397	−5.509	2.199	−1.882
2013	1.085	1.605	−169	4.397	−5.465	2.199	−1.838
2014	1.112	1.479	−191	3.947	−9.355	1.973	−2.843
2015	1.141	1.396	−199	3.947	−9.260	1.973	−2.747
2016	1.172	1.339	−163	3.705	−12.539	1.853	−3.369
2017	1.204	1.303	−116	3.543	−15.440	1.772	−3.748
2018	1.236	1.273	−51	3.543	−15.230	1.772	−3.538
2019	1.270	1.248	33	3.422	−17.759	1.711	−3.642
2020	1.306	1.227	138	3.327	−20.008	1.663	−3.542
2021	1.343	1.211	249	3.327	−19.637	1.663	−3.170
2022	1.382	1.199	368	3.248	−21.547	1.624	−2.790
2023	1.422	1.189	500	3.181	−23.221	1.591	−2.226
2024	1.464	1.179	649	3.181	−22.666	1.591	−1.670
2025	1.509	1.170	815	3.123	−23.982	1.562	−790
2026	1.554	1.161	997	3.123	−23.305	1.562	−113
2027	1.602	1.155	1.164	3.073	−24.265	1.536	1.086
2028	1.651	1.151	1.333	3.073	−23.463	1.536	1.888
2029	1.703	1.147	1.520	3.028	−24.038	1.514	3.438
2030	1.758	1.143	1.720	3.028	−23.040	1.514	4.436

* Mean value of the expected price range for phosphorous from phosphate rock(Horn and Sartorius,2009)
Source: Own calculations

As can be seen from Figure 16.2 and Table 16.1, the specific recycling costs of the cheapest process, FIX-PHOS, will already be lower than the price of rock phosphate in 2019. The accumulated differential costs up to this point amount to around € 1 million. Thereafter the process not only pays for itself from the investors' perspective, but will(be able to)provide the entire economy with cheaper phosphorous from an even more reliable source. The disadvantage: The yield from the process is relatively low and the applicability is limited to a relatively small share of sewage treatment plants. All in all, an (German) economy-wide recovery rate of approx. 2% would be feasible, utilizing this process. However, it is important especially when introducing a new technology to have inexpensive alternatives like this in order to overcome barriers to adopting the new technology.

On the contrary, not only is the yield clearly higher with the PASCH process, but also the amount of available sewage sludge(ash). On the other hand, the process does not achieve the break-even point within the period investigated(until 2030). In 2027 the differential costs will exceed the maximum of ca. € 24 million annually and accumulate to a sum of ca. €340 million. This figure should be seen in relation to the amount of phosphorous(193,000 tonnes)recycled within this period. The accumulated differential costs can be further relativised if one considers that the often suggested interim solution of "interim landfilling" this amount of sewage sludge ash for later phosphorous recovery would also cost € 290 million①.

Alternatively, (or parallel to) the PASCH process, the ASH DEC process could also possibly be utilized. It has the same advantages as the PASCH process with regard to quantities and efficiency, but only costs half. The ASH DEC process would achieve its break-even point by 2026 and by then have accumulated difference costs amounting to a maximum of € 38 million. However, the disadvantage is that no pure phosphate is obtained, which could be used in industrial fertilizer production analogous to the phosphoric acid obtained from rock phosphate, but a largely decontaminated sewage sludge ash which could be directly used in agriculture. At present, however, no sales or distribution network exists for this substance, and in addition, the handling requires farmers to make certain changes. Both factors represent barriers to a speedy market introduction which cannot be ignored.

---

① The suggestion to "dump" sludge ash containing phosphorous as an interim solution until the costs of phosphorous recycling have fallen mostly overlooks the fact that cost decreases are the result of learning effects accruing only during the actual *implementation* of the technology. According to the PHOBE project, the costs of landfilling/dumping sewage sludge ash amount to 1.50 €/kg phosphorous because of the stringent soil and groundwater protection requirements.

16.4 Germany as a lead market for recycling phosphorous from wastewater

Besides a greater independence from rock phosphate or fertilizer imports with their fluctuating and frequently rising prices, an increasing involvement of German companies in the area of phosphorous recycling would also mean that they appropriate specific know-how about developing and operating the necessary plants. This know-how can be used and is synonymous with competitive advantages when it comes to manufacturing phosphorous recycling plants and selling and operating them abroad. The possibly resulting increase in economic output can be regarded as a further argument in favour of investing in phosphorous recycling. However, certain conditions must be fulfilled to implement this potential: The necessary competences must be available on the science and research side, relevant technology providers must be present and the competition abroad must not be too big. Ultimately, the time factor plays a significant role in utilizing a potential, so that existing advantages are not lost.

16.4.1 German research competences in the area of phosphorous recycling

A first indication of the significance of German research institutions in researching technologies to recycle phosphorous can be seen in the analysis of the countries of origin of the processes depicted in Figure 16.1. Of the 20 processes shown, 14 were or are being researched in Germany, two in each the Netherlands and Sweden and one each in Denmark, Norway, Finland, USA and Canada. That Germany plays an outstanding role in phosphorous recycling research is also documented by the number of conference papers at the International Conference on Nutrient Recovery from Wastewater Streams which took place in May 2009 in Vancouver, Canada. Even if one considers that German research groups which focus particularly on the subject of phosphorous recycling were especially encouraged by the project management agency to present their results at the conference, it is still noteworthy that the number of German contributions greatly exceed those of the host country and were far ahead (of those) of the USA. In a European comparison, Spain, Austria, Sweden, Great Britain and the Netherlands stand out (the Danish papers deal exclusively with industrial fertilizers), in an extra-European comparison the leaders are China, Australia and Japan(Figure 16.3).

For comparison, in Figure 16.3 the number of News Group members of the CEEP (Centre Européen d'Études des Polyphosphates; www.ceep-phosphates.org), an

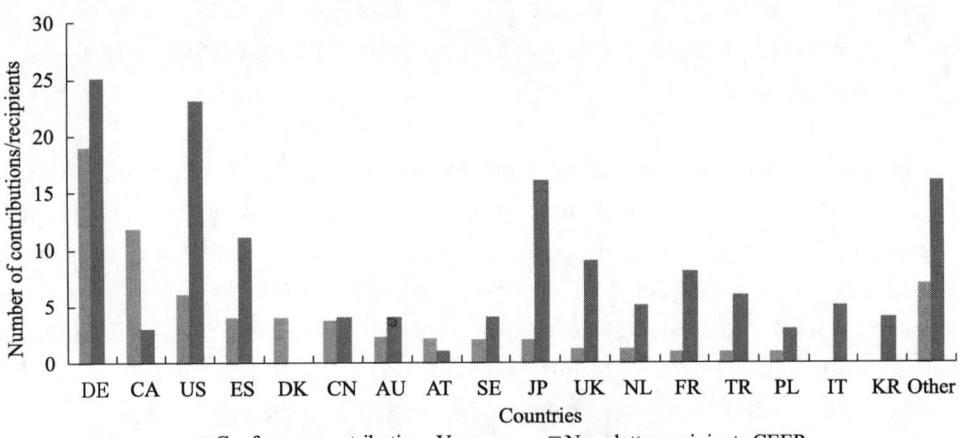

Figure 16.3 International comparison of the number of conference papers in Vancouver 2009 and the News Group members of the CEEP website (Status: March 2010)
Source: Own assessment

information forum for the European phosphate industry, is presented, which in the past has also intensively tackled the subject of phosphorous recovery[①]. The website was operated until recently in England, so that a location-related bias in favour of German participants cannot be assumed. When compared with Germany participants from Spain, Sweden, Great Britain, the Netherlands, France, Turkey, Poland and Italy perform better than they did in the papers for the conference in Vancouver, which was not surprising considering the special incentives for German participants then. However, the German participants were clearly in the majority in both cases. Interesting is also the large number of readers from USA and Japan, who obviously use the website as an internationally accessible source of information on the development in Europe.

16.4.2 Phosphorous recycling processes already implemented in Germany

A large-scale industrial process to solve the incrustation problems during sludge digestion and in the downstream pipelines and containments was developed by the Berlin Waterworks. In this so-called "Berlin Process", the digested sludge is subjected to MAP precipitation in the feed tank of the dewatering centrifuge. To separate the MAP more efficiently, initially a hydro-cyclone was used and then, more successfully,

---

① Recently the topic of phosphorous recycling was removed to the website www.phosphorus-recovery.tu-darmstadt.de of the Institute IWAR of the Technical University Darmstadt.

an airlift reactor(Stumpf et al., 2009). The MAP product is then washed and dried and is an approved fertilizer. The process is sold also under license by the company PCS Consult(Hamburg) as AIRPREX(PCS-Consult, 2010).

The SEABORNE process was developed to recycle phosphate from digested sewage sludge and liquid manure. A pilot plant which has been operating since 2000 in Owschlag(Schleswig-Holstein)(Schulz and Schultze, 2001) was followed by a large-scale industrial plant using a simplified version of the process was set up in Gifhorn (East Lower Saxony) in 2007. In order to lower the costs for chemicals, the plant is operated at pH 5, which however negatively impacts the phosphorous yield(Bayerle, 2009; Müller, 2004). The higher gas yield from the anaerobic digestion and better drainage however make the process profitable, so that the operators are able to do without subsidies. The phosphouous product (MAP) is dried and directly used as a fertilizer in farming.

In the "Stuttgart Process", phosphate is initially re-dissolved from the anaerobically stabilized sewage sludge using acid, freed from heavy metal ions using citric acid via complexing and then precipitated as MAP. This has the advantage that it can also be carried out in treatment plants which eliminate phosphorous using iron salts and can be applied in many plants without having to convert existing processes. After developing and testing on a laboratory scale in the years 2003 and 2004, the Stuttgart process was further developed, initially on a pilot scale(1 m^3 reactor volume) (2006 to 2007) whereby a recovery rate of 70% was reliably achieved. In the meantime, a model with 20 cubic meter reactor volume was built in the sewage treatment plant Offenburg-Grießheim, which can treat the sludge of 5000 to 10,000 inhabitants (MUNV, 2011). The precipitated MAP can be utilized directly as a multiple-purpose fertilizer.

The ASH DEC process which was originally developed in Austria and implemented in Löben in a pilot project is presently being further developed in the Oberursel(Germany) branch of the Finnish company Outotec. The technology was successfully tested over a longer period on a semi-industrial scale. The up-scaling to an industrial plant scale is planned. Several locations are being checked for feasibility as a commercial plant (Hermann, 2010). In the ASH DEC process, the sludge ash containing phosphorous is treated with acid and heated with chlorous compounds to produce a heavy metal-free fertilizer product whose efficacy is comparable to commercial fertilizers(TSP). After setting the nutrient composition and pelleting, the product complies with the Fertilizer Ordinance and is an approved fertilizer.

In the MEHPAREC® process an oxygen-melting-gasification of phosphorous bearing materials such as sewage sludge(or sludge ash) is carried out in a metallurgical process. In this process, the briquetted sewage sludge is gasified and its ash components are melted at 2000°C. The phosphate can be separated(at 1450°C) from the(heavy) metals and after solidification in a water tank is in a form readily absorbable by plants. The fertilizer complies with the Fertilizer Ordinance. Larger plants are already being planned for the process which has so far been implemented on an experimental scale(300 kg slag/h)(Scheidig, 2010). A feasibility study commissioned by the city of Nürnberg demonstrated that in a sewage treatment plant the MEPHREC® process, by harnessing the energy contained in the sludge(instead of ash), could be so designed that the phosphorous containing slag can be brought to market at competitive prices. In 2012 a demonstration plant with an annual capacity of 500 t and in 2014 a production plant with an annual capacity of 7,500 t will be built.

16.4.3 Competition from abroad

In the Netherlands the direct utilisation of sewage sludge in agriculture is practically impossible, because of the lack of public acceptance, due to the very low emission caps and because sufficient manure is already available as a result of factory farming. The 350,000 tonnes of sludge which are annually incurred in the Netherlands are therefore almost exclusively incinerated, especially as the goal of far-reaching volume reduction can also be reached in this way. 55 percent of the sludge is disposed of in two mono-incineration plants, the rest is burned or exported(EUWID, 2009). In the past, with the help of the DHV Crystalactors, phosphorous was crystallized out of the liquid sludge on a large scale as calcium phosphate and served as a raw material/basis for industrial phosphorous production by means of the Thermphos Process. In recent times the phosphorous concentrations sank which meant that the plant in Geestmeranbracht was no longer profitable and it was recently shut down. Now attempts are being made to use sewage sludge ash as a direct substitute for phosphate rock(Korvang, 2010) as input for the phosphorous producer Thermphos. The iron content however must not exceed a certain threshold(0.2 mol Fe/mol phosphorous). Actually, the ratio is on average 0.6 to 0.8. Two strategies are presently being pursued to solve this problem: Firstly the separate collection and burning of sludge from treatment plants using EBPR and secondly the conversion from Fe to Al salts in the chemical phosphorous elimination. The non-profit enterprise SNB which operates one of the two mono-incineration plants sees good prospects to recycle the phosphorous from 30 percent of Dutch sludge by 2015 in this way. Phosphorous recovery should thereby become economically viable, because the sludge will then no longer have to be expensively disposed of in one of the scarce Dutch landfill sites, but Thermphos will even pay for the phosphorous source sludge ash (Korvang, 2010). How seriously the subject of nutrient recycling is being taken in the Netherlands can be seen in the creation of the "nutrient platform" which was set up in December 2010 and in which approx. a dozen enterprises, associations, NGOs and political parties are jointly attempting to develop a nation-wide strategy to recover nutrients from wastewater (http://www.phosphaterecovery.com/news/current-news/launch-of-nutrient-platform/1018).

Since May 2009 three PEARL reactors have been operating in North America which produce 1500 kg of struvite daily. The PEARL process was developed in Canada (University of British Columbia) and was further developed up to industrial application by the firm Ostara in recent years. The process resembles the DHV Crystalactor. Struvite is obtained from the process water through the addition of magnesium chloride in a fluidized bed reactor. Ca. 90% of the phosphate dissolved in the process water is recovered in the process. The struvite is produced in the form of dust-free pellets, which can be directly applied as a (long-term) lawn fertilizer (named "Crystal Green"). An special feature of the PEARL process is also the business model according to which the plants are not simply sold, but the users pay for the successful operation, i. e. eliminating phosphorous from the sludge (Britton, 2009). The main focus is to prevent complications caused by too high phosphorous concentrations in the sludge stream. Recovering phosphorous is a possibility to achieve additional profits with the aid of the "waste" by-product. A variation of the process presented here is the PHOSNIX process developed in Japan (Nawa and Matsushita, 2009).

16.5 Summary and outlook

Of the considerable number of phosphorous recovery processes which have been investigated in recent years in research and demonstration projects, above all in Germany, but also in some cases abroad, two process strands were identified as economically of particular promise for the short to mid term: The precipitation or adsorption of phosphate from sewage sludge liquor (after separation from or in the sludge) as well as the manufacture of an effective, phosphorous bearing fertilizer out of sludge ash. In no case however can the recycled phosphate or phosphate-bearing fertilizer compete with the price of phosphorous acid manufactured from geogenic rock phosphate which is used in the chemical industry as the raw material for phosphorous fertilizers. Whereas ca. 1.25 €/kg phosphorous must be paid in the latter case, the cheapest phosphorous recycling processes still cost approx. 2 €/kg. However, it is already possible today, in certain cases, to reclaim phosphorous economically, if the phosphorous recycling is not the only reason, respectively particular framework conditions favour utilizing the process. Such market niches can exist, for example, if the phosphorous elimination from the sewage sludge prevents operational problems through struvite incrustations in the pipelines and tanks in the treatment plant (see "Berlin Process", PEARL) or, as is the case in the Netherlands, disposing of sewage sludge ash is so expensive that converting it into a marketable fertilizer product also makes economic sense (example: ASH DEC).

However, even apart from the existence of niche markets, due to the decline of marginal unit costs of the technology itself and the expected cost rise in producing phosphorous from rock phosphate, phosphorous recycling is not far from commercial viability. According to our calculations, phosphorous recovery from sewage sludge liquor (FIX-PHOS) could be commercially viable in approx. 10 years and fertilizer manufacture from sludge ash (ASH DEC) in less than 15 years. If it is additionally possible to identify and utilise niche markets, then the remaining time periods can be correspondingly shortened. It must, however, be stressed that economies of scale and declining marginal unit costs only take place to the extent that the technologies are actually implemented. Simply waiting for further developments is only practicable with regard to the anticipated price rises for rock phosphate—and in this case reaching the break-even will last a lot longer.

For possible German producers of phosphorous recycling technologies, the scenario examined here results in a short-term (by 2012) entry into the technology and benefiting from the most favourable opportunities up to the year 2030 in a Europe-wide market potential of € 12 respectively € 64 million for the two technology branches examined. The outlook for such a short-term entry on the part of German companies can be judged very positively, as research and development in this area in Germany can be regarded as leading-edge compared to other countries. As far as the market-oriented area is concerned, relevant activities are also taking place in Germany which are distributed over various process strands. In both cases there are significant competitors in North America (PEARL) and in the Netherlands (CRYSTALACTOR, THERMPHOS), which already have an advantage in their home countries with regard to possible market penetration. In order to maintain the existing lead at least in the area of research and development, the prior development in Germany must be continually pursued and a rapid transition to larger-scale demonstration and production facilities on an industrial scale driven forward.

References

Bayerle, N. 2009. P-recycling in Gifhorn with the modified Seaborne process. Conference Baltic 21 on Phosphorus Recycling and Good Agricultural Practice, Berlin.

Britton, A. 2009. P-recovery in North America—Ostara's Pearl process. Conference Baltic 21 on Phosphorus Recycling and Good Agricultural Practice, Berlin.

Cordell, D., Drangert, J. O., White, S. 2009. The story of phosphorus: global food security and food for thought. *Global Environmental Change*, 19, 92-305.

DWA(German Association for Water Management, Wastewater and Waste). 2005. Stand der Klärschlammbehandlung und—entsorgung in Deutschland—Ergebnisse der DWA-Klärschla mmerhebung2003. Deutsche Vereinigung für Wasserwirtschaft, Abwasser und Abfall, Hennef.

EC. 2009. Annex to the 5th commission summary of the implementation of the urban waste water treatment directive. http://ec.europa.eu/environment/water/water-urbanwaste/im plementation/pdf/implementation_report_annex.pdf.

EUWID. 2009. Klärschlamm in Holland fast ausschließlich thermisch entsorgt. *EUWID Wasser und Abwasser*, 15, 16.

EUWID. 2010. Mit weiterem Rückgang der Klärschlammdüngung ist zu rechnen. *EUWID Wasser und Abwasser*, 44, 5.

Hermann, L. 2010. Personal communication(phone, email) in March 2010 and January 2011.

MUNV(Ministerium für Umwelt, Naturschutz und Verkehr Baden-Württemberg). 2011. Land bezuschusst Modellvorhaben zur großtechnischen Rückgewinnung von Phosphor aus Klärschlämmen mit 645000 Euro. http://www.um.baden-wuerttemberg.de/servlet/is/68377

Müller, J. 2004. Anpassung der Seaborne-Verfahrenstechnik an die Bedingungen einer kommunalen Kläranlage. Presentation at a DWA Workshop on phosphorous recovery in Weimar im October 2004.

Nawa, Y., Matsushita, T. 2009. P-recovery in Japan—the Phosnix process. Conference Baltic 21 on Phosphorus Recycling and Good Agricultural Practice, Berlin.

PCS-Consult. 2010. Homepage. http://www.pcs-consult.de/html/airprex1.html. and telephone inter view with Svenja Rogge.

Pinnekamp, J., Gäth, S., Sartorius, C., et al. 2011. Phosphorrecycling—Ökologische und wirtschaftliche Bewertung verschiedener Verfahren und Entwicklung eines strategischen Verwertungskonzeptes für Deutschland. Final report of the BMBF project of the same title (FKE OZWA 0805 - 8), Aachen: RWTH Aachem.

Sartorius, C., von Horn, J., Tettenborn, F. 2011. Phosphorus recovery from wastewater-state-of-the-art and future potential. http://www.phosphorrecycling.de/attachments/042_Nutrient2011_paper+_Sartorius-et-al.pdf.

Scheidig, K., Mallon, J., Schaaf, M. 2010. Zukunftsfähige klärschlammverwertung. *KA Korrespondenz Abwasser Abfall*, 57(9), 902-915.

Scheidig, K. 2011. Beschreibung des Mephrec4®-Produktionsprozesses. Personal communication.

Stumpf, D., Heinzmann, B., Schwarz, R. J., et al. 2009. Induced struvite precipitation in an airlift reactor for phosphorus recovery. Proceedings of the International Conference on Nutrient Recovery from Wastewater Streams, Vancouver, Canada.

von. Horn, J, Sartorius, C. 2009. Impact of supply and demand on the price development of phosphate (fertilizer). http://www.phosphorrecycling.de/attachments/040_vonHorn-Sartorius-2009_P-price-development.pdf.

Author

After receiving degrees as M.S. in biology in 1984 and as Ph.D. in biochemistry in 1987 from the University of Saarland in Saarbrücken (Germany) for work in protein biochemistry, Christian Sartorius worked from 1988 to 1991 as a post-doc at the Biocenter of the Basel University on the molecular biology of key metabolic pathways of the malarial parasite. His concern for the environment and his interest in the reasons for anthropogenic environmental problems prompted him to study economics at the University of Freiburg from where he graduated as M.A. in economics in 1996 with a thesis about the role of energy in the economic process. Since then Christian Sartorius worked at the Evolutionary Economics Unit of the Max-Planck-Institute for Research into Economic Systems in Jena on the evolution of social norms and values and their role in the generation of welfare. For this work, he received a degree as Dr. rer. pol. (Ph.D. in Economics) in June 2001. From 2001 to 2004, he worked as a research associate in a project about time strategies in environmental innovation policy at the Energy Systems Unit at the Technical University Berlin. Since October 2004, he is researcher and project coordinator in the Dept. Sustainability and Infrastructures of the Fraunhofer Institute for System and Innovation Research in Karlsruhe (Germany).

His current fields of research comprise the characterization of sustainable technologies, including their ecological, economic and social impact. Moreover, he investigates the drivers and barriers for the diffusion and further development of sustainable technologies including their impacts in terms of economic growth and competitiveness. Eventually, he designs and evaluates technology-related policy instruments capable of supporting sustainable product and process innovations with special appreciation of time-strategic aspects.

The Greening of Human Resources Management in China

Torsten M.Kühlmann

17.1 Introduction

Over the last three decades China has undergone rapid industrialization, economic growth and urbanization. At the same time China has paid a high price for its accelerated development in terms of environmental devastation, including air pollution, water pollution in the vast majority of rivers, overexploitation of groundwater, generation of solid and toxic waste, destruction of the habitats of endangered animal species, near-total deforestation, rampant overfishing, depletion of agricultural land(Economy,2007). The socioeconomic impacts of the damage done to the environment are enormous (World Bank and State Environmental Protection Administration,2007). High numbers of Chinese are suffering from pollution-related diseases like cancer, respiratory problems and diarrhea. People from rural regions are joining in mass migration to the cities because of expired agricultural lands. Acid rain causes damages to crops, forests and building materials. The cost to the country's economy from environmental degradation has been estimated in 2008 to be about $ 200 billion. That was roughly 4% of the country's gross domestic product(Watts, 2010).

In response to the environmental degradation, China has installed a series of standards, regulations, and laws related to pollution control and environmental conservation since the 1980s (Stalley and Yang, 2006). Moreover, the Chinese government has been strongly promoting the implementation of ISO 14001(Zeng et al. ,2005). ISO 14001 is particularly popular in China, which now ranks as the world's single largest adopter of the standard. By 2010, nearly 70,000 Chinese companies had obtained certification according to ISO 14001 (ISO, 2011). The Chinese government has also started funding state-owned companies for reducing sources of pollution and hazards and closing down numerous firms with obsolete production technology (Economy,2007). So far, environmental policy in China was typically based on the belief in regulatory measures and one can anticipate that the Chinese authorities will promulgate additional regulations. Without doubt, the command-and-control approach has advanced progress in cleaning air, water and ground, and preventing additional environmental deterioration(Stalley and Yang, 2006; Fryxell and Lo, 2003).

On the other hand, it seems that this approach to environmental protection has been too limited as the enforcement of regulations remains to be weak in China (Zhang et al. ,2008; van Rooij, 2002). Additionally, focusing on state interventions neglects that environmental problems in China, as elsewhere, are often the result of the addition of multiple "small" behaviors rather than a consequence of newsworthy events like major spills and accidents(Boiral, 2009). A single worker throwing toxic waste away rather than recovering and storing it in an appropriate container seems to have little impact on the preservation of the environment. Yet, aggregating these acts of environmental negligence across the entire factory may provoke visible negative effects on the environmental performance of the company. Hence, at the root of many or most of environmental problems are the behaviors and underlying decisions, value orientations and social norms of the Chinese people. How they perceive, assess, and value the environment will largely affect how they behave in relation to it. Thus, beside a regulatory infrastructure for environmental protection considerable emphasis must be placed on non-regulatory approaches toward behavioral change.

One group whose participation will be outstanding for the implementation of non-regulatory approaches in China is its entrepreneurs, managers, and employees. The aggregated influence of a multitude of actions taken on a daily basis in small and large businesses significantly contributes to the quality of the environment (Fryxell and Lo, 2003). Examples include such ordinary activities as selecting modes of transport, designing products, maintaining equipment, packaging goods, and separating waste. To date, literature on companies' engagement in the protection of the environment has greatly neglected the contribution of individual employee behaviors to environmental issues(Wagner, 2011). Most research is centered on aspects such as compliance with government regulations, strategic decisions on how to respond to societal pressures, costs and benefits of responding to "go green", and the implementation of formalized environmental management systems(Jackson et al. , 2011; Boiral, 2009; Cordano and Frieze, 2000). To date, no comprehensive and successfully tested theoretical model for examining pro-environmental behavior in companies, its antecedents and consequences has been developed(Andersson et al. ,2005).

In contrast, studies dealing with environmental issues outside the workplace often address individual value orientations, environmental knowledge, social norms, and voluntary citizenship behaviors as key factors for the protection of the environment (Mobley et al. ,2010; Steg and Vlek,2009; Stern,2000). Using energy saving modes of transportation, participating in selective trash collection programs, not wasting water are all behaviors that stem from individual perceptions, evaluations and decisions. Thus, our interest in this paper is to bring together both strands of thinking in order to better understand the contribution of employee behavior and its management to an ecologically sustainable way of doing business in China. The remainder of this paper will be organized into three parts. First, we examine which factors in the individual as well as in his social context contribute to pro-environmental behaviors. Second, by integrating these insights, we develop a framework that helps us to understand how specific factors interact and are related to environmentally conscious decisions and behaviors. Finally, we discuss the implications for human resource managers in Chinese companies.

17.2 Antecedents of pro-environmental behaviors

Over the last 40 years many psychologists and sociologists have explored the roots of pro-environmental behavior(Kollmuss and Agyeman, 2002; Stern, 2000). By "pro-environmental behavior" we mean behavior that consciously seeks to minimize the negative impact of human actions on the natural world. Answers to questions like: "Why do people act pro-environmentally?" and "What impedes pro-environmental action?" are complex as environmentally significant behaviors depend on a broad range of conditions.

First, the individual predisposition to behave on behalf of the environment is presumed to be contingent upon environmental knowledge. " Environmental knowledge" or "environmental literacy" can be understood as knowledge of facts, concepts, and relationships concerning the natural environment and its ecosystems. For employees to act pro-environmentally, they need fundamental knowledge about a broad range of issues such as:

(1) The status quo of the local environment and its interrelationship with global environmental trends.

(2) The negative impact of degraded natural resources on company operations.

(3) The consequences of a degraded environment to the individual's well-being.

(4) The range of alternatives available to solve environmental problems.

(5) The compatibility of pro-environmental interventions with economic performance.

The oldest model of pro-environmental behavior was based on the assumption of a linear causal chain: The more environmental knowledge the more pro-environmental behavior (Burgess et al., 1998). This model implies that educating people about environmental issues automatically results in more pro-environmental behavior. Many environmental Non-Governmental Organizations (NGOs) base their communication campaigns on that logic (Kollmuss and Agyeman, 2002). But research showed that in most cases, increases in knowledge did not necessarily lead to pro-environmental behavior (Fryxell and Lo, 2003). Nevertheless, environmental knowledge may interact with other factors resulting in pro-environmental behavior. Without environmental knowledge it is difficult to understand one's relationship with the environment and to develop environmental concerns and initiatives.

Although public interest in environmental issues has advanced over the last years, environmental knowledge in China appears to be moderate at best. Notably, Chinese people living outside major urban areas and with lower educational background lack basic knowledge about environmental issues (Harris, 2006). For many Chinese, environmental issues primarily focus on sanitation and health, air pollution in the surrounding area and pollution of nearby water resources. People poorly understand that their own actions are causing environmental harm. There is a wide-spread absence of knowledge about global environmental trends such as climate change. However, knowledge has been increasing and spreading in recent years because of education campaigns and more coverage of environmental issues in public mass media (Stalley and Yang, 2006).

Second, environmentally significant behavior requires positive attitudes toward the intact environment and particularly toward environmentally important behaviors. Pro-environmental actions occur in response to notions that environmental conditions pose threats to valued things like other people, other species, or the biosphere and to the belief that a specific action one initiates could avert those consequences. Both beliefs combine to a favorable attitude toward that action. According to the "Theory of Planned Action" (Ajzen, 1991; Ajzen and Fishbein, 1980) attitudes toward behaviors are better predictors of behaviors than more general attitudes toward a clean environment, the use of natural resources or the protection of endangered species. For example, comparing attitudes toward climate change and driving behavior usually shows no correlation. Even people who are very concerned about climate change tend to drive. To better predict driving behavior you need to know one's attitude toward driving.

Although we assume independent, direct effects of environmental knowledge and attitudes on employee pro-environmental behaviors, an interaction of these influences seems likely(Stern, 2000). This is to say that environmental attitudes appear to be a necessary condition for environmental knowledge to shape behaviors. In the absence of such attitudes environmental knowledge has relatively little effect on such behaviors. On the other hand, environmental values if uninformed by knowledge about the environment get stuck as good intentions(Fryxell and Lo, 2003).

How do the people of China value the environment? Generally, the Chinese have a very instrumental perspective of the natural world: It exists for the good of people and deserves improvement by human interventions (Harris, 2006). Environmental problems are only important to the people directly affected by them. The Chinese have a saying along the lines of "People will clear the snow from their doorstep but not worry about the snow on their neighbor's roof".

Third, perceived behavioral control is also emerging as an important factor in pro-environmental behavior. People with a strong perceived behavioral control believe that their actions can bring about change. People with a weak perceived behavioral control, on the other hand, assume that their actions are insignificant and do not result in success. Such people are much less likely to act pro-environmentally regardless of their attitudes or knowledge, since they feel that it does not make a difference anyway. There are several situational constraints that make people believe in a lack of behavioral control. Such constraints may be lack of time, lack of money, and lack of convenience. Perceived behavioral control may also be low when one assumes that the behavior required does not correspond to one's own intellectual or physical capabilities. Situational as well as personal constraints may cause the perception of "helplessness", which has been described by Kaplan (2000) as a "pivotal issue" in explaining a lack of coherence in the context of environmentally responsible behavior. The more difficult, time-consuming, or expensive the pro-environmental behavior, the weaker is its dependence on knowledge and attitude. Knowledge and attitude have the greatest predictive value for behaviors that are not strongly constrained by context or personal capabilities. Diekmann and Preisendoerfer(1992) report that environmental attitude only significantly predicts low-cost pro-environmental behavior(e. g. recycling). But people who care about the environment such as recycling do not necessarily engage in activities that are more costly and inconvenient such as driving or flying less.

Given the generally poor understanding of environmental issues, Chinese people often do not feel capable to stop environmental degradation (Harris, 2006). The common excuse for not coping with environmental problems is"it's the government's problem". This is closely associated with the wide-spread opinion that powerful interests, such as state-owned enterprises in cooperation with corrupt local officials, cause environmental problems. Additionally, there is a lack of civil society group, that are important for spurring a sense of empowerment for environmental protection among citizens and which can act as"watchdogs"(Stalley and Yang, 2006).

Fourth, pro-environmental behaviors are influenced by social ("normative") pressures. This holds especially true when we explain the pro-environmental behaviors of individuals acting under corporate influence. Findings from a number of studies in the feild of organizations suggest that corporate values indicating commitment to ecological sustainability are an important factor in employee enactment of environmental behaviors(Howard-Grenville, 2006).

Notably in China's urban areas, norms for pro-environmental behaviors are ambivalent. On the one hand people are focused on getting rich and consumerism is manifest. On the other hand people feel that they ought to act to protect the environment. For Chinese the range of"important others"who act as referent persons is limited to family members, close friends and colleagues. Whether an organization as a whole or a society approves pro-environmental behavior is less significant.

Our review shows: A holistic explanation of pro-environmental behavior has to consider that multiple factors exert influence. To summarize, we propose a comprehensive conceptual framework that incorporates the four above mentioned factors that might have an impact on pro-environmental behavior in organizations (Figure 17. 1). This framework extends the Theory of Planned Behavior(Ajzen, 1991) which emphasizes the contribution of attitudes, social norms and perceptions of behavioral control to encompass environmental knowledge as additional predictor of environmentally significant behaviors. According to Ajzen's theory, the intention to act pro-environmentally is determined by the attitude toward the behavior, the actor's perception of social norms regarding the behavior, and the belief that the behavior will help to attain one's goals. Several studies have demonstrated the theory's value in predicting pro-environmental behaviors(Mannetti et al. , 2004; Kaiser and Gutscher,

2003; Boldero, 1995; Taylor and Todd, 1995; Sparks and Shepherd, 1992). Incorporating environmental knowledge indicates that effective pro-environmental behaviors at the workplace often call for specific and complex forms of knowledge: Know what, know why, and know how.

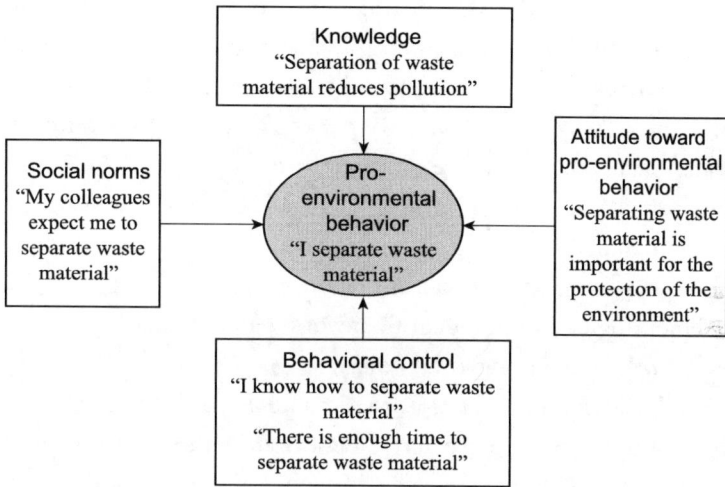

Figure 17.1 Personal and situational influences on pro-environmental behavior

Often these factors interact. For example, studies that only examine attitudinal factors are likely to find inconsistent effects because the effects also depend on other factors like knowledge or social norms or felt helplessness due to situational constraints(Cheung et al., 1999; Guagnano et al., 1995; Dieckmann and Preisendörfer, 1982).

17.3 The contribution of human resource management to the emergence of pro-environmental behaviors

As Stern(2000) holds, pro-environmental behavior in the private sphere might depend on different factors than pro-environmental behavior at the workplace. The latter is not only influenced by knowledge, attitudes, beliefs and norms, but also by the organizational context such as corporate values (Andersson and Bateman, 2000; Cordano and Frieze, 2000; Ramus and Steger, 2000). Among others, human resource management(HRM) heavily contributes to the physical and social context of work. Several researchers have argued that the involvement of HRM is a key for the successful adoption and maintenance of pro-environmental behaviors at the workplace (Boiral, 2009; Rothenberg, 2003; Ramus, 2002; Daily and Huang, 2001; Wehrmeyer,

1996). HRM can create conditions favorable to the emergence of pro-environmental behaviors and initiatives. Despite this wide-spread notion empirical studies that relate human resource management and pro-environmental activities are rare (Jackson et al., 2011; Jabbour and Santos, 2008; Renwick et al., 2008). Based upon the limited body of research, five critical HRM instruments can be identified that are frequently proposed as supporting factors for improving pro-environmental behaviors and implementing environmental management systems, like ISO 14001 (Wagner, 2011; Jabbour and Santos, 2008; Brio et al., 2007; Govindarajulu and Daily, 2004; Ramus, 2002; Daily and Huang, 2001). These are:

(1) Promoting a "green" organizational culture.
(2) Environmental education and training.
(3) Empowering employees to act pro-environmentally.
(4) Implementing cross functional teamwork ("green teams").
(5) Rewarding pro-environmental behaviors.

Figure 17.2 presents these HRM practices and relates them to the determinants of pro-environmental behaviors we have identified in the preceding sections of this paper. Obviously, an HRM practice may influence more than one determinant. For example, environmental education and training can have an impact on knowledge as well as on attitude and perceived behavioral control.

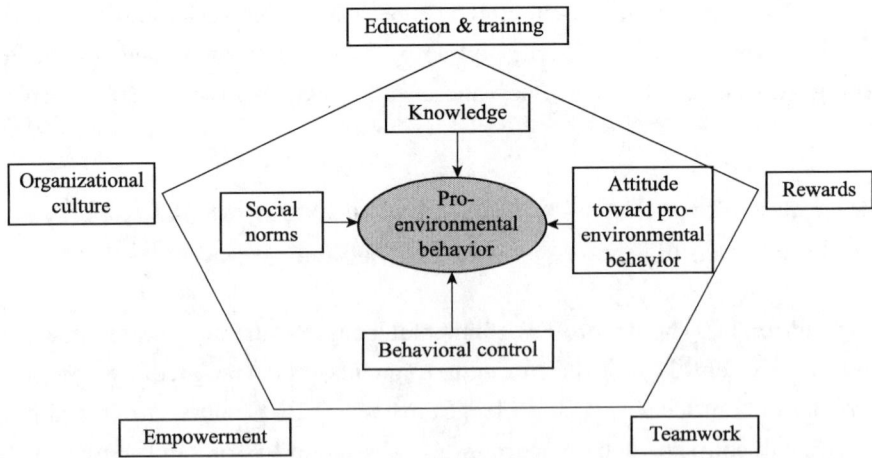

Figure 17.2 HRM approaches directed at pro-environmental behavior

In the remainder I am going to discuss these recommendations and their fit with the Chinese context. Managing employees in Chinese companies takes forms that are different from HRM practices in Western companies. Research suggests that

Chinese companies are characterized by autocratic managerial styles and centralized decision-making. Pay for performance and formalized performance appraisals are less likely to be found in Chinese firms. Additionally, Chinese companies provide less extensive formal training and education programs to their employees(Fu et al. ,2008).

These features of Chinese HRM are rooted in the cultural and institutional context Chinese companies are operating in. The"cultural congruence position"holds that behaviors and practices become acceptable, enacted and effective in a society to the extent that they are consistent with the society's values and norms. Violation of a society's values and norms will result in conflict, resistance and dissatisfaction on the part of the society's majority (House et al., 1997). Empirical evidence strongly supports the cultural congruence proposition(Newman and Nollen, 1996; Cateora and Graham, 2007; Black and Porter, 1991). Therefore, it is to be expected, that HRM practices have a great impact on pro-environmental practices only to the extent that they correspond to essential Chinese values, beliefs and institutions.

17.3.1 Organizational culture

Various studies have stressed the utility of promoting a "green" organizational culture(Howard-Grenville, 2006; Harris and Crane, 2002; Hoffman, 1993). A green organizational culture may be defined as a set of assumptions, values, and organizational norms that reflects either the desire or necessity of a company to operate in an environmentally correct way. Organizational culture offers behavioral guidelines to the employees via shared norms, values, beliefs and routines. These cultural elements can be promoted via a variety of methods. Given the high acceptance of authority and power differentials in the Chinese society(Fu et al., 2008)efforts to change organizational culture should utilize top managers, who ostensibly question the environmental impact of proposed actions and translate environmental considerations into decisions. Additionally, top managers should demonstrate their environmental commitment by adopting exemplary"green"behaviors in their daily routines(Boiral, 2009). Some literature identified the values hold and shown by managers as the most important determinant of pro-environmental activities in the corporate context (Schaltegger and Burritt, 2005; Govindarajulu and Daily, 2004). Additionally, employees who contribute critical ideas and carry out environmental projects should be recognized for their initiatives. Also the implementation of environmental management systems underlines the company's true concern about environmental protection.

17.3.2 Education and training

For Western companies the most popular approach towards environmental management includes upgrading environmental knowledge among employees and promoting pro-environmental norms and values through formal education and training programs (Jackson et al.,2011;Renwick et al.,2008). For example,building up employee knowledge about the effects of certain pollutants on the environment can encourage initiatives to prevent emissions of such contaminants. All employees of a company,and not only the ones linked to certain departments, must receive training in environmental issues in order to create a favorable situation for pro-environmental actions.

Raising environmental knowledge and awareness is constrained by several aspects of environmental problems that tax the cognitions of the learner(Preuss,1991): (1) Most environmental degradation is not immediately noticeable. We cannot perceive the ozone hole or the accumulation of greenhouse gases. We can only notice the results of pollution and destruction once severe damage has already been caused. Also, environmental deterioration in remote areas escapes our awareness. (2)Another cognitive barrier is the often slow pace of environmental degradation. Humans are very good at perceiving sudden changes but are often unable to notice incremental changes. (3)Most environmental problems are complex. Yet we are often unable to comprehend the multiple interdependencies between problem components and tend to simplify them and think in linear causal chains. This prevents us from a deeper understanding of the causes and consequences of environmental problems. It might also lead to underestimating the extent of the problem. Because most environmental degradation is not immediately tangible, incremental and complex environmental education has to draw upon understandable and vivid language,pictures,and graphs.

In the Chinese context it may be useful to capitalize on people's instrumental view of the environment. Beginning in elementary education people need to realize how and why their workplace, their income and their health depend on environmentally significant actions not only at the societal or organizational level but also at the individual level. A second avenue for imparting environmental knowledge and values might be focusing on the future business leaders namely university students. To date,most Chinese managers and workers have had effectively no formal education addressing the elevation of environmental knowledge(Fryxell and Lo,2003). Thus, environmental subjects have to be included in business education programs. Additionally, business education should include attempts to develop environmental values in future managers. The indoctrination of values and norms may be considered more legitimate within higher education in China than in Western industrialized countries. It is also possible that students' orientations may be more malleable in light of the obvious evidence of environmental damage they are exposed to. In order to attain these goals Chinese higher education should adopt more active and involving pedagogies such as field projects, experiential exercises and case studies that have been proved to be more effective in terms of knowledge adoption and value development than conventional lecture(Fryxell and Lo, 2003).

17.3.3 Employee Empowerment

Empowerment means giving employees both the opportunity and the responsibility to take steps to identify problems at the workplace and to deal with them. Empowerment is a key factor in promoting employees to act pro-environmentally(Daily and Huang, 2001; Hanna et al., 2000). Empowered employees are more likely to enact practices on behalf of the environment and are motivated to develop new solutions for environmental problems (Denton, 1999). To this end, managers need to delegate responsibility, give away decision-making power and grant scope of action (Boiral, 2007). For example, executives can delegate to employees power, time and resources to plan and experiment with the elimination of waste without management intervention. Empowerment enhances the belief of behavioral control.

But, this approach currently does not fit the traditional orientation of Chinese employees towards power distance (Fu et al., 2008; Rehu et al., 2006). Research shows that employees from high-power-distance cultures perform better when their superior instructs them on what to do than when he grants work autonomy. Therefore, empowering employees may be a long-term strategy for Chinese companies.

17.3.4 Teamwork

While individual employee activities have a share in organizations' environmental efforts, coping with environmental problems often requires a combination of several types of individual competences and collaboration of different organizational areas. The complexities of such problems mandate cross-functional teamwork. Cross-functional teams that deal with issues of environmental management are known as "green teams"(Beard and Rees, 2000). They may be defined as teams of (voluntary) workers which are formed to identify and solve environmental problems and implement programs for better environmental performance of the company. As green teams are composed of members with different backgrounds and from different departments they offer a high chance to develop comprehensive solutions and implement them in their respective home departments(Rothenberg,2003).

Being part of a group is important for members of a collectivistic society like China. Chinese people look back at a long tradition of valuing the integration of the individual into groups and assuming the responsibilities as a group member(Fu et al., 2008). Focusing on the pursuit of individual goals has always been socially discouraged. Thus, a teamwork approach perfectly fits the cultural orientation of Chinese employees.

17.3.5 Rewards

Research has shown that monetary as well as non-monetary rewards can motivate and reinforce employees to act environmentally responsible(Renwick et al., 2008; Daily and Huang,2001). Rewards also encourage the development of knowledge, attitudes and skills that help to attain the environmental objectives of a company. Thus, for companies that value sound environmental practices the reward system needs to reflect the company's commitment to environmental objectives. Many Western companies are establishing environmental objectives for their employees and integrate them into the catalogue of criteria for individual performance appraisals which in turn affects the variable portion of the amount of earnings given to an employee(Renwick et al., 2008). Increases in pay, fringe benefits, profit-sharing programs, paid time off and awards can be used to reward employees for good environmental practice. Since Chinese employees currently assess high earnings and fringe benefits as one of the most important job attributes monetary-based rewards may be one strong motivator for inducing Chinese employees to participate in environmental initiatives(Rehu et al., 2006). However, pay for performance may violate group harmony as it differentiates between group members. A more culturally congruent solution would be switching from individual-based to team-based rewards. Also recognition-based rewards may be a stimulus for pro-environmental behaviors in the Chinese workforce. Nominating outstanding employees and work units and praising them in meetings or newspaper articles has a long tradition in China. Therefore this practice might be retained and linked to the pro-environmental performance of employees.

A reward system that is supposed to support environmentally responsible behaviors requires that improvements should be part of employees' performance appraisal. Conventional wisdom holds that Chinese managers are reluctant to give their subordinates poor ratings as that would provoke a loss of face by the employee and the supervisor and impact negatively on the quality of their interpersonal relationship. Therefore, introducing a performance appraisal system may be risky. But it is not completely unfeasible. For example, the Haier Corporation, the leading Chinese producer of household appliance posts monthly appraisals of its managers in the company's cafeteria(Pucik,2005).

17.4 Conclusion

Many approaches toward changing individuals' environmentally significant behavior at the workplace have been tried. Research found that most of these approaches, if carefully executed, can change behavior. However, single interventions have had generally disappointing results. By far, the most effective behavior change programs involve combinations of intervention types. Several HR practices which have been successfully applied in Western companies to improve employees' environmentally behaviors seem to be quite compatible with the Chinese context (Kühlmann,2012). The positive impact these practices have demonstrated in Western companies may carry over to Chinese companies as well. However, despite all the indirect evidence the successful application of these procedures has still to be proved. Time has come to analyze their applicability in helping Chinese companies to become green.

References

Aditya, R., House, R. J. 2002. Interpersonal acumen and leadership across cultures: pointers from the GLOBE study. In: Riggio, R. E., Murphy, S. E. (Eds.), *Multiple Intelligences and Leadership*. Mahwah: Erlbaum, 215-240.

Ajzen, I., Fishbein, M. 1980. *Understanding Attitudes and Predicting Social Behavior*. Englewood Cliffs: Prentice-Hall.

Ajzen, I. 1991. The theory of planned behavior. *Organizational Behavior and Human Decision Processes*, 50(2), 179-211.

Andersson, L., Bateman, T. 2000. Individual environmental initiative: championing natural environmental issues in U.S. business organisations. *Academy of Management Journal*, 43 (4), 548-570.

Andersson, L., Shivarajan, S., Blau, G. 2005. Enacting ecological sustainability in the MNC: a test of an adapted value-belief-norm framework. *Journal of Business Ethics*, 59(3), 295-305.

Beard, C., Rees, S. 2000. Green teams and the management of environmental change in a UK county council. *Environmental Management and Health*, 11(1), 27-38.

Black, J. S., Porter, L. W. 1991. Managerial behaviors and job performance: a successful manager in Los Angeles may not succeed in Hong Kong. *Journal of International Business Studies*, 22(1), 99-113.

Boiral, O. 2007. Corporate greening through ISO 14001: a rational myth? *Organization Science*, 18(1), 127-146.

Boiral, O. 2009. Greening the corporation through organizational citizenship behaviors. *Journal of Business Ethics*, 87(2), 221-236.

Boldero, J. 1995. The prediction of household recycling of newspapers: the role of attitudes, intentions, and situational factors. *Journal of Applied Social Psychology*, 25(5), 440-462.

Brio, J. A. D., Fernandez, E., Junquera, B. 2007. Management and employee involvement in achieving an environmental action-based competitive advantage: an empirical study. *The International Journal of Human Resource Management*, 18(4), 491-522.

Burgess J., Harrison C. M., Filius P. 1998. Environmental communication and the cultural politics of environmental citizenship. *Environment and Planning A*, 30(8), 1445-1460.

Cateora, P. R., Graham, J. L. 2007. *International Marketing*. 13th ed. New York: McGraw-Hill Irwin.

Cheung, S. F., Chan, D. K. S., Wong, Z. S. Y. 1999. Reexamining the theory of planned behavior in understanding wastepaper recycling. *Environment and Behavior*, 31(5), 587-612.

Cordano, M., Frieze, I. H. 2000. Pollution production preferences of U. S. managers: Applying Ajzen's theory of planned behavior. *Academy of Management Journal*, 43(4), 627-641.

Daily, B. F., Huang, S. 2001. Achieving sustainability through attention to human resource factors in environmental management. *International Journal of Operations and Production Management*, 21(12), 1539-1552.

Denton, D. K. 1999. Employee involvement, pollution control and pieces to the puzzle. *Environmental Management and Health*, 10(2), 105-111.

Diekmann, A., Preisendoerfer, P. 1992. Persönliches Umweltverhalten: Diskrepanzen zwischen Anspruch und Wirklichkeit. *Kölner Zeitschrift für Soziologie und Sozialpsychologie*, 44(2), 226-251.

Economy, E. C. 2007. The great leap backward? *Foreign Affairs*, 86(5), 38-59.

Fryxell, G. E., Lo, C. W. H. 2003. The Influence of environmental knowledge and values on managerial behaviors on behalf of the environment: an empirical examination of managers in China. *Journal of Business Ethics*, 46(1), 45-69.

Fu, P. P., Wu, R., Yang, Y., et al. 2008. Chinese culture and leadership. In: Chhokar, J. S., Brodbeck, F. C., House, R. J. (Eds.), *Culture and Leadership across the World: the Globe Book of In-depth Studies of 25 Societies*. New York: Taylor & Francis Group, 877-907.

Govindarajulu, N., Daily, B. F. 2004. Motivating employees for environmental improvement. *Industrial Management and Data Systems*, 104(4), 364-372.

Guagnano, G. A., Stern, P. C., Dietz, T. 1995. Influences on the attitude-behavior relationships: a natural experiment with curbside recycling. *Environment and Behavior*, 27(5), 699-718.

Hanna, M. D., Newman, W. R., Johnson, P. 2000. Linking operational and environmental improvement through employee involvement. *International Journal of Operations & Production Management*, 20(2),148-165.

Harris, L. C., Crane, A. 2002. The greening of organizational culture: management views on the depth, degree and diffusion of change. *Journal of Organizational Change Management*, 15(3),214-234.

Harris, P. G. 2006. Environmental perspectives and behavior in China: Synopsis and bibliography. *Environment and Behavior*,38(1),5-21.

Hoffman, A. J. 1993. The importance of fit between individual values and organisational culture in the greening of industry. *Business Strategy and the Environment*, 2(4),10-18.

House, R. J., Wright, N., Aditya, R. N. 1997. Cross cultural research on organizational leadership: a critical analysis and a proposed theory. In: Earley, P. C., Erez, M. (Eds.), *New Perspectives on International Industrial and Organizational Psychology*. San Francisco: Jossey-Bass,535-625.

Howard-Grenville, J. A. 2006. Inside the black box: how organizational culture and subcultures inform interpretations and actions on environmental issues. *Organization & Environment*, 19(1),46-73.

International Organization for Standardization(ISO). 2011. The ISO survey of certifications—2010. http://www.iso.org/iso/iso-survey2010.pdf.

Jabbour, C. J. C., Santos, F. C. A. 2008. Relationships between human resource dimensions and environmental management in companies: proposal of a model. *Journal of Cleaner Production*,16(1),51-58.

Jackson, S. E., Renwick, D. W. S., Jabbour, C. J. C., et al. 2011. State-of-the-art and future directions for green human resource management: introduction to the special issue. *Zeitschrift für Personalforschung*,25(2),99-116.

Kaiser, F. G., Gutscher, H. 2003. The proposition of a general version of the theory of planned behavior: predicting ecological behavior. *Journal of Applied Social Psychology*,33(3),586-603.

Kaplan, S. 2000. Human nature and environmentally responsible behavior. *Journal of Social Issues*,56(3),491-508.

Kollmus, A., Agyeman, J. 2002. Mind the gap: why do people act environmentally and what are the barriers to pro-environmental behavior? *Environmental Education Research*,8(3),239-260.

Kühlmann, T. M. 2012. Transfer of German human resource management practices: replication, localization, hybridization. In: Stockhammer, P. W. (Ed.), *Conceptualizing Cultural Hybridization: A Transdisciplinary Approach*. Heidelberg, Springer, 95-106.

Mannetti, L., Pierro, A., Livi, S. 2004. Recycling: Planned and self-expressive behaviour. *Journal of Environmental Psychology*,24(2),227-236.

Mobley, C., Vagias, W. M., de Ward, S. L. 2010. Exploring additional determinants of environmentally responsible behavior: the influence of environmental literature and environmental attitudes. *Environment and Behavior*, 42(4), 420-447.

Newman, K. L., Nollen, S. D. 1996. Culture and congruence: the fit between management practices and national culture. *Journal of International Business Studies*, 27(4), 753-779.

Preuss, S. 1991. *Umweltkatastrophe Mensch: Über unsere Grenzen und Möglichkeiten, ökologisch. bewusst zu handeln*. Heidelberg: Asanger.

Pucik, V. 2005. Reframing global mindset: from thinking to acting. In: Mobley, W., Weldon, E. (Eds.), *Advances in Global Leadership*. Oxford: JAI Press, 83-100.

Ramus, C. A., Steger, U. 2000. The roles of supervisory support behaviors and environmental policy in employee "ecoinitiatives" at leading edge European companies. *Academy of Management Journal*, 43(4), 605-626.

Ramus, C. A. 2002. Encouraging innovative environmental actions: what companies and managers must do. *Journal of World Business*, 37(2), 151-164.

Rehu, M., Lusk, E. J., Wolff, B. 2006. Sustainable human resource management in China: a study of a German multinational corporation. *World Review of Entrepreneurship, Management and Sustainable Development*, 2(1/2), 57-72.

Renwick, D. W. S., Redman, T., Maguire, S. 2008. Green HRM: a review, process model, and research agenda. http://www.sheffield.ac.uk/content/1/c6/08/70/89/2008-01.pdf.

Rothenberg, S. 2003. Knowledge content and worker participation in environmental management at NUMMI. *Journal of Management Studies*, 40(7), 1783-1802.

Schaltegger, S., Burritt, R. 2005. Corporate sustainability. In: Folmer, H., Tietenberg, T. (Eds.), *The International Yearbook of Environmental and Resource Economics*. Cheltenham: Edward Elgar, 185-232.

Sparks, P., Shepherd, R. 1992. Self-identity and the theory of planned behavior: Assessing the role of identification with "green consumerism". *Social Psychology Quarterly*, 55(4), 388-399.

Stalley, P., Yang, D. 2006. An emerging environmental movement in China? *The China Quarterly*, 186(2), 333-356.

Steg, L., Vlek, C. 2009. Encouraging pro-environmental behaviour: an integrative review and research agenda. *Journal of Environmental Psychology*, 29(3), 309-317.

Stern, P. C. 2000. Toward a coherent theory of environmentally significant behavior. *Journal of Social Issues*, 56(3), 407-424.

Taylor, S., Todd, P. 1995. An integrated model of waste management behavior: a test of household recycling and composting intentions. *Environment and Behavior*, 27(5), 603-630.

van Rooij, B. 2002. Implementing Chinese environmental law through enforcement. In: Chen, J., Li, Y., Otto, J. M. (Eds.), *Implementation of Law in the People's Republic of China*. Den Haag: Kluwer Law International, 149-178.

Wagner, M. 2011. Environmental management activities and sustainable HRM in German manufacturing firms—incidence, determinants, and outcomes. *Zeitschrift für Personalforschung*, 25(2), 157-177.

Watts, J. 2010. China counts £130 bn cost of economic growth. http://www.guardian.co.uk/world/

2010/dec/28/china-130-bn-economic-growth[2011-09-21].
Wehrmeyer,W. 1996. *Greening People*. Sheffield:Greenleaf.
World Bank,State Environmental Protection Administration. 2007. *Cost of Pollution in China*: *Economic Estimates of Physical Damages*. Washington,D.C. :The World Bank.
Zeng,S. X. , Tam, C. M. , Tam, V. W. Y. , et al. 2005. Towards implementation of ISO 14001 environmental management systems in selected industries in China. *Journal of Cleaner Production*,13(7),645-656.
Zhang,B. ,Bi,J. ,Yuan,Z. ,et al. 2008. Why do firms engage in environmental management? An empirical study in China. *Journal of Cleaner Production*,16(10),1036-1045.
Zhu,Q. ,Sarkis,J. ,Cordeiro,J. J. ,et al. 2008. Firm-level correlates of emergent green supply chain management practices in the Chinese context. *Omega*,36(4),577-591.

Author

Torsten M. Kühlmann is a full professor of business administration in the Department of Law, Economics and Business Administration of the University of Bayreuth,Germany. He holds a Master's Degree in psychology and a Doctorate in business administration from the University of Erlangen-Nürnberg. His research interests include international human resource management, opportunism, trust and control in transnational business relationships, and knowledge transfer in MNCs. He has taught in China, Mexico and the US, and has held visiting professorships at the Technical University, Chemnitz, and at the Mining Academy, Freiberg. Amongst others, his research has appeared in Die *Betriebswirtschaft*, *Zeitschrift für Personalforschung*, *Career Development International*, *Cross Cultural Management*, *International Journal of Knowledge*, *Culture and Change Management*, *Journal of International Business and Economics* and *Journal of Business Ethics*. He is actively involved in international executive education and has consulted with a variety of organizations.

Firms' Innovation Strategies in Relation to Green Growth

Wu Xiaobo, Wu Dong[*]

18.1 Introduction

Green growth is a strategy for achieving sustainable development. It is first agreed at the 5th Ministerial Conference on Environment and Development in Asia and the Pacific, 2005. This term focuses on the sustainable economy that synergizes economic growth and environmental protection, building a green economy in which investments in sustainable management of natural capital as well as resource savings are driving forces of growth(Brock and Taylor, 2004). An economy which is in closer alignment with sustainable development objectives provides many opportunities for using financial resources better to meet development needs and reducing the vulnerability of socioeconomic systems to environmental change and resource constraints(Ekins, 1999).

Normally, the term of green growth is used to describe national or international strategies. Green growth strategies could provide more resilient that helps economies and societies become more resilient as they work to meet demands for production, transport, housing, energy, water and so on. Innovation strategies can help mitigate the impacts of adverse shocks by reducing the intensity of resource consumption and

---

[*] Corresponding author, E-mail: wudong@zju.edu.cn.

environmental impacts, while alleviating pressure on commodity prices(Aghion et al., 2009). Green growth also offers competitive advantages to those countries that commit to policy innovations. The global market for green products and services is vast and growing fast, offering countries the dual benefit of prosperity and job creation(UNESCAP,2012).

Firms play a critical role in green growth, while they are using natural resources in a sustainable manner. However, firms' objective is to maximize their profits. How to balance the profit-pursuing nature of firms and green growth is a significant research question. There might be lots of issues on externality. Firms aiming at making profit could not solve these issues by themselves, so they need some external partners (e. g. academia, government, industry, and media) to implement their innovation strategies in relation to green growth. The firms and these external partners organize a special union—social compound union, coordinating extremely well in supporting the firms' green business model innovation(Wu and Wu,2010). In this paper, we will give some cases on how Chinese firms provide an alternative concept to standard green economic growth with the help of social compound union.

This paper is structured as follows: We first introduce three innovation strategies of firms in relation to green growth in section 18. 2. Then we introduce an old Chinese wisdom—mulberry fish pond, to illustrate how green growth works in old China and express that green growth should be a muti-member system in section 18. 3. We give the definition of social compound union and its role in firms' innovation strategies in relation to green growth in section 18. 4. The core part of this paper is section 18. 5 where social compound union propelling green growth is illustrated. Two cases are presented, one is Hangzhou Public Transport Group, and the other is Hangzhou tea industry. We give out discussion to the management implications in section 18. 6, and conclusions in section 18. 7.

18. 2 Innovation strategies in relation to green growth

There are mainly three types of innovation strategies in relation to green growth for firms.

The first is green technology innovation. As the resource and energy on the earth are getting less and less, the energy conservation and emission reduction technology becomes more and more important and popular. The green technology innovation creates or improves the traditional product or process technology, making the limited resource and energy on the earth could be used longer and more effectively.

The second is green energy innovation, which means changing the traditional energy sources to some cleaner and more sustainable ones. As we all know, the traditional energy sources, such as oil and gas have lots of carbon dioxide emissions, which contributes to global warming and many global natural disasters. We must change our energy consuming structure. it's wise to develop solar energy, wind energy, hydrogen energy, tidal energy or something else to replace the unsustainable energy.

The third is green business model innovation. This type of innovation strategy is what we are interested in. The crucial role of business model in achieving sustainable advantage has been widely acknowledged. While green growth is obsoleting traditional business models, how to design innovative new ones become the vital challenge for many firms. However, there is little consensus on how to define green business model, and the connotation of green business model innovation still remains vague as well. In this paper, by introducing social compound union into the research of business model, we try to clarify the green business model with two interesting cases in Hangzhou, China.

18.3   An old Chinese wisdom—mulberry fish pond

Before we introduce the green business model innovation, we will firstly introduce an old Chinese wisdom. This is a traditional Chinese agriculture production system—mulberry fish pond, which will help us better understand how the green business model innovation worked in the old time. Mulberry fish pond is a successful agriculture production system created by the people of the Zhujiang River Delta in their long production practice. The climate there is suitable for mulberry planting, sericulture and fisheries. Mulberry trees, Chinese silkworms and four common domestic fishes(grass carp, variegated carp, dace, and silver carp)can grow well because of the appropriate temperature.

The combination of mulberry planting, sericulture and fisheries is a complex and multiple cyclic production system in which three parts are interacted and inter-promoted. The food chain in this ecosystem is as follows: The leaves of mulberry are eaten by silkworms. The silkworm feces are eaten by the fish. The pond sludge is paved onto mulberry land. The material exchange and energy conversion among mulberry, silkworm and fish are highly effective(Figure 18.1).

The mulberry fish pond system brings the advantages of the natural resources such as abundant solar radiation with high temperature and rich water sources into full play. Under some superior conditions, the plants can grow almost throughout the year. This high biomass helps the high yielding production system.

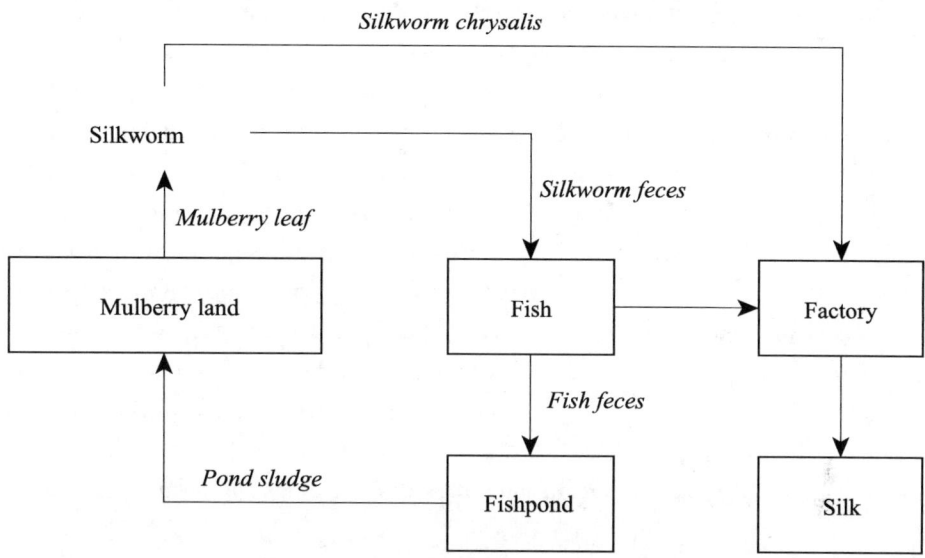

Figure 18.1　Mulberry fish pond system

The old Chinese wisdom suggests that green growth might not be done by the firm itself. In this open system, there are lots of members, and they play their own unique roles and contribute the valuable, rare, inimitable resources, finally constructing a no-waste and all-win system. Every member contributes a lot and benefits a lot from this system, and this system is all green. This mulberry fish pond system is proved to be obviously workable, making the original idea for firms' innovation strategy in relation to green growth.

18.4　Social compound union

From the old Chinese wisdom above, we have a clear understanding that it's possible to construct an innovative business model for green growth, and the green growth and economic benefits may not conflict but coordinate well. The critical factor is a highly complementary system. So we introduce the concept of social compound union which is a new social organization form developed quickly in Hangzhou, China (Wu and Wu, 2010). The traditional development of industry relies on the elite democracy which is led by the industrial elite. These elite firms do business themselves. This is their way of life, acting like lonely leaders who are powerful in their own domain but weak in the future domain such as green growth.

Social compound union links four subjects—"academia, government, industry, and media"together to participate in the affairs of industry directly and continuously in the form of participatory democracy, and to realize the industrial democracy (Figure 18.2). For example, academia could do more in new technology and knowledge creating, offering the green value proposition for the up-stream of firms' value chain. Government could do more in infrastructure construction, supporting the making or packaging of green product or service. Media could do more in promoting the green life-style to the society, making the commercialization of green product or service quickly and realizing their economic benefits. Industry could go more in cooperating with the focal firm to operate the green service well with their own expertise. The four subjects worked together on the social platform to strengthen the green value chain of the focal firm, forms a high effective business model. It is really a new way of life. The critical key is the linking of the green innovation value chains of academia, government, industry, and media. It lays the foundation for the democratic advantages of the industry and the development and upgrading of industrial firms.

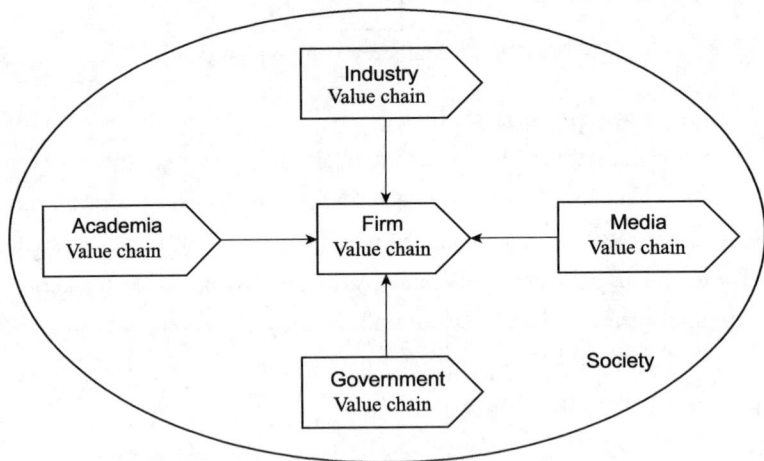

Figure 18.2 Social compound union model

18.5 Social compound union and green growth

This paper will introduce two cases to illustrate how the social compound union leads to green growth. These two cases are very famous in Hangzhou. They may represent the potential future of green growth of firms with the help of social compound union.

18.5.1 Case one: Hangzhou Public Transport Group

Hangzhou Public Transport Group Co., Ltd. was established in January 1953. It has prospered into a comprehensive enterprise mainly specializing in city public passenger transport service through more than 50 years of development. The corporation, formerly had more than 50 vehicles with 8 routes is now operating 3500 vehicles with more than 300 routes and 640 million passenger trips. Along with the economic development and improvement of people's living, they need more public transport service. But as the population grows quickly, people live in Hangzhou suffer the heavy traffic, and public transport service could not grow any more. In order to reduce the emission of carbon dioxide, Hangzhou Public Transport Group purchased many buses with green technology such as hybrid power bus and electric bus.

In face of the future, Hangzhou Public Transport Group fully realizes that continuous innovation is the only way to keep the company alive, create more developing chances and promote progress of city public transport. For the sake of green life and better traveling condition, Hangzhou Public Transport Group developed a public bicycle service system.

Hangzhou Public Transport Corporation is expanding access to its publicly accessible public bicycle service in order to provide a seamless connection of bicycle-based slow-speed traffic to metro and bus-based public traffic facilities. Hangzhou's public bicycle service grows to 50,000 bikes, surpassing Paris's popular Velib bike-share program, which offers more than 20,000. it's said that people will find public bicycle stations every 100 meters. According to statistics from Hangzhou Bus Group, the public bicycles are used an average of 100,000 times a day, with a historical one-day high of 200,000. If a rented bike travels an average distance of 2 kilometers, over a period of one year, 7,500 tons of oil will be saved and carbon dioxide emission will be reduced by 23,897 tons.

Hangzhou Public Transport Corporation also benefits a lot from this system. Hangzhou's public bicycle service provides the first full hour of service for free. After that the next hour costs a modest one yuan, two yuan for the following hour and three yuan for every additional hour up to 24 hours. Each bike was used frequently every day.

This system could not be successful without social compound union. Academia helps the design of transporting system for heavy traffic in cities. It also proposes the new technology and knowledge support for this green business model. Government helps the construction of infrastructure of bicycle parking networks. Media promotes low carbon life – style to the society. Industry such as bicycle industry offers the special bicycle for this system, and tourism industry encourages the self-cycling travel in Hangzhou.

18.5.2 Case two: Hangzhou tea industry

Longjing Tea is one of the best teas in China, and it is also the reason for Hangzhou's international fame. Longjing Tea is grown in the Longjing mountain area of Hangzhou, southwest of the West Lake. Hangzhou tea industry is very famous. Longjing Tea could be bought throughout Hangzhou. However, the best place to buy Longjing Tea is the Longjing ("Dragon Well") area of Hangzhou. The tea there is said to be the best tea available and the quality of the tea there is extremely good. Alternatively, the tea could be purchased around other attractions in Hangzhou, or from the thousands of Longjing Tea stores all around the city. However, homogeneous competition makes tea industry develop slowly. Is tea industry just a retail business for farming and selling?

Meijiawu Tea Village is located in the Longjing mountain area of Hangzhou. It was once only a poor village with over six-hundred-year history until the local farmers started to plant tea. So far it has become one of the four famous habitats for Longjing Tea and a featured tea-most farm village with rich tea culture and leisure tourism, which attracts over millions of tourists every year. The tea culture village features 160 tea houses, in which travellers can learn about the history and culture of Meijiawu Tea Village and appreciate the whole process of Chinese Tea Ceremony. Meijiawu Village is reputed for its history of serving exquisite tea.

The tea produced in Meijiawu Village is the best among all varieties of West Lake dragon tea. Local farmers usually pick tea leaves four times every year. Besides, Meijiawu Tea Village is renowned for its tea food with the favor of lightness, smooth, and slightly salty, such as shrimp in Longjing Tea, Shrimp Bucket in Bi Luo Tea, and Longjing fish. Recently, local restaurants issued several popular dishes, like carp with qingshui tea, crispy skin chicken with tea soup and idyllic stewed duck with tea soup.

Meijiawu Tea Village is a good example of green growth of the traditional economy. So Hangzhou tea industry has totally changed. Now it is not treated as farming or a farm-make-sale system any more. It realizes green growth successfully. Travellers not only enjoy the tea, but also the tea culture, tea farming, tea village, tea food, and the green way of life.

This system could not be successful without social compound union. Academia offers the technology and knowledge by conducting tea research or nutriology research, promoting the tea culture for the design of new business model. Government helps the construction of infrastructure for tea plantation tourism and the hold of tea expo. Media promotes green tea green life. Industry such as tourism industry, leisure industry and catering industry offers the special service for this system, and supports the tea industry in Hangzhou.

18.6 Discussion

Why can firms in developing countries realize green growth from innovation?

From the cases above we know that, lots of Chinese firms realize green growth by innovation. These innovation strategies might be green technology innovation, or might be green energy innovation, but the mainstream is green business model innovation. Many technical attributes of green products developed and provided by multinational incumbents from developed countries have already been far above mainstream market' actual needs in developing countries, and the green technology must be tremendously expensive and difficult to handle. Chinese firms from developing countries, can seize the opportunities of green growth but couldn't afford the extremely high costs. If Chinese firms want to construct the basis of competition in their home market away from the cutting-edge green technical performance, the main problem for them is to compete with multinational incumbents. For firms in developing countries, they might leverage the resource of the society to meet the developing countries' mass market economically than those commercialized green technology in the developed countries.

To conclude, we identify one kind of model that was named as social compound union. It offers some kind of advantage implied in innovation as given in the cases above. The multinational incumbents' trap of over-serving for customers with extremely cutting-edge green technology in developed countries provides developing countries' firms opportunities to change existing competitive basis and develop more appropriate business models for mass customers in developing countries by leveraging the power of social compound union. Firms in developing countries do not need to realize the green growth by themselves by investing too much on R&D, but with the help of social compound union. And it will finally be a successful model for lots of firms with low resources and low-level green technology.

So, in our perspective, green business model innovation with social compound union is a powerful means for enlarging and broadening markets and providing new functionality. We emphasize much more the value creation, value delivery and value capture supported by the roles in social compound union which competes against the commercialization of advanced technologies in developing countries.

How do firms in developing countries capture green value from innovation?

From above case analysis, we identify the typical ways of firms' commercialization of innovation in developing countries.

Firstly, firms should articulate an appropriate green value proposition that appeals to customers. It is of great importance for firms to commercialize their products or services. Since customers may desire some low cost latent attributes of the product or service, so the cutting-edge green technology valued by the mainstream customers in developed countries will not necessarily meet the demand of mass customers in developing countries.

Thus, firms in developing countries, disadvantaged in developing cutting-edge products but advantaged in sustaining a competitive cost structure, might achieve market success through targeting price-sensitive mass customers rather than technology-sensitive customers. How to cut the price quickly to meet the price-sensitive mass customers becomes the most critical issue for firms who are concerned about green growth. The strategy of designing the original business model to local mass customer tastes and local market infrastructure becomes vital and determinable in the intensified competition with leading green technology of multinational incumbents. Firms can also utilize their advantages in understanding and shaping local consumer tastes to bypass the multinational incumbents' leading advantage.

Secondly, except for presenting a green value proposition, firms should build a special value network with a new cost structure and special complementary assets to deliver the green value proposition. Due to the limited resources of firms from developing countries, leveraging their strategic partners' resources is the first important issue. The firms' capability to align with a value network may significantly influence their cost efficiency and profitability. On the mechanism of resource allocation, it is very difficult for Chinese firms to obtain enough resources for green technological innovation, but social compound union could provide the necessary complementary assets to promote the development of Chinese firms. Chinese firms would enhance their competence in reconstructing their traditional business, making full use of the sprawling but largely redundant partners' resource in social compound union for green business model innovation aiming at price-sensitive mass customers.

18.7 Conclusions

A firm is not only an economic organization, but also a social organization. Traditional economic mode of operation makes profit through more sales and less costs. If the market growth reached saturation and the costs are difficult to decline, the profit will be difficult to grow. This is a typical Red Sea Strategy. With this strategy, all firms entirely go into a super competition. It's impossible to realize green growth by a firm itself under this strategy, because green business requires costly investment. But the social needs of the green business are deeply strong. Therefore, firms should take the Green Ocean Strategy. By conducting the green value creating process for the society and with the help of social compound union, it's possible to construct a highly profitable green business model which fully utilizes the wisdom of academia, government, media and industry, to achieve the sustainable economic and social development.

References

Ekins, P. 1999. *Economic Growth and Environmental Sustainability: The Prospects for Green Growth*. London: Routledge.

Wu, X. B., Wu, D. 2010. Industrial democracy, the linking of innovation chain, and the upgrading and development of industrial firms. *Studies in Dialectics of Nature*, 26(8), 74-78.

UNESCAP. 2012. *Green Growth, Resources and Resilience: Environmental Sustainability in Asia and the Pacific*. Bangkok: United Nations and Asian Development Bank Publication.

Brock, W. A., Taylor, M. S. 2004. Economic growth and the environment: A review of theory and empirics. In: Aghion, P., Durlauf, S. (Eds.), *Handbook of Economic Growth*. North Holland: Elsevier.

Aghion, P., Hemous, D., Veugelers, R. 2009. No green growth without innovation. *Bruegel Policy Brief*, (7), 1-8.

Author

Professor Wu Xiaobo is Executive Vice Dean of the School of Management, Zhejiang University, China, and he is Director of the National Institute for Innovation Management (NIIM). In addition; he is the Visiting Fellow to IFM, Cambridge University; and Fulbright Senior Visiting Fellow to Sloan School of Management, MIT. He has published in journals such as the International Journal of Technology Management, IEEE Transaction on Engineering Management, Industry and Innovation, and has been granted 7 awards by the Ministry of Education of the People's Republic of China and the People's Government of Zhejiang Province. His current research interests are in information technology and management change, technological innovation and competitive strategy, and strategies for globalization manufacturing.

Professor Wu has directed many research projects granted by central and local government and National Natural Science Foundation of China(NNSFC). He has published many articles in international journals and conferences including Studies in Science of Science, PICMET, IEMC, ISMOT, Science Research Management, etc. Selected books of professor Wu's include Corporate Strategy, Supply Chain and Logistics Management, Industrialization Driving by IT: Theory and Practice, The Blue Book of Innovation Economy of Zhejiang Province and Global Manufacturing and Secondary Innovation Strategy.